The Shanghai Area

Books by Caleb Carr:

Casing the Promised Land
America Invulnerable (with James Chace)

THE DEVIL SOLDIER

Frederick Townsend Ward, 1831–1862. Ward wears
the blue Prince Albert that was his trademark, and
holds a field cap. The scars of the wound suffered at
the first battle of Ch'ing-p'u can be discerned on the
left side of his jaw. *(Courtesy of Essex Institute, Salem, Mass.)*

THE DEVIL
SOLDIER

The Story of
Frederick Townsend Ward

Caleb Carr

RANDOM HOUSE
NEW YORK

Library of Congress Cataloging-in-Publication Data
Carr, Caleb, 1955–
The devil soldier/by Caleb Carr
Subtitle: The story of Frederick Townsend Ward, the most honored and controversial
American in Chinese history.
Includes bibliographical references
ISBN 0-679-41114-3
1. China—History—Taiping Rebellion, 1850–1864—Personal
narratives, American. 2. Ward, Frederick Townsend, 1831–1862.
I. Title.
DS759.35.W37C37   1991   951'.034—dc20   91-11158

Manufactured in the United States of America
24689753
First Edition
This book was set in 11/14 Century Old Style

This book is dedicated to Simon Carr, Ethan Carr,
C. Daniel Way Schoonover, and David H. Johnson:

"And Crispin Crispian shall ne'er go by
From this day to the ending of the world,
But we in it shall be remembered—
We few, we happy few, we band of brothers."

—Shakespeare, *Henry V*

ACKNOWLEDGMENTS

Richard J. Smith of Rice University made this book a practical proposition, not only through his years of groundbreaking research in the field but by generously making his materials and insights available to me at all times. He is a scholar in every sense of the word, and has my heartfelt thanks and respect.

Beatrice Bartlett of Yale University helped me with translation and research at Sterling Library. John K. Fairbank of Harvard University took the time to read the manuscript, for which I am indebted. Needless to say, any errors or misinterpretations that occur in these pages are mine and have nothing to do with any of the above-mentioned distinguished experts.

A talented and warmhearted group of scholars in Shanghai helped me solve (insofar as it *is* solved) the riddle of what happened to Ward's memorial hall, as well as his grave and remains, after the Communist revolution. Understandably, they do not wish their names mentioned; but they know who they are, and I hope they take satisfaction from knowing that they made an immense contribution to this work.

Nancy Heywood, Paula Richter, and the rest of the staff of the Essex Institute worked carefully and patiently with me during my stay in Salem and through the ensuing months of writing. I am deeply grateful.

The staffs of the New York Public Library, the National Archives

ACKNOWLEDGMENTS

and Library of Congress in Washington, Sterling Library at Yale University, the New-York Historical Society, and the New York Society Library all rendered invaluable assistance. I am especially indebted to Angie Speicer at the National Archives, who located obscure materials at a time when the Archives' collections were in a state of confusion as a result of their being moved and photographed for microfilm.

Li Jing at Rice University, Huang Peiling at Columbia University, and Kan Liang at Yale University all provided timely translation services. Their renderings of classical Chinese were clear and of the utmost importance.

Perrin Wright and Katy Chevigny proved skilled research assistants, and I have always been impressed by their many talents. Lucy Hanbury in London was able to locate a group of critical documents on short notice, and I thank her.

Suzanne Gluck gave this project its first encouragement, and Ann Godoff gave it the green light, as well as the benefit of her sage advice. They have been more than agent and editor.

I am grateful to Linda Sykes at Photosearch, Inc., for helping me locate many images.

In the category of a new way to pay old debts, I wish to mention Donald Wilson, formerly of Friends Seminary, Reed Browning of Kenyon College, and Robert Scally of New York University, all of whom encouraged me to pursue my interests during difficult periods, and who helped me understand that an interest in history is not inseparable from a life in academia.

Finally, many people helped me keep body and soul together during the writing of this book. I wish in this connection to thank the rest of my family, as well as James Chace, Tom Pivinski, Rob Cowley, and especially Gwyn Lurie.

A NOTE ON NAMES

Because of the vast array of spellings used in the translation of Chinese during the nineteenth and twentieth centuries, all place and personal names in the following text have been adjusted to a uniform system, regardless of their source. A slightly older style of translation than the current Pinyin has been used, because it is easier for English-speaking readers to pronounce. This explains why *Beijing* is still *Peking* and why American, Chinese, British, and French speakers and writers appear to be using the same spellings, when in fact they employed many different versions.

—C.C.

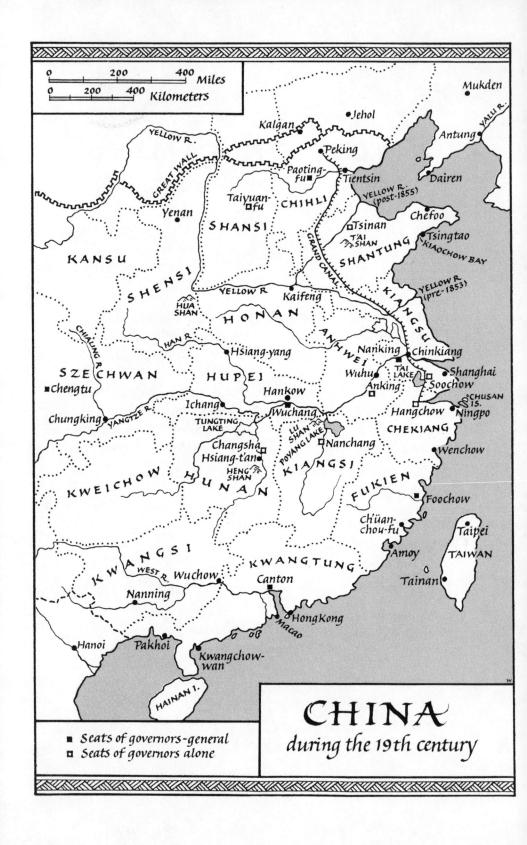

CHINA
during the 19th century

Seats of governors-general
Seats of governors alone

CONTENTS

xiii

CONTENTS

PROLOGUE

"ACROSS THE SEA TO FIGHT FOR CHINA"

In the summer of 1900 an expeditionary force of European, Japanese, and American soldiers marched into the Chinese capital of Peking, the triumphant blare of their bands and bugles announcing not only the conclusion of a successful campaign but the effective end of thousands of years of imperial rule in China. The last of the Middle Kingdom's dynasties, the Manchu (or Ch'ing), had withstood internal and external threats throughout the nineteenth century, and would hold on for eleven more years before a tide of republican revolution would engulf it completely. But all hope of recovery was in fact lost when the Western and Japanese troops entered Peking and its sacrosanct Forbidden City, the inner compound guarded by high walls that for centuries had been the residence of China's rulers. The violation of the Forbidden City by "barbarian" foreigners stripped the Manchus of any legitimate right to rule in the eyes of many Chinese, and the imperial clique was finally seen for what it was: an arrogant, corrupt group of anachronisms, whose sumptuous world of silk dragons, peacock's feathers, and divine rule had no place in the twentieth century.

The Western and Japanese governments had ordered the march on Peking because a group of antiforeign Chinese extremists known as the Boxers, under orders from the Empress Dowager Tz'u-hsi, had laid siege to their diplomatic legations and attempted to kill their ministers. The attack on the legations was a stupendously rash act, the crowning achievement of an imperial elite that had spent the last half century

1

trying to stem the advance of foreign influence in China and preserve the empire in its near-medieval state. All such efforts had been in vain: The barbarian outsiders had finally pried China open to foreign trade, foreign religion, and foreign political ideas. The bitter Tz'u-hsi had meant to make the "foreign devils" pay for their success when she authorized the attack on the legations in June 1900. But the Western diplomats and their families had once again frustrated her by bravely withstanding the siege. When the multinational relief column marched into Peking in July, Tz'u-hsi fled in disgrace, taking with her the last chance of imperial resurgence. In the conflict between unreasoning Chinese pride and relentless foreign commercial and philosophical expansionism that had raged for sixty years, there seemed to be no middle ground, and now Chinese pride had lost the long battle.

Yet there had once been such a middle ground in the Middle Kingdom, or at least the possibility of it. For the briefest of moments during the 1860s, the imperial government in Peking as well as the foreign powers had gotten a glimpse of a China in which progressive Western ideas—particularly military ideas—would be placed at the service of the emperor and his ministers to ensure the empire's survival and participation in a rapidly changing world. Unfortunately, both the Chinese imperialists and the Westerners, as if horrified by their glimpse of this strange future, had slammed the door on it; but not before the names of those who had so briefly cracked the portal open had been recorded and honored by the Chinese people. Legends quickly grew around those names, as at least one group of American soldiers discovered during their occupation of Peking in the summer of 1900. Writing a quarter of a century later, one of these men recalled,

There was much talk among the soldiers as to who had been the first to enter the Forbidden City, where no white "devil" was ever supposed to have been before. One day a group of us were arguing about the matter before a little Chinese shop, where we had stopped for one thing or another, and of a sudden the old merchant spoke up, in pidgeon English.

What did it matter, he wanted to know, which one of us had by force of arms broken into the temples of the gods? We were disrespectful of the gods, we were like burglars, for all our bravery. And we could never be the first white men to enter a sacred Chinese temple, anyway, because there was Hua, the White God. Hua had been braver than any of us—and he had been good, too. He had come from far across the sea to fight for China, and he had been carried into a sacred temple, and was there still. His was a victory of right.

The "Hua" of whom the old Chinese merchant spoke was Frederick Townsend Ward, a young soldier of fortune from Salem, Massachusetts, who had come to China in 1859 and offered his services to the imperial government in its bitter war against a hugely powerful group of quasi-Christian mystics calling themselves the Taipings. When he arrived in Shanghai, Ward was twenty-eight years old and penniless; when he died in battle three years later, he was the most honored American in Chinese history, a naturalized Chinese subject and a mandarin entitled to wear the prestigious peacock feather in his cap. He had married the daughter of another mandarin and received high praise from the emperor. But above all, he had assembled out of the most improbable elements an army that was unlike anything China or the world had ever seen: a highly disciplined force of native Chinese soldiers commanded by Western officers that was expert in the use of modern foreign weapons and capable of defeating vastly superior numbers of opponents in the field. Known to the Taiping rebels as "devil soldiers," Ward's men were dubbed the *Chang-sheng-chün,* the "Ever Victorious Army," by Peking; and after Ward died a memorial temple and Confucian shrine were built around his grave.

More than any other person or organization, Ward and his Ever Victorious Army had pointed the way toward a different kind of China, one in which Manchu chauvinism would have given way to reasoned Chinese acceptance of outside assistance. That assistance would in turn have allowed the empire to avoid a violent collision with progress and emerge as a twentieth-century power. China's failure to follow such a course had, certainly, less to do with Ward's untimely death than with the fact that the Manchus did not truly desire progress and the West did not desire China to be a power. But the momentary achievement itself, the transitory indication that an alternate future was possible, was nonetheless important—was, in a very real sense, Ward's greatest victory.

What follows is not a biography of Frederick Townsend Ward in the conventional sense, for it would be impossible to write a conventional biography of a man whose legacy has suffered so many attempts at eradication. Ward's service to the Chinese empire gave him great renown in the distant, troubled country that he adopted as his own. His memory was honored and his eternal spirit appeased (or so it was hoped) with annual sacrifices at the shrine built to his memory. But the ever-suspicious imperial Chinese government harbored lingering anxiety concerning Ward, largely because of his foreign origins. In the United States, by contrast, Ward's exploits received only passing mention in Congress and the press following his death, and then were virtually forgotten. For their part, the Ward family made repeated attempts to pry money owed to their illustrious relation out of the Chinese government, but they did little to ensure that an accurate account of his life would endure.

When the imperial Chinese government finally collapsed in 1911, Ward's legacy was further endangered. The American Legion named its Shanghai post after him and tried to maintain his grave during the era of Republican China. But China's new rulers were not sympathetic, for Ward—although his origins were American and he harbored doubts about the shortcomings of the Manchu dynasty even after he became a Chinese subject—had fought for the Manchu cause. His private misgivings about imperial corruption and repression were considered academic by most of the Republicans. Then, too, Sun Yat-sen had fallaciously but effectively traced the origins of Chinese nationalism back to the Taiping rebellion, which Ward had helped defeat. It thus comes as no surprise that Sun and his followers did little to perpetuate Ward's memory.

The brutal Japanese seizure of Shanghai in 1940 brought the destruction of many official Chinese and American consular documents, further clouding Ward's legacy. In addition, the Japanese sacked Ward's shrine and memorial hall and defaced his grave (after promising American officials that they would not). Although they later claimed to have made an effort to restore the site, the cataclysmic war between Chinese Nationalists and Communists followed too quickly on the heels of World War II for verification of such claims to be possible.

Finally, the victory of Mao Tse-tung's Chinese Communist party made it certain that assembling a record of Ward's Chinese adventure would become an exercise in detective work as much as scholarship. Like Sun Yat-sen, Mao drew badly flawed but popular parallels between his own and the Taiping movement. (Chiang Kai-shek assisted this effort by making similar comparisons between the Communists and the unsuccessful Taipings, vainly hoping that they would discourage popular support for Mao.) In pursuit of their revisionist goal, Communist scholars sometimes misplaced or destroyed invaluable relics and documents relating to the Ever Victorious Army. But the profound Communist discomfort with Ward and his legacy demanded even greater destruction: In 1955 Ward's remains were dug up, and his grave site and shrine were destroyed and paved over. The whereabouts of Ward's bones today are unknown. They have almost certainly been destroyed. A plain headstone over an empty grave in Salem, Massachusetts, is the only memorial to this most noteworthy of nineteenth-century American adventurers.

For all these reasons, the following account is not an attempt so much to reconstruct Ward's life from the inside out as to paint a picture of the man by allowing the events and people who surrounded him—and about whom we know a good deal more—to throw light on his shadowy figure. No man's life can be truly understood out of context, but in Ward's case the context is especially vital.

Put simply, that context was the Chinese empire during its penultimate period of internal and external crisis. The bizarre visions that compelled Hung Hsiu-ch'üan, the Taiping leader, to attempt the overthrow of the Manchu dynasty became, through the chain of circumstance, a very real factor in Ward's life. And the formation of Ward's character in Salem, Massachusetts, and aboard American sailing vessels during the 1840s and '50s is important to any understanding of how the Chinese empire survived. Similarly, foreign attempts to open China to greater trade and Western influence are key to understanding why Ward was drawn to Shanghai. And no account of the West's intrusion into China in the nineteenth century can be complete without an account of Ward's achievements.

The precise meaning of those achievements has always been a problem for analysts. Historians disposed to view late imperial China from the left have seen Ward as an indirect facilitator of Western penetration and exploitation: a pawn bent on shoring up a corrupt dynasty that was powerless to stop Western imperialism and a man who had no regard for nascent Chinese nationalism. Others have seen Ward as the embodiment of the imperial Chinese government's response to the simultaneous threats of internal disorder and external aggression, a response that became known as the "self-strengthening movement." In this light Ward was not an unknowing Western tool but a willing Manchu instrument, ultimately controlled by Peking and used by the imperial government to bring the Chinese army up to date. Still others have written Ward off as a simple mercenary, greedy for plunder and a servant of the Manchu cause only because the Manchus were the most desperate and convenient employers.

Yet the Frederick Townsend Ward who emerges from a careful study of events does not fit into any of these categories. Certainly, his campaigns served the Manchu cause and initially made most Westerners (whose goals in China were opposed by the dynasty) uneasy and even hostile toward him. Yet by the time of his death he was operating in close coordination with Franco-British regular forces, and Peking was expressing strong worries about his ultimate ambitions. Some who knew Ward claimed that he intended, once the Taiping threat had been eliminated, to establish his own warlord principality within China. Yet given his consistent defense of Chinese political integrity, it seems unlikely that he ever meant to carry out such a betrayal of China itself. And while he was unquestionably a soldier of fortune, Ward's loyalty to his men and to China was always more important than his desire for reward (although he certainly did expect rewards for his service). A talented officer by trade, Ward cut a remarkably poor figure as a mercenary: He made sure to secure funds for his army but rarely did the same for himself, instead accepting notoriously unreliable notes of debt from his Chinese backers. In truth, Ward had little real business sense at all; his talent was for soldiering, and he put that talent to use defending China.

But was serving China synonymous, to Ward, with serving the Manchus? This appears less certain. Ward was fully aware of the dynasty's flaws: Although they had ruled with the power of Confucian tradition for two hundred years, the Manchus were still regarded by many Chinese as invaders, whose usurpation of power from the Ming dynasty in 1644 was criminal. It may well be that Ward intended to turn against these descendants of the "Tartar hordes" once the Taipings had been defeated. Such a move would probably have been aimed not at the establishment of his own warlord domain but at the restoration of a native Chinese dynasty similar to the Ming. For their part, the Manchus initially thought that they could use Ward and became fretful when they discovered how singularly he remained his own man, a true "free-lance." Clearly they took the tales of Ward's expansive ambitions seriously. In the end, however, we will never know what marching orders the Ever Victorious Army would have received had its creator and commander lived to see the fall of the Taiping capital of Nanking.

Whatever the nature of his ties to the West and to the Manchus, Ward did prove true to the task of serving China: His organization and leadership of the Ever Victorious Army were crucial to China's military restructuring, which was an important part of the short-lived period of general reform that touched all branches of the Chinese government in the 1860s and '70s. Those reforms did not, in the end, prove fundamental enough to prevent disasters such as the Allied march on Peking in 1900 or the fall of the Chinese empire in 1911; but on the most basic level they ensured that there was a Chinese nation—rather than a collection of feuding principalities and European colonies, as had been distinctly possible—that could become a republic. For this if for no other reason, Ward's place in history is important.

It is useful to bear in mind, however, that this importance was a largely unconscious achievement for Ward. A high school dropout with almost no formal military training, Ward was neither an idealist nor a philosopher but an adventurous realist who sought to carve out a place in what had consistently been, for him, a hostile and violent world. His first thought was not for instituting comprehensive programs of reform but for his soldiers, whom he affectionately called "my people." Yet, as shall be seen, it was precisely this commitment to the people around him—rather than to the kind of political, religious, and commercial ideologies that obsessed the Taipings, the Manchus, and the leaders of the Western communities in China—that made Ward unique. The ingenuousness of his achievement does not reduce its significance. It simply helps us understand his compelling, mysterious character.

I

"A NEW RACE OF WARRIORS"

On May 2, 1860, the city of Nanking, China—nestled between a wide bend in the Yangtze River and a commanding promontory called Purple Mountain—was alive with celebration. Its citizens, who had been in open rebellion against the Manchu emperor in Peking for the better part of a decade, had endured a bitter siege during the winter, one that had finally been broken by a daring series of feints and raids by the rebel armies. After long months of privation, the way now seemed clear to bring badly needed food, arms, and treasure into the city. And so the people of Nanking lifted their voices in thanks to the god whose worship had made them outlaws in their own country: *Shang-ti,* the "Supreme Lord," whose eldest son was called Jesus and whose second son, the rebels believed, was their own leader, their *T'ien Wang* ("Heavenly King"). The scattering of the Manchu emperor's soldiers—or, as the followers of the T'ien Wang called them, the "demon imps"—before the walls of Nanking was taken as yet another sign that the T'ien Wang had truly been dispatched by Shang-ti to bring down the Manchu dynasty and establish the *T'ai-ping t'ien-kuo* ("Heavenly Kingdom of Great Peace") in China.

In the midst of the May 2 rejoicing, the T'ien Wang dispatched a message to his senior advisers and assistants, summoning them to an immediate council of war to determine the future of the great Taiping movement. The message was brought out of the T'ien Wang's sumptuous yellow palace by one of his female attendants: Taiping men were generally forbidden from entering the inner sanctum of their leader, who lived alone with a retinue of concubines and cited Solomon and his hundreds of wives as a hallowed example. Making its way from splendid residence to splendid residence, the summons finally reached the colonnades and gilded domes of the palace of the *Chung Wang,* or "Faithful King." (The T'ien Wang's lieutenants, though subordinate to him, all incorporated the word *wang,* or "king," into their titles.) The Chung Wang had been more responsible than any man for lifting the recent siege of Nanking. Indeed, his considerable military talents had ensured the survival of the rebellion for a number of years. And he had been honored in return: Once a poor mountain farmer and laborer called Li Hsiu-ch'eng, he now controlled troops numbering in the hundreds of thousands, as well as a vast fortune in silver. But in the spring of 1860 the Chung Wang was a deeply troubled man, vexed by doubts about the Taiping cause that no amount of honor or reward could ease.

Though only thirty-seven at the time he was summoned to the May 2 council of war, the Chung Wang had about him, said an Englishman who knew him in Nanking, "a trace of arduous mental and physical exertion" that "gave him a rather worn and older appearance. His figure light, active and wiry, was particularly well formed; . . . his bearing erect and dignified, his walk rapid but stately. His features were very strongly marked, expressive, and good, though not handsome according to the Chinese idea, being slightly of a more European cast than they admire." An anxious, restless man, the Chung Wang seemed to find spiritual ease only on the battlefield: "His large eyes flashed incessantly, while the lids were always twitching. From his energetic features, and the ceaseless nervous movement of his body . . . no one would imagine that he could possess such perfect coolness in battle; yet I have often since observed him in action, when, in spite of his apparent excitability, his self-possession was imperturbable, and his voice . . . unchanged, save being more rapid and decisive in moments of greatest danger."

Like many of the hundreds of thousands of Taiping adherents, the Chung Wang had joined the rebellion less out of genuine devotion to the strange amalgam of Christianity and Chinese mysticism that was the T'ien Wang's faith than out of weariness with Manchu oppression. In the two centuries since Tartar tribesmen had swept down out of Manchuria and into China, deposing the Ming and establishing their own Manchu dynasty, their rule had degenerated into a system of corruption and repression that left China's poorest provinces in a state of near-constant rebellion. Young peasants joined these uprisings almost as a matter of course: "When I was young at home as an ordinary person," the Chung Wang later recalled of the Taiping movement, "I understood nothing, but joined up in the excitement." In the ensuing decade of the 1850s, as the Taipings made their way from province to province and became the greatest threat to Manchu rule in the history of the dynasty, the Chung Wang battled his way up and out of the rebel ranks. But he also witnessed internecine conflicts among the Taiping leaders, brutal suppressive measures undertaken by the Manchus, the T'ien Wang's withdrawal into a private world of debauchery, and the slaughter of millions of his fellow peasants by both rebel and imperial troops. By 1860 the Chung Wang was weary and losing heart: "There were many people in the [T'ien Wang's] Heavenly Dynasty who did harm to the people; what could I alone do, for all my compassion? Power was not in my hands, so what could I do? . . . Once you are riding a tiger's back it is difficult to dismount."

The lifting of the siege of Nanking had not given the Chung Wang any commensurate sense of relief. In fact, his worries, especially those concerning his sovereign, had only multiplied. After the victory, said the Chung Wang, "no edict was pronounced praising the generals; the field commanders were not received in audience, nor were the court officials. The Sovereign was not interested in the affairs of government, but merely instructed his ministers in the knowledge of Heaven, as if all was tranquil." Militarily, the Chung Wang knew that the rebel position at Nanking was still far from secure. The "demon imps" would be back, and, unless the Taipings could break out of the Nanking region and secure open routes to adequate sources of supply, the imperialists would eventually crush the movement, if only through attrition. The rebels' next move would be crucial, and the May 2 council of war thus took on immense importance.

Knowing this, the Taiping chiefs arrived at the meeting wearing their most impressive regalia and armed with battle plans that each was convinced would prove the salvation of the Heavenly Kingdom. The T'ien Wang made it a point on such occasions to wear robes of imperial yellow—previously reserved for the occupant of the Dragon Throne in Peking—as well as a tall headdress reminiscent of the Ming dynasty. The Chung Wang wore a coronet of gold, in the shape of a tiger flanked by two eagles and decorated with precious stones and pearls. Rebels these men may have been—but the plundering of more than half of China had allowed their movement to take on singularly imperial trappings.

Plans for a spring campaign were proposed and discarded. The *Shih Wang,* or "Attendant King," proposed a move southeast, toward the farms of Chekiang and Fukien provinces and the rich ports of Ningpo and Foochow. But such a long march to the coast, the other wangs argued, would leave the upper stretches of the Yangtze River badly exposed and the western approach to Nanking open. The *Ying Wang,* or "Heroic King," wished to march in this direction and reinforce the city of Anking, rightly considered the gateway to the Nanking region.

It was the T'ien Wang's cousin and prime minister—the *Kan Wang,* or "Shield King"—who proposed the plan that most appealed to his sovereign. It incorporated the objects of the Shih Wang's and the Ying Wang's plans but achieved them more efficiently than either. The Taiping forces, said the prime minister, should strike out from Nanking in two great pincers, one to the north side of the Yangtze and one to the south. In a pair of wide sweeps that would shatter the Manchu forces in central China, the two armies would converge not on Anking but much farther to the west, at Hankow. The "demon imps," their attention fixed on Nanking and Anking, would not be ready for such a move. The Shih Wang's suggestion that the rebellion be resupplied through a move to the seacoast was also accepted. Ningpo and Foochow were too distant, however, to be incorporated into the Kan Wang's scheme. Instead, the port of Shanghai in the rich province of Kiangsu was selected as a target. Attacking here before moving west, the Taiping southern pincer would secure needed supplies—including twenty armed river steamships for use on the Yangtze—and hopefully establish friendly relations with the

Westerners who traded at the port and who worshiped, the Taipings believed, their own Shang-ti.

The Chung Wang had misgivings about the prime minister's plan but thought it the best of those put forward and elected to support it. That was enough for the T'ien Wang, who approved the strategy as well as the assignment of the Chung Wang to lead the vital southern army, which was to conquer the province of Kiangsu, move on to Shanghai, then wheel rapidly west and approach Hankow. Yet the Chung Wang's heart was still not at rest: He was given only one month to take the provincial capital of Soochow in Kiangsu, and the T'ien Wang's language in ordering him to do so was, in the young commander's opinion, "severe." But, as the Chung Wang observed, "things being what they were, and since I was employed by him, I had to obey."

With the plan settled, the Taiping armies were assembled and addressed by their commanders. Uniforms of red, yellow, white, and orange silk, emblazoned with the names of commanders and individual units, as well as hundreds of brilliantly colored banners and thousands of long spears, all moved in splendid agitation as the Taiping soldiers enthusiastically answered the exhortations of their chiefs. Having abandoned the shaved forehead and long pigtail that were signs of Chinese submission to the Manchus, the Taiping men wore their hair loose and uncut (earning them the epithet *chang-maos,* or "long-haired rebels"), and sometimes wound it in red and yellow turbans. And there were women in the ranks, as well: The Taipings had rejected the crippling custom of binding feet, and the daughters of the cause were able to move about freely. Taken as a whole, the Taiping hordes were an impressive and, in the Chinese experience, unprecedented sight.

Indeed, in the midst of this spectacle of color and passion, relatively few onlookers stopped to remark on the utter backwardness of the Taipings' armaments. Most carried simple swords and spears; firepower was confined to antique gingals (weighty matchlock firearms supported by cumbersome props), the occasional musket, and ancient cannons that, though often beautifully embellished, were as likely to split open as to hit their marks on firing. The arsenal was rounded out by "stink-pots"—hand-held bombs that produced burning, nauseating gases—and firecrackers, used to create panic. One British consular official, who had traveled up the Yangtze in 1853 to get a preliminary picture of the rebellion for his government, had made a point of asking about this seemingly vital shortcoming:

> I inquired how it was that the Taipings did not make greater use of the smaller firearms, muskets and pistols, the former of which I said were, with the attached bayonet, our chief arms? I was induced to ask this because, while there was a great demand among the Taiping soldiers for swords, they seemed to take little interest in guns. [The commander] said, that his people did not understand the use of them, and that they were valueless when the supply of ammunition ran out or the springs went wrong. Swords and spears, he said, seldom got out of order, were easily repaired, and he found that his people could always beat the Imperialists with them.

It was no boast. Backward as Taiping arms were, imperial weapons were no better—to date, the "demon imps" had won no crucial engagements against the rebels. And, so long as the terms of the conflict remained the same, it seemed unlikely that they ever would.

The Chung Wang marched out of Nanking accompanied by his bodyguard—a tested force of 5,000 men from his native province of Kwangsi. Then his fully assembled army of almost 100,000 troops began the trek toward Soochow: over a hundred miles through country as yet untouched by the rebellion and occupied by imperial soldiers. But the faith of the Chung Wang's legions in their commander was great, and that faith gave them powerful confidence: As one Western missionary who had witnessed an earlier Taiping advance remarked, the "personal appearance of their men in arms, and of their women on horseback . . . made the insurgents appear like a new race of warriors. . . . They all seemed content, and in high spirits, as if sure of success."

A very different sort of scene was taking place in the walled cities and towns that sat along the line of advance from Nanking to Soochow. Here nervous mandarins and imperial officials of varying civil and military ranks received word of the approach of the Taipings with visible fright. Some of this fear was inspired by rumors of rebel atrocities, but much of it sprang from the knowledge of what the emperor would do to any man who failed in his appointed task. Simple beheading was the best of these fates; the infamous "death of a thousand cuts"—in which the skin was flayed from a living traitor's body—was more commonly pronounced. Faced with the manifold dangers of a successful rebel advance, many Chinese officials chose suicide, as did hundreds of the citizens under their control.

And, even if such unfortunate Chinese could steel themselves and face the rebel approach, they had another enormous problem to contend with: retreating imperial forces, whose most common form of defense against the rebels was of the scorched earth variety. The loose discipline of the imperial troops was another result of the Manchus' two-hundred-year reign, during which the post of soldier had steadily lost social and political luster and finally become a refuge only for those who could not succeed as civil bureaucrats, scholars, farmers, or merchants. Such men were ill-disposed toward mercy or regional loyalty, and their making a wasteland of the territories assigned to them at least gave the emperor no cause for complaint.

In truth, the Taiping rebellion had seen unrestrained brutality practiced by both sides. In the face of this fact, even sinophilic Westerners had been forced to admit that, while the people of the Middle Kingdom could not generally be accused of cowardice, it would (as one Western expert who observed the rebellion wrote) "be more difficult perhaps to defend the Chinese against the charge of being cruel." This cruelty may have been qualitatively no different from that which characterized the peoples and governments of many Eastern and Western nations during the mid–nineteenth century. But, as was so often the case, the Chinese outdid the rest of the world in quantity. During the ten years since the Taiping rebellion's outbreak, the people of the Middle Kingdom endured almost unbelievable suffering: by 1860, somewhere between 10 and 20 million Chinese had died in battle, been slaughtered wholesale, or starved to death. But not before exhausting every possibility of survival: In several cities and towns ravaged by the rebellion, human flesh had been selling by the pound.

Given such an atmosphere, it was small wonder that the Chung Wang—a man known for his exceptional decency and leniency—should have inspired fanatical devotion among his people. By distributing food and money to starving Chinese peasants in the territories he conquered, the Chung Wang was able to net immense popularity on both sides of the rebellion. It was a testament to his humility and perception that he never deluded himself as to the nature of that popularity: "Today," he later wrote in his account of the rebellion, "if everyone knows the name of the Chung Wang Li Hsiu-ch'eng it is really because I was ready to distribute money; even enemy officers and officials with whom I came into contact I treated well; and because I was willing to give help to the suffering people. . . . It is not because I was talented, and I was not the head of the government."

The point was an important one. The vast body of China's peasantry had scant interest in the Taiping faith and little affection for the Manchu dynasty—the brutality practiced by both sides ensured as much. Popular loyalty in this most cataclysmic of the world's civil wars was therefore generally secured through one simple policy: decent treatment. The same citizens who might flee the advance of a Taiping general who was, for example, an ex-bandit using the cause as a cover for plundering (and there was more than one such man in the rebel camp) might easily welcome the advance of the Chung Wang. Similarly, villagers who had once risen in rebellion against oppressive Manchu officials might shift their loyalties back again if an enlightened imperial commander appeared on the scene (although in 1860 there were precious few of these).

In the century and a quarter since its conclusion, the Taiping rebellion has been represented by various commentators—from Western missionaries excited by the rebels' neo-Christianity to Chinese revolutionaries searching for the roots of their populism—as an ideological struggle. But while the religious and political components were important as detonators, the more fundamental and long-standing desire for decent treatment was the charge. Because of this, the struggle became—to an extent only grudgingly conceded by social historians—one of personalities, of individual leaders and their idiosyncratic policies.

And among these personalities, in the spring of 1860, the agitated, restless young general known as the Chung Wang was preeminent.

During the march to Soochow he once again demonstrated why. Meeting exceptionally stiff imperial resistance at the walled town of Tan-yang, the Chung Wang spent two days reducing its defenses. Upon learning that the imperial commander of Tan-yang had died during the battle, the Chung Wang ordered his body found, placed in a coffin, and buried at the foot of the town's pagoda: rare treatment for a fallen antagonist during so bitter a conflict. But, as the Chung Wang put it, "[a]live he was an enemy, dead, he was a hero; I did not bear him any hatred." The Chung Wang claimed that the imperialists lost 10,000 men at Tan-yang, and, while such numbers were invariably exaggerated by both sides during the rebellion, the victory did open the way to the town of Ch'ang-chou, the first vital position on the line to Soochow.

The capture of walled cities and towns was the outstanding feature of warfare throughout China during the Taiping period, but it had particular importance in Kiangsu province. Here the mountains and hills that surround the Yangtze farther upriver settle into a flat, rich alluvial plain, as the surging waters calm and spread into a nourishing delta. This was some of China's finest farm country: moist, rich earth laced by tens of thousands of small creeks and manmade canals. Most of these waterways were impassable to anything but small rivercraft, and their nerve centers were the towns that appeared at crucial intersections. As a general rule these towns were surrounded by high walls—sometimes as thick as they were tall—into which were cut gates in the primary directions of the compass. Some towns were actually built over the creeks and canals, and most were surrounded by muddy moats that, given the near-medieval state of China's military development, offered additional protection. Outside the walls stockades and trenches were constructed as a first line of defense, and these could be formidable. The Chinese excelled at the construction of earthworks, as well as at their destruction, usually accomplished through tunneling and mining with heavy explosive charges.

By mid-May the Chung Wang was approaching Ch'ang-chou, where he made short work of the outer defenses. The city itself held out for a few days, falling on May 20. A familiar scene then took place, as the Chung Wang recorded: "After entering the town, we did not kill or harm the people, but some were so frightened that they jumped into the water and were drowned." The Chung Wang allowed his men a full two days' rest, then proceeded southeast. The T'ien Wang's deadline for taking Soochow was drawing nearer.

From Ch'ang-chou the Taipings marched along the Grand Canal, an extensive manmade waterway built during the sixth and seventh centuries to connect the Kiangsu breadbasket with the northern provinces. Every stage of their advance brought the rebels deeper into a landscape which was strikingly unlike the rough, impoverished country of southern China, where their cause had originated. Kiangsu's cultivated fields, bamboo groves, and freshwater lakes offered a life-style that had always been beyond the grasp of peasants in provinces such as the Chung Wang's own Kwangsi. Approaching the town of Wu-hsi, the Taipings came within sight of the largest inland body of water in the region, T'ai Lake, its waters clearer than the muddy Yangtze and hemmed in by sloping hills. A sharp but relatively quick battle for Wu-hsi took place, and then the Chung Wang again paused for two days.

The approach to Soochow brought clear signs that the retreating imperial armies, aware that their hope of halting the rebel advance was vain, were turning to their usual practice of plundering and burning as they departed. The Chung Wang met with decreasing resistance and an increasingly war-weary populace as he neared what was reputed to be the richest city in all China. Soochow, known for its fine textiles and beautiful women, was a showplace of complex ornamental gardens winding among extensive waterways spanned by delicate bridges. More important, it was the administrative center of the region, the possession of which lent its captors immense legitimacy in the eyes of the peasants. On his arrival the Chung Wang surrounded the city and made ready for an assault. But the imperialists were already gone. Remarkably, Soochow was conceded without a fight on June 2—the precise termination of the T'ien Wang's one-month deadline. Upon entering the city the Chung Wang found that many Manchu officials were already on their way to Shanghai, and those who had not escaped he guaranteed safe passage back to their own people.

In Soochow, as in every town or village they took, the Taipings destroyed Buddhist and Taoist idols, denounced the teachings of Confucius, and propagated the faith of Shang-ti. But in Soochow the Taipings found their revolutionary ardor far less welcome than in poorer districts. The citizens, said the Chung Wang, were "ungovernable and wicked and would not be pacified." At last, in a signal demonstration of the power of individual leaders during the rebellion, the Chung Wang himself ventured into the villages around the city: "From all sides people came with weapons in their hands and surrounded us. All the civil and military officials with me turned pale. I was willing to sacrifice my life if the people of Soochow could be pacified; so when spears threatened my life I did not draw back. I explained everything and the people were convinced and everywhere ceased their activity and put aside their weapons." In addition to civilians, large numbers of former imperialist soldiers went over to the Chung Wang's standard. His army was gaining irresistible momentum.

But not all Kiangsu's residents were eager to live under rebel rule. As word of the remarkable events at Soochow made its way east, panic among imperial officials and peasants heightened. This was an experience wholly out of the ken of the province's farmers and merchants. Clearly the Chung Wang's Taiping horde was not to be stopped by the undisciplined troops under the command of local Manchu officers, who continued to desert in large numbers. After the fall of Soochow, a pair of the emperor's senior servants in the region wrote (or, as the process was known, "memorialized") to their master in Peking that "[t]he whole area is deserted, and there is no means by which to raise a hand [against the rebels]." The stream of refugees moving toward the coast became ever larger, their desperation ever greater.

The hopes of these frightened thousands were fixed on what had been, until fairly recently, a muddy, comparatively unimportant trading town at the juncture of the Huang-pu River and Soochow Creek, a town that was now—through the bustling, often bizarre activities of its small multinational population—fast on its way to becoming China's greatest emporium.

* * *

19

In old Chinese it meant "above the sea," but in the last century and a half the name *Shanghai* has assumed a set of connotations that have little to do with geography. And the port that the Chung Wang approached in the summer of 1860 was hard at work building that reputation. One of five "treaty ports" that Great Britain had forced the imperial Chinese government to open to foreign trade and residence following the Opium War in 1842, Shanghai was an ancient city that had known no Western resident before that year. Plagued for centuries by typhoons and Japanese pirates, Shanghai was not one of southern China's most fashionable cities. Soochow was more beautiful, Canton a greater commercial center, and almost any city had a better climate, especially in summer, when Shanghai's dank air hung heavy with cholera, dysentery, and smallpox. The crowded inner city—enclosed by a three-and-a-half-mile wall in A.D. 1554—was a notorious sinkhole of filth and crime. For all these reasons, Shanghai ranked in the collective mind of the Chinese elite as less important than the other four treaty ports: Ningpo, Foochow, Amoy, and Canton.

Yet Shanghai had advantages that the Chinese—who had long since abandoned any seafaring ambitions—had never appreciated. Located in almost the exact middle of the long Chinese coast, it was convenient to ships sailing to northern as well as to southern parts of the empire. Situated near the mouth of the eminently navigable Yangtze, it was a natural gateway to the interior. And there were other amenities. Shanghai's climate might not have been the best, but the surrounding countryside was loaded with dozens of species of game, and the shooting was excellent. (Unacquainted with shotguns, the Chinese could hardly have taken full advantage.) On a more commercial level, the general lack of interest displayed by Chinese officials toward the affairs of Shanghai made it a haven for outlaws as well as a logical center for smuggling: Soon after the conclusion of the war which took its name from the drug, chests of opium began pouring into Shanghai, creating vast fortunes for those intrepid Western "businessmen" brave enough to endure Shanghai's hostile climate and far from cosmopolitan atmosphere.

These sporting traders, smugglers, and adventurers were the founders of Shanghai's foreign community, which took root outside the walls of the inner (or, as it was soon known, Chinese) city in the years following 1842. The British were granted a corner parcel of land fronting both the Huang-pu and Soochow Creek, and they quickly set about civilizing it in typical fashion. Huge pilings were driven into the silt- and mud-covered bank of the Huang-pu, and the area was filled in with dirt. A long stretch of park was created, soon to be dubbed the Bund (an Indian term for "embankment"). In 1850 there were just over 175 permanent foreign residents in Shanghai, but there were already some twenty-five mercantile firms building large, bungalow-style headquarters along the Bund, which was destined to become one of the world's great trading strips.

In 1849 the French made arrangements with the Chinese government for their own "concession," built on land between the British settlement and the Chinese city. And soon it was the turn of the Americans, who colonized the waterfront across Soochow Creek. (In the words of one early historian of the period, "the American settlement was not created, but just 'growed.'") Streets and roads that followed meandering creeks were laid throughout all three areas: only twenty to twenty-five feet wide and little more than mud tracks when the rainy season arrived. Large wooden gates were placed at the intersections of many of these roads (their closure at night was a safeguard against rioting by the Chinese), and a primitive system of oil-burning street-lights gave a slight sense of security to nocturnal wanderers. Houses were built by the score, open-air structures that, despite their occasional expense, were designed with the summer months in mind and could be immensely uncomfortable during Shanghai's frequently brisk winters.

No question of climate or terrain, however, could dampen the amazing spirit of Shanghai's small but rugged foreign community, a spirit that was perhaps best symbolized by the fact that before the Western settlements had a municipal council they had a racetrack. The first version was built in 1850 and saw contests primarily between Chinese ponies, but by 1854 a new, larger track on the western edge of the British settlement had been constructed—complete with grandstand— and residents were soon bringing thoroughbreds from home and Arabians from India to compete. Before long foreign Shanghai had a library, a literary and scientific society, even amateur theatricals in a converted warehouse. But none of these ever achieved the popularity of the track. When races were not being run, it was open to the public as a bridal path, its infield was used for cricket matches, and it became the principal outdoor arena for the unique blend of Western civility and freebooting panache that was Shanghai society.

In all, despite its climatic drawbacks and its inattentiveness to sanitation (in the early years of the foreign settlements most sewage was simply dumped over the edge of the Bund), Shanghai in the 1850s was a far more appealing place than one might have expected to find in an empire torn by a singularly savage rebellion. One visitor described the port's foreign residents "riding or gyrating on the race course, as though they were being lounged. Those who prefer gossip to exercise frequent the Bund, a broad quay which extends the whole length of the Settlement, and which is crowded with Chinese porters all the morning and sprinkled with European ladies and gentlemen in the afternoon. The harmony and hospitality of Shanghai make it infinitely the most agreeable place of residence in China."

By 1860 there were still no more than a few thousand permanent foreign residents in Shanghai (living alongside the few hundred thousand Chinese who were crammed in and around the walled city), but there was another element that was increasingly affecting life in the settlements: transient soldiers and sailors. As trade in Shanghai grew—by 1860 more than two hundred foreign cargo ships might be docked in the port at any one time—so did the number of sailors wandering the streets of the city looking for work or, just as often, for a way to relieve their boredom between journeys. As for soldiers, England had once again gone to war with China in 1856—this time with the assistance of France—in an effort to force further trading privileges out of a Chinese government that had no wish to see foreign barbarians doing extensive business outside the five treaty ports. Although hostilities in this conflict were primarily confined to the extreme north and south of the empire, Shanghai was a common port of call for military units in transit.

As might be expected, an entire industry devoted to the entertainment and intoxication of such men grew up in the foreign settlements.

Brawling and general disorderliness became a very real problem. Because most of the city's legitimate trade was carried on in the British settlement—and because that settlement had not only a police force but a jail and magistrates willing to put people in it—this problem was considerably worse in the American settlement and especially the French concession, where municipal revenue was raised in large part through the sale of licenses for brothels as well as gambling and opium dens. Many such houses became legendary, as did the whores who worked them. By the spring of 1860 the *North China Herald,* Shanghai's outspoken proponent of British views and the official organ of the British consulate, had this to say to soldiers whose "thirst, which seems little short of that of Tantalus" drove them to drunken misconduct:

> As long as all this takes place among ourselves, and not too often, we cannot complain, but unfortunately curiosity carries the soldier among the Chinese, and it is then his peculiarities become dangerous; his martial bearing and winning ways are not appreciated by the ladies of China, as they are by those of his native country, damsels do not find the same attraction here in a red coat as they do elsewhere, his bargaining propensities are viewed with suspicion, and his presence in a Chinese shop is strongly objected to, the rough way in which he meets and overcomes obstacles, (Chinamen included) is repugnant to the Chinese mind, and the natives are beginning to find no amusement in the intoxicated soldier, and heartily to detest all those little eccentricities so common to his cloth.

An attitude of arrogance toward the Chinese was hardly unique to drunken soldiers. Disdain for their hosts characterized many if not most of the Westerners in the Middle Kingdom. On the other hand, the recent decades of closer contact had done little to improve the opinion that those hosts held of their guests. To the average Chinese the foreigners were coarse "barbarians" intent only on exploitation; to the average Westerner the Chinese were stubborn upholders of a backward order. And no group aroused greater antipathy in the foreigners than the ruling Manchus and their hirelings in the treaty ports. Whether or not the

Taiping cause had merit—and there were many foreigners, especially missionaries, who felt that its close approximation of Christianity was worthy of encouragement—the visitors certainly had no trouble understanding how it had grown so strong. As the *North China Herald* put it:

> The Great Rebellion, like an old *fungus* full of proud flesh, does not heal up; on the contrary, if popular rumors may be taken as an index of the matter, it continues to go from bad to worse. . . . The old foundations of this government are thoroughly rotten; its ranks and orders are broken; and its gorgeous decorations are in tatters. It is no mere ghoul that is devouring the body-politic. The evils are *legion;* year by year they multiply; and no mortal can tell when or what will be the end of these things.

In the spring of 1860, as Shanghai's already crowded Chinese city began to fill up and finally overflow with refugees from the west, the foreign community grew increasingly curious about the nature of the army that was headed their way. True, the possibility that the rebellion would adversely affect trade alarmed many Westerners. And, despite missionary pleas for indulgence of the rebels, the apparently blasphemous elements of the Taiping religion (primarily the T'ien Wang's repeated references to the Supreme Lord as his "Heavenly Father" and to Christ as his "Heavenly Elder Brother") became sources of deep concern in the settlements. But England and France were at war with China in other parts of the empire, and if a Taiping victory meant an end to Manchu corruption and obstinacy, it might be desirable. Thus few foreigners saw any reason in 1860 to abandon the policy of neutrality that had been their approach to China's difficulties throughout the decade of rebellion—provided, of course, that the Chung Wang promised not to harm Western residents or interfere with their commerce.

But this calm resolve began to erode with the arrival of ever more alarming reports from the field. In the beginning of June news of rebel movements around Ch'ang-chou finally reached the coast. The *North China Herald*'s correspondent put "the rebels now between Nanking and Ch'ang-chou at 140,000 (!) divided into seven large columns. This, with all the division and subtraction invariably to be applied to returns of the kind in China, still leaves it to be inferred that the Nanking garrison did break out in considerable strength." From the city of Hang-chow, conquered by the rebels, came tales of butchered Buddhist priests and general devastation: "Accurate statistics are difficult to obtain in such cases, but the reports generally concur in the statement that *from fifty to seventy thousand lives were lost* in a few days; and it is still more sad to think that a large proportion of these were suicides."

Such reports—accompanied by mounting rumors that Taiping spies were at work in Shanghai, preparing the city for conquest—had an alarming enough effect on the foreigners in Shanghai; their effect in the Chinese city and among imperial officials was devastating. Suspected rebel agents were captured in mounting numbers and dealt with summarily, as the *Herald* reported: "There have been many executions in the city during the week; the victims are said to be rebels. That they are obnoxious to the authorities from that or some other cause there is no doubt. On the bridge a short way up the Soochow Creek there are some twenty heads suspended. A most disgusting spectacle placed there to inspire terror into the minds of the dreaded rebels." At length, knowing the exact value of the few imperial troops remaining in the region, the Chinese governors of Shanghai appealed to the British and French to land troops from their warships and garrison the city.

The same Chinese government that was at war with England and France in other parts of the empire was asking for Allied help in Shanghai: It was a paradox not uncharacteristic of the rulers of China and certainly typical of the men who held effective power in the port of Shanghai. The imperial governor of Kiangsu, Hsüeh Huan, would ordinarily have exercised authority from Soochow, but he was now attempting to direct affairs in what little of the province he still controlled from the coast. Hsüeh had long experience dealing with both rebels and foreigners—he was the imperial commissioner for the five treaty ports—and it was widely rumored in the foreign settlements that his plan was to set the second group against the first. The "cunning commissioner," as the *Herald* called him, was "a rising man, and it will be the making of him if . . . he can induce the barbarian commanders-in-chief to help exterminate the enemies of the Emperor, and to retake Soochow."

But a cardinal rule in the Chinese bureaucracy was not to acknowledge involvement in such schemes unless and until they succeeded. Hsüeh Huan therefore shielded himself by placing immediate responsibility for involving the Westerners in anti-Taiping activities on the shoulders of one of his most talented subordinates: Wu Hsü, Shanghai's *taotai,* or circuit intendant. (In imperial China, the basic administrative unit was the district, controlled by a magistrate; districts then were grouped into departments, governed by prefects, and three or more departments became a circuit, placed under a taotai. Circuits were then organized into provinces.) Directly responsible for the lofty revenue of Shanghai's customs house, and no more averse to embezzlement than the average Chinese bureaucrat, Wu Hsü was, according to the *Herald,* "an extraordinary man" who possessed "the purse of Fortunatus, . . . a small army of English friends, and a crowd of servants. . . . In his capacity as Taotai and Superintendent of Customs, he has constant intercourse with English officials, and pleases them by his affability and condescension."

To the great nineteenth-century Chinese statesman Li Hung-chang—who knew Wu Hsü in Shanghai and was himself to amass a fortune through corrupt dealings—Wu was "expert in accounting and skillful in hiding deficiencies. . . . [H]is hand is deft at adjusting transactions to his own convenience. He always succeeds in confusing outsiders." Wu sharpened his skill at account juggling, bribery, and extortion—known to Westerners in China as the infamous "squeeze"—in the confines of the Shanghai customs house, which in 1854 had been transferred to an abandoned warehouse pending its move to a new, clock-towered headquarters. Through this renowned checkpoint moved massive amounts of opium (coming in) and tea and silk (going out), as well as food, textiles, and, of course, arms, to be sold at inflated prices to either the imperialists or the rebels. The extent of Wu's wealth was hardly surprising, and while the *Herald* might claim that he was in reality Hsüeh Huan's "mouthpiece and money-bag," it is entirely possible that Wu was in a position of greater de facto power than the governor.

But Wu Hsü needed to cover his activities bureaucratically just as much as Hsüeh Huan did, and to this end the taotai associated himself very closely with the successful banker Yang Fang. Yang was a native of Chekiang province who was also known to Westerners as Taki, because he headed a large financial house of that name. A director of the Committee of Patriotic Chinese Merchants, who came together to determine how best to apply their enormous wealth to the Taiping problem, Yang Fang's contacts with Westerners in China had been just as extensive and far more informal than either Wu Hsü's or Hsüeh Huan's. Originally a native agent, or compradore, for Shanghai's largest Western merchant firm—Jardine, Matheson and Company—Yang had made a fortune in banking that allowed him to purchase a mandarinate as well as a beautiful young girl for a wife (the sale of female children in China was still very common). Gregarious and by all accounts accommodating, Yang had taken the extra step of gaining a basic working knowledge of English, and both his *yamen* (office) and his home were frequented by foreigners from every walk of life.

Together, Yang Fang and Wu Hsü were involved in a multitude of commercial activities in Shanghai, everything from a "Houseless Refugees Fund"—maintained by Western donations, only a portion of which reportedly made their way to the refugees—to fitting out armed river steamers for the suppression of pirates on the Yangtze and the Huangpu. The two men's experience with foreigners made them valuable to their Manchu superiors (although they were also considered somewhat tainted by their extensive dealings with the barbarians), and their mastery of every in and out of the Byzantine Chinese bureaucracy in Shanghai made them indispensable to Westerners wishing to do business there.

Yet for all that they were the three most powerful men in Chinese Shanghai, Hsüeh Huan, Wu Hsü, and Yang Fang retained an air of nervous pragmatism. This skittish adaptability had been a large part of the reason they had come so far; and in the spring of 1860 it allowed them to see clearly that the defense of the Shanghai region and of their extensive financial and commercial empires—not to mention the recapture of Kiangsu province and the trade routes with the interior—was not an undertaking in which they could expect any help from the beleaguered central government in Peking. Attempts to reorganize the few local imperial troops that had not already deserted, moreover, held little promise of success. If a disaster greater than those that had befallen Soochow and Hangchow was to be avoided at Shanghai, a wholly new instrument of defense would have to be created.

It was natural, given their backgrounds, that Hsüeh, Wu, and Yang looked to the foreign settlements to supply such an instrument. All three knew the Westerners well: They had seen, over the years, the power of Western weapons and the efficiency of Western troops, and they were anxious to bring that power and efficiency to bear on the rebels. This meant both the defense of Shanghai proper and offensive actions against those towns in the surrounding countryside considered vital to the maintenance of trade. The three men hoped to induce the foreigners to undertake these tasks by exploiting their concern for their property and safety.

But Wu Hsü's repeated personal appeals for Allied military assistance produced no greater result than a proclamation issued by the British minister to China on May 26. Declaring that "Shanghai is a port open to foreign trade, and the native dealers residing therein have large transactions with the foreigners," the proclamation went on to promise that British troops would "take proper measures to prevent the inhabitants of Shanghai from being exposed to massacre and pillage." And, to be sure, the foreign settlements did start to make military provisions— but almost entirely for the defense of their land and interests as separate from those of the Chinese. Such measures only aggravated the fears of Hsüeh, Wu, and Yang for the safety of their own property and people. When the *North China Herald* announced that it would be "humiliating" for the British to abandon the "grand national principle of nonintervention to protect some half dozen native merchants inordinately rich and covetous, . . . a couple of third-rate mandarins, and a beggarly indifferent hostile population," Hsüeh, Wu, and Yang's course became clear. They were determined to have a defensive military unit that would offer them the considerable security of Western technology. If the regular Allied armed forces would not offer it, they would seek it elsewhere.

Or, as it happened, be sought by it. For in May an intrepid young man walked into Wu Hsü's yamen and put forward a proposal that, even by Shanghai standards, was unusual.

Known as "the Cinderella among the settlements," the American section of Shanghai was a haven for adventurers of every conceivable stripe, from outright criminals to men who craftily hid their questionable activities under the veil of commerce. In addition, the settlement was a sanctuary for many Chinese: Imperial tax laws did not apply in the foreign settlements, and the Americans were not so stern as the British and the French about ejecting natives. Separated from the French and British quarters as much by social customs and values as by the waters of Soochow Creek, the American settlement grew to have a fluid character all its own, in which foreigners and Chinese engaged in joint business ventures that covered the spectrum from marginally legal to blatantly unlawful by either Western or Chinese standards.

There was little that either the American consul in Shanghai or the American minister to China (who lived in the port, as he was not yet permitted by the emperor to reside in Peking) could do about any of this: Law in the American settlement in 1860 was confined to one marshal with no jail. Such a predicament made the American consul beholden to the British for penal space, a fact that the American minister found "humiliating." The consul, William L. G. Smith, wrote that if the British proved unable to provide such space, his next move was generally to inquire "whether the party was able to pay a fine; if, as is almost always the case, he has no means for doing this, I refuse to entertain the complaint. I have no alternative." In addition, Smith was a native of Buffalo, New York, who found Shanghai's climate not at all to his liking. By 1860 he was complaining that the combination of hard work and large amounts of quinine (used to keep malaria at bay) were making it imperative that he return home. In his agitation over his health, he was even less disposed to grapple with annoying questions of law enforcement.

Consul Smith came into contact with merchants, smugglers, sailors, drunkards, and fortune hunters every day. It is therefore understandable that when he crossed paths with a sometime sailing officer from Salem,

Massachusetts, called Frederick Townsend Ward early in 1860 he saw no reason to mention it in his consular dispatches. Ward, twenty-eight years old at the time, was a handsome man, just five foot seven but, according to Augustus A. Hayes (a fellow New Englander and junior partner in one of Shanghai's largest commercial houses), "well made and athletic." Ward sported "a black mustache, and his black hair was worn long on his shoulders. His manners were excellent, and his voice pleasant." The feature that provoked the most comment among those who met Ward, however, were his eyes. They were variously reported as being black, deep hazel, and dark blue, in all probability because their actual color was less important than their quality of gleaming restlessness. Something of a social chameleon, Ward was capable by turns of carrying on polite conversation with diplomatic envoys and holding his own in any of Shanghai's saloons. But to a man in Consul Smith's position he could not have looked like very much more than another penniless American sailor scouring Shanghai for lucrative excitement. And since Ward's search had taken him down a legal path—he had secured work as first mate on a succession of riverboats—there was even less reason to remark on his presence in the city.

But if Consul Smith had not seen fit to notice his young countryman's exceptional qualities, others had. A reputation for bravery and coolheaded daring soon netted Ward the post of first officer on an armed river steamer, the *Confucius,* which patrolled the waterways around Shanghai in search of pirates. "Pirates," in the Shanghai of 1860, could often mean Taiping rebels (and vice versa), and Ward had soon experienced scattered run-ins with the followers of the T'ien Wang. The well-armed *Confucius* was captained by one of Ward's fellow Americans, who called himself Gough and styled himself "Admiral." Gough's employer was Shanghai's Pirate Suppression Bureau, yet another organization conceived and operated by Wu Hsü and Yang Fang. Early in 1860 Gough was given the additional task of organizing a small group of waterfront habitués to scout the countryside around Shanghai and give warning of any rebel approach. The admiral demonstrated his trust in Ward by putting him in charge of the project. Ward's contacts with the rebels became more regular.

The United States, like Great Britain and France, had officially adopted a neutral stance toward China's internal difficulties. The activities of men like Admiral Gough and his young protégé Ward—though officially explained as police actions—came dangerously close to crossing the line of partisan military activity. Already during the Taiping rebellion, one American by the memorable name of Sandwich Drinker had accepted an advance of $20,000 from the gentry of Canton to organize a similar "antipirate" force and had seen his plans aborted by the American consul in that city. Drinker's intentions were judged prejudicial to China's national integrity (although American diplomats had decided that he deserved a consolation fee for his troubles, and the Chinese were thus made to pay even more money for services not rendered). No such fate befell Gough and Ward, however, quite possibly because Consul Smith in Shanghai had no interest in being so diligent. As long as the activities of the Pirate Suppression Bureau created no diplomatic incident, they were allowed to proceed.

Admiral Gough apparently did not introduce Ward to his own paymaster, the banker Yang Fang, but the network of acquaintance among so small a foreign population as that of Shanghai ensured that the meeting eventually did take place. Its architect was one of Shanghai's many commercial factotums, Charles E. Hill, an American whose fame rested on his being "the introducer into China of the Troy dredging machine." Hill was an arranger of the classic mold: "an enterprising man, with a great deal on his hands, and with the hopeful side of his nature more developed than the other," was how one American official put it. "I do not believe," Hill later claimed, "there is one man in the world who knows what I owe, or who owes me, or what I am worth." This sort of attitude—at once secretive and boastful—was common to many of Shanghai's commercial freebooters, native as well as foreign, and it is not surprising that Hill should have been friends with both Ward and Yang Fang. Hill later said that for Yang he "did more . . . than I would for any other man in China at the time."

The exact date of Ward's introduction to Yang Fang was never recorded, but the energetic young New Englander and the wily old Chinese banker apparently took to each other from the start. Yang did not, however, hold sufficient bureaucratic power to sanction projects such as the Pirate Suppression Bureau officially, and Ward's mind was beginning to fill with plans for the protection of Shanghai that went beyond the scope of the bureau. The authority needed to pursue such goals rested with Wu Hsü. Either Ward convinced Admiral Gough to arrange an introduction or the idea was Gough's own; at any rate, Ward and the taotai finally met, almost certainly in May, with Yang Fang also present.

Wu's desire to bring Western expertise to bear on the Taiping problem was well known. He could hardly fail to be interested, therefore, when Ward—who, Gough told Wu, was "well trained in the art of war"—offered to organize a small but heavily armed group of free-lance foreigners, lead them into the field, and engage the rebels. The proposed force, said its would-be commander, would prove capable of recapturing vital walled towns and in time even cities. Their pay would be according to a set scale: Ward's enlisted men would receive approximately fifty American dollars per month (although actual payment would be made in silver Mexican dollars), his officers about two hundred, and Ward himself just over five hundred, plus a handsome bonus for each town recaptured. The amount of the bonus would vary according to the size of the town; but it would, at the very least, reach into the tens of thousands of dollars.

These were heady sums for the place and time. And Wu, Gough's recommendations notwithstanding, had no hard knowledge of Ward's background or abilities. Furthermore, Peking was known to look with disapproval on the idea of using Westerners to fight the rebels. Add to this a considerable language barrier and the extent of Ward's achievement in persuading Wu Hsü to release the vast sums necessary for the training, pay, and equipment of his force becomes clear. True, Wu continued to cover himself in the usual fashion, instructing Yang Fang to take care of the actual payments (most of which were made to Ward through the Pirate Suppression Bureau). And, because Ward was apparently the only man in Shanghai willing to take the field against the rebels, Wu was in no position to be selective. Yet it was still a risk of enormous proportions.

Mere talk would not have persuaded a man of Wu Hsü's position and experience to take the gamble. Shanghai was full of large talkers, and few of these had ever gained the ear, much less the confidence, of the taotai. There was a real force at work in Ward, one that was apparent to observers and that inspired immediate acceptance of his fantastic claim that he could take a small band of men against the Chung Wang's legions and come away the victor.

That force had been formed during some fifteen years of adventuring, and during the following two and a half years it would power the evolution of Ward's small group of mercenaries into a full-fledged army that was crucial to the defeat of the Taipings. The achievement was a lasting one; for, although the conquering hordes of the Chung Wang seemed to represent a "new race of warriors" to some Westerners, the men Ward eventually led against the rebels were the true "new race." His army was a synthesis of the warlike arts of China and the West, and without it the Chinese empire might not have survived. While forging this unique weapon, Ward lived one of the great adventures in the history of Chinese-Western relations: He rose to become the Chung Wang's most talented antagonist, snatched his own measure of popularity among the peasants of Kiangsu away from the Taiping general and his cohorts, and finally died a mandarin and a general of the Chinese army—unheard-of honors for a barbarian Westerner.

All this from a man who did not live to see his thirty-first birthday: Ward's Chinese sponsors were not alone in wondering what could have enabled this American to achieve such heights with such speed.

II

"PERHAPS YOU SMILE..."

Half a world away from the rising star of Shanghai was the fading light of Salem, Massachusetts, once America's center of international trade but by 1860 wholly overshadowed by Boston and New York. When Frederick Townsend Ward was born here on November 29, 1831, the port was still fighting hard to maintain a share of the Africa, India, and China trades. But the glory days that had seen hundreds of Salem ships coming from and going to every corner of the globe were ending, and the vain struggle to compete only chafed at the nerves of an already cantankerous breed. The citizens of Salem—best known for their 1692 torture and execution of suspected witches—had built a narrow-laned town whose monotonous miles of clapboard and brick gave way to openness and a sense of physical freedom only when they ended: at the waterfront, where the wharves of great trading families such as the Crowninshields stretched out into the sea.

No city or town was more typical of the hypocrisy of pre–Civil War New England than Salem. Preaching puritanism in their churches, Salemites had participated in the American Revolution and then in the War of 1812 by turning their seafaring talents to "privateering," the gentleman's euphemism for piracy. Soon thereafter it was abolitionism that became the gospel of choice in New England parlors, yet Salem continued to facilitate that greatest of American crimes, the African slave trade. In the generations before 1861, an estimated 30 percent of all slaves were brought into the United States aboard New England vessels—and Salem was synonymous with New England shipping. Massachusetts abolitionists might write laws and tracts decrying the evils of the South's "peculiar institution," but even at the outbreak of the Civil War masters of Salem ships were being prosecuted for slaving.

The Salem masters were hard and immensely practical men, more than capable of crossing the line between pragmatism and amorality. Uncomfortable with this fact, and with the legacy of their ancestors' participation in the African slave trade, subsequent generations of Salemites chose to emphasize the port's seemingly less sordid trade with the Chinese empire. It had been a New England ship that had opened America's China trade in 1794, and in the following year a full-rigged Salem bark of 310 tons, the *Grand Turk,* had been the second American vessel to reach the Middle Kingdom. At that time only the port of Canton in southern China was open to foreigners, and at first the Salem captains brought primarily goods native to their own region: furs, lead, cotton, and the New England species of the root ginseng (the Chinese belief in the root's power to restore virility quickly exhausted the empire's domestic supply). But during the opening decades of the nineteenth century, as American traders discovered the apparently inexhaustible appetite of the Chinese for luxury goods, U.S. ships scoured the Atlantic and Pacific Oceans from Alaska to the Falkland Islands seeking the edible bird's nests, tortoiseshell, snails, beaver furs, and mother-of-pearl that would command large quantities of tea and silk in the burgeoning Canton markets.

With the coming of the industrial revolution in the West, a new commodity joined tea and silk on the list of principal Chinese exports: cheap human labor. Desperately poor or pitiably naive Chinese were swindled into disingenuous contracts—or simply abducted outright—and then packed into ships and taken abroad to live in conditions that were often as miserable as those they had left behind. Called coolies, these Chinese may not have been outright slaves. But, as in Africa, the morality of the trade did not harmonize with the preachings of New England ministers; yet, as from Africa, New England ships carried the cargo. Nearly every Salem family who could afford them had Chinese servants, and the port eventually became so identified with the China

35

trade that its parades featured local girls dressed in the finery of Chinese maidens. Underlying this charming veneer, however, was the hard reality of Chinese misfortune.

Thus one great-grandmother might recall whimsically of Salem during the pre–Civil War era,

> The wharves . . . were lined with ship-chandlers' and sail-makers' shops, warehouses, and counting rooms, the sailmakers sitting cross-legged like Turks, sewing the sails with thimbles fastened into the middle of their palm, while the odor of tar and canvas pervaded the premises. The old wharf and sail lofts that fronted the street were favorite resorts of my childhood days and I was never so happy as when allowed to wander about on the old wharf fascinated in watching the loading and unloading of ships that had rounded the point and come lumbering into the port.

Yet other Salem youngsters could detect the dark side of this romance: From his earliest days, the Ward boy called Frederick Townsend showed no attitude toward Salem other than a determined desire to leave it.

How much of this desire was rooted in a simple need to be free from the stifling town and how much was connected to the nature of life in the Ward home is difficult to say. Ward's family made certain of this after his death when, in a moment of astoundingly narrow-minded destructiveness, they destroyed his personal letters and papers. Although they were both the children of prominent families, Ward's parents— Frederick Gamaliel and Elizabeth Colburn Ward—changed residences often during their early years together and generally ended up back at the fine brick mansion that was the residence of young Frederick Townsend's paternal grandfather. Situated near the Crowninshield wharf, the house spoke elegantly of a fine past, as did the poetry with which Ward's mother embellished her personal writings. But the Ward family, like Salem itself, had passed the crest of its fortunes, and in official town records Ward's father was described simply as a "mariner." He would later add ship's master and ship's broker to his roster of occupations, but at none of these would he achieve any noteworthy success.

Frederick Townsend was the oldest of four children, and he remained close to two of his younger siblings—his brother Henry and his sister Elizabeth—throughout his thirty years. Henry, known to his brother as Harry, would eventually follow Fred to China and become his partner in a broad range of projects. Elizabeth was her eldest brother's principal confidante and correspondent. (She kept Ward's letters and papers carefully stored for decades in four large trunks; it was her executors, a group of cousins as well as her sister-in-law, Harry's widow, who saw to the destruction of these documents.) According to Ward's fellow Salemite and first biographer, Robert S. Rantoul, Fred himself was an unusually quiet child, who uttered no words for the first three years of his life, "and was at last betrayed into speech by an incident which called for action. The cat was breaking into the bird cage, and he rushed, with his first articulate words, to summon his mother. Months elapsed before he spoke again."

In one history of Salem shipping and sailing, Ward's father is described as "a stern disciplinarian of the quarterdeck," and there are many indications that he attempted to apply his shipboard principles at home. His chosen method of swimming instruction, for example, was to strip his young sons and throw them off the wharf, diving in after them to demonstrate his own technique. To be sure, the boys became expert swimmers. But Fred also became famous in Salem for repeating a unique prank: He would deliberately fall off the wharf and feign drowning simply to observe the panic created among adults above. This apparent instinct for making a game of a stern experience was destined to stick—although in later years the games would become quite deadly.

Daniel Jerome Macgowan—an American Baptist missionary and physician who went to China in 1843 and practiced medicine for nearly two decades in the port of Ningpo—was one of the first men to put together a rough sketch of Ward's China exploits. And although he had no intimate knowledge of Ward's early life, Macgowan knew enough of the friction between Ward and his father to mention it in his relatively brief account. The elder Ward was apparently "a severe man," said Macgowan, "whose severity was often complained of in after life by his son." Yet Fred's father indulged him in at least one area: sailing. Apparently intending that his oldest son should follow family tradition, the elder Ward trained his boy to be a master seaman, and by the age of twelve Fred was allowed to sail the family's fifteen-ton sloop *Vivid* on his own.

Ward's schoolmates, interviewed by Robert Rantoul at the turn of the century, still remembered with clarity his singular courage and, beyond that, recklessness. Unafraid to take the *Vivid* out at night or in foul weather, Fred often placed himself in tricky situations. Rantoul cites one case in 1843 when Fred transported a group of women, among them his own mother, to the town of Beverly. Returning in darkness, the sloop encountered a violent storm: "The situation was full of peril. Towards midnight they reached home safe to find the town awake with panic. Throughout the scene Ward sat with a firm hand on the tiller, speechless as the sphynx." The boy's brief assessment of the incident was typical: "When the lightning-flashes showed us who were there, I wished myself at home. It would have been all right if it had not been for the women."

Yet ultimately the sea was not to bind but to further separate Ward and his father. For sailing was the boy's reality, not his dream, and as he reached adolescence his hopes turned to the prospect of becoming a soldier. In 1846 the United States went to war with Mexico, and early in 1847 one of Daniel Webster's sons raised a company of volunteers and paraded them through the streets of Salem. Ward, not yet sixteen, was determined to join the effort. In the company of another Salem youth, he set out one night to follow the troops. The boys' plan and path were discovered before daylight, however, and Ward was brought back to face his father's displeasure.

Ward's mother, by contrast, viewed her son's martial longings with somewhat more sympathy—that, at any rate, was the view expressed by Charles Schmidt, later one of Ward's officers in China and a man who had, by his own reckoning, "a very intimate acquaintance" with Ward. "The seeds—the germ—of command were so strongly imbedded in him," wrote Schmidt,

> that the all watchful eye of the mother pictured to her family his future fame and *warlike* greatness. Her proposition was to send him

to West Point, that the full bent of his soul's desire might there be nurtured in its proper soil. Had he gone, no doubt his native land would have been blessed with the greatness of his genius;—would have been the happy recipient of his Great Generalship. Perhaps you smile—But if he were not a superior being, should we not see his like, now, in the hour of need—here?

(Schmidt was writing in Shanghai in 1863, when the outcome of China's Taiping rebellion was still in doubt.)

Any hope of military training was crushed, however, and Ward's father dealt with his son's rebelliousness in typical Salem fashion: by taking him out of school and packing him off for a long sea voyage aboard a clipper ship. The vessel was the *Hamilton,* captained by William Henry Allen, who had married into the Ward family. Fred, not yet sixteen, was taken on as second mate. The *Hamilton*'s destination was Hong Kong.

Still a boy, Ward was thrown into a world that belonged very much to men, a world in which keelhauling, flogging, mutiny, and murder were all common elements. Quick adjustment was called for. Fortunately, Ward had already developed many tools that served his purpose. Rantoul's interviews of Ward's contemporaries formed a revealing picture of the boy-officer:

> A born fighter, he was no bully. . . . [I]t was his ruling passion to champion the weak, and his strength, which was great, was ever on call in the interest of fair play. . . . He was a favorite with his mates,—they all concur in that judgment,—but if a boy was "spoiling for a fight" Ward did not keep him waiting long. . . . Of no more than medium stature and always slight, compact and wiry, he had the strength of an athlete, and the surviving sister [Elizabeth] recalled with pleasure the frolics of the "children's hour," when, at the end of their evening's romp, they all rode off to bed on his willing shoulders.

And then a telling comment: "What he craved was power,—not the semblance of power."

Ward did well aboard the *Hamilton,* earning Captain Allen's praise.

But the captain, like others before him, was also disturbed by the young man's recklessness. Demonstrating that he had absorbed at least some of the harsh lessons taught by his father, Ward soon gained a reputation among the crew as a strict disciplinarian. While the development of this all-important instrument of command would serve Ward well in later life, it apparently did not sit agreeably with his shipmates on the *Hamilton:* On one occasion the young second officer went over the ship's side, and, while some accounts say that he fell while chasing a butterfly, most concede that he was thrown by crew members weary of his boyish orders.

When the *Hamilton* finally reached Hong Kong, Ward got his first glimpse of the empire that would one day become his arena. Because of his age and the severe restrictions placed by the emperor in Peking on the movements and business activities of foreigners, Ward in all likelihood did not comprehend China's already alarming condition. Had he been able to examine the country more closely or with older eyes, he would undoubtedly have detected in 1847 the origins of the crisis in which he would later play so remarkable a part.

During the mid–nineteenth century a foreign resident of Shanghai, John L. Nevins, went to some lengths to collect, translate, and publish a series of Chinese tracts that he felt would demonstrate to his fellow foreigners the extreme contempt with which most Chinese viewed the West and its representatives. The tone of these tracts was uniformly scathing: "In social intercourse," the Chinese authors wrote of the foreigners,

> men show respect by removing their hats. A less degree of respect is shown by raising the hand to the forehead. . . . They kneel only before God (Shang-ti) and the pre-existent Lord of their sect. When friends meet they inquire about each other's wives but never about parents. They regard parents as belonging to a past period. . . . These people have an outward show of gentility, but their hearts are full of deceit. Their appearance is such as to easily deceive. They all live by carrying on commerce on the sea. . . . At first they confined

themselves to cheating barbarians adjacent to them, not daring to carry on their lawless practices in the Middle Kingdom. Now our Emperor, full of compassion and condescension, has deigned to hold friendly intercourse with them; but these barbarians, so far from appreciating this condescension, have availed themselves of the opportunity to give unbridled license to their lawless propensities.

During the era of Western encroachment into China an enormous gap existed between Chinese and Western concepts of "civilization" and "barbarism." The outward signs of this gap—differences in dress, manners, and business methods—seemed to many nineteenth-century Western visitors somewhat superficial, obstacles that should not and would not impede China's acceptance of other sovereign states as equals and the normalization of trading and political relations. But, as was learned by Portuguese traders and Jesuit priests during the seventeenth and eighteenth centuries, and then by British, French, and finally American merchants and missionaries in the eighteenth and nineteenth centuries, those outward differences were not decorative encumbrances that could be easily swept away. Rather, they were sturdy pillars connected directly to the ancient foundation of a culture that was radically different from anything the Western voyagers had encountered in any other part of the world.

The differences began but did not end with religion. In 1644 the Manchu invaders of China had found in place among their new subjects a "religion" that was at heart a successful ideology of social regimentation and control: Confucianism. The great sage who had taught that reverence for elders and the family was not only sacred but directly analogous to obedience to the emperor and the state was as useful to Tartar rulers as he had been to the Ming; and during the Manchu era the perpetuation of the Confucian system remained the cherished goal of China's middle and upper classes, and, most important, of the literati, the men who became the emperor's civil servants and actually administered the enormously extended family that was China. True, large numbers of peasants indulged their more mystical leanings by worshiping the idols of Buddhism and seeking knowledge of *tao*, "the way," but

Confucianism was never challenged as the ideological force that made the Chinese empire function.

Confucius's definition and elaboration of a virtuous "civilization" was not Christ's, and the vices that the Chinese sage considered "barbarous" did not always correspond to those proscribed by the Bible. The absolute subordination of the individual first to the family, then to the state, and finally to the emperor—the "Son of Heaven"—allowed for physical cruelties in China that struck early Christian missionaries (who seemed to have forgotten such Western religious atrocities as the Inquisition) as unspeakably savage. Children might be bought and sold, human lives extinguished by the tens of thousands and in horrifying ways; men of means might emulate their emperor by purchasing dozens of concubines, while their nominal wives languished in miserable servitude; imperial commissioners and officials might knowingly use duplicity to pursue their master's interests. Yet so long as these activities increased the stability of the Confucian system, they were viewed as permissible and even desirable.

For all the fault that Western visitors found with the Confucian system, however, they repeatedly ran up against one indisputable fact: For thousands of years it had worked, and worked well. Over the centuries China had become self-contained and self-sufficient, an empire that viewed itself as the center of the temporal world and whose statesmen concerned themselves not with external expansion but with internal control. As has only recently been fully understood in the West, for example, the Great Wall itself was built as much to keep China's population inside imperial borders and obedient to the imperial will as to keep foreign marauders out. Over the ages this attitude filtered from the central to the provincial and finally to the local level: A British officer who visited the city of Soochow during the 1860s noticed that its walls were "thickly studded with re-curved hooks, standing about two inches from the surface, and resembling stout nails. They were no doubt intended rather to prevent the garrison escaping than for defence."

Control permeated every aspect of Chinese life. The control of an individual over passions that might interfere with his respect for family and emperor; the control of a father over his family, and of his elders over the father; the control of magistrates and governors over their people; and, finally, the control of the Son of Heaven over them all—these were the relationships that came to define Chinese civilization. An emperor who could exercise such control was said to possess the "Mandate of Heaven," and, should his dynasty be toppled by rebellion, no doubts were cast on the validity of the Confucian order. Rather, it was explained, that dynasty had become unworthy, and the Mandate of Heaven had been transferred to a family more capable of exercising rigorous control.

Because of the powerful ethnocentricity that accompanied this philosophy, the first Europeans to reach China had been viewed as mere oddities by most Chinese. The miserable failure of the Jesuit missionaries to win converts only demonstrated to the guardians of the Confucian order that the world outside could never compete with the Middle Kingdom in strength of civilization. True, Christianity's emphasis on the individual and his private relationship to God seemed dangerous to some Chinese; but the Jesuits did not in fact bring with them any radical or subversive social doctrines. Similarly, the Portuguese traders who infested the island of Macao opposite Canton and Hong Kong could hardly be said to have represented an expansive culture of new ideas. And while China's Russian neighbors to the north were feared for their power, they, too, did not pose any significant threat to China's cultural vitality.

It was not until the British and finally the Americans reached Chinese shores that the rulers of the Middle Kingdom were thrown into panic. This fear, while prompted by religion, was on a deeper level ideological. Here were nations whose acceptance of the Christian doctrine that personal morality was more important than filial obedience had brought them to espousal of what, for the Chinese, was the virtual definition of barbarism: liberal democracy. Such a system theoretically involved not only religious but political and commercial freedom: the right of any people to participate in government, exchange ideas openly, and trade freely with other nations. These were all tremendously dangerous concepts to the Chinese; even more shocking, they were all concepts that began to take hold in China as the eighteenth century came to a close.

Where the Jesuits had failed, British and American Protestants began in the early 1800s to succeed. Granted, by midcentury there were no more than a hundred such missionaries in China. But that number must be considered significant when measured against the hostility of the overriding majority of China's rulers and subjects, and against the fact that until 1842 Canton remained the only Chinese city where foreigners were permitted to reside. (Even in Canton, the Westerners were only allowed to operate in strictly circumscribed areas known as factories.) The interior of China remained forbidden ground to traders and missionaries alike; yet the mounting success of both groups in attracting Chinese citizens revealed cracks in the Chinese system of control that profoundly disturbed many imperial officials at the central, provincial, and local levels.

The Manchu dynasty and its servants were themselves largely to blame for these developments. The intricate, shielded, and socially pervasive Chinese imperial bureaucracy had proved an ideal breeding ground for corruption, and, even before the early days of Western intrusion into China, Peking had grown inattentive to the spread of outrageously dishonest bureaucratic practices. Indeed, many high imperial officials themselves made use of such methods, buying office and influence with comparative impunity. This behavior in turn created an air of discontent among ruined members of the middle class and impoverished peasants that opened their minds to new ideologies. Meanwhile, the heavy cut taken out of the profits of Chinese merchants (a disdained class in the Middle Kingdom) by the imperial government made those merchants more anxious to do business with the West, and to do it covertly whenever possible.

Without doubt, then, the Chinese dragon—for millennia the symbol of imperial power and prestige—lay stricken by the beginning of the nineteenth century, dying of a malady that sprang from the heart and crept into every limb and appendage. But this wasting disease was aggravated by the outsiders—specifically by opium, the West's greatest weapon in the struggle to open China to increased trade. The drug underlay all Western activity in China, though most foreigners chose politely not to recognize or to discuss the fact. Once opium eating and smoking had been an indulgence of a relative handful of well-to-do

Chinese. But in the mid–eighteenth century the British East India Company had discovered that the fashion spread quickly when the available amount of the drug was increased. In light of this discovery the poppy fields of British India were tapped as never before, and between 1750 and 1839 the amount of opium imported into China multiplied a hundred times. In 1834 the East India Company's monopoly on the trade was ended, and private smugglers entered the game; within a year more than 2 million Chinese were addicts.

Economically, the illegal trade crippled China and gave the Westerners an enormous advantage. China's silver reserves poured out of the country to pay for the huge opium shipments, destroying the empire's economy and drastically inflating the number of impoverished peasants. And while legitimate Western imports never equaled the amounts of silk and tea exported by the Chinese, China's balance of trade remained unfavorable because of opium. The drug thus became a vital threat to the integrity and security of the Chinese empire and, simultaneously, the foundation on which the greatest Western mercantile empires in China were built.

The Chinese bureaucracy again betrayed the interests of the empire by facilitating the opium trade. Not only was the official, or mandarin, class populated by thousands of opium smokers and eaters but these men simultaneously made fortunes off Western bribes. Increasingly frantic edicts from Peking forbidding the use of opium were useless, and in 1838 one unusually honest mandarin memorialized to Emperor Tao-kuang:

> There are opium dens in every prefecture of the country, and they are kept as a rule by magistrates' constables and soldiers from the army, who gather together dissolute youngsters from rich local families to indulge in the pipe where they can't be seen. As most of the clerks in the magistracies share the same taste, they are sure to be protected. I beg your majesty to set a date a year from now after which all smokers who persist in their addiction will be put to death. For mark my words a man will bear the discomfort of a cure if he knows that by doing so he has earned the privilege of dying in bed,

whereas indulgence in his craving will bring him to the execution-ground.

But there were opponents of such forceful measures in the government as well, and not all of them were addicted to opium or agents of the trade. Some merely saw the practical problems: "If a man is to fall foul of the law just for taking a pipe of opium," said one such official, "prisoners will be lined up along the roads, as there won't be room for them in the gaols. The whole thing is absolutely impracticable."

In the end, the emperor gave his support to attacking not the demand but the supply side of the opium problem. In 1839 one of the great figures of Manchu history, Imperial Commissioner Lin Tse-hsü, arrived in Canton, forcefully penned the foreigners up in their factories, and flushed 20,000 chests of opium into the sea. It is possible that the Chinese did not realize the extent to which the Western presence in China depended on the drug; it is possible that they believed—of policy as of battle—that a defiant act and a great deal of noise would intimidate their enemy and cause his withdrawal. Instead, the British went to war with typically businesslike determination, and the Chinese got their first taste of Western combat.

It was a sobering experience. The British, said Chinese commanders, had steamships that could "fly across the water, without wind or tide, with the current or against it," as well as amazingly accurate cannon that were "mounted on stone platforms, which can be turned in any direction." As for the Chinese response, lamented one official, not only were the empire's cannon antiquated and her troops poorly trained and disciplined but "our military affairs are in the hands of civil officials, who are very likely admirable calligraphists but know nothing of war." The outcome was inevitable. After putting things right in Canton, the British seized the ports of Amoy, Chefoo, and Ningpo. In June 1842 a British fleet entered the mouth of the Yangtze River and, on its way to Nanking, overpowered Shanghai easily. Nanking offered even less resistance, and on August 29, 1842, an infamous treaty destined to bear that city's name was signed aboard the British warship *Cornwallis*.

The Treaty of Nanking and the supplementary Treaty of the Bogue a year later set the pattern of Chinese-Western relations for the remaining life of the Manchu dynasty. In addition to securing pledges of increased trade and tolerance of missionary activities, the English were allowed to establish settlements in four treaty ports besides Canton—Ningpo, Foochow, Amoy, and Shanghai—and were granted the privilege of extraterritoriality, of being governed by their own laws and courts while residing in a foreign country. The French soon secured the same rights the English had exacted, and in 1844 it was the turn of the Americans. Minister plenipotentiary Caleb Cushing negotiated the Treaty of Wanghia, by which the Chinese granted the United States "most favored nation" status: Any advantages already given to any other power—as well as any advantages granted in the future—were automatically conceded to the United States as well.

The Americans made much of their having obtained from the Chinese by friendly negotiation what the British had taken by force, and it was during this period that the peculiarly persistent notion that the Chinese preferred Americans to other foreigners took hold. The assertion was doubtless valid when applied to relations between Western and Chinese merchants, but U.S. officials in China repeatedly warned their superiors against believing that it had any application to dealings with the Manchu rulers of the empire. As one such official said, "It is quite a mistake to suppose that the rulers of China have any *regard* for one nation more than another; that they are more friendly, for instance, towards the Americans than towards the English; they may, perhaps, *fear* the English and Russians more than they do the Americans, but they would be glad if none of them ever came near them."

As for the opium trade, it expanded dramatically following the opening of the new treaty ports. And the spread of the drug was now facilitated by unlikely allies: Protestant missionaries. Considering Chinese paganism a worse sin than opium addiction, these Christian soldiers often found themselves transported on smugglers' ships and protected by smugglers' guns. At least one prominent missionary, the Dutchman Karl Friedrich August Gutzlaff—whose translations of the Bible and Christian tracts into Chinese were to become standard works—actually hired himself out as an interpreter for opium dealers, defiantly declaring that by using their money to finance his missionary labors he was making the devil do the Lord's work.

The Chinese were quite alive to the fact that Christianity was the spearhead of foreign commercial and political barbarism, and the ferocity of their published attacks on the Westerners' faith was not surprising: "Those who enter this religion practise sodomy without restraint," declared one Chinese pamphlet. "Every seventh day they perform worship which they call the Mass . . . [and] when the ceremony is over all give themselves up to indiscriminate sexual intercourse. . . . They call it the 'Great Communion.' . . . They reject and ignore the natural relations, and are in other respects like beasts." A further appeal was made to Chinese reason: "How is it possible for the Son of God (Shang-ti) to take the form of a man and be born?—When sin has once been committed, how is it possible to atone for it?—Before Jesus was born, in whose hand was the government of the universe?—When his body had ascended to heaven, how could he have a grave for men to worship? Preposterous stories, inconsistent with themselves!"

Such strident criticism produced results: Of the comparatively few Chinese peasants who heeded the calls of the foreign missionaries, many met a gruesome end.

But at the same time, *foreign* had a broad application among Chinese peasants. Two hundred years after the invasion of the Manchus, many citizens still considered their Tartar conquerors to fall within that category. The collapse of the Chinese economy and the humiliation of Manchu soldiers in the Opium War heightened the volatility of the disaffected, who sensed that the dynasty was weakening. That Manchu corruption was at least as responsible for China's predicament as were the Westerners was obvious even to the poorly educated, and before the 1840s were over, rebellion was in the air. "[N]othing is more likely," wrote Thomas Taylor Meadows, one of Britain's most perceptive officials on the scene, "now that the prestige of Manchu power in war has received a severe shock in the late encounters with the English, than that a Chinese Belisarius will arise and extirpate or drive into Tartary the Manchu garrisons . . . who . . . have greatly deteriorated in the military virtues; while they still retain enough of the insolence of conquerors, to gain themselves the hatred of the Chinese."

That Belisarius was not destined to rise until two years after the American clipper *Hamilton* sailed out of Hong Kong with a cargo of tea and silk early in 1848. But the *Hamilton's* young second mate, Frederick Townsend Ward, would return to China several times over the coming decade, and the opportunities offered by the empire's sickened state were ultimately to hold for him a fatal attraction.

Ward's military ardor showed no signs of cooling after his return to Salem. Many accounts state that he attempted to gain admittance to West Point but was blocked when the appointment went to a relative of one of Salem's congressmen. Whether or not this is so, 1848 found Ward enrolled at the American Literary, Scientific and Military Academy, a private institution in Vermont later known as Norwich University. His months at the academy—which offered courses in strategy, tactics, drill, and engineering—provided the only formal military training he would ever receive. Yet despite the great interest he had always shown in land warfare, and in spite of the fact that he was acknowledged to be something of a natural leader, his stay at the academy was a short one. Formal education had never been a strong suit with Ward, and his family's circumstances apparently would not bear an extended course of study. Given these factors, as well as his father's consistent hostility toward military pursuits, it is not surprising that December 16, 1849, found Ward putting once more to sea, this time on the *Russell Glover,* captained by his father and bound for San Francisco.

The ship reached its destination in May 1850, and for the next twelve to eighteen months Ward's movements cannot be traced with any certainty. He was forced for a time to remain aboard the *Russell Glover* as shipkeeper while she was in port, a duty he found frustrating. This frustration could only have been aggravated by the madness of the ongoing gold rush in California; indeed there were several reports that Ward tried his hand at prospecting.

More important, Ward claimed in later life to have made the acquaintance during his youth of the great Sardinian revolutionary and Italian nationalist Giuseppe Garibaldi, and if that story was more than fanciful boasting, the meeting almost certainly took place during this time. Garibaldi, who had aided nationalist struggles in Latin America during the 1840s, once again journeyed from Europe to the Western Hemisphere in 1850. Spending almost a year in New York, he sailed in April 1851 for Nicaragua, Panama, and finally Peru, where he remained until the beginning of 1852. This was a dormant period in Garibaldi's career, during which his personal finances, along with his plans for an Italian nation-state, were in disarray. He spent the sojourn trying to make money rather than inciting revolution. For both Garibaldi and Ward, then, these years were, as one Garibaldi biographer put it, "uneventful, unrecorded, unmemorable." But did their paths ever cross?

Ward's future second-in-command in China, Edward Forester, wrote in 1896 that he first met Ward in South America, although he did not mention a date. However, since most of Ward's remaining years are accounted for, and since none of them involved travels to points farther south than Mexico, it is possible that the meeting with Forester took place in late 1850 or 1851. This would tend to reinforce the suggestion that during this time Ward took ship from San Francisco south to Panama or even to the port of Callao in Peru. He could easily have found a post on one of the many ships that worked this commonly traveled route, and the trip would have placed him in close proximity to Garibaldi.

The actual circumstances of the encounter, even whether it took place at all, are perhaps less important than Ward's enthusiasm for Garibaldi and what he represented. The great liberator's exploits in South America—where he had fought a brutal guerrilla war in Uruguay, married a courageous native woman, and finally emerged a renowned hero—were the stuff of high romance. Garibaldi's politics may have been ultimately vague (the "liberator" was destined one day to be called dictator and to ride through the streets of Naples in a carriage with King Victor Emmanuel), but his courage, his stamina, and his talent for unconventional warfare were beyond question. These were all qualities that Ward later embodied and prized in other men. And, again like Garibaldi, Ward was inattentive and somewhat inept when dealing with life's more pragmatic questions, such as earning a living.

Late in 1851 that question came up again, and Ward took his customary step of shipping out on an American trading vessel. Now an experienced officer, he accepted the post of first mate on a bark bound from San Francisco for Shanghai. The practical decision to return to sea was in no way an indication that Ward's desire for military employment had subsided. Far from it. As Charles Schmidt wrote, "he meant some day to fulfil the destiny allotted to him. . . . In order to get at the final object of his every day study, he took to going to sea, thinking that by observing the difference of chances in other climes he might finally succeed in gaining that object easily. He did not go therefore from choice, or with the intention of becoming a great navigator."

Ward's choice of destination, however, may well have been deliberate. For by early 1852 rumors of rebellion and chaos had begun to make their way out of the Chinese empire—rumors that brought more than one foreign soldier of fortune to the treaty ports in the hope of finding a market for his talents.

The year 1850 had witnessed the sudden rise to eminence in China of two men who, though they were enemies, shared dismal personal shortcomings that were destined to bring the empire to the verge of collapse. The first of these was Hsien-feng, son of the old emperor Tao-kuang. While Tao-kuang had never been prescient or progressive in his dealings with the West (even after the Opium War he referred to the British not as adversaries but as "rebels," demonstrating his continued belief that China occupied a place above all other nations), he had not been entirely foolish. The opening of the five treaty ports had involved a strategy, albeit one of appeasement: By granting the foreigners the right to live and trade in the five cities, it was hoped that their appetite for commerce would be sated enough to make future concessions unnecessary. Therefore, while Tao-kuang was alive the Westerners were given no further cause for serious complaint.

But the ascension of Hsien-feng to the Dragon Throne in 1850 altered the situation significantly. A young libertine, Hsien-feng had an understanding of policy that was limited at best, while his arrogance was unbounded. To make matters worse, he surrounded himself inside Peking's Forbidden City with princes who advised a policy of insulting or, more often, ignoring Western ministers when they attempted to remind the Chinese government that it was pledged by treaty to open more of the empire to trade and to protect the property and safety of foreign nationals. Hsien-feng was far more interested in his concubines than in the business of governing, and the anti-Western tendencies of his court filtered unimpeded down to provincial governors and local officials. Western trade began to be generally harassed, and China's rulers demonstrated remarkably little concern for the obligations they had entered into.

Anti-Westernism might have been a satisfying indulgence for those who lived in the splendor of the palaces in and outside Peking, but it did nothing to alleviate the continuing misery of millions of Chinese peasants. To an increasing extent, the anger of these subjects became focused not on the white traders but on their own Manchu rulers. This was especially true in the impoverished southern provinces of the empire, where multiethnic populations struggled against not only the mounting demands of the imperial tax system but local organizations of bandits and river pirates. The economic crisis brought on by the Opium War had augmented the traditional Manchu inattentiveness to military needs, and in provinces such as Kwangtung and Kwangsi government armed forces did little or nothing to prevent lawlessness and the depredations of bandits. More and more Chinese peasants began to join secret societies—most notably a group called the Triads—whose main aim was the overthrow of the Manchu dynasty and the restoration of the Ming.

Out of this background emerged, in 1850, the Belisarius of whom Thomas Taylor Meadows had written. The origins of his rise were dramatically improbable, and the effects of it savagely destructive. Thirty-six-year-old Hung Hsiu-ch'üan was a relatively mild-tempered and introverted peasant from a small village thirty miles north of Canton. His principal claim to fame before 1850 was that he had failed the rigorous entrance exams of the Chinese civil service not once but four times. In imperial China, the civil service was the most honored path to notoriety, position, and success, and Hung had felt the effects of his failures deeply. After the third disappointment, in 1837, he had apologized to his parents for the shame he had brought on them, then collapsed into a grave physical illness. Marked by a high fever, hallucinations, and frightening seizures that became macabre entertainment for his fellow villagers, Hung's malady may have been epilepsy. What is certain is that the extended dream that gripped his mind during its course became the bizarre source of a powerful movement.

In his delirious vision, Hung ascended to Heaven, where he was split open. His internal organs were replaced, and he was thus reborn. An aged man with a golden beard then appeared to him, arming Hung with a sword and instructing him to bring the world back to the one true faith. Hung, accompanied by another man some years older than himself, then went through the heavens laying waste to evil spirits. In waking fits, Hung leapt about the room in which he was confined shrieking, "Slay the demons! Slay the demons!" After Hung's fever broke, he could recall his dreams clearly and felt that he had somehow been cleansed. His neighbors thought his brain had been damaged by the illness, but his behavior was benign, and for six years he lived peacefully in his village.

Then came another trip to Canton, another attempt at entering the civil service and another failure. But Hung's reaction this time, while intense, was far different than it had been on the previous three occasions. The year was now 1843: China had been humiliated in the Opium War, and signs of Manchu corruption were everywhere. Indeed, Hung's failure to gain admittance to the civil service may have been a result of his inability to pay his examiners a sufficient bribe. For all these reasons, Hung now held the imperial bureaucratic system responsible for his personal failure.

At this crucial juncture, Hung rediscovered a book that he had been given many years earlier in Canton. Written by a Chinese convert to Christianity and called *Good Words to Exhort the Age,* the text was a somewhat garbled rendering of Bible stories and Christian catechism, blended with a predictable dose of Chinese folk wisdom. At the time he received it, Hung had put the book aside without much thought. In 1843, however, he decided to read it, and as a result China would never be the same.

Suddenly and for the first time, Hung believed he fully understood the hallucinations that had gripped him during his illness. Driven past the point of madness by the intricacies and corruption of the Chinese bureaucracy, Hung became convinced that the old man in his dream was the Christian God; that the middle-aged man who had accompanied him on his demon-slaying journey was Jesus Christ; and that he himself was the second son of God, younger brother to Jesus, come to cleanse the world—with blood, if need be.

In 1847 Hung traveled once again to Canton, to the missionary school of the Reverend Issachar Jacox Roberts, where he studied the Bible for some months. Roberts was an American Baptist from the mountains of Tennessee who had come to China after being inspired by the work and words of Karl Gutzlaff, the Dutch missionary who hired out as a translator to opium dealers. Roberts remembered Hung as "a man of ordinary appearance, about five feet four or five inches high; well built, round faced, regular featured, rather handsome, about middle age, and gentlemanly in his manners." Impressed by Hung's dedication and intelligence, Roberts was also intrigued by the tale of Hung's illness: "[H]e told some things in the account of his vision which I confess I was then at a loss, and still am, to know whence he got them without a more extensive knowledge of the Scriptures." Hung, for his part, developed an enormous admiration for the Tennessee preacher. On Hung's departure Roberts gave the young convert several more Christian tracts, which were to become important to Hung's developing theology.

Returning home, Hung attracted a growing number of followers. But the group's penchant for idolatry and their condemnation of ancestor veneration aroused enormous hostility in Kwangtung province, and Hung and his disciples were soon forced to flee into neighboring Kwangsi. Here Hung established a center for his cult at the base of a mountain called Tzu-ching San.

It was fertile country for sowing discontent. Into the anarchic mix of bandits, pirates, ineffectual law enforcement, and secret societies had lately been added a new element: Local gentry, in an effort to protect their property and fortunes, had raised private bands of militia. Generally, these militia were as destructive as the bandits they were assigned to control. More and more the air of violence and lawlessness drove peasants to look for radical solutions to their desperate predicament. Taking advantage of this desperation, Hung and his followers issued anti-Manchu broadsides that were as unforgiving as they were imaginative:

> Whenever there is a flood or drought, the Manchus just sit and watch us starve, without the slightest compunction. This is because they want to make us Chinese fewer in number. They let loose avaricious and corrupt officials across the whole country, to exploit us to the marrow, so that men and women are weeping at the roadside. This is because they want to make us Chinese poor. If we investigate the origins of these Manchu Tartars, we find their ancestor was born from the copulation of a white fox and a red bitch, a union bound to produce a monster!

Thus incited, the ranks of Hung's followers at Tzu-ching San steadily swelled: Within a year of his arrival in Kwangsi, he had many thousands. Exactly where social and political discontent left off and true religious adherence began for many of these faithful was and would remain impossible to determine. But the cult's power grew regardless, and soon Hung tested that power on the battlefield.

Granting high rank to several adept military leaders who joined his movement, Hung put together a formidable army that began, in 1850, to move north toward the rich valley of the Yangtze River. Preaching stridently puritanical conduct to his followers—any sort of sexual activity during a military campaign was punishable by death—Hung led a campaign in which plunder and violence replaced other sins of the flesh. On June 11, 1851—Hung's thirty-eighth birthday—the Heavenly Kingdom of Great Peace was proclaimed, with Hung as its T'ien Wang. Early in 1852 the Taipings, who now boasted an army of some 120,000, marched on and seized the important cities of Changsha and Wuchang. The movement had taken on national significance.

Just what the political and religious precepts underlying the Taiping cause were has been argued by scholars since the rebellion first broke out. Some Westerners in China at the time—most notably Thomas Taylor Meadows, Great Britain's perceptive consular observer in Shanghai—quickly developed sympathy for the movement, seeing in it an attractive alternative to Manchu corruption and arrogance. But in fact, the Taiping leadership never developed a sophisticated or even systematic political order, and their community was structured as one large military camp. Although women were allowed to serve the cause actively, they and their children were kept strictly segregated from Taiping men. Even wives were not allowed to live with husbands. This policy was nominally intended to prevent mischievous sexual behavior, but in reality, as even Meadows admitted, Taiping women and children were effectively held hostage to ensure the loyalty of their male relatives during campaigns.

Most Taiping legal codes were similarly duplicitous. While seeming to develop a form of proto-Communism by making land ownership and the Taiping treasury communal, Hung and his lieutenants in fact used this arrangement to build immense personal fortunes. And since the *T'ai-ping t'ien-kuo* was not an actual state but rather a giant, nomadic armed band, attempts at land reform never took hold. Taiping leaders were simply unable or unwilling to develop the sort of civil administration that would have made such reforms genuinely meaningful.

As for religion, the Taipings certainly caused an uproar and brought a good deal of Western attention to themselves through their iconoclasm. Ancestor tablets were destroyed in occupied cities and towns, Buddhist and Confucian temples were sacked, and idols of every variety were destroyed. "When you bow down to lumps of clay, to wood and stone," Hung told the people, "I ask when did you lose your mind?" Yet whether Hung's faith was actually Christian has always been open to serious doubt. For many years this doubt was based on Hung's claim that he was Christ's brother: It was assumed that through this claim Hung implied his own divinity. But in fact, Hung rejected the notion of Christ's being divine. "God alone is most high," Hung declared confidently, and although he did believe that both Christ and he were God's sons, he denied that they could share in godhood. Even the original twelve disciples had, in Hung's opinion, been mistaken in their assignment of divinity to Christ: "My Great Elder Brother," Hung noted in the margin of his own New Testament, "clearly declares that there is only one supreme Lord; why then did his disciples afterwards mistakenly claim that Christ is God?" Hung's religious doctrines were in a state of constant evolution throughout the life of the Taiping movement. Indeed, toward its end their evolution obsessed him almost exclusively. Small wonder, then, that they created such confusion among Westerners.

On balance it is impossible to say that the religious element of the Taiping movement, while certainly inflammatory, was actually helpful to Hung. By denouncing the ancient faiths of China, he alienated as many peasants as he won over. After all, to many Chinese there seemed little difference between Buddhist or Taoist idolatry and Christianity: "In every temple," wrote one anti-Christian pamphleteer, "they [the Christians] are in the habit of worshipping a naked boy five or six inches long. . . . This ought . . . to be examined into." As one modern Taiping expert has written of Hung and the Taiping elite: "Competent leaders, understanding the nature of the opportunity, would have put together a different and more adequate ideology."

None of this, however, changed the fact that, in the Western communities of the five treaty ports, the notion of a Chinese Christian movement sweeping away the Manchu dynasty initially had much appeal. Some writers have suggested that Frederick Townsend Ward was among those Westerners who at first viewed the rebellion with sympathy, and, given what little hard facts were available on the Taipings in the treaty ports, as well as Ward's admiration for revolutionary adventurers such as Garibaldi, this is not unlikely. But in 1852 the movement of Westerners in the Chinese interior was still strictly proscribed, and Ward would not at this point have had the chance to make any contact with the rebels or to learn more about their goals.

Nor did he manage to find any more lucrative or exciting employment in Shanghai than signing on with one of the ships that transported opium from India up the long Chinese coast. This was not, evidently, an occupation to Ward's liking, and he soon put to sea again. Accepting the post of first officer aboard the *Gold Hunter*—a ship carrying a human cargo that has sometimes been referred to as "colonists" but more probably consisted of coolies—Ward set out for yet another part of the world where political instability had raised the possibility of violent employment: Mexico.

* * *

Debarking at the port of Tehuantepec, Ward soon made the acquaintance of one of the most remarkable Americans of his era. William Walker, "the Grey-Eyed Man of Destiny," was in 1852 just beginning his infamous career of filibustering, raising private mercenary armies and leading them into other countries to advance either his own schemes or those of wealthy sponsors. Almost a decade older than Ward, Walker was a native of Tennessee who, before 1852, had tried his hand at medicine, law, and journalism in various parts of the United States. His eclectic career had finally landed him in California. A deeply religious and humorless man, Walker was a confirmed advocate of slavery and a disciple of the expansionist solution to the South's economic woes. The creation of new slave states out of western territories would, said men such as Walker, open fertile land to slave cultivation and revitalize Southern trade. But expansion was slowed by lengthy congressional debate between the pro-slavery and Free-Soil forces, and by 1852 the impatient Walker had dreamed up his own plan for increasing the economic and political power of the Southern bloc: He intended to raise a privately financed force of adventurers, enter the Mexican province of Sonora (on the southern border of what is now New Mexico and Arizona), declare it a "republic" with himself as its president, and later, if the timing was propitious, propose its annexation to the United States as a slave state.

Walker never revealed his true reasons for invading Mexico to anyone (according to the journalist Richard Harding Davis, Walker even "messed alone, and at all times kept to himself"), and most of the men he raised for his outlandish expedition were not political partisans but simple adventurers, bent on glory and loot. Certainly Ward, who traveled north from Tehuantepec to join Walker's band, would have had nothing to do with any scheme that advanced the cause of slavery: His later statements of vehement opposition to the Confederacy confirm this. Unaware and uninformed, glad for the chance of action, Ward and the other Sonora filibusters set out in October 1853, meeting from the very beginning with misfortune.

This result was largely a product of Walker's unfortunate personality. Among a company of extraordinary characters—Ward included—whose conversation was spiced, according to one account, with "extravagant humor and improbable blasphemy," and whose chief pastimes were drinking and gambling, Walker was the sole man who, according to Davis, "did not boast nor drink nor gamble, who did not even swear, who never looked at a woman." Many of Walker's men deserted his cause even before he declared himself president of the "Republic of Lower California" on November 3, 1853. Although the exact date of Ward's departure is unknown, his leaving is generally described as a result of personality conflicts with his chief. The causes of such conflict are not difficult to imagine. One deserter from Sonora described Walker as "excessively vain, weak-minded and ambitious. His vanity makes him tyrannical—his weakness renders him cruel, his unbounded and senseless ambition has led him to believe himself born to command. His great pride was in 'standing upon his dignity;'—his men were constantly harassed with vexatious orders upon etiquette. There was not a sensible man in the entire command who did not utterly despise him."

Nonetheless, there were important lessons in the Sonora experience for Ward: Having learned the value of discipline during his ocean voyages, he now learned its limits. Ward never brooked insubordination (on one occasion he threatened to blow up the ship he was serving on when the fearful crew refused to take in sail during a storm), but he also developed what has been called the "common touch" of command: the ability to empathize with his men, to take stock of their condition and mood and structure his plans accordingly. During his China adventure Ward was to stand in singular contrast to Walker by being not only well respected but well liked by the soldiers who served under him. No description of Ward—even those of his enemies—ever accused him of vanity or cruelty; indeed, his integrity, fairness, and charm were generally conceded.

As for William Walker, after being arrested and tried in the United States for the Sonora fiasco, he went on to launch an even more ambitious expedition in 1856. Managing to secure the presidency of Nicaragua for himself, Walker was actually recognized by the American government. But his pride and arrogance separated him from his backers, and he fell ignominiously before a firing squad on a lonely stretch of Central American beach. Ward had not yet put his China plans into action when Walker was killed, and the lessons the younger man had learned in Sonora could only have been underlined by news of the execution. Ward later stated on at least one occasion that, as part of Walker's force, he had been branded an outlaw in the United States. His frequent trips back to his native country make this seem unlikely, but his shame at having served under the "King of the Filibusters" was very real.

Ward remained in Mexico following his desertion from the Walker expedition, and during this time he met Charles Schmidt. Schmidt wrote that after the Sonora experience Ward, "having found favor with the new President General [Juan] Álvarez, came very near entering his service, as most liberal offers were made to him. He declined however on account of his not liking the people, their manners and customs, all being at variance with his preconceived ideas of the way in which their governmental affairs ought to be conducted." With another American as a partner, Ward apparently tried his hand at business next, collecting scrap metal and shipping it to New York. But his commercial talents were no more impressive than ever, and the venture failed.

Schmidt's assertion that Ward objected to the "manners and customs" of Mexico, as well as to the way Mexican "governmental affairs" were conducted, is somewhat surprising—and revealing. Manners, customs, and governmental affairs have never been the usual province of mercenaries, and Ward's refusal of Mexican President Álvarez's "most liberal offers," along with his consistently poor judgment in matters of business, provide additional indications that the young American was most strongly preoccupied with concerns other than money. During his Mexican interlude Ward also picked up at least a conversational ability in Spanish, demonstrating a desire, equally unusual for a man of his profession, to integrate himself into the native landscape.

In the case of Mexico, this integration brought disillusionment with the way the country was run, and soon after his scrap metal business failed Ward set out for California. He made the trip, according to Robert Rantoul, on "a single mule." In San Francisco Ward signed on as first mate of the clipper *Westward Ho!,* which arrived from New York on February 27, 1854, en route to Hong Kong.

Not yet twenty-three, Ward had already established himself as a talented naval officer who had no difficulty securing a post on an important ship—the *Westward Ho!* was one of the "extreme clippers" that could make the China trip in just over a month—as well as a soldier of fortune of, if not equal talent and reputation, at least enormous potential. What he continued to lack were opportunities; and China in 1854 only frustrated him again.

In March 1853 the Taiping T'ien Wang, Hung Hsiu-ch'üan, had led his armies to their greatest triumph: the capture of Nanking, China's second most important city and the seat of power for the central empire. It was immediately renamed the "Heavenly Capital," and nothing seemed to stand in the way of a Taiping march to Peking and the overthrow of the Manchu dynasty.

But the rebellion stalled. Rather than taking the full and considerable might of the Taiping armies north, Hung dispatched only an expeditionary force to take Peking, then immersed himself in the affairs of his new capital. Ruling through a cabal of assistant *wangs* who rivaled the Manchus in the complexity of their intrigues, Hung became preoccupied with the construction of palaces and lost much of his political fervor. His appetite for concubines grew as his interest in the conduct of the civil war died. While his northern expedition was slowed and then defeated by imperial troops, Hung—despite his puritanical pronouncements to the faithful—assembled a large harem that became his refuge. The number of wives and concubines a man was allowed soon became codified under Taiping law: the higher the man's post, the greater the number, giving free rein to the lust of the T'ien Wang.

Hung's retreat into a closed and sensual world was mirrored in Peking by the Emperor Hsien-feng's. Those citizens of China who would not or could not pledge loyalty either to a messianically deluded peasant or to the ineffectual, arrogant libertine who sat atop the Dragon Throne now found themselves trapped between the armies of both—for the war went savagely on. Whole cities were pillaged and burned repeatedly, rivers became choked with bodies, and China teetered on the brink of self-destruction.

Most of this spectacle lay out of sight of the foreign settlements in the treaty ports, and foreign emissaries sent to negotiate with the Chinese government still fumed in exasperation about Peking's unwillingness to live up to its treaty obligations. Thus the rebellion continued to be viewed with a somewhat favorable—if cautious—eye by the Westerners. One American commissioner sent to deal with trade problems in China, Humphrey Marshall of Kentucky, informed Washington in April 1853 that "[a]ny day may bring forth the fruits of successful revolution, in the utter overthrow of the existing dynasty." And President Franklin Pierce, in his annual message to Congress for that year, announced that "[t]he condition of China at this time renders it probable that some important changes will occur in that vast empire which will lead to a more unrestricted intercourse with it."

But missionaries and other Taiping advocates could not keep reports of what the rebellion was doing to the Chinese interior and to the Chinese people from eventually reaching the treaty ports. The foreign settlements soon learned that Hung was not so much a Christian as a man who identified himself with Christ, and the anarchy and bloodshed that were everywhere rife became cause for extreme alarm. Not only was the rebellion taking millions of lives, it was giving those European powers that wished to absorb large sections of China into their own empires a rationale: the protection of their business and nationals. Recognizing this danger, U.S. Commissioner Marshall soon dropped his advocacy of the great rebellion and warned Washington that continued Taiping successes would render China "like a lamb before the shearers, as easy a conquest as were the provinces of India. . . . It is my opinion that the highest interests of the United States are involved in sustaining China—maintaining order here and engrafting on this worn-out stock the healthy principles which give life and health to governments, rather than to see China become the theater of widespread anarchy, and ultimately the prey of European ambitions."

Ward seems to have reached a similar conclusion by 1854. Certainly he never made any serious attempt to seek employment with the Taipings (as some Western mercenaries were beginning to do), and his later statements of opposition to any usurpation of Chinese imperial authority—which he called an "outrageous doctrine"—further indicate his acceptance (albeit reluctant) of the Manchu dynasty as the lesser of two evils.

That lesser evil could, however, be devilishly irritating. In 1854 Robert M. McLane of Maryland arrived in China as American minister. On attempting to meet with imperial officials in Canton (the notion of foreign ministers from "lesser" states actually residing in Peking was still laughed off as absurdly presumptuous by the Manchus) McLane experienced immediate frustration. In Canton, one high-ranking imperial official repeatedly put McLane off, complaining on one occasion that "[j]ust at the moment I, the minister, am superintending the affairs of the army in several provinces and day and night have no rest. Suffer me then to wait for a little leisure, when I will make selection of a propitious day, that we may have a pleasant meeting." This represented not merely one man's obfuscation but a comprehensive policy of avoidance and obstruction, set in Peking and designed to free China from the obligation to open her interior to greater trade and foreign penetration.

If the goal was understandable, the attitude was not. The Chinese apparently failed to comprehend that their ethnocentric arrogance was self-defeating: It only made the Westerners more determined to take by force what they were entitled to by treaty. Part of Robert McLane's assignment as minister was to assess the Taiping movement and see if it was worthy of American recognition. And while McLane—initially sympathetic to the Nanking government—soon reversed his position regarding the rebels, he also met with this rather startling reply when he requested an audience in Peking: "If you do indeed respect Heaven and recognize the Sovereign, then our celestial court . . . will most assuredly regard your faithful purpose and permit you year by year to bring tribute." Along with the tribute, McLane learned, he would be expected to kowtow to the Chinese emperor: to go down on his knees and knock his head against the floor as a sign of obedience and respect. For the representative of a nation that had been born dealing a death blow to the idea of divine representation in monarchs, it was an absurd and maddening requirement.

The unsatisfactory conduct of both Taiping and Manchu officials in

China prompted the United States, along with the other Western powers, to adopt an official policy of neutrality and nonintervention regarding the Middle Kingdom's internal difficulties. But the impracticality of such a policy soon became evident, nowhere more than in Shanghai. In September 1853 an anti-Manchu sect called the Small Swords—led by an opium-smoking Cantonese who styled himself "Marshal of the Ming Kingdom"—seized control of the Chinese city in the port and took the taotai prisoner, disrupting trade and spreading alarm in the settlements. A pair of adventurous Americans infiltrated the Chinese city and rescued the taotai, but relations with other representatives of the Chinese government were far less cordial. Imperial troops, dispatched by Peking to lay siege to the Small Swords, were typically arrogant and abusive when they crossed paths with the city's Western residents. When several of these encounters turned violent, the foreigners organized the Shanghai Volunteer Corps, an irregular force bolstered by small contingents of foreign regulars. The corps's only field action was against not the Small Swords but the offending imperial troops, in the so-called Battle of Muddy Flat in April 1854.

Disavowed by the Taipings because of religious and other differences, the Small Sword rebels were eventually reduced to cannibalism inside the Chinese city, and their movement ultimately withered and died. The final imperial attack on Shanghai's walls was made in 1854 with French assistance and was successful; but the spectacle of foreigners fighting against both rebels and imperial troops during the Small Sword uprising was portentous. In the wake of this experience, Shanghai's foreigners formed their own Municipal Council and took over the management of the Chinese Customs House for the imperial government, to ensure the free flow of trade. Such was the state of imperial fortunes that the Peking government seemed happy to approve the Western-manned Imperial Chinese Customs Service. In fact, the erosion of imperial authority caused by the Western response to Chinese anarchy was becoming severe. The Chinese needed to formulate an effective response to internal disorder and external encroachment, and they needed to do so quickly.

Unfortunately, Peking was not yet desperate enough to seek the advice and aid of sympathetic Westerners in formulating that response. Thus Ward once again could find no employment to suit him in China in 1854, and he soon departed. Always on the lookout for new opportunities, Ward was drawn this time to the great power conflict that was brewing in Europe. But China was by now exercising a powerful hold on him, and besides his native America it was the only place to which he would return time and again during the years to come.

Ward's sister Elizabeth vividly remembered her brother coming to say good-bye to her at boarding school in 1854, "on his way to the Crimean War." Through family friends, Ward had apparently secured a lieutenancy in the French army. Journeying first to France and then on to Russia, the twenty-three-year-old Ward demonstrated that his idiosyncrasies were crystallizing into patterns.

The Crimean War, pitting Great Britain and France against Russia, was a politically senseless conflict, and that senselessness was echoed in the dull-witted savagery of the combatant armies. But Ward took advantage of the dismal affair to learn a great deal about the weapons and tactics then in use among large national armies. Most important, the experience offered some practical training in the employment of modern riflemen as independent skirmishers (rather than as traditionally organized units of marching infantry) and in military engineering, particularly siege techniques. The reduction of fixed fortifications was the ultimate key to victory in the Crimea and would be of immense value to Ward later in China.

But Ward's Crimean adventure came to an end when, as A. A. Hayes recorded, "he quarreled with his superior officer and was allowed to resign." Ward's Yankee self-reliance was showing a marked tendency toward intolerance of superior authority. Indeed, for the rest of his life Ward would display simultaneously a talent for leadership and an inability to suffer constricting subordination, traits not inconsistent with his boyhood experiences in Salem. Taking his leave of the French service without penalty, Ward next surfaced in China in 1857.

It was, in all likelihood, news of war that drew him back. In 1856 France and Britain, weary of the imperial Chinese government's ongoing refusal to comply with its treaty obligations, had seized on a minor offense in Canton as an excuse for forcefully coercing Peking into more cooperative behavior. In 1857 a joint Anglo-French expeditionary force bombarded the Chinese forts at Taku in the mouth of the Peiho River, opening the way for an overland march to Peking. Once again, the Chinese were humiliated, and once again the Westerners demanded increased trade and increased safety for foreign nationals.

But the British and the French—as well as the Americans, who, though they offered no troops, sent a minister plenipotentiary to accompany the Allied expedition—wanted something else too: foreign diplomatic residences in Peking. The symbolism of the demand, if obscure today, was striking at the time. The Western nations were insisting that the Chinese finally accept them as equals, and drop their claim that China was the center of the world and foreign emissaries could therefore only be received as tribute bearers. While this demand might have seemed reasonable enough in the West, in Peking it was viewed as a more serious issue than even religious or commercial encroachment. The Manchus feared that such a concession would be interpreted within China as proof that they had lost the Mandate of Heaven and would thus lend legitimacy to the Taiping cause.

For the moment, however, the Chinese government could do nothing but accept the terms—forced on them at the city of Tientsin on June 18, 1858—and hope that they would be able to stall on actual fulfillment. In light of this result, the time seemed right for an all-out Taiping move against Peking. But the Taipings had suffered setbacks of their own. In 1856 several of Hung's wangs, jealous of one another's power, had launched an internal struggle that had cost tens, perhaps hundreds of thousands of lives. Shaken by the ordeal, Hung had decided to entrust power to members of his own family—men whose experience was questionable but whose loyalty was not—as well as to religious leaders who gave him spiritual comfort. The Reverend Issachar J. Roberts, the Tennessee Baptist who had schooled Hung in the Bible, was even asked to come to Nanking to assist the rebels in managing relations with foreigners. Only the talents of rising field commanders such as the Chung Wang kept the Taiping movement alive.

Despite these momentous events, Ward could find no more significant employment in China in 1857 than as first mate on the coastal
steamer *Antelope.* The Chinese government still would not accept the
notion of using foreigners against the rebels, despite the fact that Western mercenaries were known to be serving the rebel cause. The *Antelope* ferried passengers between the five treaty ports, and one such
traveler, William S. Wetmore, later recalled an encounter he had with
Ward when the ship went aground during a voyage through pirate-
controlled waters:

> Our captain quite lost his head and swore he would blow his
> brains out if he failed to get the ship off. The first officer, however,
> fortunately was cool and collected, and it was by his efforts that
> necessary steps were taken for protecting the steamer and ulti-
> mately getting her out of the perilous position she was in. At a later
> date . . . Ward . . . was pointed out to me, and I was certain that in
> him I recognized the quondam first officer of the *Antelope,* who had
> shown so much self-possession on this occasion.

But transporting treaty-port merchants could not hold Ward for
long, and he once more turned his back on China. Unconfirmed but
nonetheless plausible stories have persisted that he went back to Mexico to serve Benito Juárez (Ward himself later told an English officer in
China that the Mexican government had been his last employer) and that
he turned up in Texas as one of that state's famous Rangers. Whatever
the case, early 1859 found him in New York, working in an office and
for his father: twin testimonies that his fortunes were at a low point. The
elder Ward had left dying Salem to try his hand as a shipping agent, but
if he hoped that his son would or could be of assistance in the venture,
he was quickly disappointed. Ward left the East as soon as he had
secured enough funds for another trip to China. Some have said that he
completed the first leg of this journey—New York to San Francisco—
alone and on horseback, but more reliable sources have him sailing on
a clipper in the company of his brother, Harry. The two were moving
with evident purpose, and soon after their arrival in San Francisco in the
fall of 1859 they continued on to Shanghai.

Ward was just shy of twenty-eight at the time of this voyage, still full of the energy, exuberance, and recklessness that had marked his entire life. The rigors of an adolescence spent at sea, the deadly absurdity of William Walker's Sonora expedition, and the sickening waste of the Crimea had not hindered his development into an affable yet singularly iron-willed individual with a head full of great ambitions. Like many international adventurers, Ward drank and gambled in his idle hours (although he does not seem to have abused either pastime) and had a fondness for tobacco, particularly pipes and Manila cheroots. From a childhood pugilist he had developed into a more than capable close-quarters fighter, a valuable asset in maintaining discipline. Able to make and part with acquaintances easily, he had few true friends and kept his deepest thoughts to himself. All these were qualities much admired by—and, in their pure form, rare among—the world's free-lances.

Yet in his few surviving letters there is an air of isolation about Ward's individuality, an alienation that kept him apart even from his followers. Whether writing to his brother, Harry, about his personal affairs or requesting information from the soon-to-be American minister to China (and fellow New Englander) Anson Burlingame about events in America, Ward was unable to conceal a craving for the kind of conversation and companionship he could never find among the men he commanded. One astute British officer would later write that the ability to control the mercenary officers and irregular soldiers Ward organized in China rested on the commanding officer's not being "one of their style." Ward, once an inexperienced second mate of fifteen who had been thrown overboard by his crew, had by 1859 learned how to control such men successfully—but he never became one of them. Nor, for all his charm, did he ever strive to fit in among the merchants, diplomats, and military men who occupied the opposite end of the social spectrum. In fact, beneath a veneer of what one English official called "consummate tact," Ward remained a puzzling and independent man, one whose idiosyncrasies—fully revealed only on the drilling ground and in battle—inspired consternation as much as awe in both his men and the foreign communities in China.

To the America that he once again left behind in the fall of 1859

Ward seems to have had some sentimental yet little real attachment. Apparently he had, in his early twenties, fallen in love with a Salem girl of sixteen, but the girl's parents found the young sailor and soldier of fortune an undesirable suitor. The relationship was broken off when Ward was at sea, and there is no other mention of a woman in Ward's life until his final trip to China. Although Ward subsequently took an active interest in the domestic crisis facing the United States (voicing unbridled enthusiasm for "old Uncle Abe" and equally fervid hatred of "the blackguards Jeff[erson Davis] & Cabinet"), and although in letters he signed himself "an honest American," he never felt the urge or the obligation to return. Given the tensions within his family, his attitude toward Salem, his failure to achieve his dream of an appointment to West Point, and the forced end to his only known romantic involvement, such reluctance is understandable.

Ward's ultimate commitment, then, was to his restless ambition. At twenty-eight he already knew a good deal about where that ambition might lead: to what he later called "the fate of war." Yet had he known, on that last journey across the Pacific in 1859, that he would never again see or touch American soil—even to be buried in it—one doubts that he would have given any thought to turning back.

III

''AS IF BY MAGIC''

Soon after his arrival in Shanghai late in 1859, Ward was keeping company with Henry Andrea Burgevine, a fellow American and adventurer who was to become Ward's most capable and famous (some said infamous) lieutenant. Precisely when the two first met has never been firmly established. At least one authority states that while in New York, Ward convinced the penniless Burgevine to accompany him to China by spinning tales of the lucrative opportunities that had been created by the anarchy of the Taiping rebellion. In fact, the two men may have met at a much earlier date, for Burgevine, like Ward, had served in the French army during the Crimean War. Whatever its origins, the friendship between Ward and Burgevine was crucial to the events that were about to unfold in China—and Burgevine's tempestuous character, formed during twenty-three already checkered years, was to have a strong effect on the course of the Chinese civil war in the Shanghai region.

Burgevine had been born into tragedy. His father had fought for the French during the Napoleonic Wars, then emigrated to America, where he married in North Carolina and became an instructor of French at the fledgling university at Chapel Hill. A hopeless alcoholic, the elder Burgevine was dismissed by the university when its president entered a classroom and found the Frenchman drunk and the object of his students' scornful derision. In the face of this disgrace, the elder Burgevine abandoned his family before Henry Andrea was even born in 1836; he was subsequently killed in a barroom brawl in South Carolina. Young

Henry spent his first seven winters in his grandparents' home in North Carolina and his summers with his eldest sister and her husband in Ashford, Connecticut.

At seven Henry moved with his mother to Washington, where an old friend of his father's who had been elected to Congress secured the boy a position as a congressional page. Henry soon moved on to paging in the Senate, where he remained until 1853. At the same time, he received the beginnings of an excellent education—including instruction in the military sciences—at a private academy and made a number of influential contacts with Washington notables (among them Anson Burlingame, later U.S. minister to China). A bright student, possessed, like Ward, of considerable personal charm, Burgevine seemed well on his way to escaping his dark origins and moving up the social ladder in the nation's capital. But at seventeen, as he later put it, "a great desire to see something of the world" struck, and he signed on as mate aboard a ship bound for Hawaii, Australia, and ultimately India.

After picking up some rudimentary Hindustani on the subcontinent, Burgevine traveled on to the Crimea and enlisted, at nineteen, as a French private. Unlike Ward, Burgevine saw the bloody conflict through to its conclusion, earning a promotion for bravery. Then it was on to Europe and finally back to Washington late in 1856. Having, in his own words, "verified the old adage, that a 'rolling stone gathers no moss,'" Burgevine came back to his mother "older, steadier, but no richer." He gave some thought to studying law, but soon the hard reality of supporting both himself and his aging mother intruded. Drawing on family and personal connections, Burgevine tried to obtain a clerkship in the Department of the Interior. Desperate, he contacted one of North Carolina's senators, telling him that "if I do not obtain this situation by the first of July [1857], I hardly know what I shall do." But for reasons unrecorded, Burgevine was denied the post. He soon traveled to New York, where he took a job writing for a newspaper.

In adulthood, Burgevine's generally appealing personality became tainted by a tactless arrogance that was often fueled by alcohol. The effects of this unfortunate trait were first felt during his months in New York. America's crisis over slavery was fast reaching a breaking point, and Burgevine foolishly wrote an article supporting the right of Southerners to work their fields with human chattel. His paper became the object of public demonstration; Burgevine himself was fired and his home was ransacked. His mother, increasingly infirm, was dispatched to relatives in Connecticut, and Burgevine vanished into the anonymity of the New York postal bureaucracy.

Thus if it is true that Ward—himself serving as a clerk in his father's shipping office at the time—convinced Burgevine to accompany him to China in 1859, the task cannot have been a difficult one. More surprising is the fact that the two men were friends at all. Ward and Burgevine, wrote the Ningpo missionary Dr. Macgowan, "were typical of the regions that gave them birth," and, had they remained in the United States, "they would have been zealous participants in the strife that was desolating the fairest portion of the New World. One would have been fighting for the Republic and freedom; the other for disunion and servitude. As it was, they argued much and often on the slaveholders' rebellion, but always amicably." Burgevine's callousness about human life (particularly when that life was wrapped in something other than a white skin) was to resurface savagely in China, and his burning desire for wealth contrasted sharply with Ward's financial carelessness. What Ward prized most, in his own phrase, was "credit"—recognition for his acts of bravery—and he was willing to subordinate personal profit to get it. For Burgevine, by contrast, money was always the bottom line.

Yet Burgevine eventually became invaluable to Ward, precisely because of these differences. Five years Ward's junior, the bearded, tough Carolinian was educated enough to understand Ward's plans, as well as "refined" enough (in the words of one contemporary Shanghai author) to be "both engaging and insinuating" when dealing with Shanghai's foreign dignitaries. But he was also ruthless enough to hold the volatile, often drunken Western freebooters who later became Ward's officer corps in check. In the field, the two men played complementary roles—Ward the inspired leader, Burgevine the enforcer—and by all accounts their personal relationship was no more or less complicated. Above all, Burgevine had been touched by Ward's ephemeral yet pronounced ability to inspire loyalty: The charismatic New Englander was virtually the only person Burgevine did not, during his short but troubled career in China, betray.

In the late summer of 1859, Burgevine shipped out as third mate on the *Edwin Forrest,* bound for Shanghai by way of San Francisco. Some writers have claimed that Frederick and Harry Ward were Burgevine's shipmates on this voyage, though several circumstances make this doubtful. What is certain is that by this time Burgevine had accepted Ward's claim that China's distress could be the source of their own good fortune, provided that distress was severe enough to convince Chinese officials to drop their long-standing resistance to using Western mercenaries against the Taiping rebels. The *Edwin Forrest* arrived in Shanghai on October 18, and although Burgevine, like Ward, initially accepted employment on river and coastal steamers, his hopes for turning a profit on Chinese instability were not to be disappointed.

For China's troubles in the summer and fall of 1859 had become genuinely critical, and the price that any and all solutions to those troubles might command had grown proportionately large. More important for the two new American arrivals, the desperate situation faced by Shanghai's imperial officials had made the employment of Western barbarians in the imperial cause—so long disdained by the proud Chinese—a real possibility.

By 1859 the Emperor Hsien-feng's taste for liquor and indolence had caused one of his legs to swell with edema, but his profligacy continued unabated. His mind, rapidly deteriorating, became more and more fixed on the issue of how to deal with Britain and France, the powers that had forced his representatives to agree to the humiliating Treaty of Tientsin. Lord Elgin, the ruddy-skinned, heavyset British envoy who had negotiated the Tientsin terms, traveled up the Yangtze during the winter of 1858–59 to study and assess the Taiping movement, and Hsien-feng became fearful that the British would decide to support the rebellion. Elgin—accompanied by his younger, thinner, and more forceful brother, Frederick Bruce—toured both Taiping and imperial domains (though primarily the latter), and Hsien-feng might have rested easier had he known that Elgin's report to London stated that "the tone of the natives with whom I conversed certainly left on my mind the impression that they viewed the rebellion with feelings akin to those with which they would have regarded earthquake or pestilence, or any other providential scourge." In fact, by the time Bruce traveled north toward Peking to exchange ratifications of the Tientsin treaty with the Chinese government (and thus formally put the treaty into effect), the British were giving some thought to aiding the imperialists in their struggle against the rebels.

But all this was unknown inside the Forbidden City, where Hsien-feng sought the counsel of the dynamic Mongol general Seng-ko-lin-ch'in, of a trio of belligerent princes—Cheng, I, and Su-shun—and of his favorite concubine (and the mother of his son), Yehonala. Destined to rule China for half a century as the Empress Dowager Tz'u-hsi, the beautiful and wily Yehonala was in 1859 a political neophyte who craved nothing so much as the humiliation of the Westerners on the field of battle. Hsien-feng's occasional trepidation about using force against the barbarians disgusted her; and along with the three princes and Seng-ko-lin-ch'in, Yehonala pressed hard for the repudiation of the Treaty of Tientsin.

Unfortunately, the British and the French played into the hands of these Chinese war hawks. In June 1859 Frederick Bruce, now minister plenipotentiary and envoy extraordinary to China from Great Britain, appeared at the mouth of the Peiho River with a fleet of British, French, and American warships, intent on arrogantly cruising to Tientsin and then marching to Peking for the exchange of ratifications. The Westerners were informed that the Peiho River was closed and that the emperor required the foreign emissaries to debark peacefully and proceed to Peking "without much baggage and with a moderate retinue." The American party, headed by minister John E. Ward (a native of Georgia and no relation to Frederick Townsend), complied with the imperial Chinese government's demand; but Bruce and the representative of France, ignoring China's face-saving maneuver, demanded that the river be cleared of all obstruction and approached the forts at Taku in force.

Seng-ko-lin-ch'in had rebuilt and rearmed the Taku forts since their first bombardment by the British and the French in 1857, and, when the

Western allies attempted to clear the Peiho River in that spring of 1859, the Mongol general opened a murderous fire on their ships. The battle raged for days, and for once the Chinese came away the victors. Several British vessels were lost, and Bruce was forced to order a general withdrawal to the coast and finally back to Shanghai. The Americans, in the meantime, made it to Peking. But, on being told that he would have to kowtow to Hsien-feng, Minister Ward replied, "I kneel only to God and woman" and returned to the coast. Once there, however, he belied his own proud words by agreeing to exchange ratifications at the town of Peitang, as the Chinese had wished all along. The American minister was thus officially confirmed in Peking not as the ambassador of an equal power but as a "tribute bearer," and the power of the war party in the Forbidden City was firmly consolidated.

For a few brief months, China enjoyed a respite from foreign aggression. But internal difficulties more than made up for any advantages gained by the battle at Taku. In addition to the Taiping, several other large-scale rebellions had broken out during the 1850s. While never achieving the phenomenal success of the Taipings, these movements had by 1859 secured enough power to pose a significant threat to Manchu authority. Greatest of these secondary revolts was the Nien rebellion, which began in 1853 and by 1859 had caused a complete breakdown of imperial control in the Huai River basin. (The term *Nien* referred to the incorporation of small bandit groups and peasant organizations into a larger, though never fully centralized, entity.) In addition, China's considerable Muslim population—outraged by discriminatory Manchu policies and fired by a fundamentalist movement within their faith—revolted in the northwestern and southwestern corners of the empire late in the 1850s. The ensuing fighting lasted into the 1870s and was particularly bitter.

Faced with this alarming array of troubles, as well as with the ongoing problem of the civil war with the Taipings, Hsien-feng, Yehonala, and their advisers shrank ever more determinedly into the comfort of Peking's palaces and the equally unreal world of Manchu chauvinism. For this reason the Chinese victory at Taku in June 1859 was particularly unfortunate; it only reinforced the war party in the belief that compromise with either the rebels or the Westerners was an unnecessary and detestable prospect. The imperial clique continued to display the haughty, ignorant arrogance that had always characterized its rule and that, if left unsupported by other, more talented leaders would certainly have brought about the end of the dynasty in the 1860s.

But the Manchus were not left to the fate they so richly deserved. And the most important support they received, ironically enough, came from the native Chinese (or Han) elite from whom the Manchus had wrested national power in 1644. In the 1850s and '60s, a "self-strengthening movement" aimed at the modernization of China's armed forces, the reinvigoration of the Confucian order, and the elimination of bureaucratic corruption took root in China. It was led by Tseng Kuo-fan, unarguably nineteenth-century China's greatest figure and, together with Otto von Bismarck in Prussia, one of the preeminent conservative reformers of the era.

By 1854 Tseng had forsaken a brilliant career in the imperial bureaucracy in Peking to raise an army in the province of Hunan with which to fight the Taipings. Placing a premium on training and discipline rather than numbers, Tseng had put together a compact unit that relied on fighting ability rather than intimidation for success: a most unusual quality in a Chinese army, whether imperial or rebel. In addition, Tseng emphasized strong ties between officers and enlisted men, another break with imperial tradition. The Hunan soldiers also received intensive schooling in Confucian philosophy, so that they would know what they were fighting for. Tseng himself had no doubts on this score. In a typical proclamation, written at the height of the Taiping rebellion, he declared:

> Throughout history the Sages have upheld this doctrine, which expounds the pattern of men's relationships, of prince and subject, father and son, high and low, noble and humble, in an order that may no more be reversed than the position of a cap and shoe. The brigands from Kwangsi [the Taipings] have filched the ideas of the foreign barbarians, and honor the religion of the Lord of Heaven. All of them, from pretended princes and ministers down to common

soldiers, call themselves brother, and say Heaven alone is their father, and human parents are no more than brother and sister. Farmers cannot till their own fields and pay tribute, for all the land belongs to the Lord of Heaven. Merchants cannot carry on their business for their own profit, for all goods belong to the Lord of Heaven. Scholars cannot recite the classics of Confucius, for they have another work, the New Testament, containing the teachings of the so-called Jesus, while our Chinese Book of Odes and Book of History which for thousands of years have been our guides in manners and morals are used to sweep the floor with. This is a rebellion not merely against the Dynasty but against the doctrines of the Sages.

Although Tseng's origins aroused distrust among most Manchus (who, despite their genuine admiration of native Chinese culture, were never comfortable giving significant power to Han officials), his approach pleased them, and prompted tremendous enthusiasm among his soldiers. This appeal was reinforced by Tseng's strenuous efforts to live up to the Confucian ideal of the self-sacrificing scholar-statesman. A hedonist in his early days, Tseng eventually gave up wealth and comfort in the name of his cause. "He dresses in the poorest clothes and keeps no state," one Westerner observed, and his principal pastime was gardening. A long, unkempt beard and mustache hung from his broad features, and his drooping eyes were often marked by sadness, even when he smiled. That sadness may well have been not only for the wretched state of his nation but for the part he himself played in the civil war, for Tseng was a harsh disciplinarian and a stern judge. He acknowledged as much, saying that "[s]o long as respectable people can live in peace, I don't mind what is thought about my cruelty." The *North China Herald* echoed the general sentiment concerning Tseng's firm methods when it stated that "[h]e is strict, but men could always understand what he meant, and the consequence is that much fewer Mandarins have come to grief under him than usually happens."

In 1854 Tseng's methods were vindicated when he recaptured the important city of Wuchang. It was the first sign of Taiping weakness and the first time an imperial officer had reclaimed lost territory in any meaningful sense. In the years that followed, Tseng made further headway against the rebels and became set in his belief that the suppression of the rebellion was a job for Chinese troops alone. The prospect of working in conjunction with Western soldiers—whether regulars or mercenaries such as Ward—was, to Tseng, full of potential dangers. "If we borrow [Western] troops to help attack and they do not win," he wrote after 1860, "it will invite ridicule; if they are successful, the disastrous aftermath will be unfathomable." It was a point of view shared by Tseng's Manchu superiors in Peking but questioned by one of his ablest subordinates, Li Hung-chang.

Destined to play an important role in Frederick Townsend Ward's Chinese adventure, Li Hung-chang was, like Tseng, of native Chinese rather than Manchu stock. But there the similarities between the two men ended. Born in 1823 into the mandarin class, Li grew into an exceptionally tall man, over six feet, whose mental powers were equally unusual. At twenty-two he was sent to Peking to be one of Tseng Kuo-fan's pupils, and he subsequently performed brilliantly in the competition to enter the civil service. During the mid-1850s, however, he abandoned Peking and, after several abortive attempts to fight the rebels with his own army, rejoined Tseng Kuo-fan and worked his way up from the very bottom of Tseng's staff. Li's patience, determination, and talent were recognized: Tseng eventually began grooming him to replace Hsüeh Huan as governor of the embattled Kiangsu province.

One American diplomat who knew him in Shanghai wrote in 1894 that at the time of the Taiping rebellion Li was "thin, wiry, with a quick nervous manner. . . . He had a quick vibratory way of moving his head which suggested remarkable mental alertness. He was ready in conversation to a remarkable degree. He was never ill-tempered. He was positive in what he said and met an issue squarely. He was not diplomatic in the cheap sense." Indeed, Li's diplomatic talents were of the most profound order, and under Tseng's tutelage he became a capable battlefield commander as well as a superb administrator of both military and civil organizations. The one thing Li lacked was Tseng's unshakable honesty. Fatally avaricious, Li connived throughout his life to build a huge personal fortune through illegal as well as legal means. Such was his dexterity, however, that he was consistently pictured as a great patriot.

By 1859 Tseng Kuo-fan had formulated a rough strategy in which his own Hunan Army and a second force—which would be created as soon as a sufficient power base had been retaken from the rebels in Anhwei province—would act as the two arms of a huge nutcracker in crushing the Taipings in Nanking. Tseng himself was already applying pressure from the west, on the rebel stronghold of Anking. His hope was to create another army that would move to the east, defend Shanghai, and then drive the Taipings back toward their Heavenly Capital. This second army would be organized along the same lines as Tseng's Hunan force: Sound training and discipline would be emphasized over numbers, Confucian values would be drilled into the ranks, and officers would be required to develop strong links to their enlisted men. If Li Hung-chang's progress as an administrator continued, Tseng believed, the new eastern army would be safe under his command. All that was required for the scheme's success was a little time—perhaps a year or two.

The Taiping breakout from Nanking early in 1860 played havoc with Tseng's plans and put the embattled imperial government under even greater pressure. There was no eastern arm to Tseng's nutcracker in place, and Peking—rightly worried about what move the British and the French would make in the face of their humiliation at Taku—gave no thought to dispatching troops from the north to play such a role. It was a crucial moment. Although the Taipings were tactically on the offensive, their strategic goal was a defensive one: to secure Kiangsu, Shanghai, and a reliable source of supplies. If they failed, their movement would eventually perish. This urgency, combined with the anxiety of Western and Chinese merchants, made the port near the mouth of the Yangtze an ideal place to be a soldier for hire in the spring of 1860; for, despite Tseng Kuo-fan's misgivings, there was no one else for Chinese officials to turn to if the rebels were to be stopped.

The Chinese victory against French and British arms at Taku had not gone unnoticed in Shanghai: In the port to which Ward returned late in 1859 there had lately been signs of friction between the Western residents and their hundreds of thousands of Chinese hosts. Native pride was not the only cause of tension. The ongoing coolie trade had led to antiforeign demonstrations, especially against the French, whose arrogance in dealing with the Chinese far surpassed that of the Americans and even the British. When news of the battle at Taku reached Shanghai, angry Chinese citizens took to the streets and swarmed the harbor, demanding the release of coolies who they claimed were unwilling captives on a French ship. The coolies were freed, but not before two Catholic chapels had been burned. In addition, there was anger over the ongoing opium traffic, which had been legalized by the Treaty of Tientsin. Symbolic of this open wound in Chinese society were Shanghai's "opium hulks," retired, generally decrepit sailing vessels that were moored along the picturesque Bund and used as transfer stations for the tens of thousands of opium chests that came into the city annually.

The long-standing Chinese distrust of Westerners and their ways had by no means been eradicated by the complex business ties between native and foreign elements in Shanghai. Ward's achievement in gaining the confidence of two of the most powerful Chinese officials in the port—taotai Wu Hsü and the banker Yang Fang—at the fateful meeting in June 1860 was, therefore, all the more appreciable. But it was not altogether surprising. Throughout his life Ward had shown not only strong social acumen but a pronounced cultural facility, and his previous trips to China, while they had not resulted in gainful employment as a soldier, had given Ward an understanding of Chinese methods. Chaloner Alabaster, a talented and daring member of the British consular service who served as a translator in Shanghai during the period of Ward's operations, found the young American "thoroughly acquainted with Chinese manners and customs," and those who were closer to Ward confirmed that he gained this knowledge not by arrogantly forcing himself into the affairs of the native population, as Westerners so often did, but by playing his own game according to his hosts' rules.

"It is wonderful," Charles Schmidt wrote of Ward's appearance in Shanghai, "how he so easily introduced himself into the good graces of the Chinese, a people so suspicious, self willed, wily and slow to contract with a stranger in cases where the real intrinsic value of the stranger's services are *shadowed* in the future." Ward's basic method was apparent to Schmidt: "To be successful he had to *ingratiate* himself into power over his supporters; in doing so, he had to brook much, and overcome many obstacles of a sectional kind; doing so only by that necessary dissimulation without which nothing can be done with this crafty people."

Ward was well-prepared for this job of "dissimulation": He had, after all, spent his childhood and early adolescence in Salem. Many analysts have commented on the strong similarities between the New England and the Chinese merchant classes: the avariciousness, the acceptance of duplicity, and the moral posturing. In addition, Ward the disciplinarian had learned that there were many situations in which applying direct pressure to his associates was inappropriate and counterproductive, and he used this knowledge deftly in China. The Chinese considered emotionally unstable and unpredictable behavior sure signs of barbarism, and Ward's actions demonstrated a thorough appreciation of this fact. As Schmidt put it, "By a mild and gentle but determined demeanor towards all classes of the Mandarins who acted in concord with him—(on whom he had to rely for the support he required, and for the making of his fortune)—he won their belief in him." Finally, Ward's attempts to win the confidence of Wu Hsü and Yang Fang were assisted by his strong egalitarianism. As one biographer put it, "Ward, unlike many of his fellow Westerners in China, manifested no prejudice toward the Chinese."

The results of Ward's carefully considered but "determined" campaign were quick: Within days of his meeting with Wu and Yang, he was prowling the Shanghai waterfront, looking for recruits to lead against the Taipings as well as for weapons with which to arm them. The project represented a quantum leap in Ward's professional activities. True, he had prior experience working with mercenaries (most notably the Walker days in Mexico), and in the Crimea he had participated in a clash of professional national armies. But the Chinese civil war was on a scale unlike anything he had experienced. Ward could not have been unaware of this; his work with Admiral Gough had given him a very realistic idea of Taiping strength and combat methods. Yet he now seriously proposed facing this massive force with a small number of indigent sailors and soldiers selected from among the hundreds of criminals, expatriates, wanderers, and simple drunkards who had found their way to the Shanghai settlements. Ward apparently felt no trepidation in approaching this rather formidable task: From the first, his steps were deliberate and confident.

Ward's Chinese backers kept actual administration of the new contingent's finances in their own hands. As they had done with the Pirate Suppression Bureau and the Houseless Refugees Fund, Wu and Yang intended to turn a profit on Ward's corps regardless of its actual success in the field by jealously guarding (and in all likelihood skimming) the money they raised for it from local merchants. Ward offered no objection to this arrangement, so long—and only so long—as he received the funds he had been promised. He was well aware that pay was the crucial issue in a mercenary force, and he successfully impressed upon his sponsors the need for complete and timely fulfillment of financial obligations. As one anonymous Shanghai author wrote, "It is no secret that Yang would no more attempt to withhold the Contingent's pay in Ward's days than he would jump into the Huang-pu."

Nor would Ward tolerate Wu and Yang's interference in either the actual military administration of the force or the purchase of arms. Shanghai's legion of gunrunners were accustomed to unloading obsolete equipment on both the Taipings and the imperialists at absurdly bloated prices, and Ward knew that Wu and Yang would be only too likely to buy such equipment, further inflate its cost in their accounts, and pocket the difference. At first Ward did allow his backers a voice in determining the objectives of the force—in deciding where and when it would strike—but details of training and operations he kept jealously to himself.

It was a system that seemed to work. As Ward set about the initial task of organization—quickly hiring Henry Andrea Burgevine as his second-in-command—he not only earned Wu Hsü's genuine respect but established what was an apparently sincere friendship with Yang Fang. Yang had spent his life cultivating contacts inside Shanghai's Western community, but the relationship to Ward was unique, in its closeness, in its commercial complexity (the two initiated several business ventures together), and in its lack of ceremonial restraint. Ward and Yang apparently argued much and at length over financial details—encounters that became somewhat famous in Shanghai—and Ward's celebrated patience and tact often reached their breaking point. But the seasoned, personable old banker almost invariably gave in to the younger American. "Yang," wrote one observer, ". . . would be down on his knees at one of Ward's angry shouts, and knocking his head against his feet, and at the same time assenting to everything."

Ward became a regular visitor to Yang's yamen—where Westerners of all walks regularly congregated—as well as to his home, where Yang lived with his wife and at least two children: a son, whose name is unrecorded, and a daughter, Chang-mei. Nineteen years old at the time Ward first appeared in her father's life, Chang-mei was considered bad luck in Chinese Shanghai: She had been engaged to be married once, but her fiancé had died, a singular sign of Heaven's displeasure. In keeping with Chinese custom, Ward's glimpses of the young girl could only have been fleeting at this time.

With the important work of ensuring the support and respect of his backers done, Ward's next challenge was enlistment. Although by all accounts he did not display the bigotry toward the Chinese that was so prevalent among Shanghai's Westerners, he does seem at first to have shared the general belief that the Chinese could not be made to fight a modern war. Ward looked immediately to the sailors and adventurers of the foreign settlements for recruits, despite the fact that there was little in the backgrounds of such characters to indicate that they would ever make exceptional soldiers. These were, after all, men on whom the talents of some of the Western world's most accomplished and brutal disciplinarians had been wasted. Yet Ward—still very much in the process of learning his trade—evidently believed that he could tame them.

With Burgevine, Ward sought out his potential recruits in the saloons, hotel bars, brothels, and gambling dens that were their haunts. Ward was known to spend freely on these occasions, buying champagne (one of the most common beverages in Shanghai) for audiences of generally penniless indigents as he told them of the high pay and potential looting that would come with service in his corps. One British observer later recalled of such scenes: "Everybody made lots of money in those days, and it used to be the custom to 'shout' for a case of champagne at a time, to treat everyone within hailing distance—and then go off to the wars or other dangerous business on the morrow in search of more money to get more champagne with on returning to Shanghai." The same observer—displaying the hostility characteristic of the English community's attitude toward Ward during the early stages of his operations—went on to claim that Ward sometimes kidnapped intoxicated men and impressed them into service, a charge as unlikely as it is unsubstantiated. There were more than enough men in the port willing to gamble a bankrupt present on the chance for a rich and glorious future with Ward; "shanghaiing" (as it would come to be called) was singularly unnecessary.

Although most of Ward's recruits were Americans, his relatively small roster soon included citizens of nearly every Western nation: Englishmen, Prussians, Danes, Swiss, and Frenchmen all signed up, much to the displeasure of the ministers and consuls who represented their homelands. Over all of these varied recruits, Ward exercised the same intriguing hold that had won him the backing of Wu Hsü and Yang Fang. But at no time did any of them—including Burgevine—get close enough to their chief to be able to read his thoughts or predict his goals. "Although his means of selection from a high grade were abundant," Charles Schmidt wrote of Ward's enlistment activities, "he preferred men from that class of persons who were almost entirely ignorant of what they were about to do; and he did so solely from a determination to control the army under him entirely by his own power." Given the questionable reliability of many of his new Western soldiers, this was a sound policy, and in light of it as well as Ward's other achievements in the realm of personal relations, it is difficult to argue with one contemporary's assessment that "Ward was, as if by magic, apparently intended by nature, nativity and art to deal with and control the Foreigners and Natives who formed the officers, rank and file of the Contingent, as well as the Chinese superiors he had to deal with."

Establishing credit accounts at such large Shanghai mercantile houses as H. Fogg and Company and Jardine-Matheson, Ward next went shopping for provisions, equipment, and weapons. The last of these was no easy proposition, even given the large amounts of money Ward was free to spend. The Chinese desire for firearms and simultaneous ignorance of modern developments in weaponry meant that even eighteenth-century muskets—some still operating on the flintlock principle—could bring high prices from the Taipings and their imperialist enemies. Ward was interested primarily in superior small arms, in revolvers and repeating rifles that were true percussion pieces. (True percussion involved the use of percussion caps in the ignition of charges and often of paper cartridges instead of loose powder—all of which produced a drastically increased rate of fire.) These items were both scarce and expensive, and in finding them Ward made use of many Shanghai middlemen. Charles Hill, the man who had brought "the Troy dredging machine" to China, was also well-connected in the arms trade and disposed to help Ward. Others followed his lead, among them Albert L. Freeman (later an administrator of Ward's estate), who was an agent for H. Fogg and Company and who during this period had contact with Ward, in his own words, "almost daily . . . , having many business transactions with him." Yang Fang had also built up an arsenal inside the Western settlements, although it is unclear whether any of these arms were of use to Ward. In all likelihood they were the kind of obsolete equipment that could be sold for quick and dramatic profit to the rebels and the imperialists.

Although artillery was available for private purchase in Shanghai, Ward's main energies in the early days went into securing the up-to-date small arms that he prized. For his officers, Ward preferred revolvers made by the famed American Samuel Colt. By the late 1850s Colt—who had financed his early gunsmithing activities by staging lucrative demonstrations of the effects of nitrous oxide on the human body—had built an expansive factory in the United States and had even opened a smaller operation in London. His revolvers were known and valued in every part of the world, and adventurers such as Ward had played no small role in building that popularity. The highest-selling models were the Colt Dragoon—a heavy, .44 caliber six-shooter that came with either a seven-and-a-half- or an eight-inch barrel—and the Old Model Navy Pistol.

Introduced in 1851, the .36 caliber Old Model Navy was lighter than the Dragoon (weighing only two pounds, ten ounces), fired more reliably, and was the most sought after "belt pistol" in the world—as well as the preferred weapon of duelists. Colt revolvers were amazingly accurate pieces, more accurate than many rifles, and a man armed with two Colts as well as extra cylinders for fast reloading was a dangerous adversary, capable of holding off or even defeating large groups of lesser-armed opponents.

For his enlisted men, Ward sought the repeating, breech-loading rifles built by another American, Christian Sharps. Later famous as *"The Buffalo Gun,"* the Sharps repeating carbine was an advanced but solidly built and eminently reliable weapon. It took paper cartridges, which were cut open and prepared for ignition by closure of the knife-sharp breechblock, saving time and trouble. In 1848, 1852, and 1859 Christian Sharps had refined and repatented his .52 caliber weapon, which had a barrel length of thirty inches and could be fired by an average rifleman at a rate of ten rounds per minute. Superior shooters could achieve fifteen and even twenty rounds per minute: Just a dozen such men armed with Sharps rifles could produce a withering fire. Sharps had also contracted with the British government to produce some 6,000 carbines for the British army in 1855, and over the next nine years all but 2,400 of these pieces either were destroyed or found their way into private hands. British arms were among the most sought after weapons in Shanghai, and it is not unlikely that Ward would have come across some of these missing Sharps products, as well as less exceptional but still adequate rifles produced by British manufacturers.

Repeating carbines were not always available in the numbers Ward required, however, and he often had to settle for muzzle-loading muskets. In doing so, he was careful to seek models that bore the TOWER imprint on their locks: the proof of British government–supervised manufacture. Among the other long arms available in Shanghai were Prussian muskets and rifles, although only a few of these employed Johann Dreyse's famous "needle" firing system, which was shortly to help the Prussians overcome the Danes, the Austrians, and the French in a succession of wars. Ward's officers were also supplied with swords, and before long his troops were learning how to handle the peculiarly effective Chinese "stinkpots."

In short, what had only recently been a collection of much (and in some cases properly) maligned vagabonds had by mid-June 1860 become a mercenary force that caused the foreign authorities in Shanghai appreciable anxiety, not only because they posed a threat to Western neutrality in the Chinese civil war but also because they were armed to the teeth with weapons that could give a large detachment of regular Western troops a very respectable fight. And there was little reason to doubt that if foreign diplomats and soldiers attempted to terminate Ward's activities, such a conflict would take place: Many of Ward's men had been cruelly treated by their countrymen before arriving in Shanghai. The example of Ward's American recruits is typical. Under American maritime law, a ship's master was required to pay a seaman three months' wages if he discharged the man in a foreign port. But if the seaman deserted, the master incurred no such obligation. Because of this, any troublesome or supernumerary sailor was generally beaten into forced desertion or taken ashore by his officers, encouraged to drink himself into oblivion, then charged with desertion when he failed to return to his ship on time. In 1830 the desertion law had been slightly amended, and the U.S. consular service had become responsible for paying the three months' severance pay. But this was only in cases where the seaman in question agreed to be discharged. Those men who desired to keep their posts but were marked for elimination by their captains continued to face beatings and trickery.

Naturally, men who were considered undesirable for any reason by their ship's masters were also scorned by the foreign community in Shanghai: Ward and his new contingent were marked as outcasts before they even took the field. Insofar as the citizens of the settlements could ignore the well-armed mercenaries, they did so. But as Ward's ranks swelled to nearly a hundred men, such ignorance became an increasingly difficult proposition. A. A. Hayes, the Harvard-educated New Englander who was a junior partner for the Olyphant Company and who knew Ward in Shanghai, remembered that in the early days "[t]he English pronounced Ward a freebooter and a dangerous man. . . . Nor were we

Americans, I am bound to say, highly impressed at the outset by what we heard of our countryman. . . . He was regarded by most people as an outlaw, by many as a desperado."

Ward established his training camp at the town of Kuang-fu-lin, a muddy, insect-infested patch of ground some twenty miles west-south-west of Shanghai. Here the process of disciplining the contingent and preparing it for battle began, with results that could only be described as indifferent. Andrew Wilson—an English journalist and former editor of Hong Kong's *China Mail* who was later attached to Ward's force for two years and wrote an invaluable study of its operations—left a description of the Westerners Ward employed that throws light on the problem of discipline as well as on Ward's attempts to cope with it:

> As a rule they were brave, reckless, very quick in adapting themselves to circumstances and reliable in action; but, on the other hand, they were troublesome when in garrison, very touchy as to precedence, and apt to work themselves about trifles into violent states of mind. Excited by rebel sympathisers [*sic*] at Shanghai, and being of different nationalities, one half of them were usually in a violent state of quarrel with the other; but this, of course, was often an advantage to the commander.

While Ward understood that such men needed careful preparation before they could face the Taipings, the men themselves would hardly have been likely to acknowledge such a need. Even worse, Ward's Chinese backers could not be made to see it. Having hired foreigners and supplied them with up-to-date weapons, Wu Hsü and Yang Fang evidently believed that the only thing left to do was find the rebels and defeat them. Ward's attempts to gain time to prepare what became officially known as the Shanghai Foreign Arms Corps met with an increasingly impatient response from the holders of the purse strings, and Ward knew that if Wu and Yang issued an ultimatum, he would have no choice but to engage the Taipings before he was ready.

The Foreign Arms Corps's Kuang-fu-lin camp was located near the headquarters of an imperial officer who was to work in close conjunction with Ward during the years to come: Li Heng-sung. Described by one of Ward's successors as a "useful puppet," Li was a typical Chinese commander in that he had purchased his first commission. He subsequently displayed above-average determination, however, and was promoted for his courage in fighting the rebels in the Shanghai area. The Manchu military forces were divided, at their highest level, into eight armies, each of which was known by the pattern of its banner. Just below these "bannermen" in the imperial military hierarchy was the Army of the Green Standard, a national unit which, like the Banners, had once been an impressive force but was by 1860 a largely ineffective relic. Li Heng-sung's troops were Green Standard "braves" (as most Chinese soldiers were known), and despite the fact that he seems to have been a fairly capable commander and was, in Dr. Macgowan's opinion, "highly esteemed" by Ward, Li's actions were consistently hampered by the unreliability of his troops. In their very first encounters with the rebels, Ward's Foreign Arms Corps acted in conjunction with Li's braves, and before long the foreigners had learned for themselves the minimal value of imperialist assistance.

Between June 17 and June 22, 1860, the Taiping troops of the Chung Wang edged closer to Shanghai from the west and the northwest. Governor Hsüeh Huan decided to counterattack at the towns of T'ai-ts'ang and Chia-ting, and ordered Ward—through Wu Hsü—to support the imperialist attack with his one hundred men. Ward complied, and while no record of the precise role that the corps played in these engagements exists, the two towns were retaken from the rebels on June 26. Within days, however, the corps was drawn back to Kuang-fu-lin by a more important development: The city of Sung-chiang, only a handful of miles from Ward's headquarters, had fallen to the rebels. Almost immediately, Wu Hsü and Yang Fang began to agitate for a Foreign Arms Corps counterattack on this strategic location, generally considered one of the gateways to Shanghai itself.

Ward demanded more time. Sung-chiang was surrounded by a wide, murky moat as well as a four-mile wall. The city's formidable outer gates were built of strong teakwood banded with iron and were, in at least some cases, protected by inner gates of similar construction. In all, it was not a job for which Ward's men—who still lacked artillery and were untrained in siege techniques—were prepared.

But Wu and Yang were growing impatient; they desired some more significant return on their considerable investment than the victories at T'ai-ts'ang and Chia-ting. Fearful that his support would be cut off altogether, Ward agreed to make an attempt on Sung-chiang at the end of June. The result was predictable. The Foreign Arms Corps had no siege equipment, a deficiency Ward hoped to overcome by attacking at night and, with luck, achieving surprise. But the men of the corps—perhaps overly impressed by the part they had played in the two earlier victories—brought large amounts of alcohol with them on the Sung-chiang raid. By the time they were making their way across the flat, grassy terrain outside the city, they were making so much noise that the Taiping sentries were alerted to their approach. The corps suffered heavy casualties and was thrown into flight. "The miserable survivors," Dr. Macgowan wrote, "returned as stragglers to Shanghai, utterly disgusted. They were paid off and disbanded."

For the first time the Western authorities in Shanghai were given good reason to believe that Ward would abandon his mercenary plans and perhaps quit China altogether, and for the first time Ward confounded them by immediately rekindling his dream of building a private army with which to, as he later put it, "flog the chang-maos." In the face of Ward's considerable determination, Western merchants and diplomats became ever more hostile, using both the press and their extraterritorial laws to try to ensure that the Foreign Arms Corps did not prompt Taiping interference with the unequal and sinister balance of trade that they had established in China.

Of the many personal traits that served Ward well in China, none was more valuable than his adaptability. He had seen what the majority of his Western mercenaries were capable of in the field: Recalcitrant, belligerent, and besotted, they had come close to destroying Wu Hsü and Yang Fang's faith in their young commander. In the face of this disheartening spectacle, Ward dismissed almost all the men, retaining only those who had demonstrated bravery and ability and whose arrogance might be transformed, with time, into something like authority. These few would become officers. But they would need men to command, and it was now necessary to rethink old notions about who in Shanghai would make the best soldiers of fortune. Ward took to the waterfront once again to grapple with this riddle and soon made an acquaintance who facilitated a solution.

Vincente Macanaya was twenty-three in 1860 and one of Shanghai's large population of "Manilamen"—Filipinos who were handy on board ships and more than a little troublesome on land. Renowned as ferocious fighters, especially at close quarters, the Manilamen were in a class with the famous lascars of Malaysia and the pirates of the Bay of Bengal, groups that were also known to frequent the foreign settlements in Shanghai. As Spain was still in possession of the Philippines, the Manilamen were technically Spanish subjects. But by habit they were generally transients, at ease anywhere between India and Korea where laws were lax. Macanaya himself—who would, after his initial acquaintance with Ward, be known throughout Shanghai simply as Vincente—had been born in Manila and was a seasoned young man of singular courage. As Charles Schmidt, who served with and knew him well, wrote while Vincente was still alive:

> If real bravery consists in an undauntedness of spirit, a cool presence of mind, and active physical exertion, then all these qualities are combined in Vincente to a degree that leaves no doubt on the minds of the many friends who know him, and have seen him so fearless in the midst of danger. He has all the appearance of a soldier.—There is nothing rough about that appearance. [He is] gentlemanly in his ways to all, kind hearted to his friends, sober in his habits, quick in perception, frank, liberal to a fault, and with an eye always to duty, serving faithfully where he serves, beloved and respected by his comrades in arms.

Ward's trust in Vincente was almost immediate, and he quickly made the Manilaman his aide-de-camp. Still able to converse at least capably in Spanish, Ward began recruiting more Filipinos and soon had raised over eighty of them. The absence of a significant language barrier may have made Ward more comfortable among the Manilamen than among the polyglot of European drunkards who had originally filled out the roster of his Foreign Arms Corps. Certainly, Vincente and his countrymen soon justified their new leader's faith: Within days the corps was back at Kuang-fu-lin, this time training in earnest and conducting intelligence forays into the surrounding countryside. Setting a standard to which their European and American officers were forced to rise, the Manilamen ably went about the business of capturing Taiping patrols and shipping the prisoners back to the imperial authorities in Shanghai, all the while preparing for a new attempt on Sung-chiang.

By early July the activities of Ward's new force were arousing considerable criticism in Shanghai. Foremost among the Western voices calling for the permanent disbandment of the Foreign Arms Corps was that of Thomas Taylor Meadows, the British consul. Britain had a special bone to pick with the corps: In putting together his training program at Kuang-fu-lin, Ward had recognized the need for experienced drillmasters, and those of the British army and navy were renowned as the best in their field. Ward had made a particular point of enticing these valuable men away from their obligations to queen and country. A pronounced need to ensure the obedience of British soldiers and sailors was the immediate cause of Consul Meadows's antipathy toward the Foreign Arms Corps. But he had many other reasons for wanting Ward and his force put out of action.

Meadows was a sinologist of the first order. A broad, bearded man who stood over six feet tall, he had been a student of Chinese in Munich before taking up a post at the British consulate in Canton in 1842. He had witnessed the Opium War and had predicted (as he was fond of reminding people) as early as 1846 that a major rebellion would soon take hold of the Middle Kingdom. Furthermore, his understanding of China and the Chinese was not completely the result of book learning and consular duties: An avid shooter, Meadows often took hunting trips into the Chinese interior, and during these journeys he made it a point to converse with the peasantry and gauge their opinions. Like many a

Western diplomat, Meadows was appalled by the brutality and corruption of the Manchu government, and, like many foreign residents of the treaty ports, he early on saw the Taiping movement as an alternative with real possibilities.

In addition, Meadows considered the neutral stance adopted by the Western powers in China theoretically admirable but practically advantageous to the Manchu government: The first concern of the "neutral" West was the maintenance of trade in the treaty ports, and that trade benefited Peking. But while he saw the neutral policy's shortcomings, Meadows did try to use it to terminate the activities of the Foreign Arms Corps, a goal for which he worked assiduously throughout the summer of 1860. In the first week of July, Ward's men dispatched a Taiping prisoner to imperial Chinese officials in Shanghai, and the man was, according to Meadows, "disembowelled and beheaded" (although the Chinese usually tore out a man's heart rather than his lesser organs during such ritual executions). Meadows took the occasion to write to both the American consul (the less than vigilant W. L. G. Smith) and his Spanish counterpart in almost identical language:

> We have direct evidence that the Taipings have been permitting the silk to pass down freely on being told that it was for the foreign merchants at Shanghai. But we cannot reasonably expect this to continue if they find foreign auxiliaries thus engaged in active hostilities against them; . . . I have the best reasons for believing that the above force of auxiliaries were raised by, and are now commanded by one or more United States citizens, while the men are chiefly Manilla-men [*sic*]. Believing the proceedings of these [American and Spanish] citizens . . . are endangering an important branch of British trade, I now beg to bring them to your notice with a view to a remedy.

Rightly suspecting that he would get little satisfaction out of either the American or the Spanish government, Meadows also addressed a protest to his superior, British minister Frederick Bruce. The Taipings, Meadows said, had as yet shown no inclination to molest foreign trade, but activities such as Ward's might change all that. "There is certainly great reason to suppose that anger may cause [the rebels] to retaliate on the commerce of foreigners, if not on the persons of those whom business takes into the silk districts. . . . It appears to me practically impossible to maintain neutrality if we not only interpose between the rebel forces and the people and city of Shanghai but also protect the provincial authorities in it, [and] permit the authorities to raise forces, Chinese or foreign, in it."

Meadows's alarmist words found sympathetic ears among foreigners who saw any military activity in the Shanghai area—whether imperialist, Taiping, or foreign—as a direct threat to trade. But Bruce was far less impressed. Despite the fact that both men worked for the British government, Bruce and Meadows did not belong to the same breed of diplomatic official. Bruce was among those career officers who were neither sinologists by experience nor sinophiles by inclination. Forty-six years old at the time of his appointment to China, Bruce had served in the United States, Canada, Bolivia, Uruguay, and Egypt before traveling to the Middle Kingdom with his brother Lord Elgin and there was precious little scholarly love of Chinese civilization in him.

Still, Bruce was no mere mercantile stooge. He was deeply committed to the stated goals of his government, even when those goals conflicted with Western commercial interests. It may well have been that Meadows was right and that neutrality in the Chinese civil war was a noble but ultimately farcical idea for countries that enjoyed special trading privileges from the imperial government in Peking. But Bruce's instructions from the Foreign Office were that he not only prevent depredations against British trade but also vigorously enforce Britain's Neutrality Ordinance. However irreconcilable these goals may have seemed, Bruce pursued them with typical British obstinacy. Thus while he fully intended to punish British citizens who joined either Ward's force or the Taiping armies as mercenaries, he also ignored Meadows's suggestion that the British prevent imperial officials in Shanghai from raising forces for their own defense.

The inconsistencies of Bruce's attitude would only later become fully apparent. For the moment, Ward—because he was in the service of the taotai—was relatively free from British, and more generally Western, interference. The representatives of Ward's own United States were not inclined to acknowledge, much less control, his activities. Consul Smith blithely denied that Americans were involved in the mercenary doings at Kuang-fu-lin, and Minister John Ward was too wrapped up in affairs relating to the final settlement of the Tientsin treaty crisis to pay his adventurous countrymen much attention. Still, there was at least some contact between Ward the free-lance and Ward the minister at this time: After the outbreak of the American Civil War the young New Englander would write of the diplomat from Georgia's abandonment of the Union, "I find my old friend Ward Ex-Minister is a damned traitor and joined the rascals." But if Minister Ward did make any attempt to interfere with the ongoing training and patrols of the Foreign Arms Corps in 1860, it was singularly halfhearted and unsuccessful.

The failure of the diplomatic community to do anything at all about Ward's corps soon had Western merchants in Shanghai squawking. Their complaints, as was so often the case, were reflected on the pages of the *North China Herald,* which began a long and particularly vindictive campaign against the corps. The China coast newspapers generally, and the *Herald* in particular, were a phenomenon unique to the early period of Western encroachment into the Middle Kingdom, and their history offers important insight not only into the kind of foreigners who made the treaty ports their homes but into why men like Ward aroused such bitter resentment. Until the late 1860s such papers were, in the words of one expert, "one man affairs . . . directed by an editor of limited experience supported by an inadequate staff, dependent upon a narrow range of news sources." Because the foreign communities in the treaty ports were so small, most of these editors were more interested in grinding axes than in cultivating journalistic integrity, and commentary tended to degenerate into gossip-laced feuding.

In 1860 the *North China Herald* was ten years old, appeared weekly, and generally ran between four and eight pages. Its yearly subscription rate was fifteen Chinese *taels* (about twenty-four dollars), and its circulation was no more than five hundred, but it exerted an influence out of all proportion to its size. For both the British and the

American consuls as well as private business firms it served as the organ of public notice; salesmen hawking everything from "Persian Insect Powder" to cough lozenges to fire insurance advertised in its pages, as did the proprietors of dress shops, saloons, and billiard parlors; social and political events were covered in detail and described in language that was readily accessible to all; and opinions were offered straight from the shoulder. Given the contrast between its size and the scope of its concerns, the *Herald* was indeed a remarkable journal.

In 1856 the *Herald* had been taken over by Charles Spencer Compton, who had a long history of involvement in the China trade and scant liking for either the Manchus, whom he viewed with standard Western indignation, or the Taipings, whom he saw as a threat to free enterprise. Under Compton, the *Herald* occasionally expressed criticism of the rebellion, but the editor was always careful to condemn military participation by foreigners, fearing that such behavior would only bring the rebels' wrath down on Shanghai.

Thus by July 1860 a *Herald* correspondent was reporting that

> on Monday last the 9th, twenty-nine foreign sailors deserted from their ships in the harbour, having been allured by the promise of high pay, to put themselves under the orders of agents of the Taotai, and to assist the Imperial soldiers against the rebels. . . . [T]he acts of mercenaries are spreading feelings of ill-will in the minds of the natives against the private members of our community; as it cannot, for a moment, be supposed that the Chinese populace can discriminate between the character of individual Foreigners.

In fact, as was reported in the same issue of the *Herald,* Wu Hsü was using the existence of Ward's Foreign Arms Corps as a way to pacify rather than stir up the "populace": "H.E. the Taotai has . . . issued a proclamation telling the people that the rebels are very close, but that they need not fear to go and fight, as foreign soldiers are [near] Sung-chiang." But to the *Herald,* Ward and his followers continued to be a "gang" and a "disgrace," and their operations were nothing more than "depredations."

Such epithets were ironic indeed, coming from a paper that spoke for Western commercial interests in Shanghai, and it is understandable that Ward's reaction to these and similar attacks was one of indifference and even amusement. "Depredating" was an activity common to nearly every foreigner in China: The basis of most fortunes made in the treaty ports was (or at one time had been) opium, and of the remainder gunrunning, smuggling, land speculation, and confidence games made up a large portion. The righteous moralizing of Westerners whose names had been made through the spread of drug abuse or the disposal of useless weapons at inflated prices was hardly likely to disturb someone like Ward, who was well-acquainted with Chinese affairs as well as with the business practices common in the treaty ports, which he dismissed tersely as "lying, swindling & smuggling."

The opium trade not only belied the Western community's attacks on Ward but on a larger scale revealed much about the foreigners' attitudes toward the Taiping movement. The apparent anxiety of merchants in Shanghai over the rebellion's potentially adverse effects on trade were curiously inconsistent with existing circumstances, for the Taipings had never posed a threat to Western trade. On the contrary, the rebels had (as Thomas Meadows pointed out) made a special effort from the beginning not to interfere with the shipment of tea and silk down the Yangtze and Huang-pu rivers. This effort had been for the most part successful: Although figures always fluctuated, the rebellion had caused no interruption in exports. In fact, during the crucial years 1860 and 1861, tea and silk shipments actually increased. Of course, the fact that merchants were doing exceptionally well in Shanghai at the time of the Chung Wang's breakout from Nanking was reason enough for heightened fears about the effects of war on trade. But an equal and perhaps greater cause of alarm—lurking unacknowledged beneath the surface of the debate over how to deal with the rebels—was the drug trade. Opium was the one sector of commerce that the Taipings had made a concerted effort to interrupt, and in so doing they may have committed their greatest error with regard to the Western communities in China.

The buying, selling, and smoking of opium were illegal under Taiping law, and violations carried the same draconian penalty that China's Communists would use a century later to finally end the opium problem: death. That opium from British India played a huge part in both China's debilitation and the prosperity of Shanghai's Western community in 1860 is beyond question; but because British diplomatic representatives in China were so reluctant to discuss the trade publicly or in dispatches, we may never know how much influence opium actually had on official British policy.

Yet the very fact that otherwise loquacious British diplomats and politicians grew silent and evasive on this one subject speaks eloquently of the importance of the opium trade to the British empire, which had, after all, already gone to war once to preserve the free flow of the drug. At the time of the Opium War, the Manchus had been branded enemies of Britain for attempting to interfere with the drug trade. That the troublesome Taipings should have been viewed in the same light when they committed the same "attack" on "British trade" is hardly surprising. By refusing, for the most part, even to acknowledge the realities of the opium issue, eminent British statesmen were able to occupy the moral "vantage ground," as Lord Palmerston called it after the Opium War. They defended that territory tenaciously. "The Chinese must learn and be convinced that if they attack our people and our factories they will be shot"—Palmerston's policy was designed to protect opium traffickers without naming them, and, in this as in so many things, he set the pattern for British statesmen throughout the nineteenth century.

That British representatives in China took Palmerston's words literally was demonstrated in July and August of 1860, when Frederick Bruce's brother Lord Elgin returned to China and led a task force of more than two hundred British and French ships back to the forts at Taku to settle accounts for the defeat of the previous year and finally force compliance with the Treaty of Tientsin. Ten thousand British and six thousand French troops participated in the subsequent storming of the forts and march toward Peking, during which the anti-Western general Seng-ko-lin-ch'in (known as "Sam Collinson" to the British troops) was repeatedly defeated and his Tartar horsemen sent reeling westward. The Western allies apparently meant to have an exchange of Tientsin ratifications in China's capital whatever the cost.

It would be wrong, however, to say that all Englishmen in China approved of Britain's playing a part either in such armed interventions or in the opium traffic. Some found their nation's behavior in these connections so morally repugnant that they actively supported the Taiping cause, and thus set themselves up as opponents of Ward and his Foreign Arms Corps. Of these, perhaps none was more remarkable than Augustus F. Lindley. Arriving in China as a merchant naval officer in 1859, Lindley had been so appalled by the behavior of imperial officials and Western businessmen in the treaty ports, and so intrigued by reports of the Chinese Christian movement in Nanking, that he had journeyed up the Yangtze to assess the rebel movement for himself. Here he met and was greatly impressed by the Chung Wang, to whom Lindley—writing under his adopted Chinese name, Lin-le—later dedicated a two-volume account of the rebellion and his own part in it. Receiving a permit to carry on trade in Taiping territories, Lindley soon began running guns to the rebels, motivated by what he would subsequently call "feelings of sympathy for a worthy, oppressed, and cruelly wronged people; as well as by a desire to protest against the evil foreign policy which England, during the last few years, has pursued." Lindley took the field with the Chung Wang's armies, trained a group of Taipings in the use of firearms and artillery, and was even married in a Taiping ceremony.

There were other Englishmen who sought employment in the Taiping armies, although not all were motivated by as apparently lofty considerations as Lindley. For their part, the Taiping leaders, according to the Chung Wang, were circumspect about hiring Western mercenaries, considering them arrogant and unreliable. The "T'ien Wang," wrote the rebel commander, "was unwilling to use foreign troops. A thousand [foreign] devils would lord it over ten thousand of our men, and who would stand for that? So we did not employ them." This determination eroded along with Taiping military fortunes during the early 1860s, however, and more and more foreign profiteers were allowed into the rebel ranks.

Englishmen and other Westerners were not only fighting on the Taiping side in 1860 but, as in Lindley's case, running guns, securing supplies, and even enlisting recruits in Shanghai. One American, identified only by the surname Peacock, persuaded foreigners in the port to defy their various nations' bans on active participation in the Chinese civil war and to travel up the Yangtze to enlist. Some of these volunteers achieved positions of importance: One Englishman called Savage, an ex-pilot and, by some accounts, ex-soldier, held a high enough rank under the Chung Wang during the Kiangsu campaign of 1860 to be given charge of entire city garrisons. Rewards of money and rank were readily available to men who proved as capable as Savage. And while Western analysts such as Andrew Wilson might write off the foreigners who participated in the war during this period as "a few Malays and Manila-men, and, perhaps, a crazy English sailor or two," they did help the Taipings become better acquainted with modern weapons and tactics.

As for the attitude of the Westerners who fought on either side of the Chinese civil war toward each other, Augustus Lindley's words are again indicative. Lindley had only scorn for the Westerners who served the Manchus—with the exception of Ward. After the latter's death, Lindley wrote that Ward,

> whatever his failings might have been, was a brave and determined man. He served his Manchu employers only too well, and at the last, by closing a career full of peril and fidelity with the sacrifice of his life, he sealed all faults with his death, and left those who cherished his memory to regret that he had not fallen in a worthier cause. ... This adventurer originated the force that finally was the principal instrument in driving the Taipings from the dominions they had established as "Tai-ping tien-kuo." By such apparently insignificant means does the Great Ruler of the Universe overthrow the efforts and establish the destinies of man!

The first truly significant demonstration of these "apparently insig-nificant means" came in mid-July 1860, with the Foreign Arms Corps's second assault on Sung-chiang, an assault that quickly took on legendary proportions in Shanghai and, finally, throughout the Chinese empire.

Following his conquest of Soochow on June 2, the Chung Wang had dispatched columns east toward Shanghai and succeeded in capturing most of the cities and towns that ringed the port, including Sung-chiang. But in much the same way that his determination had mellowed and the pace of his armies slackened on the march to Soochow, so did the advance toward Shanghai grow ever less decisive. The Chung Wang apparently enjoyed being away from the scrutiny of his increasingly unbalanced leader, the T'ien Wang. He also took full advantage of the considerable amenities Soochow had to offer. Claiming that he needed time to enlist troops before descending on Shanghai and then moving back west and up the southern bank of the Yangtze, the Chung Wang in fact occupied himself with the construction of a magnificent residence, described by one visitor as consisting of "several sets of rooms, all connected with each other by passages and halls, but otherwise separated by courtyards variously adorned. Some have ponds, trees, soft rocks, penetrated with subterranean passages, the whole forming a labyrinth of palatial dimensions."

Meanwhile, in the war's western theater, some twenty thousand imperial troops had finally succeeded in surrounding the crucial Taiping city of Anking. The siege was not yet pressed with conviction, however, nor would it be until Tseng Kuo-fan assumed overall direction of the imperial military effort in the region. But the achievement was a sinister omen for the rebel cause. According to Augustus Lindley, the Manchu braves at first

contented themselves with the ordinary phase of Chinese warfare— watching, flag-waving, and yelling at a safe distance from any probable vicious attempt of the dangerous chang-maos. Anking, however, was a place of great strength for Chinese warfare; it formed the *point d'appui* of all Taiping movements either to the northern or northwestern provinces, and previous to any attack on their capital, Nanking, or its fortified outposts, its reduction was an absolute necessity. The city being built right on the brink of the great river, was absolute mistress of that important highway, without which, and its invaluable water communication, any extensive movement of the Manchu armies in an easterly direction became impracticable. At last, therefore, the Manchu warriors girded up their loins, that is to say, tucked up the bottoms of their petticoat inexpressibles, fiercely wound their tails around their cleanly-shaven caputs, made a terrible display of huge flags, roaring gongs, horridly painted bamboo shields, and a most extravagant waste of gunpowder, and moving forward with terrific cloud-rending yells, established themselves safely out of cannon-range of the walls, and proceeded to complete the invest-ment of the doomed city by building themselves in with a formidable series of earth-works and stockades, from which they could neither climb out nor enemies climb in.

In the face of this threat, the Taiping leadership became gravely concerned over the attitude and actions of the Chung Wang, whose preoccupation with Soochow and its surrounding territories seemed to have wiped from the young general's mind any appreciation of the important role he had been assigned in the coordinated westward attack. The Taiping prime minister, the Kan Wang, later wrote in anger that following the fall of Soochow the Chung Wang had "rested upon his oars, manifesting no anxiety whatever about the state of Anking," and some authors have speculated that the Chung Wang, weary of Taiping court intrigues and massacres, meant to establish his own warlord kingdom in the provinces of Kiangsu and Chekiang. His tested loyalty to the rebel cause makes this improbable, but in view of the pressure being applied to Anking, his behavior in Kiangsu was open to question. Anking's predicament also underscored the importance of Shanghai, which held the arms, river steamers, funds, and supplies that could restore rebel authority in the west. Taking stock of all this, and realizing that the port's capture would silence all criticism of his actions, the Chung Wang roused himself from the pleasures of Soochow and, in July, once again turned his attention eastward.

Thus Ward's decision to make a second attempt at recapturing Sung-chiang from the rebels was not based simply on pride or the need to restore his backers' faith in him. There were real strategic issues at stake. Sung-chiang and the neighboring walled city of Ch'ing-p'u (about fifteen miles to the north) were the strongest fortresses on the approach to Shanghai from the west and southwest, and the front line of defense against any attacker emerging from those directions. And while it is true that only the capture of Shanghai itself would appreciably benefit the rebel cause, the maintenance of Sung-chiang and Ch'ing-p'u—along with Chia-ting to the northwest, Kao-ch'iao to the north, the Pootung peninsula to the east, and Nan-ch'iao and Chin-shan-wei to the south—gave the Chinese and Western residents of Shanghai breathing space in which to conduct trade and receive supplies with relative freedom. Thus if the Taiping advance were to be checked, Sung-chiang and Ch'ing-p'u were the logical places for the challenge to take place. In addition, Sung-chiang held an important place in Confucian folklore and was the seat of the prefecture that included Shanghai; its recapture would provide a boost to morale and help restore the tarnished prestige of local imperial officials.

If Ward left any written record of how much these factors influenced his decision to strike again at Sung-chiang, it has not survived. But this as well as future moves made by the Foreign Arms Corps's commander indicate that he took account of such considerations almost instinctively. The British journalist Andrew Wilson found Ward not only "a man of courage and ability" but one whose "mind seems always to have been occupied with military matters as affording his proper and destined sphere in life." The axiom that an important objective (such as Shanghai) is best protected not from within but from a strong secondary position (such as Sung-chiang) would have been not only one of the basic tenets that Ward learned during his course of study at the American Literary, Scientific and Military Academy but also one that was validated during the siege campaigns of the Crimean War. An imperialist bastion at Sung-chiang would be a thorn in the side of any Taiping advance against Shanghai, as well as an ideal base from which a "flying column," or highly mobile group of raiders, could strike at other positions in the area. The decision to renew the attack was, therefore, eminently sound.

Ward would not, however, be rushed into a premature assault by Wu Hsü and Yang Fang. Perhaps doubting their decision to back the American, both men again became anxious in early July for tangible proof of his ability. But the impatience of Wu and Yang had already been almost fatal to the Foreign Arms Corps. Ward—whose career shows a singular absence of repeated mistakes—prepared for the second assault thoroughly. He may have bought time by arguing with Yang, or he may have employed the tactic that Charles Schmidt spoke of as common in Ward's dealings with "the Mandarins":

> In fact,—whenever the Mandarins ordered him to do any thing, he always said Yes, in a negative manner; in so prepossessing a way, however, that he left no doubt on their minds as to his sincerity. But he invariably put off their demands for a more leisure time, and in the interval acted according to his own views of the thing demanded, the result of action invariably agreeing with his own ideas. Then he would tell them that he had omitted through hurry, the order given him. The Mandarins seeing what would have been the result of their orders had he followed them, omitted to task him for disobedience, not daring to open their mouths for fear of letting out their own ignorance.

The most important job to be completed before taking the field again was to augment the corps's excellent small arms with artillery. Through his usual channels Ward purchased two twelve-pounder, muzzle-loading brass guns, as well as eight brass six-pounders. "Guns" referred to long-barreled cannon with flat trajectories and high muzzle velocities, which generally fired solid shot of the weight cited in the name and were most effective when battering down defenses or ripping through closely ordered units of men. Howitzers and mortars, in contrast, could achieve greater elevation and higher trajectories, as well as lob hollow shells filled with the devastating invention of Britain's Henry Shrapnel behind walled defenses. In preparing for his assault on Sungchiang, Ward had the destruction of the city's gates foremost in his mind, and he concentrated on guns, although howitzers and mortars would later play important roles in his operations.

Twelve-pounder guns were the principal ordnance pieces of the French army in 1860, and twelve-pounder gun-howitzers (which could achieve a higher trajectory than ordinary guns) were the sole artillery weapon of the United States. But Ward in all likelihood obtained British models. The British twelve-pounder was six and a half feet in length and weighed one and a half tons; the six-pounder was far less cumbersome at five feet and just under seven hundred pounds. Handling artillery in what the Chung Wang referred to as the "water-bound countryside" of Kiangsu province was a tricky task, as indeed were all military maneuvers: "[I]t is difficult for troops to move," the Chung Wang wrote, "there is water everywhere and no other routes to take [than the canals or main roads]." Training the Manilamen as well as inexperienced Westerners in the use of such weighty pieces took time, and Ward incurred the anger of the British community once again by making a special effort to recruit British gunners as trainers.

Along with artillery, Ward purchased more rifles for his growing roster of troops (who soon numbered more than two hundred), as well as machetes, scaling ladders, small boats, stinkpots, and ammunition. He had apparently learned that the Taipings could be formidable enemies and that piercing the fortifications of Sung-chiang would require every advantage his money could buy. Yet such weapons would not produce the desired effect unless Ward's appreciation of the tactics that went with them was adequate. For Ward was beginning his operations during a period of profound change in the history of warfare. That change had been initiated by the introduction of rifled barrels and breech-loading mechanisms into firearms and artillery, producing dramatically improved accuracy along with increased range and rates of fire. The tactical implications of this revolution had been sorely underestimated and even ignored by armies in both the East and the West, but the latter stages of the Taiping rebellion, along with the American Civil War and the Austro-Prussian War of 1866, would be one of the great arenas in which those implications would become savagely apparent.

In his study of the strategy and tactics of the American Civil War, the eminent British military historian and theorist J. F. C. Fuller made a keen observation that applied equally to Ward's predicament in China. Fuller believed that the "lack in the appreciation of the power of the rifle bullet has constituted the supreme tragedy of modern warfare, a drama of insanity in which millions have perished for a dream—the bayonet clinch, the flash of steel, the stab and the yell of victory." Both the

Taiping and imperialist armies in China placed a high value on "the flash of steel, the stab and the yell of victory," and they continued to do so even after modern firearms had been introduced into the war. They had little knowledge of or use for the tactics that would eventually solve the problems posed by the development of rifling, tactics that continue to characterize progressive warfare today: mobility (of individual soldiers as well as units) and hard-hitting, precise artillery support. It was Ward who introduced these tactics into China, and in doing so he placed himself among the most forward-thinking commanders of his day.

By mid-July the Foreign Arms Corps was again ready for action, as was its commander. Understanding the value of mystique in Chinese society, Ward had developed a personal style that inspired awe (and no little consternation) in the native populace as well as among his enlisted men. He abandoned the gold braid and insignia that adorned the tunics and jackets of Western commanders (and many of his own officers) and took to wearing a plain, dark blue frock coat, cut in the pattern of a Prince Albert and generally buttoned high. A white shirt and black kerchief tied loosely at the neck completed this unique uniform, which was sometimes augmented by a cape and occasionally a field cap in the French style. But most important, Ward abandoned the use of side arms and went into battle carrying only a short rattan cane or crop. This stick would become his trademark and the symbol, to many Chinese, of his superhuman daring and courage—even invulnerability. Such superstitions may have been absurd, but they were important in China and Ward cultivated them. In addition, the rattan cane had a practical application: Disciplinary floggings in the Middle Kingdom were administered with just such an instrument.

The fact that his distinctive attire and accoutrements made Ward a very distinguishable target in the field counted for less in his mind than the positive effect they produced on his men and on the collective mind of the Chinese. As this effect heightened with time, his appearance became more and more consistent. Archibald Bogle—a lieutenant and later admiral in the British Royal Navy who knew Ward in China and was with him at the time of his death—later recalled that he "never saw Ward with a sword or any arm; he wore ordinary clothes,—a thick, short cape, and a hood, and carried a stick in his hand, and generally a Manila cheroot in his mouth." In addition, the more battles Ward survived unarmed, the more he exposed himself to danger; and in exchanges with other Westerners he often expressed something very close to a belief in the superstitions about his luck and providential protection that were circulated among the Chinese.

On the night of July 16, 1860, Ward once again moved on Sung-chiang. The exact circumstances of the battle have always been a subject of discussion and argument, but one version eventually became standardized in Shanghai and is quite probably closest to the truth. Ward's plan, as in the first assault, was to achieve surprise under cover of night. But this time he took greater pains to ensure success. Most of his Western officers were left behind in Kuang-fu-lin, where their drunken carousing could only be interpreted by the rebels as an indication that the main body of the corps was idle. Ward and Burgevine, meanwhile, boarded a shallow-draft steamer with somewhere between one and two hundred Manilamen. They moved along one of the area's principal canals, but toward Ch'ing-p'u rather than Sung-chiang. This diversionary tactic was completed when Ward's men left the steamer surreptitiously and boarded a group of smaller boats while the noisy river steamer moved on toward Ch'ing-p'u. The corps reached Sung-chiang's moat under cover of a heavy fog at a little past ten o'clock. Ward moved his men toward the east gate of the city, on top of which was positioned a Taiping artillery battery armed with howitzers. The corps was able to maneuver its guns into position and train them on the gate unnoticed, and just before eleven o'clock they opened fire.

As the six- and twelve-pounders blew fragments of teak and iron away with solid shot, Ward's foot soldiers threw scaling ladders across the Sung-chiang moat and poured into the archway in front of the gate, safe from Taiping fire. With the gate shattered, Ward led a charge inside, only to find an unwelcome sight: a second gateway, also made of thick planks and wrought iron, but out of reach of Ward's guns. There seemed no way to penetrate this barrier; Ward's artillery could not be dragged across the moat. By now the Taipings had been alerted to the attack and were concentrating a heavy fire on Ward's men, who retreated into the archway of the outer gate.

Ward took a small party of Manilamen and, returning through the heavy Taiping musket fire, moved back across the moat. Here the detachment fetched twenty fifty-pound sacks of gunpowder and once more made for the east gate. Working under a protective fire provided by the Manilamen—whose careful training in the use of the Sharps repeating carbines now began to pay off—Ward's party packed the sacks of gunpowder under the interior gate and ignited them, producing a tremendous explosion. As the dust settled, it appeared that the powder had had no effect: The gate still stood. And then a small opening became visible, just wide enough for one or two men to slip through at a time.

What happened next is one of the more uncertain and embellished parts of the story of the second battle for Sung-chiang. Popular accounts had it that Ward, seeing his men hesitate with fear before the inner gate, stood, indicated the small opening with his rattan stick, and said: "Come on, boys. We're going in." At that he disappeared through the hole, followed quickly by Vincente, Burgevine, and the rest of the Manilamen. Other accounts state that it was Vincente who was first inside the walls, and this may indeed be so, but it is also true that Ward often conquered his men's trepidation by exposing himself to extreme dangers in a manner unheard of for nineteenth-century commanding officers. It was a period, generally, of rear area command; Ward's consistently forward position was another anticipation of modern tactics.

Inside Sung-chiang's second gateway was a wide ramp leading up to the Taiping howitzer battery, where six pieces were answering the fire of Ward's guns across the moat. For two hours Ward, Burgevine, Vincente, and the Manilamen fought their way up this ramp at close quarters, the Sharps repeaters going off with such well-practiced speed that they reportedly set the clothes of the Taipings afire with their muzzle flashes. In addition, the Manilamen did grim work with machetes and their fearsome *kris,* curved blades that were said to possess mystical power and were certainly effective in battle. Finally, at 1:00 A.M., Ward's men reached the howitzers. Turning the pieces around, Ward began to pummel the inside of Sung-chiang with rapid fire, killing what was later claimed to be a full third of the city's thousands of defenders.

The overall plan of operations called for Ward's small storming party to be relieved at this point by a large contingent of Li Heng-sung's

Green Standard braves, who had taken up positions a few miles away. This force was to approach Sung-chiang as soon as Ward fired a rocket signal from atop the city walls. But the Foreign Arms Corps now learned a dismal lesson in the unreliability of imperial troops. Several rockets were fired off, but there was no sign of the Green Standard soldiers. Finally, at about 6:00 A.M., when Li saw by light of day that the Taipings were in fact abandoning Sung-chiang, he moved on the city.

Only a comparative few of Ward's men were still on their feet. Sixty-two were dead and another hundred wounded. Ward himself had received the first of what would become, during the course of his Chinese career, at least fifteen wounds, this one in his left shoulder. Such injuries never slowed his pace, however: During the first six hours of his occupation of Sung-chiang, Ward established his headquarters near a Confucian temple, sent his wounded back to Shanghai, and arranged to have Li Heng-sung's men garrison and police the city. For those of Ward's men who were still ambulatory, there ensued the promised looting, a time-honored military tradition in China and one practiced by all sides in an attempt to ensure loyalty. Besides guns and ammunition, the Taipings had left in Sung-chiang stores of silver and other valuables which they had plundered during their march through Kiangsu. These were distributed among the soldiers of the Foreign Arms Corps, the greatest portions going to men such as Burgevine and Vincente, who had displayed exceptional courage. (Shanghai's Westerners affected great disdain for this practice, but during their ongoing march to Peking in the north, British and French troops would prove the most wanton plunderers of all.) Then came a proclamation ordering the inhabitants of the city and its suburbs once more to swear faith to the emperor in Peking. Finally, in the afternoon, Ward returned to Shanghai to have his shoulder treated.

The victory had immediate repercussions in every community in Shanghai. To Wu Hsü, Yang Fang, and the Chinese generally, Ward was a hero who had delivered the first significant blow to the Taiping cause in Kiangsu. To the Europeans, however, Ward was now confirmed in his status as a dangerous filibuster and outlaw, perhaps even a lunatic, and it was generally anticipated that the corps's action would bring the

Chung Wang's armies sweeping mercilessly down on Shanghai. Thus anything that could be done to minimize the battle at Sung-chiang and discredit Ward was seen as helpful in the settlements. The *North China Herald,* for example, dismissed the events of July 16–17 with the following statement: "The rebels, having exhausted Sung-chiang, and not liking the Manila-men near them, left the city, and retreated on Ssu-ching. The imperialists sent an officer to see the reason of the city's stillness, and on receiving assurance that the enemy had evacuated, rushed in and beheaded as many of the unfortunate inhabitants as they could lay their hands on."

As for the Foreign Arms Corps, *Herald* editor Charles Compton continued his attacks: "The Manila-men are still near Sung-chiang, committing their depredations. The Chinese will have a long account to settle with these gentry one of these days. Can't the Spanish Consul be induced to order them, as Spanish subjects, to return? We are sure the treaty powers would grant him assistance. It is a disgrace that such a gang should be allowed to set all laws at defiance because they are in the pay of the Taotai."

And there was this alarmist—and notably inaccurate—warning to the worried Western citizens of Shanghai: "[T]he Taotai directed all his efforts to retake the place [Sung-chiang], and drive the rebels to come near Shanghai by some other road. They are coming another way, and good care is being taken to keep up the vision of foreign gold and opium in their minds, and of the extraordinary helpless condition of the settlement."

In addition to vexed foreigners, imperial officials who had had nothing to do with the events at Sung-chiang made an effort to discount and distort reports of Ward's victory. One such man, Wu Yün—whose actual post was in Soochow but who had fled to Shanghai in the spring— claimed that Ward's attack had occurred when all of Sung-chiang's able-bodied Taiping defenders were in the field. The remaining rebel garrison, said Wu, was made up of the old and the incapacitated, and Ward faced no greater task than taking a few men, swimming under one of the water gates that bestrode the city's canals, seizing one of the four main gates, and opening it for the rest of the corps. Wu Yün's version of the story, like so many reports of Chinese imperial officials, cannot be given any great credence. As one expert on the Taiping period has written, such characters were "frequently mendacious, nearly always ill-informed, and inevitably prejudiced."

Whether heroic or criminal in aspect, the capture of Sung-chiang established Ward, Burgevine, and the rest of the Foreign Arms Corps as men of notoriety throughout Kiangsu. The most important practical result of the victory, however, was the payment to Ward of the bonus for which he had contracted with Wu Hsü and Yang Fang. The exact amount of this reward has been another of the contested details of Ward's life. Estimates ranging from 10,000 taels (or about $16,000) to 75,000 taels (or $133,000) have been offered. The actual amount probably came closer to the larger of these figures, and without doubt Ward would need the money during the months to come. For the victory at Sung-chiang opened onto not the brightest but the darkest period of Ward's fortunes: a period marked by defeat, severe injury, and finally imprisonment.

IV

"NOT AS WAS HOPED,
DEAD..."

Following the victory at Sung-chiang, Ward and his men became closely identified with that city (the corps being often referred to as "the Sung-chiang men" or "the Sung-chiang force"), and disagreements with local imperial administrators were inevitable. During these encounters Ward seems to have exhibited for the first time the limits of his tact. Rightly suspecting that the officials assigned by Hsüeh Huan and Wu Hsü to oversee affairs at Sung-chiang were also secretly charged with keeping a careful eye on the Foreign Arms Corps and its leader, Ward took effective control of the city by refusing to relinquish even nominal military authority. Such an imposition was deeply insulting to the local mandarins, whose responsibilities were both civil and military. But Ward dealt brusquely with their protests, and when the unlucky mandarins crossed paths with Burgevine—who commanded the corps during Ward's frequent visits to Shanghai—these rebukes could be more than verbal.

Ward established his permanent headquarters in Sung-chiang next to a small Christian church, and from there he addressed the manifold problems of expanding and better providing for his force. The seizure of Sung-chiang brought dozens of eager new volunteers, mostly Westerners who had gotten word of the looting and bounties that had followed the battle. But Ward—who quickly became known as Colonel Ward in view of the corps's success—had learned several important lessons during his weeks in the field. Vincente and the Manilamen had vindicated themselves in fine style, and Ward henceforward examined Western recruits with a wary eye. In addition, even more rigid discipline was maintained among those foreigners he had either kept on from the original force or hired after Sung-chiang. A typical example of how Ward dealt with insubordination, drunkenness, or abusive treatment of enlisted men by his Western officers was offered some months later by a Danish member of the corps, John Hinton. Detained by British troops for violating the various Western neutrality laws, Hinton testified that one of Ward's officers, a Prussian, had been imprisoned in Sung-chiang

> for disobedience of Ward's order. I saw him amongst a lot of Chinese prisoners, and he was very heavily ironed and shamefully treated. A few days afterwards Egan, who is Ward's Lieutenant, had a quarrel with the Colonel on account of Egan's having struck a man when on drill. Egan, in consequence, threw off his uniform and declared he would go to Shanghai. Ward swore he should not, and Egan, the same night, got very drunk, and when in bed Ward sent men and took him prisoner to Sung-chiang, where he was confined with the Prussian.

The statements of bitter Western freebooters who had journeyed to Sung-chiang expecting to enjoy a riotous life of drinking and plunder and found instead something very like regular military discipline were offered by Western businessmen and especially British officials in Shanghai as proof that the Foreign Arms Corps was not a volunteer unit but a criminal organization of kidnapped and impressed soldiers. The British—reluctant to use the term *impressment,* quite probably because it had all too often been accurately applied to Her Britannic Majesty's forces themselves—branded Ward's methods "crimping," but Ward continued to go about his affairs without apparent anxiety over British invectives. In the months to come Ward's relationship to the British community in Shanghai was destined to evolve from such open hostility toward working cooperation; but there is no evidence that he ever lost his general and characteristically American distrust of people and things British, even if he did come to respect individual Englishmen. This attitude was recognized by the British community in China, many of whom were enraged by it. One especially indignant observer, writing in the *Hong Kong Daily Press,* later observed that

> one might have expected that he would either have English predilec-
> tions, or have been able to have subdued those anti-English animosi-
> ties which characterise so many of his tribe and generation. But no,
> sir, he hates England and Englishmen from the very bottom of his
> heart. He will not have an Englishman near him, nor will he deal with
> them. All the white men about him are low Americans, with feelings
> congenial to his own. . . . [Y]ou will find that if the [Chinese] imperial-
> ists gain the upper hand, Colonel Ward and his gang will prove a very
> important anti-English element.

Of course, this view was inaccurate in its extremity; some of Ward's best officers were Englishmen, albeit deserters. But in its ex-pression of the mutual animosity that often existed between American and British citizens in the treaty ports of China (an animosity that would shortly be heightened by Britain's tacit support of the Confederacy during the American Civil War), as well as in its blind invective against Ward, it was indeed typical.

Even if Ward had been concerned with improving his image in the foreign settlements of Shanghai in July 1860, there would have been no time for doing so. Shuttling back and forth between the port and Sung-chiang with new recruits and supplies, Ward simultaneously dealt with the administrative details of both his force and the Sung-chiang area. The list of concerns requiring his personal touch was long, but two problems in particular—inadequate medical care for his men and plundering of the local populace by his officers when he was in Shanghai—netted his special attention. That attention in turn revealed much about Ward's priorities and offers further clues as to why his relations with the corps's Western officers were frequently so strained.

China was by no means a medically backward country. Its tradition of herbal healing was well-established in the mid–nineteenth century. But when dealing with the ailments of soldiers, local Chinese officials such as Wu Hsü generally substituted money for medical care. Wounded men were given cursory treatment, then paid off and, if their wounds were severe, discharged and left to seek further attention on their own. Ward attempted to change all this by establishing the first in a series of medical stations at Sung-chiang, one designed to attend not only to wounds but to noncombat-related complaints of his soldiers. These and subsequent efforts on Ward's part, as Dr. Macgowan noted later, enjoyed only "indifferent success; his surgeon being afflicted by an unquenchable thirst, which he never attempted to allay with water, being rather hydrophobic. Nevertheless, when he was free from *delirium tremens,* the troops confided in him. Once during a skirmish this staff-surgeon tumbled into an indigo pit, and would have been asphyxiated there and then, but for the intervention of an illnatured by-stander, who dragged him out for future malpractice."

While Ward's attempts to provide adequate medical care for his men did not always bear practical fruit, they did succeed in annoying Wu Hsü. The issue remained a bone of contention throughout the period of Ward's operations in Kiangsu; and the taotai complained even after Ward's death that wherever it went, the corps "always sets up a medical station. Even when the soldiers have only an ailment, they will be sent there immediately. The monthly medical expense exceeds several thousand [taels]." That Ward himself was responsible for this expense— indeed insisted on it—was indicated by the fact that once he was out of the way, Wu commanded: "From now on, when soldiers are injured during the war, they will be paid, based on the same practice for officers, a considered amount of money for nursing the injuries, while the installation of the medical station should be canceled."

As for relations with the citizens of Sung-chiang and the peasants in the nearby countryside, Ward was even more hard-pressed to realize his goals. The average Westerner, particularly the average Western freebooter, was unlikely to concern himself with the deleterious effects of plundering an already plundered populace. Loot was the principal reason such a man had signed on, after all. The Manilamen, too, initially took advantage of any chance for plunder. And it must be remembered that plunder, during the Taiping rebellion, had a distinctly human dimension: Young girls and boys were considered prized items and fair spoils. Ward early on attempted to confine looting to money and valuables, and enforced strict punishments for violators. "It is really to the credit of Ward," wrote Dr. Macgowan, "that he brought his men to refrain from plundering the people whom they were paid to protect. . . . The sight of villages fleeing for protection into cities held by rebels was never witnessed by men under Ward's command." Charles Schmidt also recalled of Ward, "Especially he was always careful that his men did not wantonly oppress the people."

But this must have been a thankless job for Ward, and certainly it was a policy that took months to become established. Even Burgevine, so valuable in maintaining discipline generally and during battle particularly, never really absorbed Ward's admittedly limited yet nonetheless real and unusual concern for the Kiangsu peasants. Thus whenever Ward's business took him to Shanghai for days or weeks at a time, he could expect affairs around Sung-chiang to deteriorate, a circumstance that further demonstrated the importance of personal leadership during the Chinese civil war: Ward's approach was often welcomed by local residents, whereas the approach of a Foreign Arms Corps contingent commanded by a man such as Burgevine might well inspire fear and even enmity.

For all these reasons, Ward continued to treat his Western officers with the harshest of hands. The usual punishments of imprisonment and "bambooing"—flogging across the back of the thighs with a short rattan cane such as the one Ward carried into battle—were sometimes augmented by capital punishment. This final recourse was not used with anything like liberality, and there is no evidence that it gave Ward any particular satisfaction. But the men in his employ were often criminals and even murderers to begin with, who held lesser forms of deterrence in contempt. Dr. Macgowan recalled a case of a "mutinous Irish captain of the force" (possibly the aforementioned Egan), who was "arrested and taken out of his quarters" as a *"pour encourager les autres"*: "It was supposed that he was beheaded; at any rate he has not since been heard of."

As he had done before Sung-chiang, Ward continued after the battle to build a cult of personality among the local Chinese. In camp, this effort eventually became embodied in the form of a dog, a large black-and-white mastiff that shadowed Ward's movements. A seemingly innocuous detail, this attachment to the mastiff was of real psychological value. Dogs were viewed as little more than a source of meat in China, and taking pains to feed and care for a large animal in a country ravaged by starvation inevitably struck most Chinese as more than eccentric: It was unnerving. Ward's attachment to the mastiff was certainly as much a matter of affection as of design, but the increased awe it won him among the natives was no less real or important.

By the end of July the Foreign Arms Corps was ready to make an attempt at another strategic Kiangsu city: Ch'ing-p'u, some fifteen miles northwest of Sung-chiang. Possession of both Ch'ing-p'u and Sung-chiang would give the imperialists effective control of the western approach to Shanghai, and it was to be expected that the Taipings, having lost the second, would defend the first of these cities all the more vigorously. Yet the actual strength of the Taiping forces in Ch'ing-p'u was unknown to Ward, largely as a result of his poor relations with imperial officials in Sung-chiang. What intelligence the imperialists gained from their traditional network of spies and informers in the cities and countryside was kept jealously hidden from the Foreign Arms Corps's commander, who made his plans, as in the case of Sung-chiang, largely in the dark.

But at Sung-chiang, Ward had at least been favored by surprise and an enemy who had no inkling that a privately financed, Western-led force might try to frustrate their advance. These advantages were now gone, and just as Sung-chiang had come to represent Ward's daring and success, Ch'ing-p'u was shortly to become the symbol of his frustrations and failures, the object of a fierce determination in the young commander that quickly degenerated into self-defeating fixation.

Like Sung-chiang, Ch'ing-p'u was a formidable fortress that sat astride a crucial intersection of canals and was surrounded by a moat. Three gates—western, eastern, and southern—were cut into the soft-cornered square formed by its walls, and it was the southern gate that

Ward made his target. The attack was to be carried out by some three hundred Manilamen and between thirty and fifty Western officers, supported by anywhere from three to ten thousand of Li Heng-sung's Green Standard braves. The Foreign Arms Corps, along with Ward's two six-pounder guns, was to be transported by a small flotilla of shallow-draft rivercraft.

Command of the Taiping forces in the Ch'ing-p'u area had been given to one of the Chung Wang's more capable lieutenants, Chou Wen-chia, who had entrusted the city garrison itself to the English ex-pilot and ex-soldier called Savage. After the fall of Sung-chiang, Chou and Savage had anticipated an imperial move against Ch'ing-p'u and prepared for it by quietly building up the number of the city's defenders: Some accounts put the total as high as ten thousand, but it was probably closer to five thousand. Most of these troops were tested veterans of the Kiangsu campaign, and, armed with muskets and trained in their use, they represented an unusually strong element of the Chung Wang's army.

All of this was unknown to Ward and the Foreign Arms Corps, who attacked in the predawn darkness of August 2. The approach to the city was made successfully: Leaving Burgevine in command of a second wave, Ward and Vincente took an advance party to Ch'ing-p'u's southern gate and there erected scaling ladders. As the men began to make their way up the wall, there was still no sign of resistance from the garrison, and it appeared momentarily that Ward would be able to repeat his Sung-chiang triumph by seizing one gate and from that vantage point raking the city's interior with rifle and cannon fire.

But then the trap was sprung. Savage and his Taipings had been alerted to Ward's advance and were lying in ambush. A devastating barrage of musket fire ripped into the Foreign Arms Corps's storming party as it reached the top of the wall, while other defenders began to pelt the men still on the scaling ladders and the ground below with heavy rocks and bricks. Ward himself received five wounds quickly, the worst to his face: A Taiping musket ball hit him in the left jaw and exited through his right cheek. According to Charles Schmidt, Vincente—immediately behind Ward—caught his commander as the latter fell backward, then somehow managed to get Ward back to the ground outside the city. "There he [Vincente] stood in the midst of a perfect hail storm of stone, firing away like a fury, whilst his companions were dropping on all sides of him, killed by the unerring aim of the rebels on the walls."

Unable to speak and bleeding profusely, Ward began to write out orders. Barely ten minutes had elapsed since the Taipings had opened fire, yet already half of Ward's force had been killed or wounded. Recognizing the disaster for what it was, Ward ordered a general retreat toward Kuang-fu-lin and then Sung-chiang. The Taipings from Ch'ing-p'u gave chase but did not press the advantage, and the remnants of the Foreign Arms Corps struggled back into the safety of Sung-chiang's walls, their wounded commander being carried for the last few miles in a sedan chair.

Despite his physical condition, Ward went quickly to Shanghai to enlist more men, buy more artillery, and try to shore up the damage done to his reputation among the Chinese by the defeat at Ch'ing-p'u. He arrived to find the Western communities gleeful over his misfortune. "The first and best item of intelligence we have to give our readers," reported the *North China Herald* on August 4,

> is the utter defeat of Ward and his men before Ch'ing-p'u. This notorious man has been brought down to Shanghai, not as was hoped, dead, but severely wounded with a shot in his mouth, one in his side, and one in his legs. . . . He managed to drag his carcass out of danger, but several of his valorous blacks [Manilamen] were killed or wounded. . . . It seems astonishing that Ward should be allowed to remain unpunished, and yet not a hint is given that any measures will be taken against him.

The *Herald*'s complaint was justified: Even Britain's Consul Meadows had come to the conclusion that, given existing circumstances, Ward could not be stopped. During the week Ward spent in Shanghai following the first attempt on Ch'ing-p'u, Meadows wrote a long and angry letter to Minister Frederick Bruce, detailing his many frustrations in trying to put an end to the Foreign Arms Corps's activities. Meadows had quickly learned that he would not get any help in this effort from the Americans: Consul Smith had written him on July 13 to say that while some Americans had gone up-country illegally, their actions were simply a matter of the neutrality laws having "been overlooked inadvertently, but I hope and believe that there is a disposition on the part of our citizens to observe the laws." Meadows had next attempted to convince the senior British naval officer in Shanghai to go upriver with a party of marines and arrest the Westerners at Sung-chiang, but, as Meadows complained to Minister Bruce, the officer "took no notice of my written request for assistance, and when I spoke to him, a day or two later on the subject, he stated that his instructions did not allow him to do police work."

From the Chinese authorities Meadows got no satisfaction whatsoever, and he subsequently came "to the conclusion that it is impossible to enforce the Neutrality Ordinance so long as the Intendant [Wu Hsü] himself is the chief instigator of British subjects to violate it." Furthermore, there was, said Meadows,

> good reason to believe that the Taipings finding themselves attacked by men furnished with superior weapons and able to use them, have resorted to the same means of defense, and that there is a body of foreigners now in their employ. The pusillanimous and unpatriotic step taken by the Intendant and other Imperial Authorities seems not unlikely to end in large numbers of the most lawless and, in many cases, ruffianly foreigners being taught the means of maintaining themselves in a career of violence and depredation in the interior of the country, beyond the controul [sic] and even beyond the ken of the foreign authorities.

But while Meadows's assessment was undoubtedly correct, he ignored the hard realities and choices facing the imperial authorities in Shanghai. Ward's Foreign Arms Corps was the only even marginally effective instrument with which to challenge Taiping authority in the interior (certainly, the British and the other foreign powers were as yet unwilling to share such a responsibility). In addition, those Westerners who, like Meadows, persistently cried that Ward's activities would bring

Taiping retribution down on Shanghai took no stock of the fact that the port was the Chung Wang's goal regardless of what Ward did. Shanghai's resources were vital to the survival of the rebel movement, and whatever the opinions of the learned British consul, it was that fact—and not the operations of the Foreign Arms Corps—that was drawing the rebel army inexorably to the coast.

While in Shanghai during the first week of August, Ward received some inadequate medical attention, purchased two powerful eighteen-pounder guns along with a dozen other new pieces of artillery, and—driven by desperation—enlisted a group of Greek and Italian reinforcements. "Being," as the journalist Andrew Wilson understated it, "an irrepressible sort of element," Ward then returned to Sung-chiang, gathered up all the able-bodied members of the corps, and marched once more on Ch'ing-p'u. This time, however, he settled in for an artillery bombardment and siege.

That Ward should have been able to recoup his position to such an extent while suffering from severe wounds is indicative of tremendous powers of physical endurance. In these, he was typical of many of the Western officers in his corps. Nearly all these men received multiple wounds during their encounters with the Taipings, and many operated effectively in spite of them. There is no doubt that they were assisted by liberal doses of strong liquor; yet their stamina was still remarkable. Ward's investiture of Ch'ing-p'u on August 9 was undertaken while he was still unable to speak as a result of the shattering of his jaw and before his other wounds had healed or even been properly attended to. The loss of blood just a week earlier had been severe, and the pain must still have been immense, yet Ward was able to design an attack that came close to forcing Savage and the city garrison to surrender.

Any chance of such a result, however, was destroyed when Savage's immediate superior, Chou Wen-chia, contacted the Chung Wang in Soochow and told him of Ch'ing-p'u's plight. This second entrance of "devil soldiers" into the Kiangsu fighting alarmed the rebel commander, who quickly mustered between ten and twenty thousand men. "We set off from Soochow by boat," the Chung Wang recalled, "arriving the following day, and went into action immediately. The foreign devils came out to give battle and the two sides met and fought from early morning until noon, and the devils were severely beaten." Ward had no hope of success against such a powerful rebel army, led by the most talented of Taiping commanders. The defeat was particularly disastrous, as Charles Schmidt wrote, because

> the rebels took all the large guns, vessels of war, stores, and money, and, by surrounding the imperial camp, killed nearly 100 Europeans, wounded nearly as many of the same, and caused a very great number of Chinese soldiers on board the vessels to jump over board and drown themselves, while the Imperial Chief Li [Heng-sung] barely escaped being taken prisoner. In this expedition Vincente also barely escaped being taken, having to cut his way through the rebels who had surrounded him.

Despite overwhelming odds against them, the Foreign Arms Corps managed to fight their way back to Sung-chiang. The Chung Wang followed close on their heels, and the gates of Sung-chiang had no sooner admitted the battered members of the corps than it was the Taipings' turn to pen Ward up. (During this action, the Englishman Savage was gravely wounded.) Ward's physical condition was now rapidly deteriorating and demanded more attention than could be given at Sung-chiang. At the insistence of Burgevine and the other officers of the corps, Ward was secretly lowered over the Sung-chiang walls to a riverboat waiting in one of the canals and was taken to Shanghai.

The corps's losses at Ch'ing-p'u had been undeniably serious and produced a profoundly negative effect on Ward's reputation in Shanghai. Yet the young American had come out of the fiasco in comparatively fortunate shape, given the severity of his strategic error in pressing the attack: For while the initial assault on Ch'ing-p'u was a logical move, it was also an obvious one, and the second attempt, rooted as it was in pride, was altogether unsound. Once it had become apparent that the Taipings were committed to holding Ch'ing-p'u, Ward would have served his own and the imperial cause better (if less dramatically) by consolidating his position at Sung-chiang and making sure that city could continue to serve as a base of operations from which to relieve the pressure on Shanghai. Because of the limited size of Ward's force, such relief could only have been achieved by striking not at points where the Taipings anticipated attacks and were gathered in strength (such as Ch'ing-p'u) but at less predictable and less fortified spots along their routes of advance and supply. And while the capture of Ch'ing-p'u might have augmented the prestige of the Foreign Arms Corps, it was certainly not worth risking the unit's very existence. Only Shanghai itself was of ultimate value to the rebels; had Ward shown patience and built his strength slowly in Sung-chiang, the role he could have played in denying the port to the Chung Wang would have been that much more significant.

These were all lessons that Ward would absorb over the long months of recuperation and rebuilding that lay ahead. For the moment, his ill-considered determination to take Ch'ing-p'u forced him to work for the defense of Shanghai not from the strategic bastion of Sung-chiang but from within the port itself, and not as the independent commander of his own free-lance army but as one among many Westerners who rallied in mid-August to meet the advance of the Taipings.

On reaching Shanghai, Ward took refuge in the rooms of Albert Freeman, the agent for H. Fogg and Company who had regularly helped him secure arms and supplies. Severely weakened and in great pain, Ward nonetheless continued to write out instructions for the resupply of his men at Sung-chiang, as well as orders for Burgevine, who was in command of the garrison. On August 12 the Chung Wang completed his investiture of Sung-chiang, although it remains uncertain whether he actually took the city. He later claimed to have done so, and some Chinese sources support this assertion, saying that the Foreign Arms Corps abandoned the defense of Sung-chiang and only returned after the Chung Wang had moved west toward Hankow late in August. But other Chinese scholars—along with numerous Western writers—claim that Burgevine was able to hold off repeated rebel assaults and that the Chung Wang, anxious to move on to Shanghai, eventually gave up the siege. In any event, Burgevine was able to keep the corps together and fighting, either within the walls of Sung-chiang or in the nearby country-side. And from his sickbed in Freeman's rooms in Shanghai, Ward kept in close touch with the force, although the effort and anxiety sapped his strength badly.

The Chung Wang, meanwhile, pressed on to Shanghai, mystified and not a little troubled about what his reception from the Westerners in the port would be. During his weeks of relative inactivity in Soochow in June, the rebel general had received several Western missionaries and what he asserted were official French emissaries in audience. From these meetings he had formed the impression that his entrance into Shanghai would be welcomed in the settlements, provided he guaranteed the safety of foreign nationals and their property. But the appearance of Ward's "foreign devils" in the military service of the imperial government had caused the Chung Wang to doubt this rather blithe assumption, as had the fact that his attempts to communicate with the Western diplomatic community in Shanghai had gone unanswered. Demonstrating the extent of the Taipings' concern that good relations with the foreigners be established, the Kan Wang, the rebel prime minister, had journeyed from Nanking to Soochow in July and addressed a communication to Consul Meadows, urging a meeting. But Frederick Bruce, hewing to the increasingly unrealistic policy of strict neutrality, ordered Meadows not to answer the communication.

The Western powers, especially the British and the French, were about to enter the most contradictory phase of their almost comically complex dealings with the Chinese empire during the 1850s and '60s. Mid-August saw Britain's Lord Elgin leading the Anglo-French task force on its punitive mission to the forts at Taku in the north, where British and French soldiers were shortly to engage in an unrestrained slaughter of imperial Chinese soldiers preparatory to a march on Peking to force compliance with the Tientsin treaty. But in regard to Shanghai, Bruce and his French counterpart had already decided that if the Chung Wang approached the port, regular British and French forces, along with whatever other Western soldiers were available and the Shanghai Volunteer Corps, would man the walls of the city and repel the rebel advance. More than one Western resident of Shanghai was confused by this apparent contradiction, and when New Englander A. A. Hayes approached an acquaintance of his in the Royal Engineers to ask about it, he received an answer that was perhaps as good as any: "My dear fellow," the officer replied, "we always *pitch into the swells*. At the north the imperialists are the swells, but down here, by Jove! the rebels are, don't you know?—so we pitch into them both."

In fact, the interests of foreign trading governments in China had not changed, whatever the details of their dealings with Peking and Nanking. The overarching goal was to force China to comply with the advantageous (for the Westerners) terms of the Treaty of Tientsin. Obviously, it would be impossible to enforce those terms if the authority of the Manchu government collapsed completely and if the Taipings extended their ban on opium to the treaty ports. It therefore became necessary to "pitch into" both the imperialists and the rebels. Such an activist policy certainly did not imply support for either party in the Chinese civil war, but neither did it represent a more genuinely "neutral" stance than had characterized Western policy since the Opium War. Thus the belligerent shift in tactics during August 1860—propelled not only by the intransigence of the war party that surrounded Hsienfeng in Peking but also by the steady advance of the Taipings toward Shanghai—did not imply any fundamental change in objective.

On August 16 the Chung Wang himself moved to the village of Ssu-ching, along the line of advance from Sung-chiang to Shanghai, and consolidated his somewhat scattered forces. As he continued the advance east he was joined by the Kan Wang, bitter over the Westerners' continued refusal to reply to his overtures as well as by reports that regular foreign soldiers were setting up defensive positions not only around the settlements in Shanghai but along the walls of the Chinese city. It seemed clear that the common worship of Shang-ti would not prove a sufficient force to unite the rebels and the foreigners, yet the Chung Wang and the Kan Wang continued to order their troops not to harm any foreign nationals or destroy any foreign property, under pain of death.

The Chung Wang's communications to the Chinese residents of Shanghai, by contrast, had a strident and threatening character. "How is it," the rebel general asked in a proclamation posted in the port by rebel spies,

> that you Shanghai people alone withstand all reason, and still listen to impish mandarins who do you nothing but injury? Your offences have now reached the climax that compels me to set troops in motion for your extermination. . . . I issue this Proclamation strongly to command and advise you; you know that an egg can't oppose a stone; make up your minds speedily, and submit yourselves. . . . I will establish my will firm as a mountain, and my commands shall be as flowing water. Immediately after I have informed you by this, my soldiers will arrive; they are not going to wait for you; don't say that I gave you no warning.

These words put panic in the hearts of many Chinese but prompted a typically pugnacious response from the foreign settlements. The Chung Wang's omission of any reference to foreigners in the proclamation was taken as a slight rather than diplomatic intention, and the *Herald* gave answer: "The 'Faithful King' will however find that we are not going to be ignored. Should he fulfil his threats, and march against Shanghai, he will meet with certain substantial proofs of our existence,—striking evidence of our prowess. John Bull at last is thoroughly aroused." With callous condescension, editor Compton added that "[a] Rebel is easier to hit than a pheasant or a snipe."

On the evening of August 17 the horizon to the west of Shanghai began to glow with the fires of burning villages, and the port's defenders knew that the rebel assault so long anticipated was about to commence. Early on the morning of the eighteenth the Taipings occupied the historic town of Hsu-chia-hui, or Siccawei, just west of the port, where Jesuit missionaries had long before established an important Catholic community. Rumors that a French priest was killed by the rebels at Siccawei (never fully substantiated) spread throughout Shanghai, steeling the resolve of the defenders. For his part, the Chung Wang quickly scattered the few imperial Chinese units sent against him, then—ever anxious to avoid giving offense to the Westerners—left the main body of his army behind and approached Shanghai with three thousand of his Kwangsi bodyguard.

At the city walls he found his worst fears confirmed. From the grandstand of the racetrack on the western edge of the British settlement to the west gate of the Chinese city, British troops and Sikh auxiliaries from India stood at the ready, supported by the Shanghai Volunteer Corps; the south gate of the Chinese city was held by Chinese imperialists, American artillery, and still more Britishers; and the eastern side of the port was garrisoned by the French. Most of the British soldiers were equipped with their army's new Enfield rifle, a weapon with impressive range and accuracy, while their artillery units were well-stocked with "canister," explosive shells packed with small iron balls. As the Chung Wang's men advanced they made contact with scattered imperialist contingents, who quickly retreated toward the west gate of the Chinese city. The Taipings followed in pursuit, then began to learn the hard lessons about Western weapons that the Manchus had absorbed during the Opium War.

"The firing of the Foreigners," said the *Herald,* "both from the cannon and rifles was excellent; as soon as canister was useless, the foe were treated to shell thrown time after time into the very middle of their flags." Raked by this brutal fire, the Taipings were thrown into tremendous confusion; but their commander's exhortations against harming foreigners were still fresh in their minds, and they did not fight back. In fact, said the *Herald* of that first afternoon, "curious to relate not a shot was fired." Instead, the Taipings moved in agitation from gate to gate, as if seeking a spot where they would be welcomed into the city by those they still believed to be their spiritual brothers.

At the western perimeter of the British settlement on the afternoon of the eighteenth, A. A. Hayes was serving with the Shanghai Volunteer Corps when, as he recalled, "a man of slight figure approached me, as I stood at the Maloo Barrier. He had collected a few fighting men, and desired to place them where they would be of some use; and so, amid the roar of artillery, the rattle of musketry, and the shrieks of native fugitives, I first met General Ward. He was a man of excellent address, mild and gentle in manner, and as kind and warm-hearted as possible.

His long hair and slight mustache were dark, and he habitually wore a blue coat tightly buttoned." Apparently recovered from his wounds sufficiently to serve, Ward had (he later claimed) been approached by the commander of the Volunteer Corps, one Colonel Neale, and asked to assist in the defense. It was Ward's endless craving for action rather than genuine need that pulled him out of his sickbed: The reluctant Taipings were no match for the Western forces already in place and were quickly halted by the ferocious artillery barrage.

The Western commanders were not, however, happy with the simple checking of the rebel advance. When it became clear, on the night of the eighteenth, that the Taipings were no real threat, parties of British and French soldiers left the defensive perimeter and entered the western, southern, and eastern suburbs of Shanghai. The British contented themselves with merely firing any structures that might give shelter to the Taipings, but the French indulged in the kind of wantonly criminal behavior that was to mark so many of their exploits in China. Plunder and rape joined arson on the list of "defensive measures." As one angry Westerner wrote to the *Herald,* the night's activities amounted to little more than "foul murder."

On Sunday the nineteenth, the *Herald* reported, the Taiping enemy further "laid himself open to some fine rifle practice," and while Sunday night was "quiet enough," Monday brought a new Taiping movement toward the Shanghai racecourse.

> Having advanced within a half a mile, they planted their banners on the tops of high graves and mounds, whilst they themselves retreated into two neighboring hamlets. The Volunteers proceeded at once to their posts at the barricades, the Royal Marines manned the several defences of the settlement, a howitzer and rocket party were sent out towards the rebel lines, and the whole settlement was rendered impregnable in less than half an hour. Now the firing and shelling commenced. The Insurgents stood it for several hours like men of stone—immovable, without returning a single shot.

For five more days this extraordinary state of affairs continued. On August 21 the Chung Wang sent an injured, angry letter to the representatives of Great Britain, the United States, Portugal, "and other countries" (he purposefully excluded the French, who he claimed had betrayed their earlier promise of a welcome in Shanghai). He accused the Westerners collectively of having been bribed by the Manchu "imps" to fight the Taipings, a most serious offense against the T'ien Wang: "I came to Shanghai to make a treaty in order to see us connected together by trade and commerce; I did not come for the purpose of fighting with you. Had I at once commenced to attack the city and kill the people, that would have been the same as the members of one family fighting among themselves, which would have caused the imps to ridicule us." Despite his hostile reception, the Chung Wang did not close the door to future good relations:

> Should any of your honourable nations regret what has occurred, and hold relations with our friendly state to be best, they need have no apprehensions in coming to consult with me. I treat people according to right principles, and will certainly not subject them to any indignities. Should, however, your honourable nations still continue to be deluded by the imps, follow their lead in all things, without reflecting on the difference between you; you must not blame me if hereafter you find it difficult to pass along the channels of commerce, and if there is no outlet for native produce.

It was an open expression of the threat to trade that Westerners had always feared was inherent in the Taiping movement, and in its wake the door to cooperation between the rebels and the foreigners began to close from the Western side. Frederick Bruce—the man who had so strongly advocated a neutral course in China, and whose brother Lord Elgin saw British and French troops storm the imperial forts at Taku on the very day that their comrades to the south repulsed the first Taiping advance on Shanghai—now openly expressed both contempt for the rebel movement and an unprecedented respect for local imperial officials in a letter to the British foreign minister, Lord John Russell:

> Every day shows more strongly that no principles or ideas of policy animate [the rebellion's] leaders. Even the extermination of

the Tartars, the only principle put forward, seems rather a pretext for upsetting all government and authority, and enabling the stronger to pillage the weaker, than an object necessary in itself, as a step towards establishing a mere national government. The framework of society is entirely broken up in the districts occupied by them, by the flight of the educated and respectable classes, to whom the common people look up with respect as their natural leaders, and who are at once their bulwark against oppression, and the guardians of order and public tranquility. . . . [The rebels'] system differs in nothing, as far as I can learn, from the proceedings of a band of brigands organized under one head.

The remarkable contradiction not only of his own earlier statements but of his government's previous position with regard to both the Chinese imperialists and the Taipings contained in Bruce's letter was apparent. The attempt to identify the interests of British trade with the welfare of Chinese peasants was a bit of self-service that stood in gross and (as ever) unexplained contrast to Britain's own aggressive posture in the north, as well as to the British community's continued condemnation of Ward's Foreign Arms Corps. One unusually honest letter to the *North China Herald* from a resident of the British settlement put it this way:

> The conduct of Ward has been justly censured in the columns of your paper. But in what does our policy differ? The circumstances are somewhat dissimilar, but the principle is precisely the same. His theatre of action was Sung-chiang; ours is Shanghai. His work was to drive the Insurgents out of the city; ours is to keep them out. He was paid for his service; our men, we are informed, are paid likewise for their service. Ward, we believe, is an old servant of the Taotai, and as such, he only continues his service when acting in opposition to the Insurgents; we have no such plea for our conduct.

On August 24 the Chung Wang left Shanghai and was soon taking the main body of his army out of Kiangsu altogether, to participate in the Taiping western campaign. Following his departure, the British indicated that they were at least beginning to perceive some commonality of interest between themselves and Ward when no less a figure than Frederick Bruce sent a secret communication to the Foreign Arms Corps's commander (or so Ward later claimed), thanking him for his assistance in the defense of Shanghai. It would be many months, however, before the British would be willing to admit publicly any indebtedness to Ward or to sanction his actions. For the moment, they chose to rely on their own resources in attempting to bring about a satisfactory arrangement of China's internal distress.

The withdrawal of the Chung Wang from Kiangsu left most of that province in the hands of Taiping units capable of defending what they had taken but not of besting British and French regulars in a major assault on Shanghai. This and other factors—the disaster at Ch'ing-p'u, the unwillingness of Ward and Burgevine to place themselves under the supervision of local imperial officials at Sung-chiang, the pronounced strains placed on Chinese dealings with the Western governments by the existence of the corps, and finally the exorbitant cost of the unit's maintenance—all influenced Wu Hsü to decide in mid-September that the time had come for the disbandment of Ward's force. There was nothing in his attitude to suggest that Wu felt any animosity toward Ward, but, like most Chinese officials, the taotai was jealously concerned with maintaining his sphere of authority, and in the Foreign Arms Corps he had seen a unit with uncomfortably autonomous tendencies. In addition, Ward's wounds continued, during September, to preclude his active leadership of the force, and Ward was the sole officer of the corps whom Wu came even close to trusting. The thought of Burgevine and the other Western "rowdies" roaming the Sung-chiang area unchecked caused the taotai much concern.

On September 26 Wu expressed this anxiety in a letter to Thomas Meadows. Stating that he had been instructed to write by Hsüeh Huan, Wu informed Meadows

that the foreigners who were engaged by the local authorities to apprehend pirates, and to assist in fighting against the rebels, have all been discharged. . . . Further these discharged foreigners, of whom there are several tens in number, and who all carry pistols on their persons are roving about the settlements and country without proper employment and are without doubt creating disturbances and troubling the orderly and well conducted people, nothing in fact being too bad that they will not do.

Wu's suggested remedy to this situation could not have been more galling to Consul Meadows: "I have therefore to request that you will send a dispatch on this subject to the chief [British] military officer, requesting him to appoint soldiers to apprehend the foreigners in question so that the country may be tranquilized."

In forwarding this request to Frederick Bruce, Meadows took full advantage of the opportunity to vindicate his earlier statements on the Foreign Arms Corps:

> That foreign ruffianism, which the Imperial Authorities were, in their unpatriotic pusillanimity, calling in to their aid, would prove a scourge to the peaceable people whom they are placed here to protect was perfectly clear to me from the first. . . . The Imperial Authorities have only themselves to blame for this mischief. . . . And now, by way of climax, these same Authorities ask for British troops to be sent out into the surrounding country to hunt for the criminals they themselves have made such in total disregard of the opinions and warnings of the resident British Consul.

Meadows tersely informed Wu Hsü that "the Chinese people have the right to seize and send to Shanghai any lawless and disorderly foreigners of whatever nation, with a view to their punishment by the Consuls of their respective countries," but that in this endeavor they would receive no British military aid.

Despite Wu Hsü's attempt to disband the Foreign Arms Corps, Ward was not yet willing to see the project come to an end; nor, apparently, was the banker Yang Fang. Paying for many of the corps's expenses with the bonus he had earned at Sung-chiang and relying on Yang to take care of the rest, Ward attempted to keep the force to-

gether, with an eye toward eventually trying Ch'ing-p'u again and re-
deeming himself. But Ward's most pressing order of business was his
wounds, particularly his jaw, which had begun to heal incorrectly. Thus
a troubling vacuum of leadership was created: Burgevine was not an
inventive enough spirit to instill any sense of purpose into the men
during the largely quiet autumn of 1860, and the corps—particularly its
officers—fell into an idleness that was at best mischievous. On October
27 the *North China Herald* reported an assault and robbery along the
Bund in Shanghai and in examining its details came

> reluctantly to the conclusion that our old friends the fillibusters [*sic*]
> must have had something to do with this robbery. . . . We have seen
> a good deal of these heroes while in the pay of H.E. the Taotai, and
> from their own lips have heard that it is part of the duty they owe
> to themselves not to allow the Chinese to encumber themselves with
> worldly goods, seeing that the fillibusters had come from far distant
> homes to root out the rebellion from among them at the risk of their
> lives. . . . On their return to Shanghai [following Ch'ing-p'u] they fell
> under the ban of the foreign ministers, and the Taotai was compelled
> to disband them. Since then we have heard but little of the fillibust-
> ers; some are still living at Taki's [Yang Fang's], and may be seen
> on the doorstep, when the weather permits, all forlorn, and smoking
> very strong pipes. . . . [E]ither Taki is keeping these men for pur-
> poses of his own against the Taotai's orders, or they are keeping
> themselves in a way that can't altogether be called by the sweat of
> their brow.

Events in northern China soon drew all remaining attention away
from the Foreign Arms Corps, which entered a shadowy period during
which the whereabouts of Ward himself became a mystery that has
never been solved. Quite probably he took ship for Paris to receive
expert medical treatment for his face. Certainly, when he reappeared in
China early in 1861, his jaw had been repaired in a fashion that did not
suggest Shanghai (although he would ever afterward speak with a slight
impediment). And among the few of Ward's personal belongings that
have survived is a photograph of a young Chinese man—quite possibly

an assistant or a servant—taken in a Paris studio. Exactly when Ward might have made such a trip is uncertain, but the fact that neither his absence nor his return was noted by either the British or the American consulate or the *North China Herald* is a measure of how much the shocking spectacle that had unfolded in the north had monopolized foreign interest in Shanghai.

After the fall of the Taku forts in late August, the Emperor Hsien-feng, his favorite concubine, Yehonala, and the Princes I, Cheng, and Su-shun sent emissaries to negotiate with the Western powers whose armies had begun a determined march toward Peking. The Mongol general Seng-ko-lin-ch'in had withdrawn to Peking after his initial encounter at Taku with the foreign troops, who were equipped with the most up-to-date small arms and artillery. Yet despite these hard battlefield realities, the war party in Peking sent negotiators more as a means of stalling for time than out of any reasoned desire to salvage what they could from a disastrous situation. Upon entering preliminary talks, the Chinese negotiators were informed by the British and French envoys that indemnities and apologies for the previous year's action at Taku were now required, in addition to compliance with all the conditions of the Tientsin treaty. The hapless Chinese representatives, recognizing the predicament for what it was, gave in, but Hsien-feng disavowed their actions and released a typical decree concerning "these treacherous barbarians":

> Any further forbearance on our part would be a dereliction of duty to the Empire, so that we have now commanded our armies to attack them with all possible energy. . . . Hereby we make offer of the following rewards: for the head of a black barbarian [Britain's Sikh troops], 50 taels, and for the head of a white barbarian, 100 taels. Subjects of other submissive states are not to be molested, and whensoever the British and French repent them of their evil ways and return to their allegiance, we shall be pleased to permit them to trade again, as of old. May they repent while there is yet time.

Increasingly, such statements were the work of the proud Yehonala and the three hawkish princes, I, Cheng, and Su-shun, for Hsien-feng himself was growing ever more ill and, in his weakness, fearful of the possible results of his arrogance. His principal desire was to flee Peking and seek refuge in his hunting palace at Jehol, north of the capital. But the bitter remonstrances of Manchu officials—"Will you cast away the inheritance of your ancestors like a damaged shoe?" wrote one group— kept him in Peking for the moment, and in mid-September he capitulated altogether to the angry harangues of Yehonala. Seng-ko-lin-ch'in was ordered to take the field again and stop the Westerners' advance. Even more fatally, several dozen French and British negotiators and journalists were seized under a flag of truce, trussed up with their arms behind their backs—the Chinese indication that the prisoners were "rebels"— and held captive in such deplorable conditions that thirteen of them, including the correspondent for the London *Times,* died.

It was the most foolish in a series of foolish moves on the part of the Chinese war party, and in its wake the Westerners became predictably outraged. Their armies pushed on toward Peking with a new sense of purpose, the French and British soldiers racing each other toward the heart of the Chinese empire in order to be the first to mete out stern punishments. On September 22 Hsien-feng fled to Jehol, confounding his subjects in Peking. But, fortunately for those terrified thousands as well as for the rest of China's millions, affairs in the capital now came under the management of Hsien-feng's half brother, Prince Kung. A scowling and, by all accounts, unattractive man who certainly shared Hsien-feng and Yehonala's distaste for barbarians, Prince Kung was nonetheless a realist who understood that "the British are merely a threat to our limbs," while the Taiping rebels "menace our heart." In Kung's opinion, his half brother had been dealing with Chinese affairs according to a badly confused set of priorities. Some kind of a peace had to be made with the Westerners, and quickly, so that the threat of a Taiping takeover could be eliminated.

Eventually, Kung accepted the Western terms for a settlement— including a firm commitment to allow foreign ministers to reside in Peking—but not before the British and the French had indulged in a particularly barbaric demonstration of their anger with China generally and over the horrendous treatment of their captured representatives in particular. One of Hsien-feng and Yehonala's favorite resort spots was the famous Summer Palace, a series of fantastically ornate gardens and residences outside Peking whose construction had been the pet project of emperors and their inner circles for generations. Early in October, French and British troops stumbled onto this invaluable display of the unreal splendor in which Chinese rulers lived, and the French, typically and immediately, began to sack the place. The British tried to restrain themselves at first, but then Lord Elgin decided that the destruction of the Summer Palace would be a suitable punishment for Chinese perfidy, since some of the Allied prisoners had been interred there. British soldiers subsequently joined in the looting, while British engineers methodically set about burning the palaces to the ground.

Whatever Hsien-feng and Yehonala's crimes, the destruction of the Summer Palace was no less criminal. It was so noted by one of the Royal Engineers who participated in the operation, a young, blue-eyed captain with a complex mind, an intense manner, and a tremendous aptitude for both conventional and unconventional warfare: Charles George Gordon. Shortly to journey to Shanghai and become a careful student of Frederick Townsend Ward's operations in Kiangsu, Gordon was destined to become one of Victorian England's greatest and most controversial heroes; and in October 1860 he demonstrated the insight that would eventually make him a man of renown on several continents by writing home:

Owing to the ill-treatment the [European] prisoners experienced at the Summer Palace, the General ordered it to be destroyed, and stuck up proclamations to say why it was so ordered. It appears that the victims were tied so tight by the wrists that the flesh mortified, and they died in the greatest torture. We accordingly went out, and, after pillaging it, burned the whole place, destroying in a Vandal-like manner most valuable property which would not be replaced for four millions. You can scarcely imagine the beauty and magnificence of the palaces. It made one's heart sore to burn them; in fact, these palaces were so large, and we were so pressed for time, that we could not plunder them carefully. It was wretchedly demoralising work for an army. Everybody was wild for plunder. The French have smashed everything in the most wanton way. It was a scene of utter destruction which passes my description. The people are civil, but I think the grandees hate us, as they must after what we did to the Palace.

The conclusion of hostilities in the north did little to resolve either the tension between the West and China or the power struggle that was taking shape within the Manchu elite between the Princes I, Cheng, and Su-shun on the one side, Prince Kung on the other, and Yehonala somewhere in between. The clever young mother of Hsien-feng's heir was beginning to see that dealing with the barbarians was a much more complicated affair than she had supposed, and in Prince Kung she perceived a man whose mind, unlike those of the three hawkish princes, might be equal to the task. At the hunting retreat in Jehol, meanwhile, Hsien-feng's illnesses worsened, and it became apparent that the question of who would rule China with what policy in the immediate future was a long way from settled. The British and the French therefore decided to retain a significant number of troops in China after the conclusion of the autumn campaign, as a hedge against even greater Chinese instability. (Of the 21,000 British troops in China at the time of the march on Peking, for example, only 10,000 were withdrawn.)

A great many of these soldiers, however, had little to keep them occupied in the north once Seng-ko-lin-ch'in had been defeated. Tales of the wide-open war being waged in the Yangtze valley were widely circulated, and many British and French officers made efforts to be transferred to what looked, in light of the Anglo-French defense of Shanghai, to be the next important theater of military operations in China. One such officer was Captain Adrien Tardif de Moidrey of the French army, whose arrival in Shanghai in late 1860 (or possibly early 1861) was of critical importance to the future operations of Ward, Burgevine, and the Foreign Arms Corps.

His thoughtful features aptly bedecked by a wide, carefully trimmed mustache and goatee, Tardif de Moidrey was a creative soldier who had taken a detailed interest in Chinese weapons and tactics during the Allied march to Peking. On arriving in Shanghai he had augmented this study with an investigation of Ward and Burgevine's operations, which at the close of 1860 had reached their nadir: On December 11 Burgevine had decided to have another try at Ch'ing-p'u but had been unable to cover even half the distance from Sung-chiang to his objective before being checked and then repulsed by the Taipings. Tardif de Moidrey met Burgevine in Shanghai at this dismal time and encountered Ward soon after the latter's return to China.

All these men had, by the beginning of 1861, been disabused of the general Western belief in the poor combat abilities of the Chinese. If properly disciplined, equipped, paid, and led, the Chinese could be the equal of any regular force in the world: Ward, Burgevine, and Tardif de Moidrey had become convinced of this during their encounters with both rebels and imperialists. The simple fact that these requirements— discipline, equipment, pay, and leadership—were never completely met on either the rebel or the imperialist side was no reason to believe that a professional Chinese army could not be created. The real problem was circumventing the traditional Chinese military hierarchy. Certainly, embattled Kiangsu province was the proper theater in which to make such an attempt: It was far from Peking and had witnessed no major victories—or even engagements—by imperial commanders. The question next became what exact form such a new Chinese army should take.

It is unknown whether Ward, Burgevine, or Tardif de Moidrey gave birth to the core idea of an independent force in which Western officers—both detached regulars and irregular soldiers of fortune—would train Chinese soldiers to fight in the Occidental style against the Taipings. In all likelihood the notion was a joint one, for at the same time that Tardif de Moidrey began to speak of forming his own Chinese artillery unit—officered by Frenchmen, equipped with Western guns, and able to support large imperialist formations of infantry—Ward and Burgevine were abandoning the idea of further association with large groups of unreliable mercenaries and speculating on the advantages of using Chinese soldiers under Western officers not only for artillery support but in all branches of service. Whatever its genesis, the idea of joint Western-Chinese operations was to prove—along with the rise of Tseng Kuo-fan in the west—one of the true turning points in the Chinese civil war, for in it lay the single hope of finally creating an eastern arm for Tseng's mighty nutcracker and thus crushing a rebel movement that, in early 1861, was still very much alive.

But the meetings between Ward, Burgevine, and Tardif de Moidrey represented only the barest beginnings of this building process. There were still enormous obstacles to overcome before the theories worked out that winter could be put into practice. The Western governments remained determined to put an end to any and all foreign involvement in the Taiping rebellion, and while local Chinese officials such as Wu Hsü had been willing to experiment with foreign mercenaries, the central government in Peking (along with Tseng Kuo-fan in the west) still saw the use of Westerners as a humiliation. Ward and his comrades would have to endure more months of hardship and refusal before their ideas would be given a chance.

The northern campaign confirmed the British in their policy of neither supporting the Manchus nor recognizing the Taipings but alternately treating with and browbeating both to get what they wanted out of China. Her Majesty's government and officials on the scene were also determined to maintain their position as the preeminent trading power in the Chinese empire. Thus when Russia offered in late 1860 to aid the Manchus by sending a naval expedition against Nanking, British attention was once again focused on the Yangtze valley. Hsüeh Huan, in his capacity as imperial commissioner for the treaty ports, advocated acceptance of the Russian offer: The imperial forces in the area could use the help, said Hsüeh, and the rivalry that would be created between the Russians and the British would be a useful revival of the traditional Chinese policy of "using the barbarian to control the barbarian." But Tseng Kuo-fan and the Peking authorities never seriously countenanced the idea, correctly supposing that it was merely a blind for Russian expansionism. The offer was rejected, and the rejection was applauded by the British, but the London government simultaneously decided that it was time to take a fresh look at the Taiping movement.

They also decided that such a look would require a British naval expedition to Nanking, for the secondhand information concerning the T'ien Wang and his followers that was being batted around Shanghai in the later months of 1860 was contradictory at best. On the one hand, Consul Meadows and his supporters in the diplomatic community had continued their muted advocacy of the rebel cause. The *North China Herald*, meanwhile, had tried to walk an independent line, although the Taiping attack on Shanghai and subsequent restriction of trade on the Yangtze had marked the beginning of a cooling toward the rebellion on the part of editor Charles Compton. Frederick Bruce, shortly to embark for Peking, voiced hostility toward both sides in the civil war. And Western missionaries continued to plead for indulgence of the rebels, whose imperfect Christianity, they said, would in time be perfected.

Adding his voice to this last group was the enigmatic Issachar Jacox Roberts, the Tennessee Baptist preacher who had early on given Hung Hsiu-ch'üan Bible lessons in Canton. In the fall of 1860 Roberts satisfied a long-standing wish of the Taiping Heavenly King by journeying to Nanking and accepting an official position that amounted to vice-minister for foreign affairs. Along with the post he received a "title, court dress, crown and gold ring," as well as the Tien Wang's promise to build some eighteen churches in the Heavenly Capital. With the aid of several other missionaries, Roberts then set about writing condensations of various parts of the Bible for translation into Chinese, in order that the Taipings might become better and more quickly acquainted with the Scripture. But into this endeavor Roberts apparently injected typical Baptist intolerance. According to Augustus Lindley, the young Englishman who was training Taiping soldiers and running guns to the rebels, Roberts's "unwise dogmatical obstinacy frequently provoked unpleasant discussion." But links to the Western communities in the treaty ports were important to the rebel leaders, and Roberts's enthusiastic exhortations to his fellow Christians that they come and participate in the glorious movement were seen as counterbalancing his "intolerant and bigoted" attitude.

Thus the many foreign voices that offered opinions on the nature of the Taiping movement hardly helped the British or any other Western government form a clear picture of circumstances within rebel-occupied

China. In February 1861, therefore, Admiral Sir James Hope of the Royal Navy was dispatched up the Yangtze with ten warships and orders to contact the rebel leadership. If this link could be established, Hope was to negotiate with the Taipings for advantageous guarantees of free trade on the Yangtze and establish new consulates in several rebel-held cities.

Hope did not at first seem a likely choice for such a diplomatically delicate mission. Known to his men as Fighting Jimmie, he was the scion of a Scottish navy family (his father had commanded a ship at Trafalgar) and had served in North and South America, India, and the Baltic before coming to China. Placed in command of British naval forces during the northern campaign of 1859, Hope had been severely wounded and was subsequently knighted for his refusal to abandon the losing effort in spite of his perilous physical condition. He recuperated in Ningpo, then returned to the north to command the naval forces for the 1860 campaign. Hope was fifty-two by this time, but neither age nor injury had in any way slowed him down, as he demonstrated during the successful assault on the Taku forts. A round-faced man with light, cool eyes and a supercilious expression, Hope possessed a bellicose attitude that exemplified the long tradition of "fire-eating" British admirals, who roamed the globe protecting British commerce and, just as often, responding to insults to the honor of British arms and of the British flag. Like so many of his spiritual predecessors in the Royal Navy, Hope spoiled constantly for fights and often seemed to care very little whom they were with.

In October 1860 Hope arrived to assume command of Britain's forces in Shanghai, a move that placed him on a course of eventual collision with Frederick Townsend Ward, whose operations were soon to rouse British ire once again. Yet the characters of the two men did not indicate conflict: On the contrary, a mutual admiration for bravery and a shared impatience with political duplicity made it seem almost inevitable that, despite the diplomatic realities of the moment, the two men would one day become friends. And in fact, by the time of Ward's death Hope considered the younger American "a very able and gallant servant" of the Chinese government, while Ward named Hope one of the executors of his estate. Any prediction of such a result in 1860, however, would have met with utter incredulity.

On February 12, 1861, Hope sailed up the Yangtze. During his expedition he successfully established the three new consulates—including one at Hankow—and secured a Taiping pledge not to interfere with British trade or come within two days' march (some thirty miles) of Shanghai for one year. In return, Hope pledged that the British would maintain strict neutrality in the Chinese civil war. But the admiral was not sanguine about either the rebellion or its leaders, who he said could be seen "in no other light than that of an organized band of robbers." And at least one possible source of future friction was left unresolved during meetings between British naval officers and the Chung Wang: The rebel commander, reported the *North China Herald,* "said Opium would be interdicted in our trade on the Yangtze. The Admiral is said to have declined to entertain the subject but declared that for any insult offered to the British flag they would be held responsible."

In March the Taipings opened the Yangtze once again to unrestricted trade, which flourished immediately. This being the case, neither Admiral Hope nor Frederick Bruce, their doubts about the Taipings notwithstanding, was in any mood to receive reports of renewed activity by Ward and Burgevine. Nor was the new British consul in Shanghai, Walter Medhurst. Thomas Meadows's unending criticism of pro-Manchu policies had finally been rewarded with a new posting in the north (although he remained in Shanghai for the moment). Medhurst—the son of an eminent British sinologist and himself an accomplished Chinese scholar—was selected as a replacement who could be counted on to follow the party line much more closely by creating an atmosphere in Shanghai that would keep rebels, imperialists, and foreign adventurers alike cowed.

But the ideas for Chinese-Western military cooperation that Ward, Burgevine, and Tardif de Moidrey had worked out over the winter were infectious stuff, so much so that in early 1861 Ward was able to convince Wu Hsü once again to back his attempts to build an irregular army. Yang Fang had shown genuine loyalty to Ward, and his involvement in the plans of this period is not surprising, but Wu's participation (or lack thereof) in Ward's schemes had consistently been based not only on his respect and affection for the young American but on a pragmatic reading of the domestic and international climate in and around Shanghai. Doubtless, then, the partial but disturbing British rapprochement with Nan-king, together with the collapse of the imperial armies in the north during the previous autumn, indicated to Wu that Shanghai's defense, as in the spring of 1860, was the concern of local officials and local merchants alone. Yet he must have known that renewed association with Ward would bring a fresh round of conflict with the Western governments. In the face of these considerations, Ward's charm and seemingly limitless enthusiasm again became decisive factors. Fully recovered now, and inspired by radically novel ideas, the New England soldier of fortune won back his spot on the seasoned taotai's payroll. Before long he was joined by his new colleague from France, Tardif de Moidrey, who began laying the groundwork for his Franco-Chinese artillery unit at Wu's and Hsüeh Huan's expense.

Ward's plan to use Chinese volunteers at this time appears to have been influenced not only by his conversations with Burgevine and Tardif de Moidrey but by the new attitude taking shape among the peasants of Kiangsu province. At several points during the fall and winter of 1860–61, the *North China Herald* had reported the appearance of armed bands of villagers who not only defended their homes against the Tai-pings but raided rebel supply lines and even took Taiping soldiers prisoner, shipping them to Shanghai for punishment. The formation of these peasant guerrilla bands had not, however, been purely the result of Taiping plundering: The equally rapacious conduct of local imperial troops had played a part as well. Having experienced the unrestrained behavior of Green Standard units, many peasants were unwilling to serve under commanders such as Li Heng-sung and took their defense into their own hands.

According to a diary kept by a perceptive Chinese observer at the time, many of these same Kiangsu peasants had, during the summer of 1860, sought refuge from the Taipings in Sung-chiang and were thus acquainted with Ward and the Foreign Arms Corps. The memory was apparently a lasting one, for the Kiangsu guerrillas would shortly be among the first men to volunteer for service in Ward's new force. Again, the power of perceptive popular leaders during the Chinese civil war was evident: Even a barbarian Westerner, if he practiced decent treatment, was preferable to marauding Taipings and plundering imperialists.

But while Chinese peasants might make capable or at least enthusiastic soldiers, Ward knew that his latest project also required superior Western officers. With this in mind, he again set about the process of weeding through the foreign mercenaries who had served in the Foreign Arms Corps and interviewing new candidates in Shanghai. The first order of business was to disassociate the new unit from the one that had made such a questionable reputation for itself following the defeat at Ch'ing-p'u. Pursuant to this goal, Ward began to refer to the Foreign Arms Corps as the Chinese Foreign Legion (although it remained known in most circles by its original name). The next pressing requirement was to hire men of at least moderate intelligence and put them in positions of responsibility. Among this new group were C. J. Ashley (who, after serving with Ward's force for several years as quartermaster and commissary general, would later enjoy a long career with the Shanghai Volunteer Corps and become one of the port's eminent foreign citizens) and an old acquaintance of Ward's, Edward Forester.

When Ward had first formed the Foreign Arms Corps he had written to Forester, who was then serving as an interpreter for several large business firms in Japan. Early in 1861 Forester was finally able to get to China and join Ward, who—on the basis not only of their earlier acquaintance in South America but of Forester's strong abilities as a linguist—immediately gave the newcomer equal rank with Burgevine. The Carolinian's weaknesses had always become apparent when the force was in garrison, and it was here that Forester was to play a part: maintaining proper procedures, acting as go-between with Yang Fang and the local Sung-chiang officials when Ward was unable to attend to such matters personally, and bringing to the affairs of the force a somewhat more professional attitude than the strong-willed but tempestuous Burgevine could boast. Forester's efficiency was subsequently demonstrated on many occasions and seemed a vindication of Ward's confidence.

It is all the more disappointing, therefore, that Forester should have proved ultimately disloyal to Ward. Following Ward's death Forester made several attempts to revise the history of his commander's operations to his own benefit, attempts that contrasted sourly with his own faithful service during Ward's lifetime. Although Forester swore under oath in 1875, for example, that he had joined Ward's force in 1861, he subsequently wrote a series of articles for *Cosmopolitan* magazine in which he described the actions of Ward's force from early in 1860, including a detailed account of the battle of Sung-chiang. Of course, the circumstances of that legendary event were readily available to any foreigner in Shanghai who cared to seek them out. But in Forester's version he himself not only was present at the battle but played an important part. And in Forester's accounts of the force's subsequent engagements, Ward was often portrayed as an absentee commander wrapped up in the distractions of Shanghai, and Burgevine as little more than a functionary. Thus it was Burgevine—hard-drinking, impetuous, violent—who in the end proved the more reliable of Ward's two lieutenants, while the calculating Forester emerged as a somewhat superior officer but a decidedly inferior comrade.

While Ward was alive, however, Forester's talents were put to good use, and in the early spring of 1861 the reorganization of the force along the lines of Chinese-Western cooperation moved smoothly—so smoothly, in fact, that the British authorities soon determined it necessary to take active measures against it. By early April the Chinese Foreign Legion was drilling at Sung-chiang, Ward having raised between five hundred and a thousand Chinese recruits as well as some two hundred Western officers. Once again, many of these Westerners were English deserters—particularly drillmasters from the Royal Navy and Marines and artillery instructors from the army—who were weary of the low pay, cramped quarters, and bad food that marked their national service. The participation of such men in anti-Taiping activities might well jeopardize the already fragile truce Admiral Hope had established with the rebels; recognizing that this danger would almost certainly prompt visits to Sung-chiang by the British authorities, Ward protected his activities with strict security in the town and his camp. Written passes bearing his signature were the sole means of entrance into either of these areas by any military personnel, and Ward kept his British deserters constantly ready to abandon Sung-chiang and move farther in country in the event of the expected British raid.

It finally came in the third week of April.

* * *

As commander of the British navy's China Station, Admiral Hope had important affairs to attend to in all five of the treaty ports as well as Hong Kong. These caused his frequent absence from Shanghai, but he took a keen interest in the port's affairs at all times, paying particular attention to the rate of desertion aboard British ships. By mid-April this rate was rising alarmingly, and Hope gave orders to Commander Henry W. Hire—captain of HMS *Urgent* and the senior naval officer in Shanghai during the admiral's absences—to confront the Chinese authorities on this subject. If Hire could get no satisfaction from those gentlemen, Hope said, he was himself to arrest the British deserters and the men who were enticing them to serve in both the imperial and the rebel causes. "I trust to your zeal and ability," Hope told Hire, "to carry out the object I have in view of stopping the desertion at Shanghai." Hire would not disappoint his commander.

On April 18 one of Hire's subordinates, a Captain Aplin of HMS *Centaur* at Nanking, captured twenty-six Englishmen who were serving in the Taiping armies. "Most of the men," wrote a diplomatic officer who witnessed the arrests,

> assert that they were enticed into drinking shops at Shanghai by regular crimps, where they were drugged, and when senseless were conveyed to certain boats in waiting. . . . Only two or three confess to voluntary enlistment without any stipulation. . . . The men were in a most miserable condition, getting no pay, but plenty of rice and spirits. They were allowed to plunder wherever they went, but seem to have had little success. They made no secret of such crimes as rape and robbery, and even hinted at darker deeds. Most of them had been present at a fight near Sung-chiang, where their leader, named Savage, was wounded, and an Italian killed. An American named Peacock, at present living in Soochow, is Captain over all; he is of high rank among the Taipings, and has the power of life and death.

This successful operation bred greater conviction among Britain's naval officers that an activist approach to the desertion problem was the correct one. On April 22 Commander Hire, accompanied by consulate interpreter Chaloner Alabaster, had an interview in Shanghai with Hsüeh Huan, at which Wu Hsü was present. Hire demanded that Hsüeh surrender all Englishmen in his service, but both Hsüeh and Wu predictably declared that they had no such employees. They admitted to hiring Tardif de Moidrey and another French officer as artillery instructors and said that they had heard that the rebels were making use of British deserters. But they were not doing the same. Hire assured Hsüeh that he had it on good authority that Englishmen in the imperial service were drilling at Sung-chiang, upon which Hsüeh urged Hire to go to Sung-chiang and arrest any such men. "Some questions," noted the interpreter, Alabaster, "were then asked relative to Colonel Ward, the Commissioner saying he had employed him for two months last year but had then dismissed him and on being told that the Colonel declared himself to be still in H[is] E[xcellency's] employ said he thought he was dead, he had heard he was wounded at Sung-chiang some long time ago while he was in his employ and thought he had died." Wu Hsü "also expressed great horror" on being told of Ward's enlistment activities, and, when both the taotai and Hsüeh promised to cooperate in capturing the deserted Englishmen and their new commanders, Hire said that he would consider it "a decided breach of faith" if they failed to do so.

The following day Commander Hire proceeded up the Huang-pu River and then Sung-chiang Creek in a gunboat, again accompanied by Alabaster as well as a detachment of Royal Marines. Startled by the appearance of regular British troops, the imperial Chinese soldiers manning Sung-chiang's gates allowed them admittance. The commander of these Green Standard braves, one of Sung-chiang's mandarins, was then sought out in his yamen. Hire presented the man with a notice that the British soldiers found posted on a column outside the yamen. Written and signed by Ward, the document prohibited entrance into Sung-chiang by any soldiers of the Chinese Foreign Legion without a pass. The nonplussed mandarin—who was placed in the unenviable position of lying to protect a group of foreign mercenaries who had consistently berated him and ignored his authority—denied that there were any foreigners in Sung-chiang. There had been in the past, Alabaster remembered the mandarin saying: "[F]oreigners constantly came and forced themselves into his presence but they were not in any way in his employ." Unsatisfied, Hire declared that he would search the town and demanded that the mandarin accompany him.

Scouring the imperialist military camp, Hire found no evidence of activity by foreigners, but then several of his marines, posted at the west gate of the town, intercepted a Chinese who bore a pass into the "barracks" of the Chinese Foreign Legion—a pass that was written and signed by Ward. Confronted with this man and this document, the mandarin "suddenly remembered the existence of such a place, still however denying that he had anything to do with the foreigners or that there were any there." Hire was next taken to a building that he was told was Colonel Ward's residence, and his men commenced turning the apparently abandoned place upside down: "Some empty beer bottles [were] found, and a trap door seemingly leading to the roof at length discovered. This was at once burst open tho with some difficulty, it being nailed down and piled over with lumber of all sorts, and a long suite of rooms discovered full of European stores, wines and evidently used by foreigners that day as some plates and dishes had been shoved away unwashed."

Hire presumed following the discovery of this shielded sanctum that although he was only a step behind the fleeing Ward, it was a long step. After happening on a roster of names of Westerners serving in the Foreign Legion, the commander decided to return immediately to Shanghai: Ward's best hope of evading capture while simultaneously avoiding an accidental run-in with the rebels would be to hide himself among the thousands of fugitives and refugees in the port's foreign settlements.

On returning to Shanghai, Hire subsequently wrote, he "waited on the American Flag Officer asking his assistance toward the detention of Ward, to which he unhesitatingly replied that [Ward] was not an American Subject, or entitled to protection as such. I then requested him to give me that in writing, which he did." Disavowed, now, by both the Chinese and the Americans, Ward apparently had no protectors, and his arrest seemed an act free from international complications. Hire returned to the *Urgent* and "ordered the Master at Arms to go on shore and bring Ward onboard." The commander then went out to dine and on returning found that Ward had been apprehended and confined on board the *Urgent:* "I informed him that he must consider himself my prisoner for the present."

Ward had been picked up on the Shanghai waterfront and was kept closely guarded during the night of April 24. Having the Foreign Legion's commander in his custody, Hire was anxious now to ascertain the whereabouts of Ward's Shanghai headquarters, said to be the center of the legion's enlistment activities but as yet not proved to exist. Dispatching agents on this mission, the commander himself sought the advice of Consul Medhurst and ex-Consul Meadows as to the eventual disposition of Colonel Ward. Both officials told Hire that "it would be best to get this ruffian Ward from the Colony" (the fact that Shanghai was not a possession of the British Crown was momentarily forgotten by all three men), and, as a first step toward this goal, Hire demanded another interview with Wu Hsü.

Before confronting the Chinese authorities, Hire returned to the *Urgent* to interrogate Ward. The principal area of uncertainty was the soldier of fortune's nationality: Without hard knowledge on this subject, it would be difficult to force any government to accept and punish the prisoner. Hire demanded to know what country Ward hailed from, to which the prisoner cagily replied: "I was last employed by Mexico. I have been a citizen of the United States but certainly am not now. I am not an Englishman for I never was in the country but once and have no relatives there, tho I have some in the United States. I do not consider this a fair question and decline to give an answer."

Ward apparently understood his captors' predicament: A man without a country could hardly be prosecuted for violating any one nation's neutrality laws. The heat was further turned up on the increasingly perplexed Commander Hire with the arrival, following the questioning of Ward, of a note from Nicholas Cleary, a Shanghai attorney. Claiming to represent Ward, Cleary demanded that Hire "hand him over to the proper Chinese Authorities at Shanghai for immediate trial upon such charges as you may have to proffer." The entrance of the "proper

Chinese Authorities" into the legal melee was a new element, and Hire proceeded to Wu Hsü's yamen.

After presenting evidence of the foreign presence at Sung-chiang, Commander Hire "expressed his regret that he could not feel the same confidence in H[is] E[xcellency's] good faith he had done at the former interview." Wu Hsü, in turn, "expressed great indignation at the conduct of the Mandarins at Sung-chiang in concealing this from him." Upon being informed that Hire had come "to request H[is] E[xcellency] either to punish Colonel Ward himself or to request Captain Hire to deport him," Wu voiced approval for the latter idea, as "he had never punished foreigners before and at any rate it would be better to deport the Colonel as if he were Chinese all he could do would be bamboo him and let him go, and he would still remain here." But Hire was subsequently informed by a legal expert that British confinement, punishment, and deportation of Ward were all questionable actions: Whatever country was entitled to exercise such measures, it certainly was not Great Britain. "My mind was then made up," wrote Hire, "to make the Chinese authorities take possession of Ward and punish him."

On April 26 the chairman of the Shanghai Municipal Council wrote to Consul Medhurst to ask that the authorities prevent "the so called Colonel Ward or his agents" from "continuing to entice members of the Municipal Police Force and others from their duty." For a man who was supposedly "crimping" foreigners into service, Ward was enjoying remarkable popularity. In addition, Commander Hire and Consul Medhurst were losing the elaborate diplomatic game being played around the prisoner on board the *Urgent:* Knowing full well that the British would eventually be forced to return Ward to him, Wu Hsü had already covered himself by protesting that if they did, there would be little if anything he could do to punish him.

The culmination of the affair came on April 26, when Wu Hsü put before Chaloner Alabaster papers purporting to show that Ward was a Chinese citizen. Apparently anticipating his arrest, Ward had mailed a letter to Consul Smith on April 24 expressing his desire to revoke his American citizenship and become a naturalized Chinese. The papers presented by Wu were, however, almost certainly forged: Peking would scarcely have approved Ward's application for citizenship at this juncture, and, even had such approval been forthcoming, there had not been time since his arrest to deliver it. But the British were not prepared to accuse representatives of the imperial Chinese government of falsifying documents, and on that same April 26, Commander Hire recalled, "an armed party came down to Jardine's Wharf, two officers came onboard when Ward was delivered up to them and marched by a strong escort of China Men into the Town."

In the wake of Ward's release, Commander Hire expressed the belief that he had, "by seizing Ward . . . , in a great measure struck a severe blow at the head of the crimping system in Shanghai." Other British officers and officials shared his confidence that the incident had severely discouraged the members of the Chinese Foreign Legion, an impression strengthened by the capture, on April 28, of thirteen foreigners near Sung-chiang by British troops. Accused of being in the imperial service, the men were returned to their various consulates for deportation, but at least one was subsequently released, and before long the British authorities were forced to accept the fact that none of their moves had in any way slowed Ward down. British soldiers and sailors continued to desert and join the Chinese Foreign Legion, and proof that the unit was still active in the interior came when Burgevine took some sixty-five Westerners and joined General Li Heng-sung's Green Standard braves in yet another unsuccessful assault on Ch'ing-p'u on May 11. (The affair was a further lesson in Green Standard unreliability: As the *Herald* reported, Burgevine's contingent "saw nothing of the 20 gun-boats and 9,000 men who were to have cooperated with them until they met them on their return about 3 miles from the city.")

Consul Medhurst and Captain Roderick Dew, who had succeeded Commander Hire as commander of British naval forces during Admiral Hope's absences from Shanghai, now decided to put an end to all these activities. They ordered a thorough search of the foreign settlements for Ward and Burgevine, one that turned up no sign of the two men or of Ward's supposed Shanghai headquarters. But roughly a week later Consul Medhurst received information from an informer, who, as Medhurst told Frederick Bruce, "to save himself betrayed his comrades":

He deposed among other things that the accounts of the legion were to be settled on a particular day and hour in the Taki hong, a house in the settlement through which the Taotai conducts his business with our Commissariat, and on Captain Dew and myself going there with an armed party, we found the soi disant "Captain" of the legion deep in accounts with the purser of the hong, and we discovered upstairs eighteen stand of musketry with a quantity of ammunition and other munitions of war. All these were seized and brought away together with the "captain," the purser, and a man pointed out as compradore to the legion. The captain claiming to be an American was handed over to his Consul, and the other men being Chinese and in the Taotai's own employ I sent to him with a letter repeating my complaints against the Authorities for lending themselves so persistently to the system of foreign enlistment. He replied that he would enquire into the charge against the men and that as the arms belonged to him he would like to have them returned. I have of course not obliged him in this particular, and I only mention this fact as well as that of his employment of Taki to shew the duplicity of which he has been guilty throughout.

In fact, the mysterious Westerner Medhurst and Captain Dew had captured turned out to be none other than Burgevine. On May 18 the Carolinian was confined in the house of the American marshal (the American settlement still had no jail), and Consul William L. G. Smith tried the case at ten o'clock that morning. Burgevine was officially charged with violating the neutrality laws and enticing British sailors to desert. But once again the Western authorities were frustrated in their attempts to deal a mortal blow to the Sung-chiang force. One officer of the Shanghai Municipal Police testified that he had seen Burgevine at Yang Fang's but also said that he had not at the time seen anyone he could identify as a British deserter. And while one such deserter was called to testify that he had served in the Ward force, he denied that Burgevine had either enticed or recruited him. In the end, Burgevine was released for lack of evidence, the whole affair producing nothing more than a cost to the American consulate of $17.50 for marshal's and clerk's fees.

Medhurst now became determined to find Ward, and on the day after Burgevine's trial British search parties again spotted and captured their quarry. The British were taking no chances this time: Ward was imprisoned on board one of their warships. Edward Forester, commanding the Foreign Legion garrison at Sung-chiang, was now in a tight spot. He had good reason to suppose that the British would march on the town and seize the rest of the legion's Western officers. As for Ward, Forester later recalled that there "seemed no hope of release or even of trial. The arrest had been an arbitrary one and the physical power was in the hands of the admiral." Hope—knowing better than to trust the Chinese to deal with the problem of Ward—evidently intended himself to make sure that the young mercenary left China this time.

In addition, while Ward was in captivity, Hope directed a strong force of British soldiers, sailors, and marines to march on Sung-chiang and demonstrate to those Westerners still at large the cost of their continued defiance. Apprised of the British move by Yang Fang, Forester "put the mud forts which we were occupying—about a mile east of Sung-chiang—in the best possible state of defense, and then sent word that I would defend my position at all hazards. The British, about eight hundred in number, marched entirely around our fort and, without firing even so much as a volley, returned to their ships." The British expedition up-country was apparently intended as a show of force, but it had little if any effect on the members of the legion.

In Shanghai, meanwhile, Yang Fang was making plans with Burgevine and Vincente Macanaya for Ward's escape from the British warship, since it seemed impossible that the British would repeat the error of releasing him into any other nation's custody. Although kept under close guard, Ward was confined in a comfortable cabin rather than the brig and was allowed daily visitors. One of these was Vincente, who managed to communicate to Ward that he should be prepared at an appointed hour during a coming night to jump through one of the large windows in his cabin (such ample openings being typical of British warships of the day). He would be picked up by Vincente, who would be waiting in the waters below in a sampan, a small river skiff propelled by a single scull. Ward could then be taken to safety at Sung-chiang.

The exact date of Ward's escape—sometime during the last week of May—is unrecorded, but the circumstances were more grist for the popular mill that was turning the Foreign Legion's commander into a folk hero among the Chinese. At the sounding of four bells (two o'clock in the morning), Ward called on the skills he had learned as a boy on the Salem wharves and leapt through the window of his cabin into the waters of Shanghai harbor. True to plan, Vincente was there and hauled Ward into his sampan while cries of alarm went up aboard the warship. As Forester wrote, "This was before search-lights on a man-of-war were even dreamed of," and by the time British launches had been manned and made their way into the dark harbor, they were faced with the sight of some thirty sampans racing in every direction: a diversion that was the final element in Yang Fang's plan. The British soon became convinced that the search was hopeless. Vincente pulled for the bank of the Huang-pu opposite Shanghai (the western edge of the Pootung peninsula), where Ward debarked and stayed hidden for twenty-four hours. He then journeyed to Sung-chiang by an indirect route. Reaching the garrison without incident, Ward remained there as the British once more turned Shanghai upside down and arrested anyone even suspected of serving or having served with the Chinese Foreign Legion.

Ward was free again—yet the British once more underestimated his determination by believing that they had dealt a death blow to the legion's activities. On June 8 the *Herald* triumphantly crowed that "[t]he force is now disbanded. Some have probably suffered capital punishment at the hands of the Chinese, some have fallen in action, some are expiating their offences against our laws in common jails, and some few have escaped it is to be hoped with sufficient examples before them never to again engage in such an illegitimate mode of earning a livelihood as enrolling themselves in such disreputable ranks as those of a 'Chinese Foreign Legion.' "

But in fact Ward returned to the task of training his Chinese soldiers and European officers with pointed zeal: Adversity, on this as on many other occasions, seemed only to give him an increased sense of purpose and a rather gleeful delight in frustrating his antagonists. Those antagonists (or at least the ones who wore the Royal Navy's blue and gold) were now growing weary, and when word of Ward's return to the drilling ground at Sung-chiang reached Admiral Hope, he threw up his hands, abandoned the policy of harassing and imprisoning the Foreign Legion's officers, and—according to Forester—invited Ward and his two seconds-in-command to attend a conference on board his flagship under a guarantee of safe conduct.

The idea that, at the height of their dramatic game of cat and mouse, Ward, Burgevine, Forester, and Admiral Hope should all have sat down on board an English warship and discussed their differences like gentlemen has exercised understandable power over the imaginations of many students of the period. But we have no one's word save Forester's that the incident occurred. Writing in the *Cosmopolitan,* Forester claimed that

> [t]his meeting was destined to have a most important bearing on the future of the Taiping rebellion. The British admiral was brought around to a new view of foreign interference with the Taipings. We gave assurances that we would no longer recruit our army from his man-of-war's-men and the admiral promised to exert all possible influence with the British minister at Peking, and with the Home Government. From that day on Admiral Hope became our strong friend and rendered us service whenever it was possible.

Always weak on dates, Forester supplied no such specific for this fabled meeting: It might have taken place any time between the late spring and the fall of 1861. Perhaps the most significant aspect of the story, however, is its oblique reference to the shift that was taking place in the British attitude toward the Chinese civil war, for it was that change that would finally transform Britain's approach to the Chinese Foreign Legion.

Ward had yet to make his way into the dispatches to Washington of either the American minister to China or Consul Smith: The United States was still interested in avoiding complications that might hinder trade. But by May 23 England's Frederick Bruce thought enough of the activities of foreigners on either side of the Taiping rebellion to inform Lord Russell, the British foreign minister, of the details:

> It will be seen that British subjects in both instances form but a fraction of the hired force. The enlisting agent on the part of the Government seems to be a man called Ward, an ex-Californian fili- buster; and on that of the Taipings, a man called Peacock. Both are of United States origin, but Ward, it appears, does not now claim to be an American citizen. The law of the United States is, I believe, very severe against enlistment in the Chinese service; but it appears their authorities find great difficulty in putting the law into operation. Ward, it appears, besides the Foreign Legion, has undertaken to drill a body of Chinese in the employment of the Imperial Government. I look upon it as perfectly hopeless to prevent foreigners entering the service of these parties as long as the pay is sufficient to attract them, and as long as the Chinese think that they will be of use in military operations.

Thus even at the time Ward was making his escape, the senior British official in China was conceding that the policy of forcefully trying to put an end to the Foreign Legion's activities was doomed. On May 24 Admiral Hope wrote to Bruce and complained that attempts by Chinese officials in Shanghai to discourage Ward were not "of that efficient character which I have a right to expect, being feigned and in the nature of a blind by delivering up a few with a view to the escape of the remainder." The British, in short, may have believed in the rectitude of a policy designed to prevent foreign involvement in the rebellion, but the lack of cooperation they experienced indicated that virtually no one else in Shanghai—whether native or foreigner—shared their conviction.

Nor did the Taipings cooperate with Britain's desire to pursue a neutral, noninterventionist course. On May 27 British interpreter Cha- loner Alabaster wrote a memorandum describing a trip up the Huang-pu River that he had just completed in the company of Captain Roderick Dew, the aggressive officer who had raided the "Taki hong" and cap- tured Burgevine. Dew had been ordered by Admiral Hope to proceed to Ch'ing-p'u, deliver a letter warning the rebel leaders that they were not to come within two days' march of the treaty port of Ningpo (the same terms that had been arranged for Shanghai), and, on his return, to capture any Foreign Legionnaires he could find at Sung-chiang. But, as Dew and Alabaster approached the walls of Ch'ing-p'u under a flag of truce (the captain "leaving his sword behind to make our peaceful object more apparent"), the rebels "opened fire with gingalls and on our stopping and displaying the letter which they certainly must have seen commenced firing their big guns, fortunately giving their shot too great elevation and as they showed no signs of desisting we retreated to the boats which were also fired on and got away as quickly as possible leaving the letter suspended on a pole we stuck in the ground."

On June 6 the redoubtable Captain Dew again made contact with the rebels—this time at the town of Chapu on the northern shore of Hangchow Bay—to warn them not to attack Ningpo. Upon landing, Dew was escorted to the local Taiping chief by rebel soldiers. The march took them through a scene of devastation: "The streets and houses," wrote Dew, "were occupied solely by soldiers, their former owners either having fled or been killed—a strange contrast to the usual life and bustle of a Chinese town." Dew soon met the Taiping chief, who declared that he was, in Dew's words:

> most anxious to be on good terms with foreigners. Did we not, under Heaven, serve the same God? He could not see why we should interfere with his attacking Ningpo; our ships and property should be protected. . . . I remarked that no cause could prosper whose path was marked by bloodshed and the destruction of the homes of the people. It was a necessity, he said, to guard against treachery and inspire fear, and I am strongly impressed by the sagacity of the remark, for I feel certain that the rapid success of the Taipings is due far more to their destructive qualities and gay dresses of yellow and red silks than to their bravery or their weapons, which seemed, on an average, to be worse than those of the Imperialist soldiers.

Admiral Hope himself issued a warning to the Taiping chief at Chapu on June 11, telling him that should the rebels attack Ningpo, "I need hardly point out to you the hopelessness of success on your part, whilst what occurred at Shanghai last year is still fresh in your memories." In addition Hope wrote to the British Admiralty, describing the Taipings as "banditti bent on free quarters and plunder" and advising direct British intervention to keep Ningpo safe. The truce with the rebels that he himself had worked out was beginning to seem to Hope a short-term policy with no application to the long run. British and Taiping goals were, in the admiral's opinion, inimical.

The increasingly antagonistic attitude of British naval officers toward the Taipings in the spring of 1860 was echoed in the reports and dispatches of diplomatic officials, as well as in the changing tone of the *North China Herald* during the period. On June 23 Frederick Bruce wrote a lengthy indictment of the rebel movement to Lord Russell at the Foreign Office. Describing frequent alliances between Taiping and bandit groups, Bruce condemned the apparent rebel inability to create any kind of political or economic institutions: "If it were possible to conceive of [the rebellion's] permanent success in its present form, China would be reduced to a mass of agriculturalists, governed by a theocracy, supported by armies collected from the most barbarous and demoralised part of the population." And *Herald* editor Charles Compton had written as early as January that "[a]ll despotisms are bad enough, but the present Insurgent movement should it prove successful, will be not only an ordinary, but a religious despotism; surely China has had calamity enough to be spared from such a bitter woe."

Yet these same men recognized the utter inability of the imperial Chinese armies to meet the threat of the rebellion. Noting that the "military art in China is in that rude and barbarous stage in which conquest is synonymous with extermination," Minister Bruce went on to warn that he saw "little hopes of communities like those of Shanghai and Ningpo escaping destruction." Foreign intervention had saved Shanghai once, but unless the Western powers were willing to take on an open-ended commitment to protect the treaty ports (and, by doing so, rescue the imperial government) from the rebels, the only hope of defeating the Taipings rested with organizations such as the Chinese Foreign Legion.

Bruce was as yet unwilling to admit this last fact, but the Chinese imperialists in Shanghai had understood it for more than a year. Tseng Kuo-fan's achievements in the west were still irrelevant to circumstances on the coast. Hsüeh Huan and Wu Hsü had seen nothing in the organization or conduct of the imperial armies in their area to indicate that any significant program of reform was under way. In June 1861, therefore, Hsüeh and Wu not only continued their carefully shrouded support of the Chinese Foreign Legion but also backed the creation of what came to be called the Franco-Chinese Corps of Kiangsu, commanded by Captain Tardif de Moidrey. Both the central Chinese government in Peking and the French minister to China had been unwilling to endorse such a project, but the French naval commander in Shanghai, Vice Admiral August-Leopold Protet, had favored it. Faced with the problem of removing Tardif de Moidrey from the French active duty list, Protet had told the captain to enter a Shanghai hospital and fake an illness while his detachment left the port. Safely on his own, Tardif de Moidrey, like Ward before him, started from humble beginnings: fifty Chinese soldiers, a handful of French assistants, and a few pieces of artillery. But the Franco-Chinese Corps was to play an important part in the campaigns to come.

If the French naval commander in Shanghai could see the realities of the moment and facilitate the involvement of Westerners in anti-Taiping activities, it is unlikely that Admiral Hope could not do the same. Thus while Forester's tale of a meeting on board Hope's flagship between himself, Ward, Burgevine, and the admiral is uncorroborated, it is entirely plausible. For, while the British diplomatic community had many reasons to resent Ward's repeated violations of Western neutrality laws, one thing only had caused friction between the British Royal Navy and the Chinese Foreign Legion: the desertions of British sailors. In his opposition to the Taipings, by contrast, Ward was at one with Hope as well as most of the admiral's officers, such as Captain Dew. And if Ward did indeed pledge at the meeting not to entice more British seamen and soldiers to desert, it is likely that Admiral Hope would have been willing to drop his harassment of Ward's operations. As it turned out, during the summer and fall of 1861 Ward placed notably less emphasis on recruiting foreigners (he even dropped the name *Chinese Foreign Legion*) and concentrated instead on using what capable officers he had to train ever greater numbers of Chinese recruits. Simultaneously—and coincidence here is doubtful—he endured no significant interference from the Royal Navy in building what came to be popularly known as the Ward Corps of Disciplined Chinese. Both facts suggest that he had indeed worked out a tacit agreement with Admiral Hope.

On July 3 Frederick Bruce wrote to Lord Russell from Peking and announced "with satisfaction that the Foreign Legion has been disbanded." But the minister was not, it seems, abreast of the latest developments in Shanghai. Bruce went on to express a hope that the "example of the value of Chinese cooperation" given by Li Heng-sung's Green Standard braves during the May 11 attack on Ch'ing-p'u would prove a deterrent to "the adventurers who infest the coast of China." But Ward, Burgevine, and Forester had already taken their operations to another plane, one on which "adventurers" played a secondary role. Ward's latest formula was at last the correct one, and within a year the Ward Corps would become not only the most reliable military unit on the imperialist side but the finest in all of China.

V

"ASTONISHED AT THE COURAGE"

In the late summer of 1860 the Emperor Hsien-feng, desperate for victories against the Taipings, had put his lingering distrust of Tseng Kuo-fan aside and elevated the eminent Han commander and bureaucrat to the post of governor-general of the provinces of Kiangsu, Anhwei, and Kiangsi. During the closing months of 1860, Tseng had tightened his grip on Anking, gateway to the Taiping capital of Nanking, with typical relentlessness. As a result, the Chung Wang was compelled to abandon his attempt to take Shanghai and marched west to relieve the pressure on Nanking. The rebel general did not go happily; but angry denunciations from the T'ien Wang—who told his young commander, "You are afraid of death"—as well as sinister hints from the Taiping prime minister that the Chung Wang's reluctance was "sure to give rise to discussion," spurred him on toward the upper Yangtze valley. The Chung Wang's reappearance in the west produced a protracted and finally frustrating campaign that lasted through much of 1861, and for the duration of that period Kiangsu province was stripped of almost all first-rate Taiping fighting units.

This situation—combined with the oppressive heat of a typical Shanghai summer, during which neither the imperialist nor the rebel armies in the region showed any inclination toward strenuous campaigning—made it possible for Ward, Burgevine, and the officers of their new corps to pursue the training of their Chinese recruits at Sung-chiang without enemy interference. Several encampments and training grounds were established outside the city walls, and within weeks Ward had a substantial force, according to Charles Schmidt, "in excellent military subjection, each one doing all the common duties of a regular garrison life, obeying his commands with precision; clothed, equipped and drilled in perfect unison with the modes of the European soldier. . . . The progress attained in so short a time was the greatest of wonders to every one in Sung-chiang."

Certainly, the sights to be seen on the Sung-chiang drilling grounds were unlike anything the Kiangsu peasants had ever witnessed in connection with Green Standard units. These local residents observed the corps's strange doings with a blend of admiration, trepidation, amusement, and sarcasm. The behavior of the corps's American commander was also very different from that of most imperialists: Ward kept single-mindedly to the task at hand and tried to impart a similar dedication to his men. As Dr. Macgowan noted, "In learning drill, the Chinese of Kiangsu proved apt scholars, and being an easy race, a certain amount of discipline was easily established. Commands were given in English, which, with the bugle calls, were soon acquired. They were trained to come into line quickly, irrespective of inverted order. Much time and patience were required to teach them artillery practice; but ultimately they became expert in that also." As for equipment, Ward continued to work through his agents in Shanghai to procure the best available arms, and by summer's end he was receiving regular shipments of not only English muskets but Prussian rifles and even Britain's latest Enfields, rifles whose rate of fire and accuracy were currently being admired (and demonstrated) in every part of Victoria's empire.

Using English commands and bugle calls as well as Western weapons were all ways to demonstrate to the men of the corps (as well as to Chinese and Western onlookers) that the unit was to be very different from any other imperial army. But no training program or type of armament aroused as much comment among observers as did the corps's decidedly non-Chinese uniforms. Ward himself paid particular attention to this detail, by some accounts designing the costumes himself. Boots and leggings were in the European mode, as were the tunics: Ward's infantry wore light green and his artillerymen light blue. Ward also retained a number of Manilamen, estimated in most accounts at two hundred, as a personal bodyguard, and these were given similarly Western uniforms of deep navy. (According to some writers, Ward frequently addressed this unit in Spanish, further tightening the bond that had first been formed when he found Vincente Macanaya roaming the Shanghai waterfront in the summer of 1860.) As headgear, the entire corps wore deep green turbans, not unlike those of British Sepoy troops in India.

This distinctive attire initially inspired hearty derision among the people of Kiangsu. The men of Ward's corps were branded "imitation foreign devils" by peasants who were used to brightly colored and frequently impractical dress being a particular point of pride with Chinese soldiers. Embarrassed by the taunts of their countrymen and occasionally bewildered by the maneuvers they were relentlessly ordered to repeat, some of the Chinese soldiers gave voice to questions and doubts: Although the men did drill well, as both Schmidt and Macgowan recorded, the English journalist Andrew Wilson reported that "their great fault" was that of "talking in the ranks." Without having yet experienced the battlefield advantages of Ward's techniques, many recruits remained hard-pressed to comprehend the value of being not only dressed but, in Wilson's words, "drilled and disciplined by Foreign Devils in a manner totally different from that to which they had become accustomed. . . . It was not until these troops became 'victorious' that their appearance was any sense of pleasure to them; but after a time they became proud of the 'imitation foreign devil' uniform, and would have objected to change it for a native dress."

It was not pride but money that secured the loyalty of Ward's recruits early on, and here Ward's relationship to Wu Hsü and Yang Fang was once again crucial. Having personally observed the training activities of the corps, Wu later noted with some awe that "every eighty soldiers carrying artillery or rifles formed a platoon, which were led by one foreign commander in the front and guarded by another one at the end; the lead soldiers carried flags and drums; following their commanders' instructions, the soldiers moved or halted, sped up or slowed down, marching systematically like fish scales or comb teeth." Bureaucratic form was given to Wu's enthusiasm with the creation of an official agency in Sung-chiang whose sole purpose was to facilitate the training of Chinese recruits in the Western ways of war. But Wu continued to shroud the activities of the corps cautiously: As late as November 1861, the taotai told Governor Hsüeh Huan that Ward's "barbarian braves" (a phrase that downplayed the role of Chinese recruits) numbered no more than 420 men, although Ward by that point had at least twice that many in an adequate state of readiness. Wu said that these troops were commanded by Ward and eight "deputy chiefs," but he was careful never to mention Burgevine, Forester, or any of the other well-known figures who were working the drilling grounds at Sung-chiang.

Whatever Wu's official worries, he and Yang took increasingly great pains to ensure that Mexican silver dollars were delivered in large quantities to Ward, thus guaranteeing the growth and loyalty of the corps. Although foreign officers could make anywhere from two to four hundred such dollars in a month by signing on with Ward, Chinese privates made only between eight and nine dollars during the same period of time, out of which they were expected to pay for their own lodging when in garrison. This was still much more, however, than could be had in any imperial unit (even Tseng Kuo-fan's relatively well-paid Hunan Army), and there was never a shortage of eager Chinese volunteers. But as the force grew, the task of securing funds for its regular payment became steadily more difficult. Between September 1861 and September 1862, the corps's total expenses would rise to more than $1.5 million: Even for Chinese bureaucrats and merchants adept at juggling accounts, it was a terrific sum, one that could not have been raised without recourse to Shanghai's considerable customs revenues. Wu and Yang could not tap those revenues, however, until Ward's force had been officially recognized by Peking. And for such recognition to be even a possibility, battlefield success was the first prerequisite.

With this end in mind, the drilling at Sung-chiang became ever more rigorous during the fall of 1861. The men were taught to respond automatically to the precise orders of their foreign officers, an effort that was helped in large measure by Ward's unflagging determination to remain highly visible at the head of the unit, in camp life as in battle. Whatever doubts the recruits might have had about the wisdom of following their officers' orders, they had no such fears concerning their commander. In the realm of tactics, two goals were paramount: to teach the men to quickly form a traditional infantry square and, once they had, to overcome their characteristically Chinese desire to discharge their weapons while the enemy was still out of range. This second problem, which had plagued both Taiping and imperial units, sprang out of the lingering faith of Chinese soldiers in the intimidating power of noise. Ward disabused his men of this belief and made certain that they would not fire until their muskets and rifles could play with devastating effect. Similarly, the artillery batteries were trained to stress accuracy rather than the terrifying effect of explosions and to concentrate their fire.

In supplying and equipping his new corps, Ward worked not only through the various business channels he had established and expanded during the previous year but also through his brother, Harry. Since his arrival in Shanghai late in 1859, Harry Ward had set up business in conjunction with his father in New York as Ward and Company and had journeyed back and forth to the United States on various trading missions. Nothing he had yet undertaken, however, could have matched the lucrative possibilities of acting as a "purchasing agent" for his brother's new army. Harry Ward was able, during the late summer of 1861, to buy, through his father, a large supply of "good percussion firelocks, in very good order," along with "two batteries of field pieces and a supply of field ammunition." But far more important, the younger Ward engineered the purchase, in September, of the eighty-one-ton river steamer *Cricket,* at a cost of $25,000.

The acquisition of the *Cricket,* first in a line of river steamers that Frederick Ward assembled during the coming year, marked a threshold moment in the development of the corps. The thousands of waterways—from rivers to manmade canals—that crisscrossed Kiangsu offered tremendous possibilities for rapid military movement, far more than the roads that ran over the often unreliable ground of the province. And while both the Taipings and the imperialists made use of the waterways for transportation, employing thousands of small boats, neither side had yet integrated this extensive network into their overall tactical and strategic planning. But by the fall of 1861 Ward had begun to see that the rivers and canals represented their own area of engagement: By heavily arming river steamers, he could make such vessels a method not only of transporting troops *to* a given battlefield but also of bringing firepower—in the form of heavy artillery mounted on moving platforms aboard the steamers—to bear on a battle *from* the water. Suddenly it was possible to see the topography of the province in a new light. The concentration of force was no longer inhibited by water but facilitated by it; indeed, the waterways became parts of rather than boundaries to the battle map, and the cities and towns located at key junctures—which had traditionally controlled the waterways—were revealed as vulnerable to attack from those same avenues.

This was more than just a new emphasis on increased mobility; it was an expansion of the theater of operations. The Taipings had long hoped to achieve such an expansion themselves: The acquisition of river steamers was one of the goals that had first brought the Chung Wang to the gates of Shanghai. But access to the ships fell to Ward instead, and his instinctive knowledge of how to use them meant that the *Cricket* and her dozen or so sister ships would soon play a decisive role. The final element in this plan was the hiring of American commanders who had worked on similar craft in the United States and whose experience with conditions much like those in Kiangsu was far greater than that of other Westerners.

During the long months of training and tactical innovation that followed the creation of his new corps, Ward also placed heightened emphasis on the need for reliable intelligence. His bitter experiences with jealous Manchu commanders who refused to share what information they possessed concerning Taiping troop strengths and movements caused Ward to address this problem in a characteristically personal fashion: by himself infiltrating and scouting rebel-held territory. Ward made these journeys, generally, in the guise of a Western hunter or trader who had secured safe passage from the local Taiping commanders. Among the few personal documents belonging to Ward that made their way back to the United States and have survived to this day are two passes from such commanders, ordering the soldiers of the Heavenly Kingdom not to harm or interfere with the movements of the unnamed "foreigner" who bore them. It is entirely plausible that Ward, exploiting the continued Taiping reluctance to molest Westerners, coolly applied for and received these passes himself; at any rate, he did, on such journeys, gain vital firsthand information concerning positions he would shortly attack. As always, he did so without apparent concern for the very gruesome fate that would have awaited him had his identity been discovered. In addition to such adventurous sorties, Ward made use of an expansive network of spies, who infiltrated not only the rebel camps but those of the imperial armies as well as the foreign settlements in Shanghai. Before long he had reliable ears throughout Kiangsu.

What Dr. Macgowan called the "secret work" of building the new corps at Sung-chiang continued through the fall of 1861. Late in the year, Admiral Sir James Hope returned from a trip to Japan to find Shanghai full of rumors about the activities of Ward and his officers. According to Dr. Macgowan, the ever-aggressive admiral went to assess the situation in Sung-chiang personally. His real purpose may once again have been to halt Ward's activities altogether: Despite their partial peacemaking earlier in the year, there was still ill feeling between Ward and Hope, which would not be fully erased for several months. Ward was known to harbor resentment over his treatment at British hands, and it is therefore natural that when he learned of Hope's approach, he

> ordered the Europeans at once to hide themselves, whilst he arranged matters so as to give the Admiral a befitting military reception with his drilled men, who were attired in foreign costume. Sir James was altogether surprised and gratified at the sight of natives so well disciplined. He desired Ward to call his officers from their hiding places—for he knew that the colonel himself could not have accomplished so much, without assistance. All officers and men were then ordered on parade, where they went through a course of easy infantry evolutions; after which Admiral Hope not only praised them, but promised Colonel Ward his cordial support in the new undertaking.

Ward took the admiral's praise and promises with a grain of salt; innate distrust of the British, bolstered by the London government's contacts with the American Confederacy as well as Ward's own experiences in China, temporarily ruled out any other reaction. Yet there were sound reasons for accepting Hope's vow at face value, for not only had the British position on the Taipings already moved significantly toward condemnation by the time of this visit but London's attitude toward Ward's activities had also shifted. As far back as August—just a month after Frederick Bruce had reported "with satisfaction" that the Foreign Arms Corps had been disbanded—Lord Russell had written Bruce to say that since the Manchus were more likely to ensure Chinese stability and prosperity than the Taipings, London would not oppose the entrance of British subjects into an "Imperial Legion of Foreigners," should Peking wish it. Of course, Peking did not yet wish it, and Russell's statement was an informal one. But events were moving quickly, and, as Dr. Macgowan noted, "The time, long predicted, when interference with the Taipings would be considered necessary, was close at hand."

In October 1861 Anson Burlingame, who had recently been appointed American minister to China by President Lincoln, arrived in Macao. The fact that official American business in the Middle Kingdom was being conducted at the time out of the home of the mission's charge, S. Wells Williams, indicated the less than vigorous role the United States had played in Chinese affairs in recent years. But during his years in China, Burlingame was to secure for the United States a prominent role in the affairs of the Manchu court. At the same time, he earned the personal respect and affection of China's rulers. In laying the groundwork for this reassertion of Washington's influence at Peking, Burlingame also struck up a friendship and correspondence with Frederick Townsend Ward, to whose activities the new minister, observing the utter chaos that ruled on both sides of the Chinese civil war, soon gave his stamp of approval.

Burlingame's was precisely the sort of decisive character that had long been absent from American dealings with China. Born in 1820, he came from a midwestern farming family and had attended the law school at Harvard. Setting up practice in Boston, Burlingame soon gained a reputation as a powerful public speaker, an advocate of Martin Van

Buren and of the Free-Soil movement. Elected to the House of Representatives in 1854, he gained fame in 1856 for an incident that had little
to do with parliamentary politics. A fellow Massachusetts representative, Charles Sumner, one day rose to give voice to violent feelings
about the South and slavery and subsequently—while sitting at his
desk—was savagely beaten with a cane by Preston Brooks of South
Carolina. Burlingame defended Sumner and spoke directly to Brooks's
cherished sense of Southern chivalry: "What! Strike a man when he is
pinioned—when he cannot respond to a blow! Call you that chivalry? In
what code of honour did you get your authority for that?"

So powerful was Burlingame's invective that Brooks subsequently
challenged his Massachusetts colleague to a duel. Burlingame agreed,
naming a spot just over the Canadian border (dueling was illegal in the
United States) as the site and rifles as the weapon. Brooks backed down,
claiming that to get to Canada he would have to travel through "enemy"
territory (the Northern states), and Burlingame came away from the
affair a hero of the antislavery forces. In 1861, however, he lost a close
race for reelection and was appointed ambassador to Austria. But the
Austrians declined to receive Burlingame, citing his strong speeches in
favor of Hungarian nationalism. Lincoln then offered Burlingame the
China posting, which he accepted.

Lincoln's secretary of state, William Seward, dispatched Burlingame to Peking with a set of instructions that were typical of the
American attitude toward China since the signing of the Treaty of
Wanghia in 1844. "I think," wrote Seward, "that it is your duty to act
in the spirit which governs us in our intercourse with all friendly nations,
and especially to lend no aid, encouragement or countenance to sedition
or rebellion against the imperial authority. This direction, however,
must not be followed so far as to put in jeopardy the lives or property
of American citizens in China." U.S. interests in China, said Seward,
were "identical" with those of Britain and France—the fact that British
and French interests were often confused and in conflict was not addressed: "You are, therefore, instructed to consult and cooperate with
[the British and French], unless there shall be very satisfactory reasons
for separating from them."

The China that greeted Burlingame in October 1861 was a nation in which such vague instructions were likely to be of even less than usual value. At the imperial hunting lodge at Jehol, north of Peking, intrigue was gaining momentum at an alarming rate. During the summer, the Emperor Hsien-feng—aware of the disgrace he had brought on his name and dynasty through his foolish belligerence and final cowardice—had indulged in a bout of debauchery that, given his health, seemed certainly aimed at self-destruction. In July he celebrated his thirtieth birthday: an edematous, besotted grotesque, obsessed with drugs and concubines. The three princes whose advice had brought about the disaster of the Allied occupation of Peking—I, Cheng, and Su-shun—still held his ear and were angling to eliminate the voices of Prince Kung and Yehonala, the mother of Hsien-feng's son, from the councils of government by having themselves declared regents for the young heir. They succeeded, gaining control of a hastily formed Board of Regents just before their decrepit benefactor died on August 22.

Yehonala and Hsien-feng's first wife, Niuhuru, were created empresses dowager following the emperor's death, Yehonala assuming the name Tz'u-hsi. But real power remained in the hands of the Board of Regents. By excluding Prince Kung—who they believed had acted treacherously in concluding treaties with the West—from crucial deliberations, I, Cheng, and Su-shun made a formidable enemy. But it was in doing the same to Tz'u-hsi that they unwittingly committed their worst mistake. Slowly, the day approached for the transfer of Hsien-feng's coffin from Jehol to Peking, a trip during which it was rumored that the three princes intended to murder the empresses dowager and blame their deaths on mountain bandits. But they had not reckoned on Tz'u-hsi's genuine gift for outwitting political opponents.

On October 5 the procession set out by foot, the late emperor's golden coffin carried by no fewer than 124 bearers. Suddenly, Tz'u-hsi and Niuhuru announced that because of the difficult terrain and the severe storms that accompanied the procession, they intended to ride ahead to Peking and await the arrival of Hsien-feng's body. Any protest that the three princes might have made was silenced by the presence of a strong detachment of the Peking Field Force, a crack unit of imperial soldiers recently assembled by Prince Kung. The Field Force detachment that accompanied the empresses dowager to Peking was commanded by Jung-lu, a young Manchu officer who was said to have been engaged to Tz'u-hsi before her "elevation" to imperial concubine.

In Peking, the empresses were greeted by Prince Kung, who had engineered their escape after receiving a secret message from Tz'u-hsi weeks earlier. Since signing the agreements with the Western powers that had put an end to the Allied occupation of Peking, Kung had reinforced his status as China's foremost statesman by pushing for the creation of the Tsungli Yamen, a Chinese foreign office staffed by competent bureaucrats ready and able to deal with the West on realistic terms. Clearly, Kung was the man best able to manage Chinese affairs, and Tz'u-hsi knew it. Their alliance produced immediate results.

When the three princes arrived in Peking, they were speedily arrested and charged with subverting the state, one of Confucian China's "ten abominations," excelled in evil only by rebellion. Specifically, they were blamed for guiding Hsien-feng down the disastrous path to war with the West. "Prince I and Prince Cheng are hereby permitted to commit suicide" read the imperial decree on the subject. "As for Su-shun, his treasonable guilt far exceeds that of his accomplices, and he fully deserves the punishment of dismemberment and the slicing process [the death of a thousand cuts]. . . . But we cannot make up our minds to impose this extreme penalty, and therefore, in token of our leniency, we sentence him to immediate decapitation."

As a result of this palace coup, Tz'u-hsi and Niuhuru were made regents for the young emperor. They sat behind golden screens in the throne room and answered questions in the boy's name, ruling on critical matters of state. But Niuhuru was weak-willed, and the dominant voice on such occasions quickly became Tz'u-hsi's. The emperor's name was changed to T'ung-chih, "Return to Unified Order," and the name came to characterize a period of imperial restoration in China. It was the clever Tz'u-hsi—her youthful impetuousness and arrogance mellowed by experience—who made this possible, through her recognition, elevation, and control of such talented men as Prince Kung, Tseng Kuo-fan, and Li Hung-chang.

171

No less important to the survival of the Manchu dynasty was the fact that the emergence of Tz'u-hsi and especially Prince Kung as the de facto rulers of China had a powerful effect on the attitudes of the Western powers toward Peking. Kung had long been recognized by foreign emissaries as the most reasonable Chinese official with whom to do business. "It is thought," Anson Burlingame wrote to Secretary of State Seward following what he called the "revolution" in Peking, "foreign interests will be conserved by this action of Prince Kung and his party in as much as they are strongly in favor of maintaining and extending peaceful relations with foreigners." British and French representatives echoed this sentiment, although many chose more cautious language. And with increasingly relaxed Chinese-Western relations came heightened Western impatience with the Taiping rebellion. Prince Kung apparently meant to live by the terms of the treaties China had signed, and an alternate choice to the Manchus as rulers of the empire steadily became irrelevant. This ever more critical attitude toward the Taipings was solidified by developments within the rebel movement.

On September 5 the city of Anking had finally surrendered to Tseng Kuo-fan. Augustus Lindley noted that "three regiments of the garrison, unable to endure the horrors of the famine raging within the doomed city, which had reduced them to cannibalism of the most frightful description, human flesh being eagerly sought at the price of eighty cash per catty (about fourpence per 1.333 lb. avoirdupois) and devoured with avidity, surrendered to the Imperialists upon condition of a free pardon, but were massacred to a man, and their headless bodies cast into the Yangtze."

In the wake of this crucial victory, Tseng Kuo-fan was given supreme military authority over Kiangsi, Kiangsu, Anhwei, and Chekiang provinces—an unprecedented promotion, especially for a Han commander. His new responsibilities made Tseng profoundly uneasy; but disturbing as the results of Anking's fall were to Tseng, they were far more so to the rebel commanders. Coinciding as it did with the largely futile Taiping western campaign, the loss of Anking left the rebels with only one option, which by now was a familiar one: to turn east and seize the riches of the coastal ports of Hangchow (which the Chung Wang had abandoned after its initial conquest in 1860) and, more important, Ningpo and Shanghai.

The Taiping predicament was exacerbated by the continuing erosion of the T'ien Wang's sanity and the attendant, predictable confusion at the uppermost levels of rebel authority. As in Peking, intrigue was rife in Nanking in the fall of 1861. Closely surrounded by advisers picked from his own family, the T'ien Wang was increasingly preoccupied with matters of theology and physical pleasure, and when he did look closely at rebel affairs it was only to become jealous of the rising power and popularity of the Chung Wang. Affairs within Nanking itself, meanwhile, were fast deteriorating, as the citizens felt the full effects of their leader's instability and the other wangs' greed. The missionary Issachar J. Roberts, now residing in Nanking, passed his hours that fall trying to engineer the sale of river steamers in the United States to Taiping agents. But by season's end, Roberts had come to see that the rebellion was not the happy cause he had imagined he was setting out to join months earlier. In a nervous year-end report, "which I never expect to publish while living among this people," Roberts wrote that

> [t]he aspect of things here have two very different phases—the one bright and promising, the other dark and unpromising. . . . The bright side consists chiefly in negatives, such as, no idolatry, no prostitution, no gambling, nor any kind of public immorality, allowed in the city. . . . But when we come to the religious aspect of this revolution, together with other evils both political and civil, we have a very dark side, which has grieved my very heart exceedingly, and often inclines me to leave them; but then I pity the poor people, who have immortal souls, and are really the sufferers, and greatly to be pitied for time and eternity.

Speaking of the man who had once sat in his Bible class, Roberts pronounced: "As to the religious opinions of the T'ien Wang, which he propagates with great zeal, I believe them in the main abominable in the sight of God. In fact, I believe he is crazy, especially in religious matters, nor do I believe him soundly rational about anything." The character of the ruler was reflected in the state: "Their political system is about as poor as their theology. I do not believe they have any organised Government, nor do they know enough about Government to make one, in my opinion. The whole affair seems to consist in martial law, and that, too, runs very much in the line of killing men, from the highest to the lowest, by all in authority."

Venting personal bitterness, Roberts stated that the T'ien Wang

> wanted me to come here, but it was not to preach the Gospel of Jesus Christ and convert men and women to God, but to take office, and preach his dogmas, and convert foreigners to himself. I would as lief convert them to Mormonism, or any other *ism* which I believe unscriptural, and, so far, from the devil. I believe that in their heart they feel a real opposition to the Gospel, but for policy's sake they grant it toleration; yet I believe they intend to prevent its realization, at least, in the city of Nanking.

Roberts detailed the starvation that was increasingly prevalent, as well as the "traps" set by rebel leaders "to catch men and slay them," and finally the propensity of the rebel leaders for "pulling down houses" and turning common families out into the cold in order to create space for new palaces. "And hence," he concluded, "I am making up my mind to leave them unless the prospects brighten up considerably to what they are at present. . . . May the Lord direct my steps!"

Roberts's report was subsequently made available to English-language newspapers on the China coast and to foreign diplomats, and it reinforced the general Western dissatisfaction with the Taipings. That dissatisfaction became outrage and active opposition when, in the beginning of December, the Chung Wang once again appeared at the head of a massive, eastward-moving army. His initial target this time was not eastern Kiangsu but Chekiang province. Perhaps remembering his reception at Shanghai a year earlier, the Chung Wang this time marched on Ningpo and Hangchow, and, while he met no active foreign resistance, his conquest of the two cities went a long way toward sealing the fate of the Taipings within the Western communities.

Condemnation did not come immediately; indeed, the capture of Ningpo in the beginning of December was used by the foreign powers and especially the British as something of a test case, to see how the rebels would behave when in control of a treaty port. The Taipings, said the *North China Herald,* "shewed pluck in capturing the city, while they evinced no desire to molest foreign residents, or revenge themselves, as usual, on the unoffending inhabitants. If such is the case, and . . . they are sincere in their peaceful designs, they shall have justice done to them at our hands. While we denounce those of the rebels who act as cold-blooded, blasphemous imposters, we shall give 'the devil his due' if any party of them act otherwise." But in reality such statements were disingenuous, for there was little the Taipings could have done to prevent their eventual condemnation by the Westerners given the new circumstances in Peking. Just a week after making the preceding statement, the *Herald* announced that

> [t]hese insurgents are so far politic as to invite us to trade as usual, even on more liberal terms than heretofore, so that they be recognized as the ruling power in the district. But in honour, in justice, aye, even in expediency, can we do this[?] Such conduct on our parts individually—not to speak of the representatives of the Treaty Powers—would be a most serious infraction of the several treaties entered into with the constituted Government at Peking. . . . [A]t the present juncture we are more than at any other period of our connexion with China, bound to support the existing Government of the empire.

Thus by year's end the Taipings were being charged with treachery for having violated the yearlong truce Admiral Hope had negotiated with them in March 1861, and before long Taiping methods of government were being decried by loud voices throughout the Western settlements. One missionary wrote from Ningpo to say that "[i]t is impossible to particularize one-tenth part of the cruelties that are daily and hourly witnessed by us in this place, where no doubt the Taipingites are on their best behavior." And before long the British consul in Ningpo, a man known for harboring anti-Taiping sentiments even before the occupation of the port, was writing to inform Frederick Bruce that

> not one single step in the direction of "good government" has been taken by the Taipings; not any attempt made to organize a political body or commercial institutions; not a vestige, not a trace of anything approaching to order, or regularity of action or consistency of purpose, can be found in any of their public acts; the words "government machinery" as applied to Taiping rule, have no possible meaning here; and in short, *Desolation* is the only end obtained, as it has always been wherever the sway of the marauders has had its full scope, and their power the liberty of unchecked excess.

Late in December Admiral Hope once more journeyed up the Yangtze to try to gain assurances from the Taipings that they would not attack any more of the treaty ports. Hope felt personally insulted by the new Taiping eastern offensive, and his mood was even more than usually belligerent. When asked, he refused to guarantee that the treaty ports would not be used as bases for Chinese imperial troops. And when told that he could hardly expect the Taipings to respect the ports' neutrality under such circumstances, he threatened not only an active Western defense of the cities "but such further consequences as your folly will deserve." Hope had no authorization for such statements from his superiors, who almost certainly would have disavowed them. But the lines were being drawn for a significantly expanded conflict in the Yangtze delta. And in January 1862 the Chung Wang completed this process by once more marching into Kiangsu and toward Shanghai.

While officers such as Admiral Hope might have been anxious, by the end of 1861, to fight the rebels with their own troops, statesmen such as Frederick Bruce were not yet convinced of the desirability of bringing the rebellion to a complete end. If nothing else, the war continued to spur the Manchu government on toward reform, and, whatever his preference for Prince Kung over other Chinese statesmen, Bruce was determined to drive China further down that path. For many months

to come, Bruce would insist that "every consideration of sound policy indicates that Nanking is the *last* place we wish to see taken, as while in the hands of the Taipings it gives us a hold both on them and on this recalcitrant government." Thus the British prime minister, Lord Palmerston, might thunder that "these Rebels are Revolters not only against the Emperor, but against all laws human and Divine," but to condemn was one thing, to intervene actively with regular forces another. And it was by no means clear that Great Britain was prepared for the latter prospect during the opening days of 1862.

All this meant that Admiral Hope and officers like him had to find more inventive ways of meeting the Chung Wang's challenge. There were only some six hundred British regulars in Shanghai in January 1862, along with four or five hundred French. Bolstered by the Shanghai Volunteer Corps, this did not represent an impressive force; the Chung Wang had at least a hundred thousand men moving in several powerful columns toward Shanghai from the south, the west, and the northwest. Bellicose language and a defiant attitude could not stop this horde, propelled as it was by heightened desperation.

Hope was soon joined in Shanghai by the commander of the British army in China, General Sir John Michel, who, like Hope, was an imaginative officer ready to explore unorthodox solutions to the Taiping problem. Small, thin, and immensely energetic, General Michel had built a reputation in India by waging an unconventional campaign against a group of rebels that saw him personally march through fifteen hundred miles of rugged, dangerous terrain. Michel had commanded a division during the Allied advance on Peking and had been present at the burning of the Summer Palace. On arriving in Shanghai, he quickly acceded to Hope's view that British forces, if employed at all in the region, would have to be formed into "flying columns" that could be rushed to support imperial Chinese units in moments of crisis rather than dissipated in a circumferential defense of the Shanghai region.

In choosing such a strategy, Hope and Michel were supported by the commander of France's forces in Shanghai, Vice Admiral August-Leopold Protet. Like Michel, Protet had seen extensive and adventurous colonial service and knew more than a little about waging an unconventional campaign against a hostile native force. And, like Hope, Protet was a fire-eater who itched constantly for action. It had been Protet who had encouraged Tardif de Moidrey to organize his Franco-Chinese Corps. Indeed, Protet had made the project possible, by advising Tardif de Moidrey to feign illness when his unit had received orders to leave Shanghai. Anxious to have his own chance at the Taipings, Protet eagerly consented to be a part of Hope's flying column strategy.

But for such plans to proceed the governments involved would have to sanction joint offensive action by their armed forces, and in the diplomatic realm there were serious impediments to this. Whatever the cooperative inclinations of Western military officers, the diplomatic representatives of France and Britain viewed each other with less than trusting eyes. Informed of the steady progress of Tardif de Moidrey's Franco-Chinese contingent, the British consul in Canton wrote to the Foreign Office in London and accused the French of "trying to make political capital out of the Chinese embrouillement." This transparent expression of Britain's fear that France would shortly rival Her Majesty's representatives at their own game was underlined in talks between Frederick Bruce and the Chinese central government in Peking. Bruce informed the Chinese that if they needed foreign officers to train soldiers they should "apply for Prussians." He made his reasons plain to Lord Russell: "Prussia is Protestant, she represents a large trade in China, and she is not a powerful naval force—Her officers would be less troublesome, and would create little jealousy, than those obtained from any other Treaty-Power—They are also comparatively indifferently paid."

In short, British diplomats not only prevented their own officers from commanding either foreign or native troops in offensive field actions, but intended to see to it that the French did not do so either. For several enterprising Frenchmen, however, such obstacles meant comparatively little, especially when measured against the military and monetary allure of training Chinese units to meet the coming onslaught of the Chung Wang. Foremost among these was Prosper Giquel, the French director of the Ningpo office of the Imperial Chinese Customs Service. The Customs Service was by this time headed and staffed by

Portrait of Ward by an unknown Chinese artist. Ward probably sat for this oil work in early 1862, when his fame and prestige among Chinese and Westerners alike had reached dramatic heights. Note that the left side of Ward's mouth does not display the droop caused by his jaw wound and facial scars; the artist did his best to disguise this feature. *(Courtesy of Essex Institute, Salem, Mass.)*

View of Shanghai in the 1860s. Taken from the American side of Soochow Creek, this picture shows the British Settlement across the water and the great mercantile houses stretching away along the Bund. Warships similar to the one from which Ward made his daring escape in 1861 can be seen in the distance, and a group of sampans are in the foreground. *(Library of Congress)*

Henry Andrea Burgevine. This engraving—the only known likeness of Burgevine—ran in *Harper's Weekly* in 1866. Ward's ill-starred second-in-command had died while in the custody of imperial Chinese officials a year earlier. *(Harper's Weekly/Brown Military Collection)*

The walls and moat of Sung-chiang. This photo gives a good idea of the task Ward's comparatively small force of Western officers and Filipino soldiers faced when they stormed the city in July 1860. The walls are stone, and the moat is of an appreciable width and depth. *(Courtesy of Essex Institute, Salem, Mass.)*

The northern campaign: the Taku Forts, August 1860. Taken after British and French troops had successfully stormed the forts that guarded the approach to Peking, this photo offers proof of the Chinese genius for elaborate defense: The thick earthen walls are guarded by rings of wooden and bamboo spikes, as well as deep ditches. Ward faced similar obstacles during his Kiangsu campaign. *(Bettmann/Hulton)*

The northern campaign: Allied troops enter Peking, October 1860. A popular French rendition of the conclusion of the Franco-British march on the Chinese capital. Despite its melodrama, the image depicts many real details of Chinese methods of warfare: banners, large crowds of soldiers dressed in elaborate uniforms, and an ultimate reliance on spears, bows and arrows, and a few obsolete firearms. *(Roger Viollet)*

A Chinese-Western artillery battery. It is unclear whether this is a unit of Ward's Ever Victorious Army or a detachment from one of the various Franco-Chinese contingents, but the photo gives a good idea of why such troops inspired consternation and (initially) derision among Chinese peasants—they were a distinctly un-Chinese sight. Note the Western officer to the left and the Chinese noncommissioned officer carrying a saber in the center. *(Courtesy of Essex Institute, Salem, Mass.)*

Edward Forester. Photographed at the time he published his very questionable reminiscences of the Ever Victorious Army and the Taiping rebellion in 1896, Forester still displays the determination that allowed him to survive brutal imprisonment by the Chinese rebels. *(Cosmopolitan/Brown Military Collection)*

Admiral Sir James Hope. Even sitting for an official portrait could not mellow Fighting Jimmie's air of bellicose, even smirking, arrogance—just as wounds and political complexity never dampened his taste for personally battling any real or perceived challenge to British influence and his own good name. *(Greenwich Hospital Collection, National Maritime Museum)*

Anson Burlingame. The famous orator and former U.S. congressman stands at the center of the mission that he led for the Chinese government to the Western powers following the expiration of his term as American minister to China. Burlingame was the first such minister to reside in Peking, where he became a trusted friend of the imperial clique. *(Harper's Monthly/The Bettmann Archive)*

Tseng Kuo-fan, Li Hung-chang, and Tso Tsung-t'ang. The great Han commander and bureaucrat Tseng Kuo-fan is shown tutoring his two most eminent pupils. Li was later governor of Kiangsu, while Tso achieved great success as governor of Chekiang. Note Tseng's famously unkempt beard. *(Wan-go Weng/Columbia University Collection)*

Li Hung-chang. China's most famous nineteenth-century statesman was photographed at the time of his appointment to the governorship of Kiangsu province, where he met and worked closely with Ward. Li's oft-noted perspicacity and presence are evident. *(Bettmann/Hulton)*

Photographic portrait of Ward. In this image all surface traces of Ward's wound have been removed, although the left side of his mouth still displays the slight droop that impaired his speech. Once again, he wears his unadorned Prince Albert, buttoned high. *(Courtesy of Essex Institute, Salem, Mass.)*

Chang-mei. Yang Fang's daughter was probably photographed at the time of her marriage to Ward in March 1862, when she was twenty-one. Her shaved forehead and traditional dress stand in some contrast to the typical props of a Western photographer's studio. *(Courtesy of Essex Institute, Salem, Mass.)*

Ward's battle standard. Chinese soldiers traditionally carried into battle banners bearing the names of their commanders, and Ward followed this custom. The character denoting his Chinese name, "Hua," appeared in deep green against a light green field bordered in red. *(Courtesy of Essex Institute, Salem, Mass.)*

Ward's Manchu boots and mandarin cap. Ward was buried in the rest of his mandarin robes. The blue rank button is missing from his cap, but the prestigious peacock's feather has survived. *(Courtesy of Essex Institute, Salem, Mass.)*

Adrien Tardif de Moidrey. The French captain who may well have been the originator (but was more probably, along with Ward and Burgevine, the co-author) of the idea of having Western officers train Chinese soldiers in the use of Western weapons and tactics. *(Steven Leibo,* A Journal of the Chinese Civil War*)*

Prosper Giquel. The young French officer and customs commissioner in Ningpo who studied Ward and Tardif de Moidrey's methods and copied them with great success in Chekiang province. Alone of the daring Western innovators that led Chinese troops against the Taipings, Giquel survived the war and continued to render valuable service to the Chinese government. *(L'Illustration/Sygma)*

Charles George Gordon. Photographed at the time he took command of the Ever Victorious Army, Gordon exhibits all of his characteristic jaunty recklessness and extreme sensitivity. *(Bettmann/Hulton)*

Tz'u-ch'i. A remarkable view of the stout walls before which Ward was mortally wounded. *(Courtesy of Essex Institute, Salem, Mass.)*

The musket ball that killed Ward. For thirty years, as he progressed from lieutenant to admiral in the British navy, Archibald Bogle carried this innocuous but deadly missile with him as a keepsake. *(Courtesy of Essex Institute, Salem, Mass.)*

Ward's memorial hall in Sung-chiang. Built in 1876–77, the hall was in subsequent decades maintained by a keeper who can be seen in the shadows to the right. Ward's shrine was just inside the building, and his grave was in the courtyard. A paved public park (called, ironically, a "resting place" by Shanghai residents) now occupies these grounds. *(Courtesy of Essex Institute, Salem, Mass.)*

Ward's shrine. On the altar sits a brazier for incense, and to either side are the blue columns bearing the original gold inscriptions praising Ward. *(Courtesy of Essex Institute, Salem, Mass.)*

Ward's burial mound. Photographed years after Ward was interred, the tumulus has become overgrown by plants and bamboo, and his dog's grave is no longer even visible. The walls to the right and left were erected to guard the memorial compound from neglect and vandalism. *(Courtesy of Essex Institute, Salem, Mass.)*

Ward's empty grave in Salem. At Harmony Grove sits this less than romantic but only surviving memorial to America's most remarkable nineteenth-century adventurer and one of history's great free-lance captains. *(Courtesy of Essex Institute, Salem, Mass.)*

Westerners, an arrangement accepted by the Chinese because of the dramatic rise in revenues it produced. Understandably, it was also the focus of particular animosity from anti-Manchu factions. When Ningpo fell, therefore, Giquel quickly closed his office and journeyed north to Shanghai.

Giquel had been a soldier during the Anglo-French campaign in China in 1857 and had stayed on to master the Chinese language and eventually sign on with the Customs Service. Just twenty-six years old in 1861, he arrived in Shanghai to find the foreign settlements furiously trying to arrange for the city's defense. Giquel quickly offered his services as an interpreter during various meetings between French, British, American, and Chinese representatives. But it was the activities of Frederick Townsend Ward and Adrien Tardif de Moidrey that particularly fascinated him.

Securing the post of interpreter for Admiral Protet, Giquel was given a chance to get a closer look at the Franco-Chinese Corps of Kiangsu. By the beginning of 1862, Tardif de Moidrey had satisfied his backers' requirements by drilling his Chinese artillerymen to a high state of readiness, and he was allowed to expand his unit to two hundred. The Franco-Chinese Corps was an ideal adjunct for the kind of campaign that Admiral Hope, General Michel, and Admiral Protet hoped to fight: a compact, hard-hitting force capable of quick movement and—because of its familiarity with Western tactics and commands—of integrating itself into a larger Allied force. Giquel learned many lessons from Tardif de Moidrey, lessons that he was to apply on his return to Ningpo. But in his attempts to gain firsthand information concerning the activities of the Ward Corps, Giquel was far less successful.

Indeed, few Westerners in Shanghai had heard any news or had any glimpse of the Ward Corps for quite some time. But in the initial confusion and subsequent panic prompted by the Chung Wang's advance, no one stopped to remark on the fact. As during the Taiping eastern offensive of 1860, refugees poured into Shanghai from the interior, carrying what belongings they could, drastically overcrowding the Chinese city and the Western settlements, and bringing horror stories of Taiping occupation. The Chung Wang, meanwhile, declared openly that he intended to take Shanghai no matter who participated in its defense, and the only military units in the city that had a real chance of stopping the rebels before they reached Shanghai's walls, the Anglo-French regulars, were prohibited from taking the field for offensive actions. Once again, it was a dismal scenario, and once again, when cause for hope emerged, it came out of Sung-chiang.

At first, it was only a succession of rumors. One of the strongest of the rebel columns moving on Shanghai was coming from the north-west and by early January had reached the vicinity of the important town of Wu-sung. From Wu-sung the rebels could hope to close the mouth of the Huang-pu River, a disastrous prospect for Shanghai. But an Allied counterattack was as yet impossible. The Taipings thus had time to entrench themselves, and into these fortifications they moved some of their best-equipped and best-trained troops. A British officer who had unusually close contact with the Taipings during one of their attacks on Wu-sung, Captain George O. Willes, later reported to Admiral Hope that

> [f]rom a personal interview with two [rebel] officers, and being for some time within thirty or forty yards of the skirmishers, I am enabled to say that they were armed with muskets, which they handled efficiently. The two officers were dressed in Chinese cos-tume, but with . . . single-barrelled [*sic*] European pistols. . . . [H]aving had an opportunity of seeing the Imperialist troops in the Peiho expedition, I was quite astonished at [the rebels'] apparent equipment and organisation.

In mid-January these same Taipings, having grown fairly accus-tomed to what Captain Willes called the "smart but ineffective fire" of their imperial opponents, encountered an unprecedented and unwel-come sight: a detachment of Chinese soldiers in Western uniforms, bearing down on their entrenchments. Like the armies of such imperial commanders as Tseng Kuo-fan, this unit carried a banner emblazoned with the name of their leader: a light green standard, bordered in red, with a dark green Chinese character denoting the name *Hua*. Hua, the

Taipings would soon learn, was the Chinese name adopted by the young American who had trained and was leading this unit. (The name was a phonetic approximation, much like Augustus Lindley's "Lin-le.") In the ensuing encounter, the rebel soldiers, despite numerical superiority, were driven from their positions by the highly disciplined "imitation foreign devils," and before long word had spread throughout Shanghai and along the China coast that, after six months of careful preparation, Colonel Ward was back at work.

The success at Wu-sung was followed up quickly. In their eastward march from Soochow, the Taipings had once again secured Ch'ing-p'u and then established strongly entrenched bases at several towns in the area: Ying-ch'i-pin, Ch'en-shan, T'ien-ma-shan, and Kuang-fu-lin (Ward's original training ground in 1860). The rebels consolidated their occupation of Kuang-fu-lin by filling it with twenty thousand troops. A week after his appearance at Wu-sung, Ward took five hundred men of his corps and, according to Dr. Macgowan, attacked Kuang-fu-lin "without artillery, and made a bold rush on the rebel fortifications. The enemy seeing, for the first time, their own countrymen in foreign attire, and led in a disciplined way by gallant officers, were filled with dismay, and fled precipitately."

Banking not only on the superior arms and training of his men but also on the psychological impact of their appearance, Ward had taken an enormous risk at Kuang-fu-lin. The gamble had paid off, and Ward repeated the tactic during the first week of February at Ying-ch'i-pin. He launched a surprise attack against greatly superior numbers, killing and wounding thousands of stunned rebels and driving the rest back to Ch'en-shan and beyond. During this action Ward sustained some five wounds, the most serious of which was the loss of a finger to a Taiping musket ball. Characteristically, he did not pause to recuperate but on February 5 took Burgevine and six hundred men of the corps and attacked T'ien-ma-shan. The pattern of victory was the same: a surprise rush against the rebel entrenchments, then a wild pursuit during which thousands of rebels were killed, wounded, or captured.

Wu Hsü's joy over Ward's successes was unrestrained. On February 5 he sent a personal letter to Ward, congratulating "the General" (although Ward had not yet received such a rank from the Chinese government) on his successes at Kuang-fu-lin and Ying-ch'i-pin:

> I have received reports from battalion commander Li [Heng-sung] and others that the rebels have attacked the barracks in Kuang-fu-lin since the new year, and that you, General, repeatedly led troops to engage them, and you are invincible. Yesterday, I heard that at 9:00 a.m. on the fifth day of this month [Chinese calendar], a large number of rebels attacked and occupied Ying-ch'i-pin. Then again, your excellency led five hundred men of the Foreign Arms Corps to attack the nest of rebels, and defeated several tens of thousands of them. . . . I was very pleased when I heard this news. A blemish in an otherwise perfect thing is that your finger has been wounded. . . . The soldiers of the Foreign Arms Corps have rendered good service in these battles, and they are all praiseworthy and should be given rewards respectively. I have already discussed this with Yang Taki personally. As to the details of how to reward the soldiers, your excellency can name a sum to Taki, who will send the money at once. . . . The only thing (which is not good) is that your finger has been wounded, I do not know if this will affect the every-day life of your excellency. I hope that you will pay much attention to your health and recover very soon. This is the most important thing.

The letter was not signed but concluded "Signature is in another place"—a Chinese expression indicating that the receiver would know who the sender was without the latter identifying himself, and a sign of Ward and Wu's unusually close relationship.

Just a day after writing this letter, Wu received a note from Ward detailing the success at T'ien-ma-shan. The taotai again sat down to write: "You have obtained a great victory. I was so delighted after reading your letter. The victory you have just had shows that your troop is well-trained and impenetrable. In addition to sending your letter to the Governor [Hsüeh Huan], I am looking forward to your coming to Shanghai, so that I can seek your counsel personally." On receiving the details of Ward's successes, Hsüeh Huan, in a subsequent memorial to the throne, acknowledged the American's personal leadership in this series of attacks and his "great contributions" to their success.

Inspiring as Ward's victories were, however, the sheer weight of numbers was with the Taipings, and following the defeat at Wu-sung (an event important enough to rate a line in the "Latest Intelligence" section of the London *Times*), Ying-ch'i-pin, Ch'en-shan, and T'ien-ma-shan rebel units quickly surrounded Ward's several encampments in the Sung-chiang area, as well as the walls of the city itself. Once again, Ward's daring had proved an annoyance to the Chung Wang, one that the rebel commander intended to erase with overwhelming odds. Taiping storming units immediately went to work on Ward's defensive positions, and the outlook was not hopeful.

In Shanghai, news of the fighting in the Sung-chiang area had quickly followed reports of the Wu-sung engagement. Yet the citizens of Shanghai's Western settlements—desperate as they were for any sign of effective resistance to the Chung Wang's legions—did not reprise their familiar vitriolic denouncements of "the filibuster Ward." The *North China Herald,* along with the other China coast English-language papers, remained momentarily silent, as if awaiting events; when it did acknowledge the situation, on January 18, it was only to say that "[b]esides this body of armed men [the Taipings near Wu-sung] there are two others approaching Shanghai, one from the direction of Soochow, which during the day was in fierce combat with the Imperialists at Sung-chiang; the other body from Hangchow."

Alarm in Shanghai had continued to mount as January came to a close and it was learned that the central Taiping column alone—the force moving east from Soochow—numbered eighty thousand men. On January 25 the *Herald* reported "that up to the hour of going to press, the advance of the insurgents is imminent, and our naval and military authorities are on the *qui vive* to repulse them should they appear within range of the posts occupied by the troops, marines, and blue-jackets. The firing in the direction of the Pootung [eastern] side of the river has continued at intervals during the day. As we write the booming of distant guns reaches our ears, which are estimated at about five miles distant."

During the first week of February, any hope that the men at Sung-chiang might hold out against the Taipings dwindled.

And then came another unexpected report. Far from being overwhelmed by the rebels in their district, the Ward Corps had survived every Taiping attack; indeed, they had turned the final assault into a disaster for the soldiers of the Heavenly Kingdom. The Taiping commanders had thrown some 20,000 men at Sung-chiang, only to find that Ward, anticipating the move, had placed "masked" or hidden artillery batteries in the main path of the rebels' advance. When the Taipings had come within close range, these batteries opened fire. The Taipings suffered 2,300 casualties immediately. Reeling under the shock of concentrated artillery fire, the rebels were next assaulted by a strong detachment of Ward's infantry, who quickly seized between 700 and 800 prisoners. In the ensuing confusion, Ward was able to recapture many boats laden with arms and provisions that the rebels had taken during their occupation of the area. In all, it was a daring display of offense as defense, and the *Daily Shipping and Commercial News* did not overstate the issue by declaring that "the Taiping rebels have sustained a severe defeat, which may have a wholesome effect on the bands of marauders in the vicinity of the city and settlement of Shanghai."

On February 15 it was the turn of the *North China Herald,* Ward's old nemesis, to acknowledge his achievement:

> It would appear that during the week the [rebel] bands infesting the northern suburbs [of Shanghai] have either retired towards the coast, or what is more probable, made a westerly detour towards the south where a large body of Taiping insurgents has been hovering on the outskirts of Ming-hong between Shanghai and Sung-chiang, after having been defeated in their attack upon the latter city by the bravery and discipline of the Imperialist troops under the command of Colonel Ward—who has trained a regiment of fine able-bodied men in the European system of military tactics.

Gone forever were accusations of lunacy or criminality; for the remainder of his life, Ward would be treated with uniform respect, if not deference, in the pages of the *Herald.*

Ward's friend Augustus A. Hayes took note of this transformation in the attitude of Shanghai's Westerners with appropriate irony. "One day," he later recalled of that time,

> it was known that a powerful Rebel force was approaching Shanghai. Then came again the familiar call to arms, the preparations to receive women and children on board the steamers, the daily orders and bulletins.
> Then, however, followed something new and surprising. The Rebels had, we heard, been met and defeated with tremendous slaughter,—and by whom? By a native force, admirably drilled, equipped and disciplined, fighting by European tactics, and led to victory—complete, overwhelming victory against an enormous numerical superiority—by our lately despised American *filibustero*, General Ward. Public opinion changed at a jump. It must have been with a grim satisfaction that Ward awoke, the morning after this battle, to find himself famous.

Nothing in Ward's subsequent behavior indicated that he paid any more attention to the praise he received from Shanghai's Western citizens than he had to their insults. He secured payment for his troops, used his expanded contacts to procure more and better weapons, and continued to apply his energies to enlarging and drilling his corps at Sung-chiang. The attitude was an appropriate one, for, despite the kind words in the English-language papers, the distrust that official representatives of the Western powers, particularly the British, had always felt toward the commander of the Ward Corps remained intact following the successes near Sung-chiang. It would take more and greater victories to finally destroy those barriers.

The enthusiasm of Wu Hsü and Yang Fang for the new Ward Corps during the fall and winter of 1861, and the two men's confidence that the unit could play an important role in stemming the Taiping advance, were not universal among Chinese merchants and civil leaders in the port. The native elite of Kiangsu province especially tried to find other ways of bringing foreign power to bear on the rebel threat. Wu and Yang were, it should be remembered, Chekiang men, although they held positions of power in Shanghai; as such they were viewed with no little jealousy by many Kiangsu notables. This regional rivalry played a distinct part in prompting a powerful group of Kiangsu officials—most notably Feng Kuei-fen, a leading scholar from Soochow—to look beyond Wu and Yang's pet project for help.

In November 1861 some half-dozen of these Kiangsu men—including not only Feng Kuei-fen but Wu Yün, the Soochow official who had attempted to discredit Ward's victory at Sung-chiang in 1860—sent emissaries to Tseng Kuo-fan asking for assistance in meeting the Taiping threat in their province. Tseng replied that while he hoped to be able to dispatch an army to Shanghai soon, he could not yet spare troops for the job. The Kiangsu leaders, unimpressed by such outlandish and as yet unproved schemes as training Chinese soldiers to fight in the Western style, decided next to seek direct foreign military aid from the representatives of the Western powers in Shanghai. Specifically, they approached one of Great Britain's more seasoned representatives, Harry Parkes. Parkes had been one of the British officials whose capture and abuse had prompted the burning of the Summer Palace in 1860: His views on a coordinated Chinese-Western response to the Taiping threat were understandably skeptical. In cautiously declining the latest Chinese request that foreign regulars take the field against the rebels, Parkes fell in line with the attitude not only of British minister Frederick Bruce but of Western officials generally. The rebels might have been viewed with steadily decreasing sympathy by the foreign powers, but joint action and offensive operations by their regulars remained steps too long for any of them to take.

The Westerners, characteristically, had their own ideas about meeting the rebel challenge. Early in January 1862, a Defense Committee was formed by the Shanghai Municipal Council, and this committee quickly decided that, while they did not wish to act in concert with imperial Chinese forces, all expenses incurred by foreigners in their efforts to protect the port should be met by their Chinese hosts. There was a mercenary quality to this proposal, one that had previously made the idea unacceptable to the British Foreign Office. But times had, apparently, changed, and, even more important, the Chinese were anxious to pay. As always in the Chinese bureaucracy, an official organ for the disbursement of these funds had to be established, and soon Governor Hsüeh Huan had called into existence the United Defense Bureau. The bureau had four Chinese executives whose task was to coordinate payment and military logistics in Shanghai with representatives of the foreign powers.

The Chinese were enthusiastic about the bureau, believing that it would inevitably draw the foreigners into offensive action against the rebels in the interior. With this end in mind, the bureau was authorized to raise enough funds to pay and supply as many as ten thousand foreign regulars. But on January 12, during a gathering at the British consulate, the Chinese representatives learned just how unrealistic their plans were. The French, with Prosper Giquel as interpreter, initially seemed obliging: They were ready to defend not only the foreign settlements but the Chinese city as well and, beyond that, to engage the Taipings outside Shanghai. But the British quickly squelched such ideas. Despite the misgivings of Admiral Hope, British diplomatic representatives stuck to Frederick Bruce's clearly delineated line of defensive measures within Shanghai. Even defense of the Chinese city was not considered important or wise. Rightly suspecting that the "United" Defense Bureau was a Chinese contrivance aimed at getting foreigners to do the work of imperial forces, the British remained cool.

Besides inadvisable, the Kiangsu leadership's plans for foreign intervention remained academic so long as Peking refused to allow foreign soldiers to operate in the Chinese interior. The imperial government's concern over this matter had not vanished. Tseng Kuo-fan was still bitterly opposed to the idea, convinced that if the foreigners were successful in such operations they would only use their victories to gain greater influence in internal matters of state and if they were unsuccessful it would "invite ridicule." But Tseng's views were now opposed, and effectively, by the Kiangsu men, who spoke through Hsüeh Huan. Late in January, Hsüeh memorialized to the throne, summarizing the opinions of the Kiangsu elite by reviewing other cases during which Chinese imperial dynasties such as the Han and the T'ang had used foreign warriors for their own purposes.

Great as their respect for the views of Tseng Kuo-fan was, Tz'u-hsi and Prince Kung were both impressed by Hsüeh Huan's argument. In addition, Tseng had unconsciously undercut his own case by capturing Anking: The Chinese imperialists no longer looked utterly incapable of meeting the rebel threat, and the prospect of accepting foreign help in the treaty ports and perhaps even in the interior was far less humiliating. The Empress Dowager Tz'u-hsi and Prince Kung both paused to reflect on the subject, and their reflections were influenced by events in the Shanghai region: Ward's successful engagement of the Chung Wang's advancing army offered additional hope that the Chinese could accept some kind of foreign aid without mortgaging their integrity.

Seeing that the scheme of training Chinese soldiers to fight a modern war now had political value, the British quite predictably reacted to Ward's success by vigorously inserting themselves into the training business. Here was a job that was suddenly something more than the fantasy of a handful of Western free-lances, was, in fact, far too important, and too full of potential influence, to be left to men such as Ward and Tardif de Moidrey. Ever able and willing to shift course drastically, the British established their own training ground for Chinese troops at Tientsin in February 1862.

The driving force behind the project was General Sir Charles Staveley, who had commanded a brigade in John Michel's division during the Peking campaign and who was shortly to assume Michel's duties in Shanghai. The two men were very different: Michel had experience in unconventional warfare and respect for those who could wage it well, even if such men, like Ward, lacked formal training or experience in a national army. In addition, Michel was by nature gregarious and not disposed to condemn men from Ward's walk of life out of simple prejudice. Staveley, on the other hand, represented the more unfortunate type of British officer abroad: skilled and undeniably brave, but ambitious, aloof, and narrow-minded. Staveley's sister had married the brother of Charles George Gordon, the young captain of engineers who had so forthrightly recorded the activities of Allied troops at the Summer Palace, and Gordon served as Staveley's chief of engineers. Observing his brother-in-law with the same careful eye that had watched the burning of the Summer Palace, Gordon pronounced that "[t]he worst feature in his character is his selfishness & a certain want of consideration for others."

Staveley's training operation at Tientsin went well, and he became rather inordinately proud of it—too proud to believe that any American mercenary could do the job as well or better. Nor was Staveley the only Englishman convinced that the task of supplying China with modern armed forces was one for which only Queen Victoria's officers were fit. Soon after the Tientsin program was launched, a former head of the Imperial Chinese Customs Service, Horatio Nelson Lay—like Staveley a remarkably arrogant and ambitious man—sketched out a plan for the creation of a modern Chinese navy: a fleet of British gunboats, officered by British sailors, answering only those orders of the Chinese government that Lay himself believed advisable. The project was doomed to failure; British arrogance had for once exceeded the bounds of possibility. But its mere conception was nonetheless revealing.

Thus there was, in the beginning of 1862, more than ample reason for Ward to keep a very watchful eye on British representatives and soldiers in the Shanghai region. This atmosphere of mutual distrust was heightened by news from the United States. That Great Britain had been flirting—whether capriciously or not—with recognition of the Confederate States of America was well-known, and late in January word was received in Shanghai that in November an American warship had seized two Confederate emissaries traveling on board a British mail packet, the *Trent,* and sent them as prisoners to Boston. The British government had immediately demanded a formal apology for what was an illegal act, and war fever had been whipped up on both sides of the Atlantic. The U.S. government eventually disavowed the action, and the British were placated, but not before the effects of what came to be called the *Trent* affair had been felt in every corner of the globe where American and British citizens lived and carried on business together.

In Shanghai British officers were heard to say openly that if war between the United States and Great Britain did come, Her Majesty's naval forces intended to seize and even destroy American assets and property. The situation momentarily drew Ward's attention away from the fighting west of Shanghai, and his subsequent actions revealed the loyalty that he still felt toward the nation he had disavowed a year earlier. At the time of the *Trent* affair, Ward remarked to A. A. Hayes: "I was an American before I was a Chinaman; and these Englishmen will find it out." Ward then confided "to a few confidential friends" the details of a characteristically daring plan that was to be implemented in the event of war. The scheme involved not only his Chinese troops but a group of coastal pirates whose acquaintance Ward had made during his various tours on coastal and river steamers and whom he now occasionally paid for their services and support. Hayes later recalled that Ward

determined to mass, quietly and secretly as he could easily do, a large body of his disciplined troops at a town some twenty miles distant, from which a forced march could readily be made without any warning. Entirely under his control was a guild of what one might politely call privateers, or junks manned by desperadoes of a piratical class thoroughly armed. A large body of these privateers he proposed ordering into the river before the settlement, and distributing among the few naval and many merchant vessels flying the British flag. On board such junks is carried a fearful engine of destruction known by a name unmentionable to ears polite [stinkpots]. It is a species of hand grenade of earthenware, easily broken, and filled with a composition not only possessing the destructive qualities of Greek fire, but capable of suffocating those among whom it strikes. It is this which places any vessel, however heavily armed, in a dangerous position when at anything like close quarters with a Chinese pirate. On the day, grimly said General Ward, on which his British friends should begin the seizure of the property of Americans, the latter would have warning from him of what was to happen during the ensuing night. Of such happenings it was needful for him to enter into but a few details. They were summed up with the quiet remark that the next morning would see the British portion of Shanghai "a heap of smouldering and looted ruins."

Though extreme, Ward's plan was wholly feasible: The Ward Corps had already grown to a sufficient size to be able to engage the limited number of British troops in Shanghai. All that was needed was determination and recklessness, and, as Hayes concluded, "To any one who should read this statement, and pronounce it overstrained or fanciful, I would simply remark that the reader did not know General Ward."

The crisis over the *Trent* affair quickly passed when news was received that the United States and Great Britain had agreed on terms that avoided conflict. But animosity between Englishmen and Americans in Shanghai—indeed in all the treaty ports—as a result of Britain's attitude toward the American Civil War did not fade. Hayes noted that the United States had only one warship in China's waters, "and no one of her officers will forget to his dying day the savage manner in which the rules forbidding her hospitality were enforced." The British residents of Shanghai seemed to take delight in the Union's dismal fortunes during the first years of the war: "Mail after mail brought venomously garbled accounts of Union disasters. It was hard at times for Americans to bear up against the temporary depression caused by such news, and by the atmosphere about them."

In fact, the gap between Ward and the British community might well have remained unbridgeable but for one factor: Ward's rapidly evolving personal relationship with Admiral Hope. The events of February 1862 seem to have been critical in hastening the development of what would become a fast friendship. Since his failed second mission to Nanking in December, Hope had been longing for a chance to personally vent his anger over what he considered rebel perfidy against the Taipings. But he had been restrained by his diplomatic superiors and by Peking's uneasiness at the thought of using Western troops. It is therefore natural that he should have felt a certain vicarious satisfaction when the Ward Corps attacked the Chung Wang's legions in precisely the way the admiral himself had hoped to do: as a flying column. More important, Hope correctly perceived that the Ward Corps could serve as a useful blind. By acting as support troops for the disciplined Chinese, British and French regulars might take the field without being accused of direct intervention against the Taipings.

Hope's reasons for cultivating Ward's friendship were, then, apparent. But for his part, Ward remained wary of the man whose officers had twice arrested and imprisoned him, and he made no secret of this resentment during conversations with Hope in February. Anxious to put an end to such feelings, Hope assured Ward that "[b]ygones are bygones, you are on the right road now & you shall have all the support I can give you." Words, of course, counted little with Ward, but Hope soon backed his pledges up not only by making efforts to see that Ward gained access to a greater variety of British arms and supplies but by personally accompanying his former antagonist, at great risk, on one of Ward's intelligence-gathering missions in the field.

On February 16 Hope and Ward disguised themselves as a pair of recreational hunters and journeyed north from Shanghai. Following the eastern bank of the Huang-pu River through the Pootung peninsula and venturing into rebel-held territory, they reached their destination: the town of Kao-ch'iao. Like Wu-sung, Kao-ch'iao was a gateway to the Huang-pu, immensely important to the security of Shanghai. But while Wu-sung had been denied to the rebels, largely through the daring of the Ward Corps, Kao-ch'iao had been taken with relative ease when the Chung Wang reappeared in eastern Kiangsu. The seizure of Kao-ch'iao heightened the likelihood that the Taipings would close off the Huang-pu and hasten the capitulation of Shanghai. In acknowledgment of the town's importance, the rebel commanders had moved an unusually strong force of some ten thousand men into its entrenchments (Kao-ch'iao had no formal wall), then made preparations to support the movements of the other Taiping columns to the south.

Dislodging the Kao-ch'iao garrison was a formidable proposition, but, recognizing that it was vital to the survival of Shanghai, Hope and Ward prepared for the job. Maintaining their hunting charade, the two onetime adversaries carefully observed and analyzed the fortifications that the Taipings had constructed. As nonchalantly as they had come, the irrepressible Western soldiers then left Kao-ch'iao and returned to Shanghai. Armies were martialed in preparation for what would be a crucial test, not only of the Ward Corps but of Shanghai's Western regulars and of the ability of Ward, Hope, and Protet to work together effectively in the field.

Admiral Hope would later explain his unprecedented—and unauthorized—decision to support the Ward Corps in its advance against Kao-ch'iao by telling the Lords of the British Admiralty that on "every occasion on which I have reported the state of Shanghai since my return here, it has been my duty to bring the devastation and atrocities committed by the rebels in its immediate vicinity very prominently under their Lordships' notice." Stating that the rebel occupation of Kao-ch'iao made it likely that the free access to Shanghai by trading and supply ships would be "impeded, if not altogether stopped," Hope asserted that he "considered the case to be one calling for my interference, in which opinion Admiral Protet entirely concurred."

Hope further supported his position by describing the activities of the new Ward Corps, the first such mention made in British naval dispatches: "During the last 6 months, a Chinese force of about 1500 men, to be raised to 4000, has been embodied, armed and disciplined under the authority of the Viceroy of the province by Colonel Ward, an American, at Sung-chiang, a walled town about twenty-five miles southwest of Shanghai, and a district of country in its vicinity has been placed under his charge." Ward had, said Hope, been ordered by Hsüeh Huan to take Kao-ch'iao. But because of his perilous position at Sung-chiang, Ward could only spare 600 men for the job. British and French "interference" (a unique and suitably vague term) was therefore doubly justified: on the one hand to ensure freedom of trade, on the other as support for the only genuinely effective imperial unit in the area.

On the afternoon of February 20, 336 British sailors and marines (Sir John Michel declined to dispatch any British army units), along with 50 or 60 French troops, accompanied a detachment of 500 men from the Ward Corps down the Huang-pu. Ahead of the expedition sailed the British warship *Coromandel,* commanded by Captain George Willes and carrying Chaloner Alabaster—the intrepid British consular aide and interpreter—as an observer. Alabaster later reported that on the evening of the twentieth the *Coromandel* "got to within a quarter of a mile of the village [Kao-ch'iao], to European ideas a large town, full of banners, and strongly stockaded, and retired without molestation, observing a considerable number of murdered villagers along the way." According to Dr. Macgowan, "every house" in Kao-ch'iao was "pierced for musketry," while coffins, "emptied of their contents and filled with earth, together with trunks of trees, rendered approach difficult."

The expeditionary force was joined during the night by some hundred additional French troops, as well as another hundred of Ward's men. With the Frenchmen came two howitzers as well as Admirals Hope and Protet, who immediately assumed command of their respective contingents. Ward, Hope, and Protet then laid out an order of battle that would become a blueprint for future operations. To avoid international complications, the Allied troops would be held in reserve, offering support through long-range rifle, artillery, and rocket fire (the British had brought six-pounder rockets along for the occasion). The Ward Corps, meanwhile, would act as storming troops and bear the brunt of the actual fighting. At dawn on the twenty-first, Ward led his units into position and wasted no time in assaulting the rebel fortifications.

Ward's men, wrote Alabaster, began their attack "by driving the rebels out of some detached houses, and checking the advance of a strong party sent to [Kao-ch'iao's] relief." The French detachment had gotten their two howitzers into place and commenced fire along with the British rocket battery, directing their fire at "the place where the banners seemed thickest." Ward's disciplined Chinese troops kept up "an incessant fire along the line which was warmly returned." Ward's tactical goal was reminiscent of his first success at Sung-chiang: to seal his objective off, seize one gate or point of entry, and then turn the rebel fortifications into a trap, from which many of the defenders would be unable to escape. With the help of volley fire from British marines, Ward and his men managed to seize a long bridge or causeway that ran from the rebel stockade back into the town itself. This causeway, Edward Forester recalled,

> was turned into a slaughter-pen. The enemy were packed in so closely, and we were at such short range, that our fire did terrible

execution. So demoralized were the rebels, that no attempt was made to resist when we reached the gates. . . . The rout was complete. Not only was the enemy in wild retreat, but their panic had spread through the entire army. At the south gate they fell over each other in a frantic endeavor to escape. But once outside only the shores of the Yellow sea awaited them, and upon its sands Death waited with open arms. Our handful of men pressed them so fiercely that the rebels had no time to take to their boats. In despair they leaped into the water, to be drowned by wholesale.

This much of Forester's account of the battle of Kao-ch'iao, while colorful, is corroborated by other eyewitnesses; Forester, however, went on to claim that Ward "feared" failure at the causeway and that he, Forester, rallied the men to victory. Furthermore, he made no mention of the part played in the battle by Burgevine, who actually led one of the first units into the city and received a rather serious head wound, which he merely stanched before proceeding with his attack. Forester's craving for glory again did heavy damage to his credibility.

When the Allied detachments finally joined Ward's men inside Kao-ch'iao, wrote Alabaster, they were "unable to come up with the rebels, although we saw them retreating in the distance." In addition to the many prisoners taken, the attackers liberated a large number of chained coolies who had been impressed into the rebel service and who, along with local villagers, took no little delight in revenging themselves on the Taiping captives after the battle.

Fire was set to the town, although its origin was uncertain. Alabaster claimed that the rebels had lit buildings as they abandoned their positions, although others contended that Hope's troops put the torch to a store of grain they discovered. The men of the Ward Corps were allowed to loot, as their contract with their commander had stipulated. But Ward interceded to limit the abuse of Taiping prisoners. The day after the battle, corps commissary C. J. Ashley discovered that imperial commanders in Shanghai intended the wholesale slaughter of a large group of captured Taipings. In Dr. Macgowan's phrase, Ashley "hastened to inform Ward, who caused the butchery to cease."

The battle for Kao-ch'iao had not been protracted, but it was, as

195

Alabaster acknowledged, "very sharp, the rebels making a very good defense; but Ward's men, till they got into the town, when dispersed to loot, behaved admirably, and the loss, exclusive of Chinese, was only one man killed, and three or four scratched." The Ward Corps's casualties were also slight, given their role in the assault: by some accounts seven men killed, by others ten, and between forty and fifty men wounded. "The Chinese troops," Hope told the Admiralty, "took the village today in very good style, many of them behaving with much gallantry, supported by the French and English force which was not seriously engaged." This last fact was particularly important, for much as Ward had demonstrated that his men could function in smooth conjunction with Allied troops, he had also shown that they could undertake major operations independent of them.

The attackers learned from their prisoners that the Chung Wang himself had been expected in Kao-ch'iao that very day, and that the rebel general had intended to launch an assault on Shanghai from the north. Ward's and Hope's move had been timely indeed. "I am in high hopes," Hope wrote, "that the severe check the rebels have experienced will prevent their being seen, in the immediate vicinity of Shanghai, for some time to come." Hope's prediction took no stock of the fact that the Chung Wang was now in personal command of the rebel forces in the area. Never a man to back away from a "check" such as he sustained at Kao-ch'iao, the Chung Wang only became more determined to realize his goal of taking Shanghai. But it was now apparent that he would face far greater obstacles than had been placed in his path in 1860, for there were forces in the field in February 1862 that could and apparently would hamper any rebel approach to the city's walls rather than wait inside Shanghai for a Taiping assault.

For at least one American, the battle of Kao-ch'iao was a surprising, and in all likelihood shocking, introduction to life in the Shanghai region and the activities of the Ward Corps. George Frederick Seward was a nephew of the American secretary of state and had recently, at the age of twenty-one, been appointed American consul in Shanghai. On February 21 he was aboard a coastal steamer that had sailed out of Hong Kong bound for his new post, and, when the ship passed into the mouth of the Huang-pu River, Seward was afforded an excellent view of the violent proceedings ashore. Kao-ch'iao also brought Ward to the attention of American minister Anson Burlingame: "Admiral Hope," Burlingame later told Secretary of State Seward, "informs me that he was astonished at the courage of the Chinese, led by Col. Ward, at Kao-ch'iao. It is thought by many that they are superior to the Sepoys and that they, when properly instructed, will not only be capable of defending themselves but equal to aggressive war."

Reaction to the Kao-ch'iao victory in Western Shanghai was perhaps best exemplified by the fact that, in describing the event, the *North China Herald*—which had once openly hoped for Ward's death—used the word *gallantly* in describing the actions of the corps.

Kao-ch'iao netted Ward considerable attention from soldiers and advocates on the Taiping side of the Chinese civil war as well. Augustus Lindley, still loyally serving the rebel cause, later wrote bitterly that

Admiral Hope, in his attack upon the Taipings, associated himself with one Ward, an American filibuster, in the service of the Manchus. Previous to this, and to the Admiral's unsuccessful attempt to juggle the Taiping authorities into another agreement not to approach Shanghai, the said Ward was persecuted and reviled very fiercely; but no sooner did the Admiral and his colleagues think it necessary to pull in the same boat, than the Yankee filibuster became their pattern and ally. The whilom *rowdie* companion of *ci-devant* General Walker, of Nicaraguan memory, mercenary leader of a band of Anglo-Saxon freebooters in Manchu pay, and sometime fugitive from English marines sent to weed his ruffians of their countrymen, suddenly became the friend and ally of the British and French Admirals, Generals and Consuls. The surprise of Ward can only have been equalled by his gratification upon finding his very questionable presence, and still more doubtful pursuits, patronized and imitated.

In England, Colonel William H. Sykes—a former Indian army officer and now member of Parliament for Aberdeen who was one of the last Taiping partisans in the House of Commons—condemned Admiral Hope's support of Ward and the participation of British troops in anti-

Taiping actions: "A Christian's blood runs cold," said Sykes, "at the contemplation of such slaughter of human beings, who earnestly ask to be considered our friends." But the public mood in Britain had shifted irreversibly, and the London *Times*'s assessment of Sykes was indicative: "[T]hat assiduous member [is] a standing warning against a superstition which has long existed in the House of Commons, that because a man has been in India thirty years ago, he must necessarily know something about China in the present day."

The day after Kao-ch'iao, Admiral Hope scouted the territory around the town and found it largely deserted by the Taipings. Presumably, he made this excursion in Ward's company; at any rate, the two held important talks following the battle concerning their future strategy. On returning to Shanghai, Hope revealed the essence of their conclusions in a letter to Frederick Bruce. Telling the British minister that he had "considered it necessary" to lend "certain moral support" to the Ward Corps, Hope went on to

> strongly recommend that the French and English commanders should be required by yourself and M. Bourboulon [the French minister] to free the country from rebels within a line commencing at Chia-ting on the Yangtze above Wu-sung, through Ch'ing-p'u to Sung-chiang on the [Huang-pu] River, and thence across to a walled town opposite on the Yangtze, by which means a district of country amply sufficient for the support of Shanghai would be protected, and the town secured from the present state of chronic panic so detrimental to trade.

In the months to come, this idea would gain notoriety as "the thirty-mile radius," and Hope's concluding remarks to Bruce clearly revealed the plan's author: "Colonel Ward, upon whose experience of the Chinese I am disposed to place very considerable reliance, assures me that if Imperialist garrisons were placed in the towns I have named, with the troops under his command employed as a flying column, he could effectually prevent the return of the rebels within the limits I have named, even if they were disposed to attempt it—an event very unlikely to occur."

Once again, Hope underestimated the Taipings; they were indeed "disposed to attempt" the clearance of the thirty-mile radius. And both he and Ward overestimated the ability of imperial Chinese army units in the region to garrison captured towns. None of this, however, detracted from the soundness of Ward's idea or from the noteworthy fact that he was now in a position to advise his former antagonists. The turnaround in his fortunes was, however, just beginning.

On February 27 General John Michel, who was in the process of resigning his command of British army units in China, accompanied Admiral Hope on a visit to Sung-chiang. Michel was preparing a list of recommendations for the British government and for his successor, Sir Charles Staveley, regarding the Taipings and future British military policy. His purpose in visiting Sung-chiang was to determine whether the Ward Corps should play a role during the coming months of what now appeared unavoidable conflict with the rebels. Ward obligingly brought his men out to parade before the British commanders, and, as Michel reported to Frederick Bruce the following day:

> I saw one regiment of 700 or 800 men in line, and some 300 or 400 others at drill. I examined them with some minuteness, and can judge pretty well what they are worth. Their arms are good percussion firelocks, in very good order. The regiment in line stood for some time on parade as steady as an indifferent European regiment. They know some company and some battalion drill, and also our manual and platoon exercises; they charged in line very fairly. They were all clothed in a good serviceable uniform, with turbans, and I understand are paid regularly 8½ dollars per month. . . . I am of [the] opinion that 1,000 men of this description and thus drilled, are quite competent to deal with many thousands of rebels, and that an augmentation of this force would enable Colonel Ward to clear the country by degrees. I consider this force, if duly supported, the military nucleus of better things. . . . I believe that no better means could be found than the Chinese Government handing over to this officer, or aiding him to enlist some 8,000 or 10,000 men, and perhaps more eventually—in fact, such a number as he may be able to officer and drill; that funds be placed at his disposal to pay for such

troops regularly; and that he be aided in procuring arms, ammunition and guns.

Michel's perception of imperial Chinese officials and commanders in the region was just as insightful:

> The Viceroys of districts will of course be unwilling to hand him over any portion of their rabble (called soldiers), as probably they pocket much money which is supposed to be spent in providing troops, arms, and ammunition, besides, perhaps, from their jealousy of this new element. Colonel Ward should therefore be invested with some large powers. . . . I consider that soon a prestige would attach to his army, which would do as much as the fighting of his troops, and by extending the system the silk districts would be recovered, and eventually the rebel head-quarters [Nanking] would be gained.

Michel's recommendations regarding Ward personally were perhaps the most sensitive portion of his communication, and he seems to have known it: He took care in underlining that "Colonel Ward's interest will be so strongly enlisted in carrying out this matter energetically, that whatever he may be, and whatever feeling there may be as to trusting him to any great extent, I am convinced that no dread of that sort should deter the Chinese Government from giving him frank, energetic and real support; not that support which will be given by jealous squeezing Viceroys, but direct from Peking, supported energetically by your Excellency."

Ward's character and his ultimate purposes were serious concerns not only of British diplomatic officials but of Minister Burlingame of the United States as well. Burlingame already had knowledge of the Ward Corps's second-in-command, Henry Burgevine, who had been in Washington during Burlingame's terms in Congress. Early in March, Burlingame made arrangements to meet Ward himself and to sound him out, sending a report on these encounters to Secretary of State Seward on March 7.

Ward was, said Burlingame,

an American to whom my attention was first called by Admiral Sir James Hope who wished to introduce him to me and who commended him warmly for his courage and his skill. He is instructing the Chinese in the use of European weapons and has about two thousand of them (Chinese) trained whom he has led in a most desperate manner, successfully, in several recent battles. I know nothing of him save what I have learned from Sir James Hope[,] the Chinese and himself. He says he was born in Salem Massachusetts— went to sea when a boy—became mate of a ship and then was a Texas Ranger—California gold miner—instructor in the Mexican service—was with Walker, for which he was outlawed by his Government; at the Crimea and then joined the Chinese army where he has gradually risen to influence and power. He is now their best officer and for his recent successes has been recommended by the Chinese and the English for greater promotion. He says he is a loyal American and though a Chinese by adoption he desires above all things that his country shall have its full weight in the affairs of China.

In the weeks to come, Burlingame would be as personally won over by Ward as Admiral Hope had been. But while Burlingame's friendship would be of enormous emotional importance to Ward, it was Hope who provided the material assistance Ward very much needed to expand his corps. On March 5 Hope wrote to the Admiralty to say that while he had once believed that the training of Chinese soldiers in modern military methods was a job for French and British regular officers, he now considered it "clear that the Force organising under Colonel Ward is very preferable for this purpose in virtue of its character being more completely Chinese and therefore more calculated to lead to that self dependence on the part of the government without which China will never be restored to peace." Hope then took the extreme step of asking that the British government—using imperial Chinese intermediaries— make available to Ward "at cost price . . . such guns, Arms, Ammunition and other military stores as can be spared to him both here and in India." In addition, Ward and his Chinese and Western business partners should be allowed to purchase arms and especially river steamers in England. Should any "legal difficulties" be encountered because of the Neutrality

Ordinance, "they should be removed by Order from the Foreign Office."

Far as he had gone in his recommendations, Hope went one step farther: British soldiers and noncommissioned officers who wished to join the Ward Corps should be allowed to do so. The benefits of adopting all these measures would soon become apparent: "I have little doubt that at the expiration of a few months [Ward] will be in possession of Soochow, will have cleared this province including the Silk districts[,] and will have so tranquillised the Country in this vicinity as to render the occupation of Shanghai by Foreign Troops unnecessary."

The imperial Chinese government was still trying to come to grips with the idea of using Western troops to counter the Taipings in and around the treaty ports when word of the battle of Kao-ch'iao was received in the Forbidden City. Peking had just announced that since there were inadequate imperial forces in Shanghai to meet the new advance of the Taipings, Chinese officials in that city would be permitted to make use of Western troops. And a week later Tseng Kuo-fan had reluctantly accepted the idea of permitting Anglo-French forces to operate in the treaty ports, although he continued to vigorously resist the notion of foreign troops campaigning in the interior. But on February 25 Hsüeh Huan memoralized to the throne and by introducing Frederick Townsend Ward and reviewing his career presented the imperial government with a risky but potentially very effective way out of its dilemma.

Hsüeh began by acquainting the throne with the details of Ward's arrival in China and his early successes in 1860 and went on to describe his victories in January and February 1862, including his scouting mission with Hope before Kao-ch'iao. The Kiangsu governor's tone was uniformly respectful, and he took every opportunity to remind Peking that Ward had long ago petitioned to become a Chinese subject—a petition that had yet to be answered by the throne:

> Wu Hsü attests that Ward excels in both courage and intelligence and knows military affairs well, a fact that is shown by his effective training of soldiers. It is a rule that all foreigners who are not governed by the consuls are within Chinese jurisdiction; Ward

has acknowledged in a written statement that he wants to be a Chinese subject and to change to the Chinese style of clothes. [In Manchu China, the wearing of native dress and the shaving of the forehead were vital symbols of a foreigner's acceptance of Chinese cultural superiority.] Considering the above factors, it seems we should not discourage Ward's zeal to submit to the Chinese way of life. This is the whole story of this matter, and I hereby petition the Throne to grant Ward the fourth rank [mandarin's] button and let him continue to train soldiers at Sung-chiang and cooperate with the government troops in fighting the rebels.

Hsüeh did not mention the fact that Ward's "written statement" that he wished to "submit to the Chinese way of life" had been made largely in order to avoid prosecution and prolonged imprisonment by the British. Rather, Ward was portrayed as an earnest supplicant, one who richly deserved not only official recognition as a Chinese subject but elevation to the status of fourth-rank mandarin. (The "button" of which Hsüeh spoke was a small colored sphere that was worn in the crown of every mandarin's cap. Colors denoted rank: The fourth-rank button was dark blue.) Hsüeh was well aware that both Ward and Burgevine— who soon followed Ward's lead by applying for Chinese citizenship, and whom Hsüeh also recommended for fourth-rank status—had manifold reasons for requesting Chinese citizenship. The two men hoped that official recognition from Peking would further protect them from foreign interference as well as clear the way for a dramatic expansion of the size and operations of the Ward Corps. Their enthusiasm for "the Chinese way of life," as they had experienced it, was limited at best. But Hsüeh, along with Wu Hsü and Yang Fang, shared Ward's desire to make the funding and operations of the corps easier by gaining imperial sanction, and he painted his picture of the young commander in the best possible light.

The effort brought results. In a responding decree, the Emperor T'ung-chih—or rather, the Empress Dowager Tz'u-hsi and Prince Kung—declared that Ward had "turned out of admiration toward Chinese customs and with a sincere heart is helpful and obedient, surely worthy of admiration and esteem." Ward was granted the fourth-rank button as well as a peacock feather for his new mandarin's cap; Burgevine soon received the dark blue button as well. The event caused much comment in the Western communities in the treaty ports, and when word of Ward's transformation made its way back to London, the *Times* took note of it in its "Latest Intelligence" column with the unembellished and rather bemused headline "Colonel Ward has been created a Mandarin."

Further rewards were to come. But Ward and Burgevine had little time to concern themselves with ceremonial machinations, for the end of February brought new emergencies in the field. The severe check that the Taipings sustained north of Shanghai led them to redouble their efforts to close on the port from the west and south. Early in March, Ward turned to meet these threats. The corps—its movements now carefully followed by Western and Chinese officials not only in Shanghai but in Peking as well—met the approaching rebel armies with typical audacity and gave the Taipings additional lessons in the virtues of Western military methods.

During the week following the battle for Kao-ch'iao, Admiral Hope embarked on more trips into the districts around Shanghai, ostensibly, as the *North China Herald* put it, "for the purpose of reconnoitring on the Pootung or east bank of the [Huang-pu] river." Yet given Hope's character and behavior, it is difficult to dispute Augustus Lindley's claim that the admiral "went roving about the country for a week in search of some one to fight. His warlike spirit was gratified at a place named Hsiao-t'ang, in the vicinity of Ming-hong (nearly twenty miles away from Shanghai), a fortified village occupied by several thousand Taipings."

Hope was again accompanied by Chaloner Alabaster, who provided another eyewitness account. Apparently Hope, in the process of "reconnoitring," was fired at by the Taipings from behind their very considerable fortifications at Hsiao-t'ang. The admiral then determined to show the rebels, as Alabaster put it, "that they could not fire on Europeans with impunity." (The fact that Europeans had already attacked the rebels with similar impunity and were thus understandably viewed as enemies was conveniently ignored.) Hope and Admiral Protet again loaded HMS *Coromandel* and six gunboats with weapons and men, and on Friday, February 28, a battery of mountain howitzers and six-pounder rocket tubes was landed about three miles from Hsiao-t'ang. A pair of British naval guns and two French howitzers, the same models that had been brought to Kao-ch'iao, soon followed. During the night a detachment of French soldiers who were guarding the guns were surprised by a party of lantern-bearing Taipings, who came to get a look at the Western artillery and were easily driven off.

Toward dawn on March 1, Admiral Hope landed with 35 artillerymen and 350 sailors and marines. The first group was headed by Captain George Willes—who had observed the Taipings at Wu-sung and then commanded the *Coromandel* at Kao-ch'iao—and the second by Captain John Holland of the Royal Marines. Admiral Protet arrived next with 300 Frenchmen. The two Allied commanders were then joined, said the *Herald,* "on the spot by Colonel Ward and a detachment of his disciplined Chinese," numbering about 700. The combined force proceeded to march on Hsiao-t'ang, which in most accounts was said to be defended by 5,000 to 6,000 Taipings. They arrived at the town just before 8:00 A.M.

Hsiao-t'ang's defenses were much like Kao-ch'iao's and indeed were typical of most Chinese entrenchments. Described by the *Herald* correspondent as being "of a very formidable nature," they consisted at their perimeter of several alternating rows of sharpened wooden stakes and deep trenches studded with pointed sprigs of bamboo. Behind these rows was a fifteen-foot earthwork topped by gun emplacements and a barricade constructed of "boxes filled with earth and stones, coffins, bags of cotton, sandbags, tables, and furniture—in fact everything that could be stuck together to form a barricade, thickly loopholed for musketry—a place that could not be stormed without the loss of a great many men, unless assisted by artillery."

The expeditionary force halted some five hundred yards from these defenses. Curiously, there was no scattered, inaccurate musket fire or defiant screaming coming from Hsiao-t'ang. Nor was there the usual collection of bright banners proudly displayed. "At first," said the *Herald* correspondent, "it was supposed that they had evacuated the place, when parties of skirmishers from Ward's corps sent to the right, fearlessly crept up under cover of the graves, and soon began to exchange shots with the enemy, upon which all doubt as to their having evacuated the place was removed."

Exchanges of fire suddenly flared up all along the line. Hope and Admiral Protet held the left side of the Allied position, while the Ward Corps attacked from positions on the right. "A shell or two was then thrown in," said the *Herald,* "which proved to the rebels that their foreign assailants were in earnest." The Taipings answered with a hail of small and long arms fire, as well as a few rounds from some light guns. On the left, British marines steadily approached the rebel positions. But they were outpaced by Ward's men, who worked their way around the corner of the defenses on the right in order to cut off the Taipings' escape route to the south.

Hsüeh Huan later informed Peking that Ward—as always at the head of his troops, urging them on with his rattan cane—"was wounded at seven points on his body" as he fought his way through the rows of rebel trenches and stakes. Despite superior numbers, a strong defensive position, and unquestioned bravery, the rebels could not match the Allied force in discipline, quality of arms, or mastery of modern skirmishing tactics. The British naval guns eventually opened a serious breach in the Taiping lines, and at this, said Alabaster, the "place was taken by assault; Ward's men getting in at one corner immediately after we got in at another, and the rebels getting jammed in a street, there was immense slaughter." The Taipings attempted to flee, but, as the *Herald* recorded, "Some of Colonel Ward's men had got round on the other side, and were in hot pursuit." Hsüeh Huan recorded that meanwhile, inside the town, "Ward continued to lead his army in the fight, burning the rebels' barracks, demolishing the rebels' fortifications and killing countless rebels. . . . [E]ven when he was wounded, he did not retreat, and eventually wiped out the rebels' camp." British and French troops poured into the town along with the balance of the Ward Corps, and after some bitter hand-to-hand fighting the battle came to an end.

Nearly a thousand Taipings had fallen, along with three or four

Europeans serving alongside them. Several hundred more rebels were taken prisoner. The British and French had lost one man killed and some twenty wounded, and Ward's losses were similarly light. One of his fifty wounded, however, was a heavy blow. Burgevine, like Ward, had been consistently forward in the fight, inspiring his Chinese soldiers to impressive acts of courage. The *Herald* wrote that "[a]s for the Chinese organized under Colonel Ward, they seemed to know no fear, and, perhaps, exposed themselves too much." Certainly Burgevine did: Hsüeh Huan noted in his memorial to the throne that during the street fighting "some rebels hid in a house, and when Burgevine broke in, he was wounded, a bullet hitting him on his right leg, penetrating his belly and coming out his left leg. He was rescued and sent back." In fact, the Taiping musket ball that struck Burgevine made a clean hole about half an inch in diameter through his pelvis. Burgevine at first insisted on continuing his military duties and thus aggravated what was already a very serious wound. He would never fully recover from the injury, although he was to spend most of the spring and summer of 1862 trying. In addition, the wound gave Burgevine what he needed least: an additional reason to drink. By attempting to ease the chronic pain that tormented him for the rest of his life with alcohol, the Carolinian heightened the erratic and volatile side of his character to an eventually tragic extent.

Those Taiping soldiers who were able to escape Hsiao-t'ang fell back on the town of Nan-ch'iao, a few miles to the south. But when elements of the Allied expeditionary force appeared in pursuit, the rebels continued their flight by moving northwest and regrouping with the much larger Taiping army that was occupying Ch'ing-p'u. Clearly, the main rebel threat to Shanghai was now emanating from the west. During the days following Hsiao-t'ang, this threat was demonstrated when the imperialist commander Li Heng-sung—reportedly spurred on by the striking success and rising fame of the Ward Corps—martialed his Green Standard troops and attempted to check the Taiping advance at the village of Ssu-ching, on the line from Ch'ing-p'u to Shanghai. Given the quality of the Taiping army in Ch'ing-p'u, the outcome was predictable: By the second week of March, Li's army was surrounded and cut off. Ward, despite the multiple wounds he had received at Hsiao-t'ang, immediately decided to attack in support of the beleaguered Green Standard troops.

In his attempt to relieve Ssu-ching, Ward was unassisted by British or French troops. With between seven hundred and a thousand soldiers of the corps, as well as several pieces of his own artillery, he moved against the rebels on March 14. According to the *Herald,* Li Heng-sung "was on the point of giving in when this timely succour arrived." Like the corps's previous pair of engagements, the battle for Ssu-ching was comparatively short and very sharp, Ward's men once again facing enormous numerical odds for which they compensated with disciplined movement, effective rifle fire, competent artillery support, and proficient use of their gunboats.

Ward himself, Hsüeh Huan told Peking, "was the first to break into the enemy's position," where he "gunned down two rebel officers in yellow clothes [a mark of particularly high rank] and seized a yellow silk flag with a dragon design." This event threw the rebels into apparent fear and confusion: Flying into a panicked retreat, during which hundreds were captured and an even greater number killed, the Taipings crowded onto a "floating" bridge over a canal, which collapsed under their weight. Many hundreds were drowned. "Ward then moved on," said Hsüeh, "to help the battle on water, capturing twelve gunboats and burning more than a hundred other [smaller] craft." The casualties of the Ward Corps were somewhat higher on this occasion, chiefly because a rebel magazine was ignited in their midst, producing an enormous explosion.

The victory was important on many levels. First, the immediate goal of saving Li Heng-sung and his men had been achieved, although just what effective function these troops could serve was becoming less and less clear. Second, the imperial Chinese government now had a fighting force of proven quality in eastern Kiangsu, one which, unlike the Green Standard units, could engage much larger Taiping formations successfully. Recognizing the vital role that the corps had seized for itself, Hsüeh Huan immediately authorized Ward to enlarge it. But most important, Ward had again demonstrated, as during the battles in January and early February, that such victories did not require the cooperation or the support of Western regulars. Given enough men and proper equipment, the Ward Corps could make it unnecessary for the foreign powers to intervene with their troops, while establishing itself as the vital eastern arm for Tseng Kuo-fan's nutcracker strategy.

The advantages of enlarging the corps seemed clear, yet almost as soon as these several factors were recognized and appreciated by the Chinese government and the representatives of the Western powers, they became sources of suspicion and anxiety. Ward himself was responsible for this. Chinese officials, once intrigued by Ward's desire to turn to Chinese ways, suddenly discovered the actual limitations of that desire. The best-trained, best-equipped, and best-led army in the empire was in the hands of an adventurer who, it became known, refused to wear the mandarin's robes he had been granted or to shave his forehead according to the Manchu style. For the representatives of the West, by contrast, it was precisely Ward's signs of devotion to China—his close association with Wu Hsü and Yang Fang, his well-known contempt for Shanghai's Western mercantile community, and his support of Chinese political integrity—that were disturbing. Clearly, Ward was answering to a set of values of his own devising, and in mid-March his roguish behavior reached its apogee when he married, in a traditional Chinese ceremony, Yang Fang's twenty-one-year-old daughter, Chang-mei.

VI

"HIS HEART IS HARD TO FATHOM"

No single episode in Ward's mysterious life is more difficult to assess than his marriage to Chang-mei. Indeed, the event remains the clearest symbol of just how complex and ambiguous Ward's motivations actually were. Ambition, avarice, and affection were all factors in the young American commander's decision to ally himself intimately with the family of his most loyal backer, Yang Fang—but in what proportions these elements were blended is a matter for conjecture. One clear conclusion can, however, be drawn from the event: By March 1862 Ward had cast his lot irreversibly with China. Fame, failure, and death were all possible ends to the course on which he had embarked. But whichever fate it was to be, Ward would meet it not as a foreign adventurer intent only on profit but as a Chinese subject whose ambitions—whether pointed at greater elevation within the Manchu hierarchy, at the overthrow of that hierarchy, or at the establishment of a private warlord domain—were to play an important role in the future of the empire that had so consistently drawn him back from escapades in other parts of the world.

Certainly, the marriage ruled out any possibility that Ward, after years of being branded a notorious scoundrel, might capitalize on the success of his new corps to become one of the leading citizens of Shanghai's foreign settlements and of the Western element in China generally. Hallett Abend—a *New York Times* correspondent in China during the 1930s who authored a somewhat fanciful biography of Ward—claimed that by March 1862 Ward had become one of the most desirous social catches of Asia's then most colorful international community. Added to the fact that Ward was young and a bachelor, and Shanghai's most exclusive hostesses, particularly those with marriageable daughters, began to compete to lure him to their dinners, their teas, their receptions, their balls. . . . Much sought after, he appeared briefly between his marches and his battles, and was greatly lionized during several short intervals between campaigns. And then, by his own act, he cut himself off from this charmed circle, and to this day no one knows the precise motivation for the act, publicly performed, which abruptly made him a social outcast.

Whether Ward was ever so enthusiastically "lionized" by Shanghai's hostesses is questionable. Many of Abend's statements were based (or so he claimed) on an examination of records that were destroyed by the Japanese during the Second World War. But it is certainly true that the marriage to Chang-mei—coinciding as it did with Peking's approval of Ward's long-standing petition to become a Chinese subject—perpetuated the distance between Ward and many other Westerners just when that gap might have been narrowed. Of course, celebrity among Shanghai's foreign residents had never held any value for Ward, and it is therefore unsurprising that he should have given so little thought to how his marriage might be interpreted in the settlements. Yet Abend was right to presume that Ward would have made some effort to explain the "shocking mésalliance" to his brother, Harry, and sister Elizabeth, who remained among his closest confidants. Any letters that might have embodied such efforts were destroyed, however, and we are once again forced to examine an important episode in Ward's life not by studying his own words but by deducing from circumstances.

Perhaps the easiest aspect of the affair to understand is Yang Fang's desire to have Ward enter his family. On a purely practical level, it was unlikely that Yang would ever have found a native Chinese husband for Chang-mei: Though the child of a wealthy father, as well as a healthy and attractive woman, Chang-mei was tarred as a woman of "bad luck" because of the demise of her first fiancé. Such superstitions outweighed Yang's position and fortune in the minds of most Chinese, and Chang-mei had little to look forward to but a life of maiden servitude in her father's household. By 1862 this fate seemed confirmed, for Chang-mei was twenty-one: already old for a Chinese bride. The fact that during the beginning of that year a suitor did appear could only have been a relief to Yang Fang, and the additional fact that that someone was Frederick Townsend Ward transformed the merchant banker's relief into genuine joy. For by March 1862 the celebrated "Hua" had risen to a position in the Chinese hierarchy that rivaled Yang's own.

Victory at Kao-ch'iao had secured for Ward a fourth-rank mandarinate with peacock feather and enrollment as a Chinese subject. Similar honors had been awarded to Burgevine. Following the battle at Hsiao-t'ang, Governor Hsüeh Huan had again memorialized to the throne, asking that both Ward and Burgevine be raised to the third rank. The request had been granted, and the spherical buttons that adorned the mandarin's caps of the two Westerners were changed from dark to light blue. Yet Peking was uneasy about granting such high honors to men of foreign origin, and an imperial edict expressed concern over the fact that Ward and Burgevine had been supported in their operations by Admirals Hope and Protet: "China's use of foreign troops is only an expedient measure. We should bestir ourselves, so that the foreigners will only enhance our power and prestige. It is not right to rely on foreign aid while our own armies flinch and hesitate."

Hsüeh Huan used the flinching and hesitation of imperial forces in Kiangsu to press for further honors for Ward, who commanded the only effective government troops in the province. Following the battle at Ssu-ching—during which, very significantly, Ward was not aided by the British or the French—Hsüeh sent another memorial to Peking. He pointed out that Hope and Protet appreciated not only Ward's courage and skill but his status as a Chinese subject as well: "Several times they [Hope and Protet] have asked us to treat [Ward] well. American Minister Burlingame also knows that Ward has subordinated to China and that Ward has been fighting bravely; he praised Ward. So these foreign emissaries all know the matter well and they will not make objections [to our giving Ward Chinese titles]." In addition, Hsüeh believed that further honors would tie Ward more closely to the imperial cause:

"When Ward was informed of the fourth rank button that had been granted to him, he was extremely pleased and inspired. On the fourteenth day of the second month [Chinese calendar], he fought at Ssuching and raised the siege of the base. Truly and unusually capable, this Westerner enjoys merits and is fond of winning. He has always longed for the Chinese red button [the highest mandarin rank] and would deem it a great honor to wear it."

Finally, Hsüeh made the unusual request that Ward be granted a commission in the imperial Army of the Green Standard. It was an unprecedented honor for a Westerner and one that heightened the general air of uncertainty that surrounded the subject of the Ward Corps in Peking. Specifically, Hsüeh asked that Ward be made a regimental colonel of provincial troops; if this were allowed, said the governor, Ward "would be pleased and would exert himself even more in attempting to repay the kindness." Despite Peking's nervousness, Hsüeh's point was well taken and his latest request granted. In recognition of his valor on the battlefield, Ward was even permitted to wear a prestigious embroidered tiger on his official robes. But Peking's worries never disappeared. "It is heard," read an imperial edict issued just after Ward was made a Green Standard colonel, "that Ward does not wear the rank button that has been granted to him, nor has he cut his hair [to the Manchu style]. Is Hsüeh Huan's former report that Ward wished to be a Chinese subject and change his clothes true? Hsüeh Huan should report honestly whether this foreigner will genuinely appreciate the colonelcy that has just been granted to him."

Prince Kung and the Empress Dowager Tz'u-hsi were consistently alive to the fact that, while Ward's services to China were considerable and admirable, his new position as a Chinese officer in command of the empire's most effective military unit might make him a most dangerous man should his loyalty to the Manchus ever waver or turn. As a freelance outsider whose services could easily have been dispensed with, Ward had ironically been less of a threat than as a legitimate Chinese subject and officer. For this reason, the need to tie his fate to that of the dynasty through a complex system of controls and rewards became all the more urgent.

It is quite possible, even probable, that this was another reason why Yang Fang favored his daughter's marriage to Ward: The more varied and personal Ward's entanglements with the imperial establishment, the less likely his abandonment of the cause. The central paradox in this situation—one that Yang as well as his superiors in Peking either could not see or were powerless to counteract—was that in attempting to control Ward by granting him rank and favors, they all became steadily more dependent on him. This was especially true at the provincial level, where the bureaucratic fates of men such as Hsüeh Huan and Wu Hsü became directly tied to the continued success of the Ward Corps. Having started down a path in which their own success depended on Ward's victories—victories that, in turn, depended on continued elevation and reward—Hsüeh, Wu, and their superiors had no choice but to keep the rewards and elevations coming.

All of this made Ward a most eligible match for the daughter of a successful businessman and aspiring provincial official such as Yang Fang. And there is no evidence that the proposed union—which may actually have originated with Yang rather than Ward—inspired any negative feeling in Chang-mei herself. The fact that Ward was a foreigner and a soldier might have prompted condescension among the Manchus in Peking, who viewed the profession of arms with little of the romance that it enjoyed in the West. But the Kiangsu and Chekiang native elites, who daily faced the direct threat of a Taiping attack, generally saw the Ward Corps as an important, or at the very least necessary, organization. Indeed, at the same time that Hsüeh Huan requested unprecedented honors for the unit's commander, he asked (apparently at Wu Hsü's urging) for official recognition of the corps itself: "Because of the extreme effectiveness of the 'Foreign Arms Corps,' " he memorialized, "I have selected [for them] the name of the 'Ever Victorious Army' [*Chang-sheng-chün*]." In granting this title China's rulers further demonstrated their desire to integrate the corps into the traditional Chinese military hierarchy. As Richard J. Smith has pointed out:

> Perhaps Hsüeh chose the appellation simply because it sounded
> auspicious and appropriate, but the possibility also exists that the

Kiangsu governor may have had in mind the precedent of Kuo Yao-shih, a barbarian *(Ch'i-tan)* commander who submitted to the Sung [dynasty] and who later led a military force with an identical designation. The parallel is particularly striking because Ward's contingent, like its Sung namesake, at times received criticism for having become proud and unmanageable.

While undoubtedly pleased that his corps should receive such recognition from Peking, Ward continued to refer to the unit in private as "my people": *Chang-sheng-chün* apparently meant as little to him personally as did his mandarin dress, his fiancée's status as a woman of "bad luck," and the repeated desire of Chinese officials that he shave his forehead. Although Ward was solidly loyal to the empire, his interest in China's more antiquated social customs and folk wisdom went only as far as their usefulness in impressing, manipulating, and controlling the local populace. In this connection he did find the "Ever Victorious Army" title of immense use, and for that reason the name stuck. Andrew Wilson, who witnessed the evolution of the Ward Corps, offered a singularly clear explanation of the importance of the force's new name, which, he said

> must not be taken in a literal but in a transcendental and celestial sense. The Chinese have a fine faculty for inventing happy names. . . . Nor are such titles merely hollow sounds. . . . [T]o the Chinaman these titles have a vital significance, and the turn of a phrase will often influence his whole conduct towards the subject designated. No principle is more constantly enforced in the Chinese Classics. . . . When inquiry was made of Confucius as to what was the first thing necessary to improve the government, he answered, "What is necessary is to rectify names"; and very expressively he said, that "to have a bad name is to dwell in a low-lying situation, where all the evil of the world flows in upon one."

Official recognition of the Ever Victorious Army only facilitated the development of Ward's close personal ties to Wu Hsü and Yang Fang, and in these ties may lie the most logical explanation for Ward's marriage to Chang-mei. By early 1862 Wu Hsü—one of the most powerful figures in Chinese Shanghai, a man who could outwit experienced foreign officials as easily as he could juggle account books—was referring to himself in letters to Ward as "your younger brother" and even "your foolish younger brother": both Chinese terms denoting genuine humility and close friendship. The continued importance of Ward's relationship with Wu cannot be overstated, for in imperial China personal connections were the key to control and hence success. Ward's ties to the Shanghai taotai, not to mention his complete civil as well as military control over Sung-chiang, demonstrated the extent to which he had successfully manipulated the Chinese system to his benefit. Ever a man of caution, Wu was consistently aware that in tying himself closely to Ward he gave his young protégé influence over his own position. Yet such was his real belief in Ward's capabilities and in the military (and financial) potential of the Ever Victorious Army that he willingly took the risk.

The same was even more true of Yang Fang. Ward's relationship with Wu Hsü existed largely off the books, but with Yang he became an actual business partner. Officially, Yang was made co-commander of the Ever Victorious Army when it was formally recognized by Peking, although his activities continued to be confined to raising money and arms in Shanghai. Soon Ward and Yang had expanded their joint dealings by entering the steamship business together, buying and chartering river vessels for service with the Ever Victorious Army as well as for extracurricular shipping activities. Sometimes Ward's brother, Harry, was used as a front for such operations, the management of which was generally left in Yang's hands. Again, Ward's preoccupation with military matters and his inattentiveness to business details probably cost him, for a man such as Yang Fang would not have been above juggling his accounts of dealings with even his closest associates.

Indeed, Harry Ward claimed after his brother's death that Fred had given Yang Fang 150,000 taels to invest in the government salt monopoly, one of the most profitable schemes going in imperial China. Yang consistently denied that any such transaction had ever taken place, and this as well as other claims made against Yang by the Ward estate subsequently created much bitter feeling. But in truth, Yang's denials of any debts to Ward or his heirs were less an indication that the friendship between the two men was false than a demonstration of the nature of friendship among Chinese merchants and officials. During Ward's lifetime Yang was personally loyal to his young comrade and partner—loyal in friendship and, undoubtedly, duplicitous in his financial dealings. The only area in which Ward consistently called Yang to task was in paying the men of the Ever Victorious Army fully and promptly; to expect Yang to behave forthrightly in other areas without similarly stringent supervision would have been naive. Like so many Chinese of his caste, Yang cheated not out of malice but when and where he could; his personal attachment to Ward was nonetheless genuine.

For all of these reasons, Ward's marriage to Chang-mei can be seen as a method not only of further tying the newly Chinese commander of the vital Ever Victorious Army to the imperial cause but of tightening the personal bonds between Ward and the Chekiang clique that Wu and Yang controlled in Shanghai. Emphasizing the importance of these interpretations, many analysts have ignored or downplayed any personal considerations that might have been involved in the marriage. After all, Chang-mei, living in a traditional Chinese household, would not have been permitted to see Ward very often during his visits; even if she had, her knowledge of English was almost certainly confined to some rudimentary pidgin, while Ward's command of Chinese was never appreciable. Personal attachment between the two appears, on the surface, to have been unlikely.

But inconvenient details undermine any purely political or mercenary interpretation of Ward's marriage. First, while union with a Chinese family might have been expected to heighten Peking's trust in Ward, in fact it did not: The marriage was not a significant topic in memorials and imperial edicts written during Ward's lifetime, probably because the specific Chinese woman he selected was the daughter of a non-Manchu known for his misuse of the imperial financial system. Ward's elevation to a third-rank mandarinate and his original commission in the Army of the Green Standard occurred before Peking even knew of his marriage to Chang-mei, and his further promotion to brigadier general—made later in the spring of 1862—was based, as his colonelcy had been, on battlefield achievements.

Then, too, Ward's ties to Wu Hsü and Yang Fang were already considerable and in place when the engagement was announced; while it is reasonable to suppose that all parties concerned might have desired a strengthening of those bonds, the marriage actually accomplished less in this direction than did the purchase of steamships and the expansion of the Ever Victorious Army. In addition, if Ward took a wife solely for business reasons or for appearances' sake, it is safe to assume that he would not have removed her from the security of her family's home in Shanghai to share his dangerous and uncomfortable life in Sung-chiang. Yet more than one Western witness claimed that Ward and Chang-mei spent the hot, perilous summer months of 1862 together at Ward's headquarters.

But no single aspect of Ward's marriage was more indicative of its complex genesis than his own behavior during the betrothal and the wedding itself—behavior so out of character it seems impossible that it was not a product of genuine emotion.

If Hallett Abend's description of Chang-mei as a "pathetic" young woman seems at first unkind, it should be remembered that the lot of women in imperial China was not generally speaking a pleasant one. The case of Chang-mei's nominal mother (who may or may not have been the girl's biological parent) provides an apt example. According to Dr. Macgowan, Mrs. Taki, as she was known to foreigners, had been purchased during childhood along with her sister by a "Chinese Barnum." She had then been "made to study the art of making riddles, of shining in conversation, and to be prompt in humorous repartee," while her sister had been trained as an acrobat. Both girls exercised their talents publicly for their master's profit, but they eventually became obstreperous and were resold, the acrobat to a district magistrate for three thousand taels and the *"spirituelle"* to Yang Fang for a much larger sum. Yang was free to enjoy the privilege of every successful Chinese man— concubines—hence the doubt as to whether his first wife actually gave birth to his daughter. It was not unusual that Chang-mei's heritage should have been a subject of so little concern, for in a Chinese home the arrival of a female child was not an event worthy of particular note. When one adds to this dismal background the cloistered youth of a well-to-do Chinese girl, and the tragic conclusion of her first betrothal (which made her a virtual social pariah), Abend's assessment of Chang-mei emerges as sadly appropriate.

Another early Ward biographer, Holger Cahill, claimed that Ward waged a "campaign for the hand of Chang-mei." The assertion is impossible to prove or disprove, but it is true that the betrothal and wedding were the only times during which Ward indulged in traditional Chinese ceremonies. What scolding edicts from his new imperial masters in Peking could not achieve, deference to his young bride apparently could—and did. Acting through a go-between, Ward provided Chang-mei's family with a *pa-tzu,* or engagement card, on which were inscribed Chinese characters that detailed his birth down to the hour; Chang-mei and her parents supplied Ward with her *pa-tzu,* and both cards were examined by astrologers to determine the pair's heavenly compatibility. (One early-twentieth-century American scholar speculated, quite plausibly, that Ward paid his astrologer to tailor his findings to ensure a perfect match.) While these divinations were in progress, Ward kept a steady stream of traditional gifts flowing to Chang-mei's home: geese and other fowl, fruits, cakes and wine, money, and material for his bride's wedding dress.

For his part, Yang Fang composed a letter to be sent to Ward's father in New York, a copy of which has survived. In it, Yang expressed gratitude that Ward's father would permit the marriage without being present to investigate his daughter-in-law's family. Yang further revealed his genuine joy at the union. Addressing the elder Ward as "Your excellency Hua, elderly gentleman of noble character and high prestige," Yang declared: "I am indebted for your kindness in not despising the poor and humble, and trusting in people's words, and agreeing to my little daughter's marriage to your son. What kind of happiness can compare to this? Now I am receiving formalities from you, and I am forced to accept all of the betrothal gifts. We wish that they will have a happy life for a hundred years, and that their offspring will be prosperous for five generations."

The days before the actual wedding ceremony were filled, for

219

Chang-mei, with sewing, worshiping at the altar of her ancestors, and weeping, as per Chinese custom. On the day of the ceremony she put on her multiskirted dress, gave final offerings to her ancestors, and entered a red sedan chair. She was borne to what has sometimes been referred to as "Ward's house" but must have been a residence belonging to Yang and perhaps used by Ward and other officers of the corps, for Ward was at the time just beginning to build his own house in the French Concession. Holger Cahill's description of Chang-mei's reaction on entering her husband's home is in all probability another apocryphal tale, but it is consistent with the young woman's background and Chinese tradition. Chang-mei, said Cahill, "expected to pay homage to her husband's ancestors and she found it strange that he had no ancestral altar in the house. She decided, however, that her foreign husband did not look un-Chinese, for he was as dark as a son of Han, and he wore his Chinese robes and the insignia of his rank for the wedding ceremony."

Ward's appearance in his mandarin's costume offers considerable evidence of the importance he placed on the wedding. He might have felt scorn for many of the Western citizens of Shanghai, but according to Wu Hsü he had no desire to open himself to their ridicule—or to that of his trusted comrades in the foreign armies—by parading around Shanghai in Manchu garb. Wu told Hsüeh, who in turn informed Peking, that Ward fully intended to "change his clothes" when his corps reconquered Soochow (which, incidentally, offered evidence that as early as March Ward was making expansive plans for the Ever Victorious Army). But he refused to make such a change any earlier. On this one day, however, he endured bemusement and in all likelihood some taunting (good-natured and otherwise) in order to keep his bride from losing face in her own community. To those who knew Ward and were present at the ceremony—Westerners as well as Chinese—it must have been something of a shock to see the man who so habitually wore an unadorned blue frock coat appear in black Manchu boots, the unmistakable pillbox cap of a Chinese mandarin (complete with blue button and peacock's feather), and a knee-length robe with an embroidered tiger across the torso. It was a moment to be remembered: The next time Ward would be similarly dressed he would be lying in his coffin.

According to Cahill, the wedding festivities lasted for two days, and as this too is in general keeping with Chinese custom it is reasonable to suppose that it is an accurate statement. Ward offered still more gifts to Chang-mei and her family, including one especially personal item: a small seal or *chop,* whose Chinese characters literally translated to "must not forget each other" but were in spirit much closer to the English "forget me not." Because the exact date of the wedding is unknown, it has always been unclear whether the two-week honeymoon that many sources say followed it was interrupted by the battle for Ssu-ching or whether that battle preceded the wedding; whatever the case, by mid-March Ward—a man for whom women and romance had never played an evident role—was a married subject of the Chinese empire.

Ward and Chang-mei's life together was destined to be short but, as several subsequent events and circumstances indicated, more intimate than many analysts have supposed. The fact that Ward decided to build his own house in Shanghai just at the time he was married is the first indication of this: Again, he could easily have left Chang-mei at her parents' home rather than supplying her with what looked to be a very fine new residence in the city. Then there are the reports that the couple were together in Sung-chiang during the summer: A man such as Ward, who ran a very tight, professional military camp, would surely not have encumbered himself with a new Chinese bride in such a place for mere show. But the strongest testament to Ward and Chang-mei's closeness comes from a biography—only recently brought to the West by Richard J. Smith—of one Shen Chu-jeng, a Chekiang native who claimed to have been adopted as a youth by the Wards.

Written by a close friend of Shen's daughter, the biography relates a typical story of the Taiping rebellion: When the rebels reentered Hangchow in December 1861, the thirteen-year-old Shen witnessed the massacre of most of his family. Captured by the Taipings and impressed into military service (the rebels had whole units composed of young boys), Shen remained uncertain of his mother's fate until he one day encountered his wet nurse, who had also been captured. The woman informed Shen that his mother had committed suicide by throwing herself down a well. Despondent, Shen followed the rebel force at knife point until it arrived at Sung-chiang. Finally able to slip away from the Taipings, he soon made a propitious acquaintance: "At this time, the Westerner General Ward had just defeated the Taipings at Ying-ch'i-pin. He thus came to meet Shen and adopted him. The general taught Shen his military tactics and strategy and enlisted him in the boys' army. When Ward's wife, who was from the notable Yang family in [Chekiang], realized Shen's family background, she became very sympathetic to this poor orphan and tried her best to take care of him."

This is the only known reference to Ward's having any children, adopted or otherwise (Chang-mei bore no offspring), or to his having formed a detachment of young boys. But Shen claimed to have participated subsequently in several crucial battles and to have continued serving in the Ever Victorious Army after Ward's death. Although he glorified his own role, the details of events he cited are consistent with known facts, and his story has credibility.

A final pair of incidents further—and perhaps fatally—contradict the political interpretation of Ward's marriage to Chang-mei. When Ward lay mortally wounded and in tremendous agony, he spoke of just three people, expressing concern that they be taken care of: his brother, Harry, his sister Elizabeth, and his wife, Chang-mei. Politics and appearances were of no consequence at the time, for Ward had been told that he was near death. And within a year of his passing, Chang-mei succumbed to a mysterious illness; the only known explanation or identification of the malady came from Shen Chu-jeng's biographer, who called it "extreme grief."

To emphasize these facts is to probe for insight into Ward's personal motivations as much as to seek a storied romance. And when we turn away from Ward's Chinese connections to the subject of his Western friends and comrades, we find further evidence that those who count him simply a scheming mercenary both assign him skills he did not have and do him something of an injustice.

During the weeks he spent in Shanghai in the spring of 1862, and for months after his departure for Peking in midsummer, American minister Anson Burlingame played something of the role of spiritual godfather for Ward and his senior American officers. From Burlingame these younger men sought news from home; for him they eagerly performed favors; and to him they proudly related tales of their exploits, seeking, it seems, validation from their senior compatriot. A man of tremendous vitality and insight, Burlingame did not disappoint the young adventurers, and many of the few real insights we have into their inner workings—particularly those of Frederick Ward—are available through the minister's papers.

By the end of February Ward had conceived a plan in which Wu Hsü and other Chinese officials (it is unclear whether the imperial government was involved) would give Harry $200,000 to $300,000 with which to buy quality river steamers and other weapons in the United States and Great Britain. Harry was to begin his journey in early March, and on the seventh Burlingame obliged both Ward brothers as well as Wu Hsü by writing to Secretary of State William Seward:

> I have given letters of introduction to the President and your-self, at the request of the Chinese authorities, to a young man called H. G. Ward[,] who goes out by this mail to purchase gunboats and arms for the Chinese Government. Ward has been . . . selected through the influence of his brother[,] called Col[.] Ward, but now I believe general, in the Chinese service. . . . His younger brother who goes out for the Government seems to be a sprightly young man. I know nothing of his ante ce dents [*sic*], and cannot vouch for him beyond what I have written.

As it turned out, Burlingame took quite a chance in vouching for Harry Ward at all: Although the younger Ward did commission the building of at least four steamers for the Chinese government in the United States, and may have purchased other arms for shipment to Shanghai, he subsequently ended up selling the boats to the Union Army for use during the American Civil War. Harry never returned to China. The question of what happened to much of the money he had been given was pursued by the Chinese government for many years but without real vigor, suggesting that the project may have been a private scheme of Yang Fang and Wu Hsü. Still, for Burlingame to have given the younger Ward letters of introduction to both Secretary of State Seward and President Lincoln demonstrates both that persuasive charm ran in the Ward family and that the American minister was quite susceptible to it.

Burgevine and Forester, too, were on good terms with Burlingame. Burgevine, of course, had known Burlingame in Washington and was acquainted with the new minister's wife and children. On at least one occasion Burgevine facilitated the delivery of a supply of lemonade and soda water to Burlingame in Peking—the kind of favor that was probably performed regularly—and Burlingame later repaid such kindnesses by pushing hard for Burgevine to be named Ward's successor in command of the Ever Victorious Army. Burlingame was no more confident about the vagaries of Burgevine's or Forester's characters than he had been about those of Harry Ward. But just as he had been persuaded to provide Harry with important letters of introduction, so did he put aside misgivings about the seconds-in-command of the Ever Victorious Army and plead their cases, when necessary, both in Peking and to Washington.

But it was Frederick Ward who inspired the most unqualified affection and approval in Burlingame. Much of this sentiment can be attributed to Ward's infectious, positive attitude, but it was also a result of Burlingame's genuine admiration for Ward's battlefield achievements. Burlingame had not been immune to the evolution of opinion concerning the Taiping rebellion that was symptomatic of most Americans who actually journeyed to China. He had expressed some evenhanded curiosity about the rebels before the trip, but arrival in Shanghai had brought him face to face with tens of thousands of Chinese refugees fleeing the interior, as well as with increasingly stark reports concerning the Taiping movement. Even short excursions outside the port were enough to plant hostility toward the rebels in almost any foreign official, which generally resulted in a vocal desire that some more efficient force than imperial Chinese armies be brought to bear on the savage problem. Burlingame was no exception, and in Ward's army he, like Admiral Hope and General Michel before him, saw a potential instrument for the reestablishment of order. In late March, Burlingame expressed these sentiments in a letter to Secretary of State Seward, saying:

The rebellion still rages but as yet it has made no direct assault upon Shanghai. Since the 2nd of February six battles have been fought within thirty miles of this place with great loss to the rebels. . . . Without giving you all the details of these battles, I will write in general terms that while there were not more than twelve hundred men, at any one time, on the side of the Imperialists, there were said to be from five to twenty thousand men on the side of the rebels—and while the rebels are superior to the Imperial soldiers in this part of the Empire—and nearly always beat them when the Imperialists are led by native officers—they are unequal to the Chinese, trained and led by Europeans or Americans. They were beaten in every battle with great slaughter.

Although it had been Admiral Hope who had first brought Ward to Burlingame's attention, the connection through Burgevine almost certainly widened Ward's access to the American minister. By summer the two men were corresponding quite informally, and one August letter from Ward to Burlingame offers the most complete surviving commentary by the commander of the Ever Victorious Army on the state of China, events in America, and his own affairs generally.

"I have not written to you for some time," Ward opened, "but I have been so horribly busy that I have done I fear nothing properly, unless it is to flog the chang maos." Citing recent battles, Ward played up the bravery of his own men:

So you can see my people have been hard at work—with I am sorry to say severe loss to me, some 400 men being killed or rendered useless to me hereafter—it is the fate of war though and I suppose I take the same chances and fortune favors me. The Rascally officials here though rob one of what one treasures most (Credit) when one risks one's life—but I fancy the truth will eventually leak out. I have told Butler my secretary to give you the particulars of my little fights as I think it will serve to kill a few moments as I think Peking must be excessively dull and monotonous—let it be though confidential for he is such a devil of a fellow that there is no answering for his pen when once started.

225

Decrying the self-serving statements and activities of both Chinese officials and Western merchants in Shanghai, Ward exhibited a fear that Peking would never get an accurate account of either his own actions or those of the Ever Victorious Army: "We have a bad set here—and if you ever speak to Kung Wang [Prince Kung] about such things I wish you would say a word about my people. . . . Now I have written you a long chit and I trust you will understand that I am so horribly pressed for time & detained by these infernal Shanghai bores that any apparent negligence on my part in not writing to you sooner will be pardoned."

Before closing, however, Ward took time to warn Burlingame against what he considered a great danger. By the summer of 1862 the leaders of Western Shanghai had become so convinced of the inability of the imperial government either to protect them or to properly manage the port's affairs that a "free city" movement had sprung up. Its proponents favored international supervision of Shanghai and an end to imperial authority—in essence, the theft of an entire city. In condemning the movement, Ward revealed much of his feeling about China:

> There is one thing though that I really think your attention should be drawn to, and that is the Free City movement of the merchants here. It is certainly one of the most outrageous things to be mooted at such times as this by money makers that I really think they should be snubbed. . . . It is only causing very hard feelings and to tell you the truth I fear I shall be by the authorities considered from my position as one of the exponents of this squatter sovereignty—and as I am down on any such rascally filibusterism, and also mean because the parties mooting it are the first to shreik [*sic*] for aid whenever they come to grief and let better people get broken heads for their villainy, that if they have addressed you on the subject you would use some of our old New England plain sense and speech and let them understand the ultimate consequences of any such outrageous doctrines.

Then came a final observation demonstrating that, his Chinese citizenship aside, Ward was still attached to the troubled country of his birth: "Grand news from home. Jeff[erson Davis] and the Secesh party catching it. If old Uncle Abe does not give them thunder this fall then I am mistaken. If he wants a subscription to build the strongest[,] darkest & deepest Hotel in the country for the blackguards Jeff & Cabinet I am up for 10,000—all I am afraid of is that they will all loot enough to keep themselves the remainder of their lives in Europe—I hope McClellan is in Richmond before this."

Typically, Burlingame would later portray this last rather wild proposition as a "patriotic" offer by Ward to "contribute ten thousand taels to the Government of the United States, to aid in maintaining the Union"; the same almost avuncular indulgence that Burlingame had always shown toward Ward lasted even beyond the young commander's end. Nor is it difficult, on the basis of such letters, to see why: Ward had expressed a real commitment to China (even as he acknowledged the shortcomings of the empire's "Rascally officials"), a strong aversion to the "infernal bores" and "money makers" of Shanghai, and, despite his own past, a condemnation of "filibusterism"—all positions that matched Burlingame's own. There was no sense of Ward voicing these opinions simply to ingratiate himself with the American minister, for Burlingame was, in the summer of 1862, not in a position to perform any significant favors for the Ever Victorious Army. The correspondence and friendship between the two men was thoroughly genuine.

Close as Ward was to Admirals Hope and Protet, as well as to a select few of the Western officers in his army, none of these relationships was as completely free from reserve and maneuver as that with Burlingame. Hope later wrote that Burgevine, for example, "stood higher in Colonel Ward's estimation than any of his other officers"; yet there are no personal references to Ward—admiring or otherwise—in Burgevine's surviving written statements. As for Forester's attitude, it is worth noting that after Ward's death Admiral Hope—worried that the unit he still referred to as "Ward's Disciplined Chinese" might change its title—wrote in a rather warning tone to tell Forester of his wish that "in remembrance of our friend it will always retain that name." Certainly Forester dealt with his former chief most prejudicially—and inaccurately—in his published reminiscences. Nor has time turned up any laudatory statements from officers of the Ever Victorious Army who survived to enjoy long lives of participation in the affairs of Shanghai, such as C. J. Ashley, Ward's commissary general. Only Charles Schmidt, the mercenary officer who had first met Ward in Central America in the early 1850s, left any testament to his commander:

"General Ward," Schmidt declared in an undated memorandum that was probably written during the late 1870s,

> was beloved and respected by all who knew him. Although not a highly educated man, he was shrewd and had common sense, and while in action he was very brave. This was not a reckless bravery, but a cool and daring bravery so requisite in a good leader. He would never send a man to a place where he would not go himself if required, but if he saw any person show the white feather, he would dismiss him instantly. He showed great tact in his difficult position, and managed to keep his own in spite of the intrigues and flatteries of British officers & periodical difficulties with the Chinese government officials who did not always rightly interpret the General's motives for certain actions. . . . He was ever active and alert, trying to improve his force in order to accomplish that which he had undertaken to do for the Chinese government.

As it had from the first, then, Ward's determination to finish the job that he had set out to do for the Chinese empire continued to put him at odds not only with representatives of foreign powers and corrupt Chinese bureaucrats but with many of his own officers, whose first and often only concern was pay and loot. Yet as the Ever Victorious Army expanded Ward remained singularly able to handle such men, and to get the best out of them. A. A. Hayes wrote of the officer's life in the army, "It was a terrible service. Ward spared neither himself nor those under him. The officers, conspicuous figures among the native privates, suffered fearfully." Ward had weeded out the most unreliable of his Westerners, but many of those who remained, while exceptional soldiers, were plagued by the same proclivities that had almost caused Ward's first force to be stillborn in 1860. Ward kept a close eye on and strict control over such behavior. Hayes recorded the example of the army's chief of artillery, a highly competent Englishman named Glasgow, who, Hayes wrote,

> had been a non-commissioned officer in the British service, and so brave and skilful that promotion was twice in his grasp, only to be forfeited by excesses. On a memorable day, when he was with Ward, he had a battery in the open, pounding at the walls of a city. To him came his slight, boyish-looking commander. "That battery is making bad practice," said he. "Advance it one hundred yards." The position was enfiladed by bullets, and men were dropping every moment; but from that order there was no appeal. Glasgow shrugged his shoulders, took a surreptitious pull at a flask, and gave the word. Another half hour, and he could cease firing, for the small man in the blue coat was in the breach, with the forlorn hope of the Ever Victorious Army.

Though able to make effective use of men such as Glasgow, Ward by all accounts looked forward to the day when employing them would no longer be necessary. By the spring of 1862 he had already begun elevating promising Chinese privates to noncommissioned rank, and, as Admiral Hope reported on several occasions after Ward's death, Ward intended "to bring forward some of his best [Chinese] sergeant majors as Captains of Companies." At least one such man, Wong Apo, was so promoted during Ward's lifetime, in recognition of his repeated acts of bravery. Again, Ward's unusual confidence in the military potential of the Chinese—an attitude facilitated by his equally unusual lack of racial prejudice—offered a glimpse of the future available to a Chinese ruling class willing to absorb progressive Western methods.

It was this implicitly egalitarian attitude toward the Chinese that finally made Ward more popular among his men than among Western diplomats, his own officers, or Chinese officials in Shanghai and Peking. By March 1862 the Ever Victorious Army had become the embodiment of nearly all its creator's hopes and fantasies: an efficient, well-organized unit of native soldiers who understood and could execute the most up-to-date Western military maneuvers. The men were mustered at seven each morning, paraded twice a day between training sessions, and dismissed at six in the evening. The activities of the various units became specialized: By the end of the summer of 1862 there were two artillery battalions (one light and one heavy), a rifle battalion, three additional infantry battalions, and an "elite force" of some six hundred particularly well-trained Chinese shock troops. The skill of these soldiers aroused awe even in unsympathetic Chinese observers, such as the Soochow scholar Feng Kuei-fen. Admiring the Ever Victorious Army's ability to form a defensive square, Feng noted that the troops thus deployed looked "like a loaf of bread with pins sticking in it."

The army was in a constant state of growth and evolution. In his memorial to the throne following Ssu-Ching, Hsüeh Huan had told the emperor that "I, your servant, commended Ward, telling him to enlarge the Ever Victorious Army, so that we can have more capable soldiers in future battles." Already commanding close to two thousand men, Ward soon received authorization to move the army up to three thousand and beyond. Some witnesses claimed that Ward had personal ambitions to expand his force to twenty-five thousand. Even those who, like Wu Hsü, were well-disposed toward Ward recognized that such a force would be able to defeat any army in China. Wu himself pronounced that the "ideal number of the *Chang-sheng-chun* is three thousand"—large enough to do the job facing them, small enough to be controllable.

Control: As always it was the primary worry of Chinese officials at both the imperial and provincial level. Nor did this concern begin or end with the actions of the Ever Victorious Army; it dominated the official Chinese assessment of Ward personally. Perhaps the most dangerous quality for a man to lack in imperial China was restraint, and, for all his enormous personal charm and skill at disciplining troops, Ward's unwillingness to subscribe personally to a social or political philosophy of anything other than his own devising implied an enormous lack of restraint, of respect for external control. Because of this, Peking was finally unable to separate Ward the man from the military reforms he embodied in the Ever Victorious Army. As a result, those reforms were never allowed to be of long-term use to the Chinese empire.

*   *   *

Ward's military innovations, like those of Tseng Kuo-fan, were seen in Peking as little more than temporary expedients. The Ever Victorious Army, like Tseng's Hunan Army and the Anhwei Army that Tseng had placed under Li Hung-chang, was unshakably loyal to its commander; in the case of the Ever Victorious Army, perhaps even more than to the emperor. Although he had "subordinated" to China, Ward was, like Tseng, a man from outside the Manchu elite; worse still, he had been born a barbarian Westerner, which doubled the danger inherent in his troops' loyalty to him. In addition, the Ever Victorious Army—again like Tseng's armies—was basically an instrument of provincial rather than imperial power; Peking had little say over its training or specific objectives. Thus while the distrust that had marked Hsienfeng's attitude toward both Tseng Kuo-fan's armies and those of freelances such as Ward was unquestionably tempered under T'ung-chih, Prince Kung and Tz'u-hsi fully intended to disband any such sources of decentralized power once the Taiping threat had been removed.

But therein lay the problem for the Manchus, as well as yet another paradox. The rebellion could not be ended without Tseng's and Ward's armies; the more power those armies were given, the sooner that end would come. But to place no limits on their ascendancy would make the postwar job of disbanding them all the more difficult—perhaps impossible. This danger was especially acute in the case of the Ever Victorious Army, which even Tseng distrusted. He would later dismiss Ward's troops as "disdainful, extravagant, utterly coarse," while complaining that "their maintenance is very expensive." The pride that Ward had worked so hard to instill in his men, and that propelled them to acts of extreme bravery on the battlefield, thus became another source of distrust for Chinese officials. By the end of March, Tseng had decided it was high time to dispatch Li Hung-chang's Anhwei Army to Shanghai, to assist in the port's defense and, if need be, to serve as a check on the Ever Victorious Army.

Despite all this very real concern, however, expediency remained the rule in a war that was far from decided: By late March Peking had sanctioned not only Ward and his Ever Victorious Army but the use of foreign regulars. Tseng Kuo-fan continued to protest the employment of such troops in the interior, but Peking had begun to consider the possibility of joint action by Tseng's troops, Ward's men, and perhaps even the foreign regulars as far inland as Soochow and, eventually, Nanking. Still, China's rulers made these deliberations in an air of general nervousness, and their behavior exhibited a fear of treachery that was almost self-fulfilling. Seemingly aware that Ward's commitment to China might not imply equal devotion to the Manchu dynasty, the imperial clique stayed constantly on the alert for signs of insincerity from the commander of the Ever Victorious Army. As a result, much was made in Peking—perhaps understandably—of events and statements that were less than sinister, sometimes even trivial, while the very real service that Ward rendered to the empire was not fully appreciated until after his death, when it was safe to do so.

An incident early in the 1862 campaign illustrates the unfortunate way in which battlefield expediencies could lead to philosophical alarm in Peking. According to Dr. Macgowan, a rebel party laden with plunder suddenly found itself surrounded by Ward's men. In a typically short, sharp action the rebels were defeated, and Ward ordered their boats and goods burned. Local villagers had gathered in the hope of plundering the rebel contingent, and at their head was a blue-button mandarin. Ward declared that there was to be no looting, but the mandarin heedlessly led his villagers in among the defeated rebels. At that point, Ward ordered one of his soldiers to shoot the mandarin. But, as Dr. Macgowan observed, "the order was regarded with dismay. The soldier refused— partly because the blue-button was only doing what each soldier desired to do; but chiefly, because shooting an officer [mandarin] was tantamount to patricide. Colonel Forester then himself shot the offender— the moral effect of which was more salutary than the shooting of a whole squad of privates."

Macgowan's phrase "tantamount to patricide" was no exaggeration: The summary execution of a high-ranking mandarin in front of a large number of Chinese soldiers and peasants was an open challenge to the Confucian order, even though the man's behavior and the military situation demanded it. Peking, all too ready to see a pattern in Ward's behavior that might clearly indicate disrespect and even disloyalty, could not help but be alarmed by such actions, even though Ward carried them out to advance the cause of internal stability in China.

By many accounts, Ward's penchant for making broad statements about his army and his ambitions also made the Manchus question whether he was a loyal servant. A. A. Hayes later remembered that Ward "habitually spoke of his means, etc." in a "random way," while Admiral Hope observed during the summer of 1862 that Ward "talks a little fast sometimes as to what he will do, American fashion." Ironically enough, Ward's natural tendencies in this direction may have been exacerbated by his association with Chinese officers and officials: Blatantly ungrounded self-glorification was a fundamental feature of the Chinese bureaucracy. At any rate, during the summer of 1862 Ward managed to create several grandiose impressions among Shanghai's Westerners as to his eventual intentions. And, while it is easy enough to speculate that he may have done so simply to see what effect such talk would create (in much the same way he threw himself off the Salem wharves as a boy to gauge adult reactions), it is true that Peking took such talk very seriously. Hayes, noting Ward's elevation to "a position never attained by any other foreigner in the Chinese service" (a position that only heightened Peking's fears), went on to reveal that "[h]e had received unexampled promotion, and knew that upon the expected capture of Nanking he would be raised to the rank of a prince of the blood royal. It is also a fact that his consuming ambition aimed at the restoration of the old Chinese dynasty to the throne so long held by their Tartar conquerors."

This rumor, which Hayes so blithely (and without evidence) cited as a "fact," was well-circulated among Westerners in China: Tseng Kuo-fan's most eminent biographer was just one expert who acknowledged that "there are many who believe that [Ward] cherished a design to carve out for himself an empire in China." The Chinese government, which had eyes and ears throughout the settlements, could not have been unaware of such talk, and it is easy to imagine the kind of anxiety it must have engendered in the Forbidden City.

Typically, the imperial government's response to what they perceived as Ward's lack of restraint was an attempted exercise of greater control. For this reason, all the correspondence between Hsüeh Huan and the throne concerning Ward's acceptance as a Chinese subject, as well as his elevation to third-rank mandarin and brigadier general, was two-tracked. On the first and most obvious level there was appreciation for Ward's contributions to the imperial cause, but on the second level there was a more shielded—yet more important—hope that such honors and rewards would bring Ward finally and completely under Manchu sway. This effort can be seen as analogous to Prince Kung's belief that by granting treaty concessions to the Westerners and subsequently living by the terms of those treaties China would not be giving strength away but gaining greater control over the treaty powers.

Both policies were successful—to a degree. John K. Fairbank is certainly right to see the treaty system in nineteenth-century China as an extension of the ancient tribute system—in the minds of the Chinese, at any rate. In this light the creation of the Tsungli Yamen (the imperial Chinese foreign office) and the extensive machinations of Prince Kung were not so much concessions to the West as sophisticated ways to try to "pacify and control men from afar," as one imperial edict put it. Certainly, such efforts did not imply any Chinese acceptance of the superiority of Western culture or methods of doing business; as Fairbank points out, "[T]he treaties themselves did not remake the Chinese view of the world. To China they represented the supremacy of Western power, but this did not convey the Western idea of the supremacy of law."

Kung and Tz'u-hsi's approach to both Ward and Burgevine (who had followed Ward's example not only by petitioning for Chinese citizenship but by marrying a Chinese woman) reflected this same underlying attitude. Fairbank's summary of the results that Peking hoped to bring about through its complex system of rewarding and elevating the two Americans is worth quoting at length:

> The record concerning individual mercenaries like Frederick Townsend Ward conforms to the following pattern: first, the foreign adventurer displays his bravery and devotion to the imperial cause

by fighting the rebels with great ardor and daring, even to the point of being seriously wounded. Secondly, he seeks the equivalent of "Chinese citizenship," that is, to be enrolled in the Chinese population register, forgoing the jurisdiction of his own foreign consul. In addition, he adopts Chinese customs—for example, Chinese dress— and may even marry a Chinese wife. Finally he is given Chinese military rank and assimilated into the command of troops. . . .

In all these dealings with foreign military figures, the Ch'ing [Manchu] officials . . . feel it essential that if a foreigner is to lead a force of Chinese troops he must have imperial military status. This is conferred upon him personally from the emperor, as on any Ch'ing official. In return the foreigner is reported to be respectful, submissive, grateful, and loyal. As far as possible he is taken into the Chinese cultural order, parallel to his entrance into the Chinese power structure. When Ward and Burgevine are considered to have "turned toward civilization," seemingly forsaking their allegiance to their homeland, it is a serious and important point. Their opportunism must be watched and their sincerity kept under inspection, but the fact that they, almost alone among the foreign community of the time, have made a gesture of seeking registration as Chinese subjects makes it possible for them to lead a strategic military force in a vital sector of China. The Ch'ing officials control them through a personal relationship, which is the essence of control in the Chinese bureaucracy.

Such, of course, was not the situation as it actually existed but as China's rulers wished their own people and the outside world to see it. The imperial clique consistently portrayed themselves as *leading* military commanders such as Ward—as well as events in the Taiping rebellion generally—rather than being led *by* them. But in fact imperial policy concerning Ward, the Ever Victorious Army, and the Chinese civil war was almost always reactive. Never were specific goals or innovations set up ahead of time, personalities found to implement them, and results obtained that were in keeping with the original plan. From the earliest days of Tseng Kuo-fan's Hunan Army through the establishment of Ward's Ever Victorious Army, the various emperors and their advisers in the Forbidden City had been one step behind events, trying to assert their control over men and developments that consistently raced ahead of them.

In Ward's case, a careful examination of the details of his participation in both the Chinese "cultural order" and the imperial "power structure" reveals the startling extent to which he established his own pattern of relationship with the Chinese government. True, Ward did display "his bravery and devotion to the imperial cause by fighting the rebels with great ardor and daring," but he did so for a stipulated fee. The recapture of cities continued to net Ward handsome bonuses (although he sometimes accepted, quite unwisely, promissory notes from his backers in lieu of these bonuses), and this system was deeply resented by the imperial government. Similarly, Ward did seek Chinese citizenship, but he scorned the avarice and cowardice of his Chinese superiors and on at least one occasion had such a man put to death: an open challenge to the Confucian order.

As for adopting Chinese customs, Ward was anything but consistent. He showed respect for those customs that he found admirable or useful, but he steadfastly refused to oblige his imperial masters by either shaving his forehead or wearing his Chinese clothes. He did don his mandarin's robes once, but only out of deference to his wife and her family, a fact that must have piqued his superiors in Peking. Not only did Ward refuse to put himself into traditional Chinese garb but he obliged his soldiers to wear Western uniforms and taught them English drill commands. The "imitation foreign devils"—or, as the Chung Wang called them, "devil soldiers"—were initially embarrassed by all this, and by the ridicule of their fellow Chinese, but success in battle gave them great pride, just as it heightened Peking's discomfort with them.

Ward did marry a Chinese wife, but Chang-mei was the daughter of a Chekiang merchant who commanded little respect in Peking, as well as a woman of "bad luck" (the imperial clique, especially Tz'u-hsi, were nothing if not superstitious). And while Ward was given Chinese rank, this was as much an expression of concern and the need for control as it was of satisfaction. Finally, Ward's leadership of "a strategic military force in a vital sector of China" predated Peking's acceptance of his request for Chinese citizenship. As always, China's rulers were forced to give Ward what he wanted in order to keep him fighting. Imperial edicts subsequently tried to take the attitude that the government's plan all along had been to nurture Ward's development as a loyal Chinese subject. His promotions were portrayed as the natural reward for his successful completion of a process over which Peking had always been in control. But in fact Ward had shrewdly accrued to himself a measure of influence and independence unheard of even for a native Chinese officer, and robbed the imperial government of much of its freedom of action.

Yet did all this mean that Ward was disloyal or intended one day to commit one of the "ten abominations," subversion of the state? Certainly Ward was never anything but steadfastly true to China's interests, but China's interests and those of the Manchu elite were already becoming distinct considerations. Still, nothing in Ward's actions ever smacked of treason against the Manchus. His "fast" talk in Shanghai apparently did contain occasional references to the reestablishment of a native Chinese dynasty with himself in a position of power and influence, but such statements can more than easily be explained by his frustration with "Rascally" imperial officials. Or it is possible that he quite seriously intended to carve out his own principality. Certainly, the person who believed such ambitions beyond him "did not," in A. A. Hayes's phrase, "know General Ward."

That such pervasive uncertainty should have whirled around one man's actions explains why imperial edicts issued after Ward's death displayed simultaneous remorse and relief. Ward's services would certainly be missed by Peking, but the constant anxiety he prompted would not. Already, in the spring of 1862, that anxiety was becoming explicit at the provincial level: In April Hsüeh Huan memorialized to the throne and expressed second thoughts about Ward's conduct during the battles at Kao-ch'iao and Hsiao-t'ang. Certainly, Hsüeh was trying to excuse his own military incompetence, and that of his subordinate commanders, by criticizing Ward, but the memorial reveals the quandary into which government officials had been thrown:

> As for the fact that Ward refused our army's help in his allied
> action with British and French troops, in which they broke the

rebels' fortresses at Kao-ch'iao and Hsiao-t'ang, Ward's intention was to demonstrate his own capability and monopolize the achievement. . . . In all now there are about three thousand men [in the Ever Victorious Army]. Having observed Ward's capabilities, I think that this is the highest number he can command; if there are any more than that, I am afraid that he will not be able to train them thoroughly. Furthermore, there is something that I feel I should report, although it may be only my excessive suspicion. Ward is an American. . . . I thought that during this war against the rebels it is hard to find fine generals, so I sent in several memorials to petition the Throne's favor for him. But recently I have noticed that Ward is becoming more and more arrogant, treating the Ever Victorious Army as if it were his own. He makes his own decisions about the army's actions; whenever a battle is fought, he takes action before official orders reach him. His disobedience has become obvious. And after every battle he asks for a heavy reward, and it is not easy to satisfy his appetite. It is understood that foreigners love money and fame, but Ward's character is still too extreme and his heart is hard to fathom. I, your servant, dare not guarantee that he will be consistent [in his loyalty], and I will try to restrict him generally and thwart his arrogance. If his army becomes too large, it will be a tail too big to wag.

Ward shrugged off this growing storm of controversy with typical confidence. He continued to treat the Ever Victorious Army "as if it were his own" and to keep tight control over its training and objectives. His every action indicated that he meant to stay in China and expand his activities: His partnership with Yang Fang became increasingly successful, involving ever more river steamers, and the building of his house in Shanghai went on. In late spring he wrote happily to his brother, Harry, in New York: "I bought the 'Martin White,' a slow tug boat a little while ago for Forty One Thousand Taels and have got her at work on the river, making money fast they say. I have not had time to overhaul the accounts, but believe she will clear me 4 or 5000 taels per month[.]—I have got my house started in the French Bund, [a] fine lot 370 feet, front house 100 by 96 and I think will suit. My material comes from all over the province and costs but little." This was not to be any temporary residence, as another letter to Harry a few weeks later indicated: "My house is progressing slowly, was down last evening to see it—Basement built up 13 feet but it is all to be finished in four months. Figure Thirty-Four Thousand Taels [almost $55,000]." Apparently, Ward was looking beyond the defeat of the Taiping rebels to a day when he would be able to spend considerably more time in Shanghai.

But at the time Ward wrote these letters the downfall of the Heavenly Kingdom was far from achieved or even assured. From his luxurious seat of regional power in Soochow, the Chung Wang viewed the setbacks his armies suffered in Kiangsu during the opening months of 1862 with deep concern. In mid-March he issued orders to his field commanders in the Shanghai area to hold their ground and await his arrival: The Chung Wang intended again to take the field personally and lead his troops into Shanghai in order to establish Taiping authority over the port once and for all. It was the rebel general's last real chance to give his cause a new and perhaps long-term lease on life by gaining access to Shanghai's wealth and trade. And the only meaningful opposition he faced was the mysterious Hua's devil soldiers and a comparative handful of foreign regulars.

VII

"ACCUSTOMED TO THE ENEMY'S FIRE"

Alarmed as the Chung Wang was by the several reversals his armies suffered at the hands of Ward's disciplined Chinese and their foreign allies in the early spring of 1862, the rebel general's decision to make another attempt on Shanghai was influenced at least as much—and probably to a greater extent—by developments within the Taiping hierarchy. His own power had created jealousy not only in the increasingly withdrawn and unstable T'ien Wang but in other top rebel leaders and his own officers as well. "The T'ien Wang," the Chung Wang later wrote, "saw that I now had a large army and feared that I might have secret intentions—there were machinations by jealous ministers as well. . . . My subordinate officers were angry and bore resentment in their hearts. . . . [E]ach thought only of his own future, throwing administration and regulations into disorder." By occupying Shanghai the Chung Wang would not only impress the T'ien Wang with his loyalty but simultaneously demonstrate to ambitious rebel generals that he was still the Heavenly Kingdom's most formidable commander, a deadly adversary in any internecine conflict of the type that had decimated the rebel armies during the 1850s.

For all these reasons, the Chung Wang's eastern campaign during the late spring and summer of 1862 was characterized by greater force and conviction than had marked his incursion into Kiangsu two years earlier. The Taiping forces did not move with zealous abandon in March 1862: On the eighteenth, for example, the Chung Wang wrote to the rebel commander in Chia-ting, northwest of Shanghai, telling him not to attack the imperialists but to strengthen his present position. Chia-ting was a vital link in the chain of towns that composed Ward and Hope's thirty-mile radius around Shanghai, and the Chung Wang knew that it was a logical spot for an imperialist attack. In addition, the Taiping commander at Chia-ting was told to build new fortified encampments in the areas around Chia-ting and Ch'ing-p'u, posts that could accommodate the large numbers of Taiping soldiers who would accompany the Chung Wang on his return to eastern Kiangsu. All these preparations were aimed at the final elimination of Sung-chiang as a base of operations for Ward's troublesome devil soldiers, after which the Chung Wang could move his entire army against Shanghai without worrying about a pocket of resistance in his rear.

Ward and Hope were fully aware of the extreme danger of allowing the Taipings to entrench themselves firmly in such close proximity to Shanghai. So, too, was the new British army commander in China, General Sir Charles Staveley, who arrived in Shanghai late in March to take up Sir John Michel's duties. With him Staveley brought more troops, raising the number of British regulars in the port to about 2,500—roughly half of the overall British force in China. Even more important, Staveley transferred additional artillery units from the north, including batteries armed with Britain's new Armstrong guns, twelve-pounder fieldpieces with rifled barrels and breech-loading mechanisms that were out and away the best guns in China. Capable of firing highly explosive shells farther, more accurately, and at a faster rate than other cannon, the Armstrongs had already proved their worth during the Peking campaign, and they were soon to become the most feared weapon in the Shanghai theater of operations.

Fresh from his training of imperial soldiers at Tientsin, Staveley continued to regard Ward's Ever Victorious Army with a skeptical eye after his arrival in Shanghai. In his lingering jealousy and suspicion of Ward, Staveley lagged behind not only other Allied officers in Shanghai, such as Admirals Hope and Protet, but most of Britain's diplomatic corps in China as well. By March nearly every representative of the Crown from Frederick Bruce down was beginning to grasp Sir John Michel's point that, whatever Ward's personal motives or goals, his army could play—indeed was playing—an extremely useful role in strengthening and reforming the imperial Chinese government.

Though still of the opinion that the Taipings provided a useful spur with which to move the Manchus toward reform, Minister Bruce wrote to the British Foreign Office on March 26 to say that "[t]he weakness of China, rather than her strength, is likely to create a fresh Eastern Question in these seas." That same day Bruce wrote to Hope, suggesting a possible third trip by the admiral to Nanking, to negotiate new safeguards against rebel molestation of trade. Given the British and French governments' now demonstrated determination to prevent such depredations, Bruce supposed that the Taipings would be "more disposed to be reasonable" than they had in the past. In addition, Bruce suggested the formation, "at Foochow, Canton, etc., of corps like that of Mr. Ward, to protect them against marauders, and to be substituted for the thousands of useless rabble, who now eat up the resources of the state." Bruce's idea of a third trip to Nanking was never pursued— Hope was far happier fighting the Taipings than talking to them—but in his March 26 dispatch to Lord Russell at the Foreign Office Bruce echoed and elaborated his second suggestion, which was destined to produce important results.

"In the Chinese force organized and led by Mr. Ward," Bruce stated, "I see the nucleus and beginning of a military organization which may prove most valuable in the distracted state of China. If the Government is wise enough to adopt this reform, it may save itself; if not, the organization of this description of force at the chief ports will at all events preserve them from destruction." Describing the 40,000 imperial Chinese troops in and around Shanghai as a "worse than useless horde," Bruce pointed out that the funds needed for their maintenance could be better used to "equip and pay a disciplined force of from 20,000 to 25,000 men, who would be irresistible by any Chinese rebel bands." Of course, such a force would also be irresistible by any imperial Chinese army, which was precisely why Peking was determined to prevent its development. But such Manchu concerns for the perpetuation of their own power only exasperated Bruce, who went on to "suggest most strongly that 10,000 stand of smoothbore muskets be supplied without delay from India for the arming of [Ward's] men. I suggest either that these arms be given gratis, or that time be allowed for payment."

Bruce then revealed the rather surprising extent to which his opinions on Ward's activities had come full circle, and how fully he appreciated the larger political and diplomatic implications of those activities: "It may be objected to the policy I have recommended in this and other despatches, that there may be danger in introducing an improved military system into China. To this it may be replied with truth, that any risk arising from this cause is far less serious than the danger, commercial and political, we incur from the unchecked growth of anarchy throughout China." Thus Ward had evolved, in the mind of Britain's chief diplomatic officer in China, from a potential cause of anarchy and conflict with the rebels in early 1860 into the most advantageous answer to those same problems in 1862. This development occurred simultaneously with Ward's identification as a potential threat to Manchu authority by provincial officials and the imperial clique in Peking. Ward could not have helped but realize that these twin developments made it imperative that he take the field again, and quickly: By taking advantage of the Western powers' current enthusiasm for his army and acting in conjunction with the newly reinforced foreign regulars, he could gain important victories that would disarm his critics in the imperial government. And so, in the first week of April, Ward bid his new Chinese wife good-bye and once more led the Ever Victorious Army against the rebels in a series of assaults that were coordinated with attacks by Hope, Staveley, and Protet.

On Thursday, April 3, General Staveley took a thousand men from three regiments—the Ninety-ninth, the Fifth Bombay Native Infantry, and the Twenty-second Punjab Native Infantry, all units that would see heavy service against the Taipings in the weeks to come—and marched west-southwest from Shanghai to the deserted town of Chi-pao. In Chi-pao he rendezvoused with about 450 marines and sailors under the overall command of Admiral Hope. Individual naval detachments were commanded by a group of officers whose names were cropping up more and more in British dispatches concerning actions against the Taipings:

Captain George Willes, who had intrepidly investigated rebel fortifications and armaments at Wu-sung and scouted Kao-ch'iao earlier in the year; Captain John Borlase of the *Pearl,* who would shortly demonstrate an enthusiasm for fighting the Taipings that rivaled Hope's own; and Captain John Holland of the Royal Marines, a pugnacious officer with a singular appreciation of brute force and an equally singular disdain for tactical complexity.

In Chi-pao this British force was joined by several hundred of Ward's soldiers, along with three hundred French marines and sailors under Admiral Protet. In addition, one hundred of Adrien Tardif de Moidrey's Franco-Chinese Corps arrived, with a half-dozen rifled howitzers and guns. The British had brought along about ten pieces of artillery, including several of Hope's large naval guns and Staveley's devastating Armstrongs. In all, the expeditionary force that assembled at Chi-pao was an unusually powerful one, and on the morning of April 4 it marched due west toward the rebel bastion of Wang-chia-ssu.

Though an unwalled town, Wang-chia-ssu had been fortified in a manner that typified the Chung Wang's new determination not to lose ground in eastern Kiangsu. Perhaps having learned from their several experiences of being trapped in their own strongholds, the Taipings had built not one but a series of stockades, each surrounded by the usual network of ditches spiked with bamboo. These stockades interlocked, allowing the various rebel detachments—some four or five thousand men in all—to support each other; at the same time, because of their separation, the fate of all the stockades was not necessarily dependent on any one. It was an impressive example of the Chinese genius for defense, one that would put the Allied expeditionary force to a genuine test.

The general Allied plan of attack at Wang-chia-ssu called for an initial assault from the west and north; the rebels, it was assumed, would flee south, where they were to be intercepted by Ward, who was marching north-northeast from Sung-chiang with another thousand to fifteen hundred of his troops. At first all went well: At 8:00 A.M. a dense fog lifted to reveal the Taipings brandishing hundreds of banners atop the two-mile expanse of their various stockades, and the French and British artillery, along with Tardif de Moidrey's guns, immediately opened up a devastating fire. For half an hour the pummeling continued, the rebels trying for a time to answer with their gingals and smaller guns but eventually growing altogether silent. Already Taiping soldiers could be seen escaping from various stockades. But the main body of the Ever Victorious Army was nowhere in sight. Those of Ward's men who were present were dispatched to deal with the fleeing rebels, and although they did, according to an eyewitness account published in the *North China Herald,* "considerable execution" among the fugitives, most of the rebels were able to escape. By 10:30 the Taipings were in full flight under pressure of a frontal assault by the British troops, but Ward's main force still had not appeared, and the rebels continued to stream south toward safety.

Whether Ward was held up by another rebel force or by difficult terrain has never been clear. The fact that when he finally arrived in the early afternoon he was without artillery suggests that he had been delayed in trying to get his guns through the soft earth between Sung-chiang and Wang-chia-ssu, and had finally abandoned the effort and gone ahead with just his infantry. Whatever the case, only several hundred of the Taipings at Wang-chia-ssu had been killed, and the survivors subsequently withdrew into an even more powerful series of interlocking stockades—garrisoned by a much stronger rebel force—at Lung-chu-an, half a dozen miles to the southeast. The body of the Allied force returned to Chi-pao, its commanders understandably disappointed. The day had done nothing to raise General Staveley's estimation of the Ever Victorious Army, and, as if to restore the slightly tarnished name of his force, Ward elected to pursue the Taipings to Lung-chu-an. Admiral Hope accompanied him.

The only real blunder Ward had made to this point—his assault on Ch'ing-p'u in August 1860—had been a result of wounded pride. So, too, was the second mistake of his career: attacking Lung-chu-an on April 4, 1862, without waiting for artillery support. Edward Forester—in a puzzling moment of humility that suggests more a desire to portray himself as the driving force behind the Ever Victorious Army's field operations, mistaken and otherwise, than it does genuine honesty—later wrote that he was responsible for the hurried assault against the rebel stockades. But once again his claims are uncorroborated and unsupportable. Much more plausible is Augustus Lindley's description of the attack, as seen from the Taiping side:

> Drawing his mercenary sword, and brushing back the Yankee locks, General Ward gave the word to assault in a tone of assured victory. The disciplined Chinamen, led by their foreign officers, rushed forward bravely enough; but the Taipings had not been half destroyed by shot and shell; neither at that time had they lost their best troops in conflict with the British and French. . . . Consequently, after three attempts to storm the stockade, when five officers and seventy men [of the Ever Victorious Army] were placed *hors de combat*, Admiral Hope advanced to call off the men, and was rewarded with a Taiping bullet lodged in the calf of his leg. Ward, having none of the resistless artillery to mow down the patriotic Taipings, found them more than a match for his men—disciplined, led by foreigners, and well armed as they were. A retreat was therefore sounded, and the British Admiral was ignominiously carried away upon a litter borne by sundry cursing Celestials [imperialists].

In assaulting Lung-chu-an, Ward had rashly thrown his fifteen hundred men, unsupported by artillery, against some eight thousand Taipings who fought behind the safety of strong entrenchments. The odds against success were too astronomical even for Ward. Returning to Chi-pao with the wounded Admiral Hope—who, according to Forester, waited in line for six hours behind other, more seriously wounded men before having his leg treated, by which time the admiral's boot was "filled to overflowing with blood"—Ward joined the other Allied commanders in planning a more considered and coordinated assault on Lung-chu-an. General Staveley, predictably, declined to dispatch his army troops on this latest adventure; rather he agreed, with apparent point, to hold Chi-pao "in case of a reverse," as the *Herald* correspondent put it. Admiral Hope was forced by the wound in his leg to remain in Chi-pao, and the British naval units were placed under the command of Captain Borlase. Admiral Protet agreed to participate, as did Tardif de Moidrey, and at 7:00 A.M. on April 5 this force set out for Lung-chu-an.

During the night the Taipings had reinforced their stockades. Ward's men were sent out toward these strengthened positions in skirmishing order, while the British and French contingents took up positions behind their guns, which were about three hundred yards from the Taiping fortifications. As the artillery opened fire, Ward's men began to move in a large semicircle toward the rebels, under cover of various graves and burial mounds outside the town. Without risking or losing a man, the French and British continued to hammer away at Lung-chu-an, and very quickly Ward was in position to lead the final assault, which was observed by the *Herald* correspondent: "Ward's men pushed on beautifully and in excellent order from cover to cover; while the rebels, notwithstanding the heavy pounding of the artillery, kept up a brisk fire upon them, by which five men were killed and two officers with seven men wounded. Having stolen up to within a hundred yards, Ward's men made a most gallant rush—cheering in the English manner—causing the rebels to abandon their outworks." According to Captain Borlase, the rebels, seeing that Ward's men were quickly moving around to cut off their retreat, "immediately decamped." And, with that, the chase was on.

After setting fire to the seven interlocking stockades of Lung-chu-an, the men of the Ever Victorious Army, along with the French and British contingents, herded the rebels into and out of other nearby encampments, driving them ever farther from their larger bases. By afternoon the Allied expeditionary force was back in Chi-pao, having completed what the *Herald* termed "the strongest and most successful attack by foreigners upon the Taiping rebels near Shanghai which has yet occurred." There were apparent lessons to be drawn from the day, and Ward, upon returning to Sung-chiang, quickly set about absorbing them.

Clearly, the Taipings' new strategy of firmly consolidating their positions before advancing meant that assault troops such as the Ever Victorious Army would more than ever require strong artillery support. The *Herald* may have overstated the case when it declared that "with a powerful artillery force every rebel post in the province might be taken with ease," but the essential point was correct. Ward had demonstrated that his disciplined infantry battalions were the equal of any foot soldiers to be found in China; mobile and daring, they represented a true flying column. But if the Ever Victorious Army was to be able to stand on its own merits at all times and in all situations, Ward would have to be sure that he could bring not only his infantry but the artillery units he was training at Sung-chiang, as well as his small but growing flotilla of armed steamers, to bear on any battle in the province. By relying on Western guns he was doing more than giving Allied artillery a role in the fighting; he was making the Western forces indispensable to success.

This point was again driven home on April 17, when Ward took four hundred of his men and joined an Anglo-French assault on Chou-p'u, the Taipings' strongest position on the Pootung peninsula (the body of land lying between the Huang-pu River and the sea). General Staveley brought elements of the same three British infantry regiments—the Twenty-second Punjab, the Fifth Bombay and the Ninety-ninth—while Admiral Protet headed a contingent of four hundred French sailors and marines. Admiral Hope was still recovering from his leg wound, and command of the British naval detachments again devolved on Captain Borlase. In all some two thousand Allied troops supported by a dozen guns took part in the action, which followed the same pattern as the successful assault on Lung-chu-an: The men were ferried in British gunboats, and, on arriving before the interlocking stockades of Chou-p'u, Ward's troops spread out as skirmishers and storming parties, while the Allied troops remained behind the safety of their guns.

At two in the afternoon, according to Captain Borlase, the guns opened "a most destructive fire," under cover of which Ward's men moved into position to intercept the Taipings when they evacuated the town, it being by now assumed that the rebels would not hold up under the concentrated fire of the British and French naval guns, Tardif de Moidrey's howitzers, and Staveley's Armstrongs. Sure enough, within half an hour the four to five thousand Taiping defenders had begun to flee, and many were shot down as they did: Borlase put the enemy dead at three hundred, but Augustus Lindley claimed that no fewer than six hundred lost their lives. Ward's men fought their way through ditches spiked with bamboo and stormed the inner fortifications, and within hours the action was over. It was a particularly satisfying day for the attacking soldiers, because Chou-p'u was found to be full of Taiping loot. The *Shanghai Daily Shipping List* stated that

> [a]s the houses were ransacked, great quantities of valuable jewels, gold, silver, dollars, and costly dresses were found, which was fair loot to the officers and men. . . . It was a glorious day of looting for everybody, and we hear that one party, who discovered the Taiping treasury chest with several thousand dollars in it, after loading himself to his heart's content, was obliged to give some of them away to lighten his pockets, which were heavier than he could well bear—a marked case of *l'embarras des richesses.*

Matters of loot aside, the need for Ward to develop a more mobile and impressive artillery arm was apparent, and in the weeks to come it was this branch of service that received his special attention. Having experienced many times the difficulty of moving land guns through the Kiangsu countryside, Ward placed steadily greater emphasis on expanding his fleet of steamers and beefing up their armaments. He already had at his disposal the *Cricket* and the *Zingari,* and in late April or early May he either chartered or bought three more vessels, the *Rose,* the *Pao-shun,* and the steamer whose name would come to be most closely associated with the operations of the Ever Victorious Army, the *Hyson.* The British journalist Andrew Wilson described the *Hyson* as "a small iron paddle-steamer, of about ninety feet long and twenty-four feet wide, drawing three to four feet of water, and carrying one 32-pounder on a moving platform at her bow, while at her stern there was a 12-pounder howitzer. A loopholed protection of planking ran round the bulwarks to a height of six feet, and the steam-chests were protected by a timber traverse. She averaged eight knots per hour."

Steamers such as the *Hyson* would play an especially critical role in attacking towns that were not removed from the waterways of Kiangsu. But landlocked operations would also require heavy artillery support, as Ward had seen at Wang-chia-ssu, and he continued to push for the procurement of up-to-date land guns. It was a slow process. In the spring of 1862 Ward was able to acquire little more than some serviceable American twelve-pounders, but by the late summer and early fall the Ever Victorious Army was being outfitted with advanced British and French pieces as well. Ward's emphasis on artillery endured after his death: According to Wilson, when the Ever Victorious Army's artillery arm reached its height some months after its creator had been killed, it had "two 8-inch howitzers, four 32-pounder guns, three 24-pounder howitzers, twelve 12-pounder howitzers, ten American 12-pounder mountain howitzers, eight 4½–inch mountain howitzers, fourteen mortars, brass, 4½ to 8 inches, and six inch rocket tubes." Wilson's somewhat laconic statement that this "was a heavy force of artillery in the circumstances" reflected how fully Ward, during his tenure in command, put the Ever Victorious Army on a course toward independence.

Soon after the battles of Wang-chia-ssu, Lung-chu-an, and Chou-p'u, Li Hung-chang and his long-awaited Anhwei Army began to arrive in Shanghai, opening a new chapter in the military and political history of the port during the Taiping period. Ferried down the Yangtze on British vessels, the Anhwei troops were a very different breed of soldier from the largely useless and often destructive imperialist Green Standard soldiers who operated in the Shanghai region. Thus far the Green Standard contingents had been unable to competently garrison any of the important positions won by Ward and the Westerners. In Chou-p'u, for example, Ward's men, along with elements of the Twenty-second Punjab Regiment, had held the town during the night following the attack, then turned it over to Green Standard soldiers for permanent garrisoning. But the nervous Green Standard men, left on their own, quickly abandoned it. The Taipings were thus free to return and rebuild their fortifications in the Chou-p'u area as soon as the Ever Victorious Army and the foreign contingents turned their attention to other sections of the thirty-mile radius. It was hoped that the Anhwei Army would be able to finally provide badly needed, effective garrison troops. Its commander, however, had other ideas.

Li Hung-chang's caution concerning foreign military activities in China, as well as his personal ambition, dictated that he would not allow the troops that he and Tseng Kuo-fan had so carefully trained and indoctrinated to play a supporting role to Western regulars, or even to the Ever Victorious Army, at least until Li was better acquainted with the imitation foreign devils and their commander. Li's first concern on reaching Shanghai was, in fact, not fighting the rebels at all but slowly and carefully assessing the immensely complex situation that faced him in the port. Having received his final civil and military schooling at the feet of Tseng Kuo-fan—a man who did not tolerate corruption or the subordination of Chinese interests—Li was deeply disturbed by much of what he found. "The Taotais Wu and Yang Fang," he wrote to Tseng in mid-April, "and the officials and gentry of the Joint Defence Bureau, in managing diplomatic relations, behave in too humble and flattering a manner. His Excellency Hsüeh [Huan] barely maintains a proper attitude, and often has quarrels with the foreigners. They do not treat him very amicably, and often quarrel with him over joint military action in the interior."

Li's soldiers did not arrive in Shanghai all at once but over a period of weeks, giving him an excuse for not going on the offensive immediately. In addition, Li did not become acting governor of Kiangsu until mid-May; for the moment, overall responsibility for imperial military movements remained with Hsüeh Huan. During the grace period afforded by these two factors, Li continued to observe and report back to Tseng concerning affairs in Shanghai without engaging in any significant military operations. Worried as he was about the honesty and capabilities of his fellow Chinese officers and officials as well as about the ultimate intentions of the Western powers, Li—who always viewed affairs with unusual and incisive detachment—did not fall prey to exaggerated suspicions about Ward. Ordered by Peking to "fraternize" and make "small rewards" to "Ward and others who seek both fame and fortune," Li went on to exhibit genuine admiration for the commander of the Ever Victorious Army, although he never gave full credence to Ward's change of nationality. For the remainder of his days Ward remained a "foreigner" to Li, albeit "the most vigorous of all" foreigners in his actions against the Taipings.

Ward also developed a qualified respect and admiration for the man who soon became his imperial superior. Li Hung-chang was obviously, in style, training, and leadership ability, far superior to the Chinese officials Ward was used to doing business with in Shanghai. At the same time, Ward could see that Li—whatever his condemnations of Wu, Yang, and the rest of their clique for corruption—was no less ambitious or averse to political and financial maneuvering than any of them. To Ward, Li was "the Devilish Governor," yet while there was perception in the epithet, there was little real hostility. And certainly, during the battles they fought together in the summer of 1862, the two men demonstrated something that transcended personal suspicions and jealousies. For it was Ward and Li, acting in concert, who most clearly revealed that if the Chinese were willing to suspend their cultural arrogance, accept the assistance of ambitious but loyal outsiders such as Ward, and adapt to Western ways of war, they might not only quell rebellion within their borders but establish themselves as a power to be reckoned with internationally.

In mid-April, however, the victories of summer were still many battles away. On April 22 Admiral Hope, General Staveley, and Admiral Protet met in Shanghai to sign an agreement formalizing their determination to clear the thirty-mile radius around the city in conjunction with the Ever Victorious Army. Specifically, the Allied commanders declared that occupation of Chia-ting, Ch'ing-p'u, Sung-chiang, Nan-ch'iao (south of Shanghai), and Che-lin (south of Nan-ch'iao) was necessary to "keep the rebels at a distance, which will preclude the continuance of that state of alarm which has prevailed during the last few months, and which has been so detrimental to [Shanghai's] commerce." The agreement noted that Ward was currently in possession of Sung-chiang and intended to fortify Ch'ing-p'u similarly, once it had been retaken. Hsüeh Huan had pledged garrison forces for the other cities, but, recognizing the value of this commitment, the Allied agreement added that "it will also be expedient to place 200 troops, half English and half French, in support of the Chinese, until Colonel Ward's force is sufficiently augmented to enable him to replace them by 300 of his men."

Within days of signing this agreement, the Allied commanders were surprised to learn that Hsüeh Huan, determined to play a role in the thirty-mile-radius fighting, had ordered his Green Standard troops to attack a Taiping encampment at Nan-hsiang, on the line from Shanghai to Chia-ting. The assault took place on April 25 and, even more surprising, was successful, the rebels being driven to another, stronger encampment a mile away. On the following day General Staveley—as if to prove he would not be outpaced by the imperialists—ordered a march on Nan-hsiang, where he intended to link up with British naval units in preparation for a large-scale march on Chia-ting. Moving quickly through a dozen miles of devastated countryside, the British troops succeeded in reaching Nan-hsiang that same day and were joined there by naval units under Captain Willes and marines under Captain Holland. Early on the morning of the twenty-seventh, elements of the Thirty-first Regiment and the Royal Artillery also reached Nan-hsiang, many by boat. Immediately, skirmishing parties probed the nearby Taiping position, which was surrounded by stockades and ditches.

Ward, in the meantime, was leaving little to chance in preparing his army for its part in the looming attack on Chia-ting. Loading his men and several guns aboard his steamers as well as another thirty smaller gunboats, he made the approach to Chia-ting by water: At last the Ever Victorious Army would be in a position to cover its own attack with its own guns. Back on the route from Nan-hsiang to Chia-ting, General Staveley received a rude shock when, without coordinating his movements with his French comrades, he attacked the Taiping positions outside Nan-hsiang and was beaten back. Making as little of this incident as possible, the *North China Herald* reported that Staveley quickly recouped and was soon on the road to Chia-ting again. But the sight of British regulars retreating before rebel fire must have wounded Staveley's pride deeply, although he could take some solace in the fact that Ward had not yet arrived to witness the humiliation. The Ever Victorious Army linked up with the Allied units on the twenty-eighth, at which point the badly outclassed Taipings in the area began a hasty retreat to the northwest. Close to 3,000 French and British troops, along with Tardif de Moidrey's Franco-Chinese Corps, Ward's 1,400 men, and several thousand Green Standard soldiers, now moved in a general advance on the walls of Chia-ting.

The Allied force spent April 30 reconnoitering the city's defenses and getting their various artillery units into place. The former assignment was entrusted to General Staveley's brother-in-law and chief of engineers, Captain Charles G. Gordon. Gordon's ability to read and map terrain quickly was exceptional, and he charted Chia-ting in a manner that would characterize the rest of his tour of duty in China and, indeed, his entire life: with utter disregard for his own safety. Deeply religious and sometimes suspected of harboring a martyr complex, Gordon was at his best in situations of immense physical peril. His maps of the thirty-mile radius, often drawn as Taiping musket balls and bullets rained around him, eventually became vital to every commander in the region. Gordon dismissed the achievement with typical disdain, noting simply that he had been "in every town and village in the thirty miles' radius. The country is the same everywhere—a dead flat, with innumerable creeks and bad pathways. There is nothing of any interest in China; if you have seen one village you have seen the whole country." But Gordon did see other sights, at Chia-ting and elsewhere, that impressed him more than the Chinese countryside: most notably the disciplined Chinese soldiers of the Ever Victorious Army, and the inventive command techniques of its creator.

By the following morning the Allied expeditionary force was ready for its assault on Chia-ting. "Daylight on the 1st of charming May," Augustus Lindley recalled, "was ushered in by the roar of a large park of foreign artillery." The French and British troops had taken up positions outside Chia-ting's southern and eastern gates, while Ward attacked from the west and the Green Standard units were assigned to cover any Taiping attempt to escape through the city's north gate. Chia-ting's well-built walls were some three miles in circumference, and for two hours Ward's guns and those of the various Allied units battered at them incessantly, during which time the city's six thousand defenders were thrown into a state of utter confusion. Several Taiping units composed of young boys took part in the defense, and Lindley recounted one sad tale that gave a taste of the fiery terror produced by the artillery bombardment:

> Three little fellows, each armed with a small matchlock, were
> seen by a friend of mine to rush forward directly a large shell would

knock down a portion of the parapet and fire off their puny weapons at the foe. They were too small to reach the loop-holes, and so waited till the 32-pound shot of the besiegers made a hole for them to use. To avoid the deadly rifles they never used the same hole twice, but nevertheless were all killed, for my friend, when passing round the walls, found their bodies lying close together and crushed by a mass of fallen stonework.

Under the relentless pressure of the guns, the Taipings began to withdraw toward the avenue of least resistance: the imperialist detachments to the north. Seeing this, the other Allied units dashed to the walls, raised scaling ladders, and began their assault. "There was a great race," wrote Dr. Macgowan, "between the English, French and Chinese to be the first to plant their respective colours on the city walls. All three claimed to be first. The Sung-chiang contingent strongly claimed this honour; although, from apprehensions of the atrocities they might perpetrate, they were ordered not to enter the city." Ward was being careful that his men should not spoil their reputation either in the countryside or in Peking through the kind of wanton pillaging that the French and British units engaged in immediately after they entered Chia-ting. Charles Schmidt recalled ironically that the French troops "seemed to be in the very best humour that day, for they carried off everything that could be got away. It was a romantic sight to see the soldiery leaving the city, followed by bullocks, sheep, goats, boys and women—all considered as loot. . . . In fact the French troops showed a bad example to the new Chinese levies, in committing all sorts of cruelties, which were all laid to Ward's force."

The behavior of the British troops was not much better than that of their French allies: The *China Mail* commented that "[t]here is another matter of regret, and that is, that while we are stigmatizing the rebels as robbers and bandits, we should take their treasures and divide it amongst ourselves. . . . There is every reason to believe that England's chivalry is likely to be kept a profound secret from the people of China so long as her affairs are under the present guidance."

Taiping casualties—most of which occurred during their retreat from the city—were severe: Augustus Lindley put them as high as 2,500 killed. Five hundred of Ward's men were detached to garrison Chia-ting, along with two hundred British troops and the imperialist units. The rest of the Ever Victorious Army then boarded their steamers and gunboats for the trip back to Sung-chiang. But the mood of the troops was less than triumphant. As Dr. Macgowan wrote: "Those who returned to Sung-chiang were sulky and insubordinate, through not being allowed to plunder. What booty some of them managed to get was taken from them by the English provost-sergeants. It was usual to accord three days furlough, which was granted on this occasion also; and then drill instruction and recruiting were resumed." In addition, "a German band was engaged," perhaps to raise the morale of soldiers who were hard put to understand why their commander had stood by and watched the Allied troops strip Chia-ting without allowing his own men to participate. But Ward's reasoning was sound: Excessive looting, even had Ward been personally disposed to it, would at this critical juncture have marked the Ever Victorious Army as just another oppressive imperial army, to be feared as much as the rebels by Kiangsu's peasants. The growth of both Ward's cult of personality and the mystique of his contingent required extreme restraint.

Soon after Chia-ting the British Foreign Office, impressed with Ward's activities, approved both the strategy of the thirty-mile radius and the idea of expanding the Ever Victorious Army to the remarkable size of ten thousand men. On May 6 a British Foreign Office memorandum to the Lords of the Admiralty stated that "Her Majesty's Government are of the opinion that stores, and even guns and muskets which can be spared, should be sold to Colonel Ward . . . at cost price. Lord Russell will instruct Her Majesty's Minister at Peking to advise the Chinese Government to furnish Colonel Ward the supplies he may require, and to do their utmost to raise his force to ten thousand men." Such a notion was out of the question to the Manchus, who did their very best to plead poverty and every other excuse for not making it possible for Ward's army to grow beyond the four to five thousand it eventually did reach. But this expanded and high-level British support meant that Ward would have considerably less trouble procuring rifles, muskets, pistols, swords, ammunition, and other equipment for his men, as well as new pieces of up-to-date artillery.

The British attitude toward the Ever Victorious Army was indicative of London's increasing impatience with Chinese anarchy and the Taiping rebels. In perhaps the most famous embodiment of this impatience, Captain Roderick Dew—the aggressive British naval officer who, in 1860, had scoured Shanghai looking for Ward, captured Burgevine, and subsequently been fired on by the Taipings outside Ch'ing-p'u—retook the Chekiang port of Ningpo on May 10. The operation was reminiscent of Ward's capture of Sung-chiang in 1860, a fact that was not altogether surprising, for in temperament the two men were much alike. By 1862 their relationship had evolved so far that Ward was able to refer to Dew as "my friend and moreover a fine fellow & officer." Dew's exploits at Ningpo offer clues to the origins of this friendship.

Since capturing Ningpo in December 1861, the Taipings had garrisoned it with between twenty and thirty thousand troops and tried to avoid conflict with the Westerners who lived and traded in the treaty port. But in mid-April, with Allied contingents actively campaigning against the Chung Wang in the Shanghai area, the Taipings in Ningpo had become testy: Some shots were fired at a British gunboat by unidentified rebels, and several Chinese inside the British settlement were reportedly killed by similar fire. Admiral Hope, still nursing the leg wound he had received at the hands of the rebels at Lung-chu-an, was in no mood to hear of high-handed Taiping actions against his officers in Ningpo: Captain Dew was immediately dispatched aboard HMS *Encounter,* with orders to warn the Taipings that such behavior would bring forceful British intervention.

Dew received no apologies from the Taiping commanders in Ningpo when he arrived on April 24, and tension mounted. At this point the taotai of the city arrived with a fleet of Chinese junks commanded by one A-pak, a piratical acquaintance (and sometime hireling) of Ward's. The taotai and A-pak met with Dew and the French naval commander and asked for their help in an attempt to reestablish imperial authority over the port. Dew refused to participate without provocation, but he knew that such provocation was not far off. The Taipings had built a series of impressive fortifications overlooking the British settlement and installed in them a battery of sixty-eight-pounder guns that could not be fired without at least some risk to British residents. Dew warned the Taipings that if any such firing took place—even if the rebels were only defending themselves—he would return fire on the city. All A-pak had to do was move his junks past the foreign ships in the harbor, draw the inevitable Taiping fire, and British participation in the battle would be ensured. Such was the sequence of events on the morning of May 10.

With the *Encounter* and a handful of British and French gunboats—including the *Confucius,* on which Ward had served years earlier—Dew launched a determined assault on one of Ningpo's gates as soon as the Taipings fired on A-pak. The naval guns blazed away at the Taiping position while Dew took two hours off for lunch; then the *Encounter*'s captain personally scaled the gate at the head of several hundred British and French sailors. Suffering heavy casualties, Dew's party reached the top of the gate, hauled up a howitzer, and began to rake the inside of the city with artillery fire. The rebels stood this punishment briefly, then began a general withdrawal to the city of Yü-Yao, some thirty miles away.

Without any higher authorization than some vaguely encouraging words from Admiral Hope, Captain Dew had committed a major act of aggression against the rebels. What he found inside Ningpo's walls, however, convinced him that his course had been the right one. Dew later wrote: "I had known Ningpo in its palmy days, when it boasted itself one of the first commercial cities of the empire; but now, on this 11th May, one might have fancied that an angel of destruction had been at work in the city as in its suburbs. All the latter, with their wealthy hongs and thousands of houses, lay leveled; while in the city itself, once the home of half a million people, no trace or vestige of an inhabitant could be seen. Truly it was a city of the dead."

Within a week, a detachment of four to five hundred men of the Ever Victorious Army had arrived in Ningpo to assist in garrisoning the port by guarding its western gate, and by month's end the city's activities were returning to something like normal. But Dew endured heavy criticism for his impulsive action from both his naval superiors and

British diplomatic officers. Determined nevertheless to follow up his initial move, he set about organizing a small defensive force of disciplined Chinese soldiers led by British officers. In doing so he ran into the additional opposition of local mandarins, who had little desire to see the British extend their control over yet another treaty port.

The French, witnessing the various controversies that swirled around Dew's actions, saw an opening. The Imperial Chinese Customs Commissioner for the port, the Frenchman Prosper Giquel, had returned following Ningpo's liberation, ready not only to reopen his customs house but to make use of the careful military study he had done in and around Shanghai. Conferring first with Ningpo's mandarins and then with the French naval commander in East Asia, Giquel gained support for the idea of a corps of disciplined Chinese led by French officers. The unit would play much the same role that Ward's Ever Victorious Army was filling in Shanghai and would establish France rather than England as the most influential Western power in Ningpo. The Chinese provincial officials agreed, out of a desire as much to play the two foreign nations off against each other as to reform the Chekiang military; they were, however, less forthcoming with funds for Giquel's project than Hsüeh Huan, Wu Hsü, and Yang Fang had been for Ward's. But Giquel did manage to have a talented French officer, Albert Édouard Le Brethon de Caligny (who had commanded the *Confucius* during Dew's attack on Ningpo), named commander of the new unit. And, although the few hundred Chinese recruits they raised were early on armed with obsolete—even dangerous—firearms, and although the British strongly condemned the project, Giquel's and Le Brethon de Caligny's determination ensured future success.

The man who had served as Giquel's model in the meantime was making ready to assault the city that two years earlier had been the site of his only catastrophic failure. The capture of Ch'ing-p'u, and after it Nan-ch'iao and Che-lin, represented the final step in the Allied-imperialist plan to clear the thirty-mile radius. In preparing for his part in the Ch'ing-p'u assault, which was scheduled for the second week in May, Ward assembled an even stronger contingent than he had brought to Chia-ting. There would be no repeat of the grisly humiliations of 1860:

Some eighteen hundred men, supported by the steamers with their big guns as well as batteries of howitzers, were drilled to a high state of readiness.

Ward's consistent emphasis on discipline, both on the battlefield and off, was by this point showing not only in his men but in the general condition of Sung-chiang and its environs. The Allied expeditionary force of about 2,600 men discovered as much when they steamed up the Huang-pu from Shanghai to consolidate with the Ever Victorious Army before marching on Ch'ing-p'u. As one eyewitness put it in an account published in the *North China Herald:*

> The city of Sung-chiang has latterly become much improved under Colonel Ward's protection. Very nearly all the suburbs, which were destroyed by the rebels when in possession of the place, have been rebuilt; and although there are a large number of shops, yet they scarcely seem adequate for the wants of the population,—which is very large. Good fish, mutton, and beef is to be had here in abundance. . . . The city walls have been repaired, and embrasures cut for guns, in imitation of the English method. They are manned with cannon on ship-carriages, working on roughly-made platforms, with due provision of shot alongside each. The guard-houses are tenanted by Ward's drilled Chinamen,—who present a very creditable appearance. The sentries had evidently been ordered to pay the proper compliments to foreign officers, and carried arms to every uniform that presented an inch of gold lace, with great propriety.

On May 8 the combined expeditionary force—joined by several thousand imperialists under Ward's old associate Li Heng-sung—embarked for Kuang-fu-lin aboard countless steamers, gunboats, and smaller craft. "Every one was in immense spirits," according to the *Herald* account, "the laugh resounded, and jokes and repartee passed from boat to boat increasing the volume of merriment as they were bandied about by hundreds of mouths. . . . Such a Babel of sounds filling the air; commissaries cursing, coolies groaning, voluble Hindustani, guttural Chinese, and good broad English and Irish resounding on all sides." Moving at a leisurely pace, the flotilla finally reached Ch'ing-p'u on the ninth, under a steady rainfall.

By the morning of the tenth the rain had stopped, and the expeditionary force began to take up positions before the walls of Ch'ing-p'u and attend to the business of reconnoitering. Once again, Captain Charles Gordon braved rebel musket fire to make a detailed map of the city's defenses: The *Herald* account stated that he got within fifty yards of the Taiping perimeter. A rebel deserter was interrogated and revealed that many of the city's defenders were impressed peasants with little enthusiasm for the job before them; thus heartened, Ward and his comrades decided to wait for the ground to dry before making their attack.

Ward deployed his men before the eastern and northern walls of Ch'ing-p'u, while Li Heng-sung's men guarded the west gate and the Allied forces prepared to attack the southern gate. At dawn on May 12, the firing commenced. Considering the rather colorful trip that had preceded it, as well as the emotional value that Ward could not have helped but attach to Ch'ing-p'u, the battle itself was brief and anticlimactic. The rebel deserter's report that many of the defenders were less than dedicated proved true: About an hour before the artillery barrage stopped, said the *Herald* correspondent, "a man came from the city into Ward's camp and offered to give it up if we would cease firing. He was not to be trusted and his offer was refused." The Taipings subsequently left the city in haste: Ward's men and the Allied soldiers, on entering the city, found "bowls of food still smoking," as well as "kettles of hot tea . . . which the rebels had left in their speedy retreat from the walls."

By 8:00 A.M. the battle was over. Ward deposited fifteen hundred of his men in the town as a garrison, under the command of Colonel Forester (Forester's rank, like most of those in the Ever Victorious Army, was conferred by Ward and did not represent a commission in the Chinese service). Once again, Ward did not permit his men to plunder the city (although he received a thirty-thousand-tael bonus for its capture), and he quickly took those men who were not staying with

Forester back to Sung-chiang. Within days, however, the Ever Victorious Army was again on the move, marching with the Allied expeditionary force against Nan-ch'iao.

The casualties suffered by Ward's force and the other Allied contingents thus far in the thirty-mile-radius campaign had been exceptionally low, all the more so when measured against the staggeringly disproportionate losses inflicted on the Taipings. In the battles to date Ward's killed and wounded could be measured in the tens, while the Allies rarely had more than one or two men killed during a battle. This low casualty rate, along with the plundering permitted by Allied commanders and the relatively small amounts of actual marching that had to be done during the campaign, had all given the undertaking what Richard J. Smith has called an "almost carnival atmosphere." Nan-ch'iao looked to be more of the same. A smaller city than Ch'ing-p'u, its loose brick walls only about three-quarters of a mile in circumference and surrounded by a simple ditch and dike, Nan-ch'iao was occupied by a large number of Taipings who had no ordnance that could match the artillery Ward and the Allies were bringing with them. Allied spirits during the approach to the city were once again high.

On Friday, May 16, the expeditionary force arrived at Nan-ch'iao, and on the seventeenth Admiral Protet and General Staveley undertook a personal reconnaissance of the city's defenses. Ward, as always, assumed his position at the head of his troops, preparing to storm Nan-ch'iao after the guns had done their work. In the afternoon the artillery barrage began, and before long the usual sight of Taipings fleeing the city was noticed. At this point, General Staveley ordered the guns to cease fire and, together with his staff, began to dash about the walls looking for a suitable spot for storming. He was followed by a French contingent under Admiral Protet, moving at double time. And then, according to the *Herald* correspondent, "lo and behold! the cunning defenders, who, with the exception of their guns' crews and a few musket parties, had been lying behind and at the bottom of their wall to escape from our fire, uttered most appalling yells, manned their walls, and gave us a well-sustained sharp fire of small arms, well-directed."

In an instant, the carnival atmosphere was dispelled, for among those who fell in the hail of Taiping fire was Admiral Protet. A rebel musket ball hit him full in the chest, and he was flung back into the arms of his soldiers. The admiral was quickly taken to safety, but his wound proved mortal. Protet had been one of the antirebel commanders most liked and respected by French, British, and Chinese soldiers alike: Good-natured and aggressive, he had pursued the clearance of the thirty-mile radius without partisan sentiment. It scarcely seemed possible that the Taipings should have been able to claim such a victim; and, in the aftermath of the admiral's death, they might well have wished that they had not.

Never known for their mercy or restraint, the French troops went somewhat mad as news of Protet's fate spread. Nan-ch'iao was quickly stormed by the Allies along with the Ever Victorious Army, upon which Ward's men stepped back to watch the French troops vent their sorrow and anger. As Augustus Lindley recalled:

> Mercy seems never to have entered the minds of those Christian warriors, who loudly inveighed against the Taipings as "blood-thirsty monsters," &c., &c.; for when victory crowned their unparalleled feats of arms, no effort to save the defenceless and unresisting fugitives was ever made, but while those who had thrown down their arms were vainly trying to hide or flee from the deadly rifle, or stood blocked in the gateway of the tower, the valorous conquerors calmly and easily continued to shoot them down so long as they remained within range.

Resentment was still running high as the expeditionary force pressed on to the city of Che-lin, a few miles to the south. Ward and the Allied commanders learned from informants that Che-lin's two-mile wall, surrounded by canals and a wide, heavily bambooed ditch, were impressively fortified and contained somewhere between five and ten thousand Taipings armed with serviceable artillery and British Tower muskets. After wresting some buildings that lay outside the city away from the rebels on May 19, the expeditionary force opened up a typically devastating artillery barrage on the twentieth. The only unusual event of the morning occurred when a Taiping leader, riding through the camp of the Western forces, was taken for an imperialist and allowed to pass on. The rebel leader subsequently "rode for his life and got to his friends inside the city," reported the *Herald,* but the inside of the city soon became the least healthy place to be. The French and British effected two breaches in Che-lin's walls and before long were inside. The French troops raced through the city full of a vengeful fire that quickly infected the British. Lindley wrote that "[t]he defenders driven from the ramparts or killed, the gallant Allies rushed through the small town, *indiscriminately massacring every man, woman and child within its walls.* The Taipings had so earnestly endeavoured to shut out the besiegers that they had most effectually blocked themselves in, and were consequently butchered almost to a man."

One British officer who followed in the wake of the French wrote that, indeed, "[a]lmost every house we entered contained dead or dying men," and the *Overland Trade Report,* another of the English-language China coast newspapers, reported that "[s]ince the death of Admiral Protet the French troops have been behaving like fiends, killing indiscriminately men, women and children. Truth demands the confession that British sailors have likewise been guilty of the commission of similar revolting barbarities—not only on the Taipings, but upon the inoffensive helpless country people."

Had Ward not been present, there seems little doubt that his Chinese troops would have felt free to join in this destructive frenzy. Already there were reports that the Ever Victorious Army detachment sent to Ningpo, commanded by Major J. D. Morton, had been guilty of plundering and extortion in its administration of the port's west gate. Such reports offered further proof that only Ward stood between his men and an utter breakdown in discipline: a position he had occupied since the very first days of his corps.

It is impossible to say how long the Allied troops would have continued their brutal activities south of Shanghai had they not been restrained by events in other parts of the thirty-mile radius. General Staveley himself stated that his troops burned Che-lin to the ground, following which he ordered them to prepare "to advance on the next rebel town," even though the capture of Che-lin marked the realization of the goals set out by the Allied commanders during their meeting on April 22. Once freed to plunder, it seemed, the French and British troops, along with their commanders, were not easily brought back to the essential goal of defending Shanghai. Fortunately, the Chung Wang himself inadvertently provided the necessary reminder.

Following their successful actions at Nan-hsiang and Chia-ting, the Green Standard units in and around Chia-ting had become overconfident and attempted an attack against a rebel force at T'ai-ts'ang—some ten miles farther northwest than Chia-ting—during the third week of May. Perhaps smelling disaster, Li Hung-chang had refused to allow his Anhwei troops to participate in this action, which resulted in a disastrous rout of the imperialist forces by the Chung Wang on May 17. Knowing that the Western troops and Ward's men were occupied to the south, the Chung Wang next decided to surround not only Chia-ting but Sung-chiang and Ch'ing-p'u as well. Although none of these cities fell immediately, the Chung Wang did succeed in cutting off the lines of communication to Chia-ting and Ch'ing-p'u, retaking Kuang-fu-lin, and once again threatening Shanghai, with a force of between 50,000 and 100,000 men.

When Ward received word of the Chung Wang's movements, he quickly returned to Sung-chiang, consolidated its defenses, and tried unsuccessfully to open a line of supply to Forester in Ch'ing-p'u. Both Ward and Forester then settled in for what looked to be a pair of very determined sieges. The Taipings, Forester recalled, built a stockade around Ch'ing-p'u, "about a mile from the walls, and began a series of attacks. Time and again they made desperate attempts to scale the walls with ladders. We were kept busy night and day. . . . I tried to counteract this by making frequent sorties under cover of night or a heavy fog. These dashes were bloody affairs and always resulted in heavy loss to the enemy. But they could spare ten where I could spare one, and the material reduction of my force began to be disastrous."

General Staveley, for his part, had been thrown into something as much like panic as any haughty British officer would ever be likely to exhibit in such a situation. On May 23 Staveley wrote to Frederick Bruce to say that he would be unable to come to the aid of Ch'ing-p'u because he was leaving directly for Chia-ting, to relieve the pressure on that city. But by the twenty-sixth he had seen enough of the Chung Wang's forces and been sufficiently impressed by the cowardice of the imperial units in the region to withdraw the British garrison from Chia-ting. "As it is impossible to foresee what may be the result of the hostile attitude of the rebels," Staveley told Bruce, "and as the Imperialist troops are utterly worthless, I have considered it advisable to have all the troops that can be spared at Shanghai." Admiral Hope disagreed vehemently, but the move was approved. Besides spelling doom for Chia-ting (which fell soon after the British evacuated it), Hope knew that Staveley's policy meant probable disaster for Ward and Forester. But Staveley was far from factoring Ward's army—which he almost never mentioned in his dispatches—into his thinking.

Indeed, should the Chung Wang's latest offensive have ultimately destroyed the Ever Victorious Army, it might well have fit into Staveley's plans, for ever since his arrival in Shanghai, the general had been jealously attempting to take over the training of Chinese recruits from Ward. On May 28, at Staveley's urging, Li Hung-chang—now governor of Kiangsu—signed an agreement pledging to transfer two thousand imperial troops to Staveley for training. Supported by the British consul in Shanghai, W. H. Medhurst, as well as by Admiral Hope and Minister Bruce, Staveley immediately began pressing for an increase in that number. The difference between Ward's disciplining Chinese troops and a British officer doing so was clear to all Chinese officials: Whatever the throne's doubts about the commander of the Ever Victorious Army, he had never worked for the expansion of foreign influence. Wu Hsü, Li Hung-chang, and Prince Kung consistently tried to hamper Staveley's project, but they were also careful not to cause an actual breach with the British, for Li still did not feel that his Anhwei troops were ready to assume the principal burden for defending Shanghai and recapturing surrounding towns. If Ward and Forester should be annihilated, British support in the region would be more important than ever. And without meaningful British cooperation, the fate of the Ever Victorious Army was doubtful indeed.

Much depended, therefore, on how Ward handled this latest crisis, a crisis which represented, along with everything else, his first direct confrontation with the famed Chung Wang.

Although they had faced detachments of each other's armies many times (most notably during the second battle of Ch'ing-p'u in August 1860), the Chung Wang and Ward had not yet personally pitted their talents against each other on the same battlefield. The siege of Sung-chiang in the spring of 1862 was, therefore, deeply symbolic: The former peasant laborer Li Hsiu-ch'eng and the ex–ship's mate Frederick Townsend Ward, having established themselves as the most talented commanders on their respective sides in the Chinese civil war, squared off at the heads of two powerful armies, each of which represented an alternate path that might, had either man been successful in the long run, have led China away from the institutionalized obsolescence of the Manchus. As the Chung Wang, Li Hsiu-ch'eng now led a brightly dressed, vast host of courageous zealots that he had forged into the best of the Taiping armies; as the legendary Hua, Ward had built a smaller unit, drably clothed in Western uniforms but brilliantly trained and capable of holding its own against much larger enemy forces. Neither man could have known that their attempts to bring China into a new era—the one through a socioreligious movement, the other through military innovation—would, in the end, demand the sacrifice of their lives and finally come to naught. But this ultimate result does not reduce the significance of the twin efforts, or of that remarkable moment in early June when the two leaders planted their standards opposite each other and prepared to do battle across the fortifications of Sung-chiang.

Yet for all its apparent drama, the Chung Wang's attempt to take Sung-chiang was foolish and in many ways reminiscent of Ward's fixation on Ch'ing-p'u two years earlier. By wasting men and supplies in his effort to recapture the cities and towns of the thirty-mile radius, the Chung Wang played strategically into the hands of his enemies. For by late May 1862 Tseng Kuo-fan was bearing down hard on Nanking, and he would shortly be in a position to invest it. Whatever happened in Kiangsu would be meaningless if Nanking were lost; by merely engaging the Chung Wang until Tseng could complete his encirclement of the Taiping capital, Ward served his function in the larger strategic plan, in much the way that a boxer's left hand might maneuver an opponent's head and body into position for a finishing right. In this sense, Ward had already proved his superiority to his antagonist, although whether he would live through the siege of Sung-chiang to enjoy the achievement remained to be seen.

The Chung Wang's investment of Sung-chiang quickly became close, although the rebel leader did not succeed in breaking the water line of communication to Shanghai. Admiral Hope—still angry over General Staveley's decision to withdraw from the thirty-mile radius— took every opportunity to ship arms, supplies, and small detachments of British sailors and marines up the Huang-pu, and on May 31 he shot off an angry letter to the secretary of the Admiralty, declaring that Staveley's strategy was having an "evil moral effect" on the entire Shanghai region. The Taipings, said Hope, were creeping back into towns abandoned by the imperialist forces and the Western allies, both west and east of the Huang-pu. Furthermore,

> rebel forces, in large numbers, are now encamped about the hills in the vicinity of Ch'ing-p'u and Sung-chiang, and they are occupied with the siege of both these places. In the former there is a garrison of . . . Colonel Ward's Chinese troops, and, had the place been properly armed and provisioned for six months, and the breaches [created by the Allied guns on May 10] repaired, I should have had no fear for the result. Unfortunately this was not done, and there appears every prospect of its eventual capture by the rebels.

Hope did say that he supported the idea of Staveley training Chinese troops, but he also called for greater assistance to Ward and his army, including the granting of authority to Major Morton in Ningpo to raise 2,500 men for that city's defense.

In Sung-chiang, meanwhile, one of Hope's officers, Captain John Montgomerie of the *Centaur,* was doing his best to help Ward hold off the Chung Wang. Sung-chiang's plight was worsened by Ward's inability to break through to Ch'ing-p'u and either relieve it or withdraw the garrison and consolidate the Ever Victorious Army at Sung-chiang. Captain Montgomerie accompanied Ward on an abortive attempt to reach Colonel Forester in Ch'ing-p'u, and, on returning to Sung-chiang, Montgomerie elected to keep his small detachment of men with Ward in the city, where they played an important—though often exaggerated—role in Sung-chiang's defense. On May 30 the rebels launched a concerted attack on the city and managed to seize a large supply of arms and powder as well as one of the *Centaur*'s gigs. To prevent any greater losses, Ward on June 1 burned the city's suburbs, which had been so painstakingly rebuilt over the previous two years. On the following day, Ward and Montgomerie took several hundred men on a daring raid outside the walls to recover as much of the lost equipment as they could lay their hands on. The fight was a sharp one, but by nine o'clock that night Ward had recovered at least some of the arms and with Montgomerie had succeeded in getting all their boats inside Sung-chiang's westernmost water gate.

For the next three days the Taipings made repeated and concerted efforts to storm the city, all of which were repelled. Montgomerie noted that each of these attempts was preceded by the erection of an artillery battery outside the walls by the rebels but that on each occasion the battery "was successfully destroyed by guns from the city." By June 5 the Taipings were becoming unnerved, and on that morning, according to Montgomerie, the "Chung Wang sent a letter to Colonel Ward, demanding that the city might be delivered up to him." A copy of this letter was preserved by Augustus Lindley, and, although he attributed it to one of the Chung Wang's generals rather than to the rebel commander himself, the tone (and Montgomerie's eyewitness testimony) confirm it as the work of the Chung Wang: "Had you not invaded my territories, I should not have troubled you; the people would have remained undisturbed. Would not this have been better for both sides?" Castigating Ward's Chinese soldiers as men who "eat the bread of the Ch'ing [Manchu] dynasty, serving a stranger," the Chung Wang saved his final message for the leaders of the devil soldiers: "As for you, O foreign troops, you had best return to your native country, as quickly as may be; for, being a distinct race, why should you contend with me, or why should I be compelled to overcome you? . . . If you are resolved and will fight with me, I fear, indeed, your trade will suffer."

Captain Montgomerie noted that to these bombastic statements, "of course no answer was made."

At Ch'ing-p'u, Colonel Forester was showing similarly admirable pluck, despite his own bleak predicament. In the last days of May the rebel general besieging the city, having felt the full force of the defenders' determination to hold Ch'ing-p'u, dispatched a message to Forester under a flag of truce. Taking the usual proud tone, the rebel general's demand for surrender pointed out the futility of resistance and chastised Forester's men:

> Now, the most detestable are the strange devils and foreign demons, and he [the rebel general] has heard that among you there are men disguised as foreign demons, throwing away their lives for nought; nevertheless he has left the south road open, and the garrison are allowed to leave the city, and save their lives, in the guise of villagers; not one of them will be killed; or should they wish to stop, and send in their submission, it is allowed them to do so.

These were lenient terms, although it was questionable whether their author could be trusted. And Forester was facing problems within Ch'ing-p'u that might have tempted him to accept the offer: According to Dr. Macgowan, Forester "was obliged to relax certain wholesome rules. Opium (for smoking) had to be served out to prevent mutiny." Forester's own account stated that this sentiment for mutiny broke out not among the Chinese troops but—predictably—among his European officers. Indeed, it was some "thoroughly loyal and faithful" Chinese sergeants major who warned their commander of the plot. Forester quickly locked up the guilty parties, but his situation scarcely improved: "Fighting, fatigue and famine had worn us out, and now, with all my European officers in prison, I had nothing but Chinese to depend upon." This last item is (once again in Forester's case) uncorroborated, but that Forester still found the courage to answer the rebel general's surrender demand with gusto on June 1 was proved when a copy of his reply later made its way to Admiral Hope. In it Forester declared,

> You say if I do not give you the city to-day or to-morrow you will attack it and kill us, and I write to tell you that it is impossible for me to do so. My master, Ward, having given me charge of this city, with plenty of troops, guns, stores, munitions of war, etc., I am bound to hold it, whatever numbers come against it, and prevent your taking it; and I have given all my officers orders to do their best to do so, as I dare not give it up on my own responsibility. I regret you do not approve of us foreigners stopping here, but if you want us you must come and take the city.

Ward's and Forester's desperate straits made Li Hung-chang's ongoing refusal to commit his army fully in the field finally unsupportable. General Staveley continued to decline to do more than defend Shanghai, and so long as Li Hung-chang was unwilling to commit the body of his Anhwei forces, Staveley's position was all the more justified. "The Western soldiers," Li wrote to Tseng Kuo-fan on May 29, ". . . always seem to suspect that I, Hung-chang, am not willing to cooperate with them. They say that they will soon withdraw the Western troops back to their home countries; that many foreigners have been wounded and killed in action here. If China is unwilling to cooperate, they will have to evacuate their troops. I, Hung-chang, shall say some tactful words to comfort them; if I can meet their wishes, I shall do so." But Li continued to refuse the idea of joint operations between his troops and the foreign regulars in China's interior. He told Tseng on June 3, "Recently I have repeatedly memorialized the Court on the inappropriateness of joint campaigning. Hope and I, Hung-chang, have met as many as four times—all because he called first—and I have to treat with him as the occasion arises. Even were the situation to become desperate, I would never ask for his help or be willing to serve foreigners."

By the first week of June, however, the situation west of Shanghai was indeed desperate, and Li was genuinely moved by Ward's brave stand. "Ward," he told Tseng, "who valiantly defends Sung-chiang and Ch'ing-p'u, is indeed the most vigorous of all. Although until now he has not yet shaved his hair or called at my humble residence, I have no time to quarrel with foreigners over such a little ceremonial matter." Li's dual desires—to prove his men the equal of foreign soldiers in defending China and to offer some kind of assistance to Ward—finally prodded him into action during that first week of June. Ordering his commanders to engage the rebels on both sides of the Huang-pu, Li achieved a string of victories that surprised the Allied commanders and succeeded in drawing at least some of the Chung Wang's attention away from Sung-chiang and Ch'ing-p'u.

On June 6 Hope ordered more British regulars to Sung-chiang on his own authority as naval commander in Shanghai. At the same time, most of Major Morton's detachment of the Ever Victorious Army in Ningpo, having been informed of the desperate struggle of their leader, returned north and immediately began to battle their way toward Sung-chiang. At the village of Tou-fu-peng, not far from Sung-chiang, the Ever Victorious Army troops engaged a strong rebel force and fought them into the night. Under cover of darkness the detachment reached and set fire to the rebel stockade and entrenchments at Tou-fu-peng. The fire became a beacon, visible from the walls of Sung-chiang, and Ward, seeing it, martialed his troops—along with the British and imperialist units in the city—and attacked in the direction of the flames. Together, the two parts of the Ever Victorious Army were able to inflict a stinging defeat on the Chung Wang.

By June 9 Admiral Hope had grown weary enough of the defensive British posture in Shanghai to ascend the Huang-pu himself with about two hundred British regulars. Reaching Sung-chiang successfully, the admiral decided to join Ward in another attempt to break through to Forester in Ch'ing-p'u. With Ward's steamers *Hyson, Cricket,* and the newly acquired *Bo-peep* leading Hope's *Kestrel* and the French gunboat *Étoile,* the combined force made for Ch'ing-p'u, pausing just long enough to sweep some four thousand rebels out of Kuang-fu-lin. On the tenth Ward succeeded in breaking through to the beleaguered Forester: "I well remember the day they reached me," Forester later wrote, "for I had about given up all hope of ever getting out alive." Ward and Hope immediately decided that, as Ch'ing-p'u could not be held, its artillery and stores should be removed to the boats and the town itself burned. This action would subsequently be the source of much debate among Chinese officials, some of whom claimed that it demonstrated Ward's disloyalty and penchant for pillaging. But in fact it was nothing more or less than an extreme step taken during an equally extreme emergency.

With Ch'ing-p'u in flames, the Western and imperialist forces began their withdrawal to Sung-chiang, when one of the more famous and mysterious events of the campaign occurred: For some reason, Forester returned to the town just as the rebels were entering it. Forester himself later claimed that he had climbed a guard tower to scout enemy movements and was surrounded while above by rebel troops. Augustus Lindley stated that the Ever Victorious Army's second-in-command went back for forgotten loot. And the bewildered correspondent of the *North China Herald* could discover no reason at all. The rest of the force waited an hour for Forester to return, but he never did. "It is conjectured," said the *Herald,* "that he has fallen into the hands of the enemy or been shot by them."

In fact, Forester had been captured, beginning long and grisly weeks of imprisonment during which he was shackled, forced to walk to Soochow, berated and spat on by passing rebels, tortured, and compelled to witness the executions of other prisioners while being told that his turn was coming soon. But in reality the Taipings knew better than to execute such a valuable prisoner: Li Hung-chang eventually agreed to pay a large ransom in arms and money for Forester's release. Yet the imprisonment changed Forester. He emerged with his health badly impaired and his spirit almost broken, and in this bitter experience may well lie the explanation for some of his mysterious actions after Ward's death.

Deprived, now, of both Burgevine (who was still recovering from his wound) and Forester, Ward returned to Sung-chiang to experience a somewhat bittersweet triumph: Finally frustrated by the determination of the devil soldiers in Sung-chiang, the Chung Wang had decided to withdraw to Soochow and concentrate on regrouping and resupplying in preparation for another attempt on Shanghai in July or August. The Chung Wang later explained this move by citing the deteriorating situation in Nanking:

> We closely invested Sung-chiang, but just as we were about to succeed, General Tseng's army [a force commanded by Tseng Kuo-fan's reliable brother, Tseng Kuo-ch'üan], came down . . . with a sound like splitting bamboo, reached Nanking and threatened the capital. In one day three messengers, with edicts from the T'ien Wang urging me to hurry [back to Nanking], arrived at Sung-chiang. The edicts were very severe, who would dare to disobey? There was nothing I could do, so I withdrew the troops from Sung-chiang without attacking the town, because of the severe summons.

This self-serving and transparently false account of events was viewed skeptically even by Augustus Lindley. It was clear that the Chung Wang was taking advantage of the T'ien Wang's summonses in order to extricate himself from even greater humiliation at Ward's hands.

This conclusion is supported by the fact that the Chung Wang did not return to Nanking after retreating to Soochow but began exploring alternate strategies for reaching and taking control of Shanghai during the summer. He explained his actions to his ruler by saying that while Tseng Kuo-ch'üan's forces had arrived at Nanking fresh and well-supplied, his own were weary and required rest and provisioning. The T'ien Wang did not buy the excuse and sent another edict to Soochow: "I have three times commanded you to come to the relief of the capital," said the Heavenly King, "why have you not set out? What do you think you are doing? You have been given great responsibilities, can it be that you do not know my laws? If you do not obey my commands, [you will find] the punishment of the state difficult to endure!" But the Chung Wang continued to procrastinate, neither marching west nor making another move east.

The rebel general's indecision created tremendous opportunities for anti-Taiping advances in the Shanghai region, opportunities that General Staveley could not or would not exploit. He continued to hew to the line of defending only Shanghai. Ward, for his part, had not regrouped and reorganized his force enough to undertake a major offensive. But fortunately Li Hung-chang, emboldened by his recent successes, was willing to expand his role in the fighting and ordered his commanders to effect a pincerlike attack on rebel forces in the area of Hung-ch'iao, just southwest of Shanghai. On June 18 the pincers closed, reportedly resulting in the deaths of a thousand rebels and the capture of two hundred more. That same day Li wrote to Tseng Kuo-fan, saying, "This pleases me exceedingly, since it at once changes the atmosphere of military affairs of recent years. To-day, according to intelligence from spies, the various brigands near Ssu-ching and Sung-chiang have all fled." With his personal power consolidated, Li also felt more free to criticize the way officials such as Wu Hsü and Yang Fang were dealing with foreigners and the Ever Victorious Army: "The services of foreigners may still be required," Li told Tseng on June 23, "but the accounting ought to be clear." This criticism of Wu and Yang's methods never bled over, however, into any indictment of Ward.

But if Li viewed Ward with an admirably clear and detached eye, Peking's vision was increasingly clouded by suspicion and hostility. And by offering the prospect of a competent all-Chinese military force in Kiangsu, Li's victories aggravated rather than eased this condition. The seed of doubt planted in the imperial clique by Hsüeh Huan's early worries about Ward's arrogance and ultimate ambitions had grown steadily in the ever-suspicious atmosphere of the Forbidden City. As early as May 24 an imperial edict had stated that "[t]o have the British and French attack the rebels will lead to many abuses, and even Ward has a mind unreceptive to control." Li, by contrast, presented no such problems.

Great Britain's growing support of the Ever Victorious Army (General Staveley's personal misgivings notwithstanding) also accelerated the growth of suspicion in Peking. The more British representatives called for the expansion of the Ever Victorious Army, it seemed, the more determined the imperial clique became to limit that expansion. Responding to news of Prosper Giquel's and Le Brethon de Caligny's attempts to build a Franco-Chinese Corps in Ningpo, Admiral Hope wrote to Admiral Protet's successor in Shanghai to say "that the object is not to have a number of separate corps there, English, French and Chinese, but that all the men drilled there should be turned over to Colonel Ward's force, which is a Chinese force authorised by the government at Peking, and to which the troops trained by Captain Dew are attached." Again, Hope advised Frederick Bruce to persuade the Chinese government to allow Ward to raise 2,500 men in Ningpo, but again Peking tried to avoid the issue.

The reasons for this avoidance were made clear during June. Ward knew full well that abuses had been committed by detachments of the Ever Victorious Army not under his direct control, particularly the men under Major Morton's command in Ningpo. "I can manage my men," Ward was later reported to have said at about this time, "but not my officers." Dr. Macgowan echoed these sentiments, adding that the Chinese soldiers themselves—not just the Ever Victorious Army's Western officers—were guilty of misconduct when away from Ward's sternly watchful eye: "Ward's legion, unfortunately, could not, in his absence, be trusted with provost duties. They could not resist preying upon the people they were expected to protect." But Ward also knew that jealous Chinese provincial officials would exaggerate these incidents in their reports to the throne in an effort to discredit him. Prince Kung was told by local officials, for example, that Ward had gratuitously burned not only Ch'ing-p'u but Chia-ting as well—a report never corroborated. Tales of Ward's misuse of funds for his army began to circulate among these same officials, even though it was the efficient fiscal administration of the Ever Victorious Army (as opposed to Ward's personal finances, which were often in confusion) that remained one of the primary reasons for the unit's success.

Rightly suspecting that Kung was being given a warped view of himself and his army, Ward wrote to the prince directly in June: a fairly serious breach of official protocol. In his memorandum, according to Kung, Ward "stressed his contribution" and requested "greater power so that he can move his army more freely." Kung, in his reply, "delicately discouraged" Ward from similar communications in the future, and the incident only heightened the imperial clique's suspicions. "Although Ward is serving China," Kung pronounced, "he is still a foreigner. His nature is basically unrestrained and his heart is even harder to fathom. . . . I now petition the throne to order Li Hung-chang and Tso Tsung-tang [another of Tseng Kuo-fan's talented students, who had become the new governor of Chekiang province] to watch him carefully, and to make him gradually fall under our control so that he will not ruin himself with his arrogance."

Li Hung-chang's victories in June offered China's rulers hope that they would soon need neither foreign regulars nor the Ever Victorious Army; thus Hope's continued calls for the expansion of Ward's force and Staveley's repeated demands that he be given men to train at Shanghai went unanswered. Enraged by all this, Frederick Bruce sent a blunt message to Prince Kung on June 28, saying that he felt compelled to "lodge a very serious complaint against those who direct the operations of the Chinese soldiers at Shanghai."

"Your Imperial Highness is aware," Bruce went on,

> that it had been agreed between them and the allied Commanders that the latter should re-capture the cities within a certain radius of Shanghai, and that the Chinese would furnish garrisons for the places so taken. . . . Instead of confining themselves to the part assigned, the Chinese abandoned a strong position held by them [Chia-ting], and marched forward some 7,000 or 8,000 men to attack a town called Tai-ts'ang single-handed. The result was what might be anticipated, as long as officers are so ignorant of war as to oppose men undisciplined and badly armed, to . . . a large body of rebels who are wise enough to furnish their bands with better arms than those manufactured in China. . . . Thus the fruit of the late successes has been almost entirely lost. . . . I have also to report that Governor Li has only placed 300 men at the disposal of General Staveley to be drilled. . . . If the Imperial Government does not make sufficient efforts to justify me in stating to my Government that the retention of foreign troops in China will not be required for a lengthened period in order to preserve the Chinese towns from destruction, your Imperial Highness may depend upon it that either they will be withdrawn or the revenue of the port will be taken and applied to

the payment of the force required for its protection. No Government will for long go to the expense of holding places for a foreign Government which is unable or unwilling to hold them itself.

This was a serious indictment but one that Kung, in a long-winded reply, simply sidestepped. Saying that he would review Bruce's various points, Kung added, "As to the instruction of troops in foreign drill, the true reason why there has not been greater eagerness shown on this point, is that the expenses of the army are enormous." And that, as far as the prince was concerned, was that.

Bruce's threatened withdrawal of foreign troops from Shanghai did not, of course, ever come about; the port was entirely too important to British interests. But the controversy surrounding the defense of Shanghai threatened to bring military cooperation to a standstill, which would offer the Chung Wang favorable conditions for a new assault. At the end of June the antirebel forces held only Sung-chiang and Nan-ch'iao, the latter still occupied by a small Allied garrison. Taiping units had been able to move back into every other important city and town in the radius, and so long as ministers bickered in Peking and General Staveley refused to leave Shanghai, there seemed little hope that, should the rebels choose to strike again, an effective response could be mounted.

The situation, however, was salvaged in dramatic fashion in mid-July, not by British officers or imperial decrees but by the combined talents of Ward and Li Hung-chang.

During the first week of July, as Ward regrouped at Sung-chiang and occasionally engaged in minor area actions, Li Hung-chang ordered his Anhwei troops to press the rebels more vigorously on the eastern, or Pootung, side of the Huang-pu River. On July 7 Li succeeded in recapturing Feng-hsien, an important town near the shores of Hang-chow Bay, and from there advanced toward the rebel stronghold of Chin-shan-wei to the southwest. Chin-shan-wei, even more than Nan-ch'iao, represented the southern key to the Pootung peninsula; if it could be wrested back from the rebels, both Shanghai and its inland trade would be that much safer.

By the end of the first week in July, Ward was ready to march south and join forces with Li. Indeed, in the wake of the Chung Wang's withdrawal from eastern Kiangsu with his best troops (which neither Li nor Ward could have known was temporary), both imperialist commanders were beginning to look beyond the liberation of the Shanghai region and toward a linkup with Tseng Kuo-fan's troops at Nanking. Participating in the capture of the rebel capital was a cherished goal of Ward's: One of the items found among his personal effects after his death was a detailed map of Nanking. In a letter to Tseng on July 10—written as his own troops and those of the Ever Victorious Army were beginning joint operations in the Chin-shan-wei area—Li felt secure enough about Ward and his army to hazard proposing the project to his mentor:

> Ward has more than four thousand men. . . . The Taotai Wu has offered the valiant services of Ward to help an assault on the Shui-hsi Gate at Hsia-kuan [in Nanking]. He would be able to sail there in a few days. As I, Hung-chang, dare not give immediate permission, you, my Teacher, may kindly send me your instruction, and ask my elder Yuan [Tseng's brother Tseng Kuo-ch'üan] what he thinks of it. . . . [Ward's] Army is like a foreign army, and Admiral Hope treats it with favour. But the men are provided with Chinese rations and money. As they have often heard of the great name of my Teacher, they will obey your orders.

For the moment, Tseng Kuo-fan was reluctant to use the Ever Victorious Army in the Nanking area. He did not rule out the possibility in the future, but he felt that Ward's army first needed to further test and prove itself in Kiangsu. This was just as well, for in mid-July Ward had more than enough to keep him busy in the Shanghai area.

On July 16 about a thousand of Ward's men hurried to engage a rebel column near Chin-shan-wei that had fought its way past a detachment of Li's army in an effort to reestablish the Taiping presence in the Pootung peninsula and cut the imperialist lines of supply and retreat. Ward was able to frustrate this rebel threat before sundown on the sixteenth, and after dispensing with it he immediately coordinated with Li's forces for a nighttime assault on Chin-shan-wei itself.

The battle plan at Chin-shan-wei was Ward's, made during a council of war with the other imperialist commanders. Although most still regarded him as a foreigner, the Chinese officers listened and obeyed as Ward directed that Chin-shan-wei be invested on all four sides and subjected to a powerful artillery bombardment: the same basic scheme that had been used with repeated success during the thirty-mile-radius campaign. This time, however, the guns all belonged to the Ever Victorious Army, and the storming troops—though some were led by Westerners—were all Chinese. It was a signal moment.

According to Li Hung-chang, the rebel garrison in Chin-shan-wei began to withdraw from the city during the night, even before Ward's guns had opened fire. Possibly the garrison had heard of the fate of other cities that had been subjected to pummeling by guns manufactured in the West. Or Li may well have invented this detail to downplay the importance of Ward's participation in the battle and magnify his own role. Despite Li's respect for Ward, it would not have been the first nor would it be the last time that such misrepresentation occurred. By all accounts, at any rate, Chin-shan-wei was in imperial hands by the morning of July 17. Ward later told Burlingame that his men were responsible for the city's capture "although I find the Governor has credited himself and [his] troops with it, but then as they had been badly whipped the day previous to my taking it and had retreated to the rear you can imagine how much credit they really deserve."

Ward and Li Hung-chang's rivalry was thus in evidence once again at Chin-shan-wei, but there continued to be no real sense of bitterness about the competition. Immediately after Chin-shan-wei, Ward and Li again discussed an assault on one of Nanking's water gates, to be made by the powerfully armed and ever more numerous river steamers of the Ever Victorious Army. Li had not yet received Tseng Kuo-fan's thoughts on such an idea, and, on the chance that his teacher might agree, Li ordered Ward to prepare his men for the operation by moving north and seizing the port of Liu-ho, on the Yangtze. A rebel trading center occupied by Taiping troops as well as pirates working in affiliation with the Heavenly Kingdom, Liu-ho served as a base from which the rebels could harass the trade of Shanghai and Kiangsu province generally. Its recapture would involve amphibious operations, making it a logical spot to rehearse an attack on Nanking.

Ward embarked for Liu-ho from Wu-sung on July 29 with four of his steamers and, upon arriving at what he called the "piratical den," immediately began to destroy the rebel fortifications with his mounted guns. After an extensive bombardment Ward's infantry landed and attacked. The fighting was bitter, but the Ever Victorious Army soon gained the upper hand: The rebel defensive works were, in Ward's own words, "destroyed completely," and a collection of merchant vessels and captives held by the rebels were set free. Ward learned that the Taipings in Liu-ho had been planning a major raid against Ch'ung-ming Island, situated at the mouth of the Yangtze and vital to the safety of Shanghai's trade. Like the battle for Kao-ch'iao in February, Ward's success at Liu-ho had been particularly well-timed.

Following his return to Sung-chiang, Ward was informed of Tseng Kuo-fan's desire that the Ever Victorious Army "try out their guns" a bit more before participating in any attack on Nanking. Tseng suggested the recapture of Ch'ing-p'u and Chia-ting, and, accordingly, Ward began to make plans for another attempt on the city that had been so troublesome to him. Li Hung-chang agreed to play a role in the assault and instructed Ward's old associate Li Heng-sung to clear an approach to Ch'ing-p'u so that the body of the Anhwei Army could move west unimpeded. On August 5 Li Hung-chang's troops arrived before Ch'ing-p'u's rebuilt outer works, where they were soon joined by Ward and the Ever Victorious Army.

Before Ward had left Sung-chiang, he had received a letter from Wu Hsü reminding him that, once Ch'ing-p'u was taken, he should not allow the Ever Victorious Army to engage in any looting activities that would give ammunition to Ward's critics in the Chinese bureaucracy. Referring to himself again as "your foolish younger brother," Wu told Ward that "your only duty is to attack the city. As soon as the city has been taken over, give it to Colonel Cheng [one of Li Hung-chang's officers]. . . . Please do not let the Ever Victorious Army enter the city, in order to avoid blame and condemnation in the future. This is most important and I beg you to give it your attention." Wu's admonitions were hardly necessary: Ward was only too aware, after the thirty-mile-radius campaign, of the cost of allowing troops to run wild after taking a city. In drawing up his battle plan, Ward assigned no garrisoning role to his two thousand troops; instead, they were to perform their traditional function of breaching and storming.

Li Hung-chang's various imperialist units were assigned to the north, east, and west gates of the city. The Ever Victorious Army would launch the main attack on the southern gate, supported by Li Heng-sung's troops. The battle began on August 7. Ward's steamers opened fire on the Taiping defenses—the *Hyson* even managing to pound its way into the city moat—and the Ever Victorious Army along with the Chinese troops busied themselves destroying the rebel outworks. On the following day, Ward attacked the south gate but was repulsed. According to the *Peking Gazette,* the official Chinese government organ, this failure resulted from a "want of courage" on the part of the Chinese units attacking in support of Ward. Once again frustrated by Li Heng-sung, Ward awaited the arrival of five hundred of his own men from Sung-chiang. The additional troops joined him on August 9, and Ward prepared to attack again on the tenth.

According to Forester, the Ever Victorious Army's artillery at this latest battle of Ch'ing-p'u was commanded by an Italian colonel called Sartoli. Dr. Macgowan referred to this man as Major Tortal, but both agreed that he was, in Forester's words, "an expert in gunnery who had gained his experience under Garibaldi." (Whether or not Ward had met Sartoli earlier in life is unknown; it is nonetheless noteworthy that so many of Ward's officers had served in campaigns and with leaders that Ward himself either had actually or was rumored to have been involved with.) On August 10 Sartoli's batteries set to work on the south gate of Ch'ing-p'u again and soon effected a ten-foot breach in the walls. Ward himself then led a storming party toward the walls, although according to Dr. Macgowan it was Ward's Filipino aide, Vincente Macanaya, who was first into the breach. Unfortunately the Italian Sartoli insisted on joining the storming party and was killed on the walls. But Ward pressed on. "The work of General Ward's men was steady and sure," said the *Gazette,* ". . . and under the shelter of the smoke, they scaled the wall. With firedarts [rockets] and bayonets they advanced against the Rebels and killed numbers of them. Seeing this the Imperialists rushed in a body and took possession of the city."

Immediately, the Taipings began a hasty withdrawal through the north and west gates, where imperialist units were lying in wait. Hundreds of Taipings were killed during ensuing ambushes. These, however, were secondary actions. Even in Peking, it was clear who had pulled the laboring oar during the attack: "General Ward," said the *Gazette,* "has, many times before, led his men against this city of Ch'ing-p'u . . . , but especially in this battle he was regardless of personal danger in leading and urging his soldiers on to the slaughter. For this he is worthy of our highest praise." In reporting the battle to Tseng Kuo-fan, Li Hung-chang similarly gave the lion's share of the credit to Ward, describing his comrade as leading "his men forward while at the same time, he kept firing with rockets and guns. Most of the outrageous brigands on the walls fell and our troops made an assault to get in." Ward himself summed up the action to Burlingame by saying simply, "I took Ch'ing-p'u in fine style by breaching and storming."

Some three thousand imperialist troops were deposited in Ch'ing-p'u as a garrison, after which Ward returned to Sung-chiang, then went to Shanghai. He called on Li Hung-chang and once more asked that his army be allowed to play a role in Tseng Kuo-fan's siege of Nanking. "Ward has seen me to-day," Li wrote to Tseng on August 14, "and urges me to transfer him to help attack Nanking. He says that he could arrive there in three days—without fail. After victory, the wealth and property in the city would be equally shared with the Government's troops; and so forth. As I, Hung-chang, have received your Excellency's letter saying that there are already enough troops without further reinforcement, I ask for the matter to be deferred pending your instruction."

Denied a part in the Nanking fighting, Ward soon turned his attention south to Ningpo, where the Taipings were gathering for what looked to be a concerted effort to retake the port. As he began to make provisions for taking a large body of troops to reinforce Major Morton's detachment (in what would be his first action outside Kiangsu province), Ward also took time to write to Burlingame and warn him of the "free city" movement that was gaining momentum among Shanghai's foreigners.

On July 26, the *North China Herald* had echoed many Westerners' sentiments about the constant problems of lawlessness, refugees from the interior, and inefficient imperial administration in Shanghai by declaring that "the formation of one central and responsible executive power emanating from a legislative assembly, empowered to draw up a code of laws for general purposes, is becoming an absolute necessity." Li Hung-chang was aware that the foreigners were quite serious in proposing this usurpation of Chinese authority: He told Tseng Kuo-fan on August 14, "Whether this arrangement is possible remains to be seen. Permission to do so, of course, rests with the Tsungli Yamen. . . . As I, Hung-chang, replied in an official letter to the Tsungli Yamen, no guarantee can be given that they [the foreigners] will not get possession of the city. In such a case everything would depend on the Court's decision. It is like walking on ice. I am very worried."

For his part, Ward had no illusions about the laxity and corruption of Chinese officials in Shanghai: "Actually if I had not my foot so deeply in the mire," he told Burlingame on August 16, "I would throw them all overboard." Yet Ward would not put his weight behind what he called "squatter sovereignty," again demonstrating that his ties to China were quite genuine. The fact that Li Hung-chang never seriously questioned Ward's loyalty (even if he did sometimes try to take credit for battles that rightly belonged to Ward) further shows the extent of Ward's commitment. By late August, Li was heightening his attacks on Ward's principal Chinese associates, Wu Hsü and Yang Fang, complaining that they were using irresponsible and illegal methods to raise money to pay the Ever Victorious Army. Wu especially, said Li, "is to be guarded against like a bandit or a brigand. How difficult it is for one who is in authority!" Yet there was no such criticism of Ward, no suggestion that simply because he was being paid by Wu and Yang he was also a party to their "fraudulent tricks."

In fact, far from being a party to Wu's and Yang's more extreme frauds and embezzlements, Ward was ultimately a victim of them. In his August 16 letter to Burlingame, Ward claimed that not only Wu and Yang but Li Hung-chang as well "actually owe some 350,000 tls. [taels] to me & my friends for advances made on acct. of wages, etc." While the figure is impossible to prove—it would later be the subject of a decades-long lawsuit by Ward's family against the Chinese government—the basic accusation is almost certainly true. Ward was in the habit of supplying his men out of his own pocket when the flow of money from Shanghai was slow: Prompt and regular payment of his men remained one of the keys to his success. In supposing that all these accounts would eventually be put right, Ward took risks with his personal finances that ultimately proved disastrous.

But in mid-August, as Ward prepared to go to Ningpo, there seemed little reason for him not to be confident about his affairs. He had realized many of his military goals and was on the road to realizing still more. The opposition of Chinese officials and the distrust of the imperial clique were securely counterbalanced by the success of his growing army. And, as for the military forces of the Western powers, Ward and Li Hung-chang had shown that they could be successful without them. The time had now arrived, "to which Ward had long looked forward," according to Dr. Macgowan, "when he could take the field without the aid of foreign troops." The battles of Chin-shan-wei, Liu-ho, and Ch'ing-p'u—as well as Ward and Li Hung-chang's joint planning for possible Ever Victorious Army participation in the siege of Nanking—exemplified the synthesis of Chinese and Western methods toward which Ward had been working for more than two years. It is understandable, therefore, that he should have looked so eagerly toward the expansion of his operations into Chekiang province.

But that expansion was postponed. In the latter half of August the Chung Wang made another bid for Shanghai, with an estimated 100,000 men. In turning to face this threat, Ward and Li Hung-chang conducted their last and most crucial joint campaign.

In August 1862 a young lieutenant of the British Royal Engineers—Thomas Lyster—arrived in China, where, a few years later, he was destined to die of a series of illnesses brought on by the severities of the climate. But during his time in China, Lyster wrote numerous letters home that were later published by his father. Honest and unusually compassionate, the letters mark Lyster as a keen observer of Chinese-Western relations on a variety of levels. On August 18, for example, he wrote from Hong Kong:

> Some of our fellows amused themselves by tying the tails of Chinamen together. I am afraid we bully them a good deal. If you are walking about and a Chinaman comes in your way, it is customary to knock his hat off, or dig him in the ribs with an umbrella. I thought it a shame, and remonstrated with the fellow who was with me to-day for treating a poor beggar of a Chinaman in this way; but he assured me that if you make way for them they swagger and come in *your* way purposely. The French soldiers treat them even more roughly than we do.

Lyster soon arrived in Shanghai, where he was thrown together with another young officer of engineers, Captain Charles Gordon. "This is an immense place," Lyster wrote of Shanghai. "There is a surplus population here now of 70,000 villagers, driven in by the Taipings, which makes provisions very dear. . . . I suppose you know all about the Taipings. They number about 100,000, and are nothing but a band of marauders. They come down on a village, rob it, slay all the inhabitants they can lay hold of, and then burn the place. . . . I scarcely ever go into the country without seeing some poor people dead or dying." The death toll in the countryside was indicative of the sharp fighting that characterized the Chung Wang's latest offensive.

Before long, Lyster had met one of the campaign's most illustrious combatants: "I was introduced to General Ward, the American, who is an officer in the service of the Chinese Government; in fact, he has been made a mandarin; he is a quiet-looking little man, with very bright eyes, but is a regular fire-eater; he has saved £ 60,000. He is married to a Chinese."

Ward was never more of a fire-eater than during the days before his introduction to young Thomas Lyster. Western military leaders downplayed the severity of the Chung Wang's August advance into eastern Kiangsu, perhaps because their troops played so little part in the fighting. Indeed, English-language newspapers and Western consular officials had reported little or nothing of Ward and Li Hung-chang's early August victories, because no foreign troops had been involved. But this attitude did not reduce the actual seriousness of the situation. The Chung Wang knew that he would soon have to comply with the T'ien Wang's demands that he return to Nanking; should he be able to report the capture of Shanghai upon his arrival, his ruler's bitterness might be assuaged. Thus the latest Taiping attack quickly became a fierce one.

By mid-August, just a week after its recapture by Ward, Ch'ing-p'u was again besieged, by a Taiping force of twenty thousand. The imperialists in the city, now bolstered by a detachment of the Ever Victorious Army, managed to inflict a severe check on the rebels after an intense battle lasting several days. Next the rebels—moving from town to town in desperate search of any sign of weakness that might indicate an open road to Shanghai—engaged Ward and the imperialists on the northern side of the Huang-pu. Two key towns west of Shanghai were surrounded, besieged, and bypassed, but Li Hung-chang quickly dispatched forces to meet the various rebel columns as they advanced. Ward also led detachments out of Sung-chiang toward Shanghai to relieve the pressure on Li's troops.

Bolstered by Ward's men, Li ordered a series of attacks in the vicinity of Chi-pao and Hung-ch'iao—just a few miles from Shanghai itself—during which the main rebel force was successfully halted and then driven north. The Taipings tried to counterattack on August 28 but could make no headway: By the following day, they had been pushed past the familiar ground of Nan-hsiang and in the direction of Chia-ting, which they still held. Whatever the Chung Wang had expected to meet on the road to Shanghai, the sight of Li Hung-chang's exceptionally effective Anhwei troops acting in conjunction with the devil soldiers must have surprised him; yet he made no mention of it in his own account of the campaign and ascribed his eventual retreat to the continuing harangues of the T'ien Wang.

On August 31 Li reported to Peking that the main Taiping force had once again pulled out of the Shanghai region. Li's reputation was greatly enhanced by this latest defense of the port, as was Ward's, and Li's subsequent order that Ward resume his preparations for going to Ningpo gave rise to speculation that the governor was jealous. Certainly Ward's position within the Chinese hierarchy had become uniquely powerful. "It is a fact," A. A. Hayes recalled of this period of Ward's life, "that an official of very high rank, whose name is familiar in modern Chinese history, was kept waiting by [Ward] at his door, later brusquely bidden to enter, and then roundly abused for presuming to think that Hua would come to the door to meet him; to which treatment the official meekly submitted." There is good reason, then, to wonder if Li (who may well have been the official Hayes spoke of) sent Ward to Ningpo to prevent any further eclipse of his own fame. Indeed, so convinced was Li of Ward's importance in both the Chinese and Western communities that he wrote to Tseng Kuo-fan on September 8:

> Ward commands enough authority to control the foreigners in Shanghai, and he is quite friendly with me. Wu [Hsü] and Yang Fang both depend on Ward. If my Teacher gave them an order, these "rats" would all endeavour to comply with it. Ward is indeed brave in action, and he possesses all sorts of foreign weapons. Recently I, Hung-chang, have devoted all my attention to making friends with him, in order to get the friendship of various nations through that one individual.

These were heady assessments of Ward's position and influence, but there is no indication that such talk changed the young commander's behavior or attitude at all. In a September 10 letter to Burlingame, Ward displayed all the charm, humor, and boyish deviousness that had marked his entire life. As Ward's last surviving written statement, the letter is worth quoting in its entirety:

> My Dear Mr. Burlingame—
> I have written to you once or twice but not yet had the honor or pleasure of an answer, but fancy you are so occupied with the gaieties of Peking that you forget us poor devils at Sung-chiang.

Matters about the same here, as usual the same amount of lying, swindling & smuggling as ever, no improvement. The mail has just arrived and I hear your wife also, I intended when I heard of her arrival to have immediately called on her, but fear I am compelled to leave chop chop for Sung-chiang. So much for being a soldier; and I fear I shall not have the pleasure of meeting her unless it is at Peking.

If I was only certain that my chits arrived safely I would give you some news but really do not like to put some things on paper unless there is a certainty of their getting in the proper place. Anything I can do for you here simply hint at it and it will be done—do it sans ceremonie and it will be truly executed. Our country is in a bad state and there is considerable crowing in some quarters. My brother is in New York hard at work, I greatly fear he will volunteer [for the Union Army] instead of coming out here, as he is getting decidedly belligerent in his tone and excessively patriotic. I find my old friend [John] Ward Ex-Minister [to China] is a damned traitor and joined the rascals [the Confederacy]. I beg of you to write me, tell me about Peking and Prince Kung and let me know how to write you without fear of its being otherwise overhauled.

And believe me as ever—an honest American
And your humble servant to command—
F. T. Ward

Shanghai, Sept 10, 1862

Many of Ward's most pronounced characteristics resurface in this document: his eagerness for approval, his loyalty to yet curious detachment from the United States, his concern for his brother, and his clear-eyed perception of affairs in Shanghai. Above all, there is evidence of the adroitness that had allowed him to manipulate those master manipulators—the Chinese bureaucracy—so well. Li Hung-chang would seem to have had good reason to fear Ward's rise. Yet on balance, given their personal relationship, it seems that Li dispatched Ward to Ningpo less out of bureaucratic insecurity than out of a simple wish to gratify his foreign comrade's "fire-eating" tendencies. For, talented as Ward was at using the Chinese political system, Li was ultimately to prove the grand master of the game.

If Ward's fame did not affect his behavior, his battlefield successes did: He became steadily more reckless, almost as if he believed the Chinese superstition that he led a charmed life. In the first two weeks of September, Ward shuttled back and forth between Shanghai and Sung-chiang, preparing for his expedition to Chekiang province. During one of his visits to Shanghai, he called on A. A. Hayes, who remembered being quite concerned about Ward's approach to his safety and affairs:

> On a late day in September, 1862 . . . I looked up from my writing to see him standing by me. I could not think of this smiling, amiable man as a great commander and a future ruler. I only remembered then that when I, a few months before, lay sick of that terrible Shanghai fever, which is said to combine all the bad features of other fevers with a few of its own, he had taken time from his cares and duties to come and sit beside a young countryman's bedside. He asked me to lend him my Arab horse, which of course I was glad to do. Later in the afternoon, walking in a street of the settlement, I met him, sitting erect in the saddle. We stopped, and I was patting my horse's neck and talking to the general, when the impulse seized me to speak to him as I did.
>
> "General," I said, "you are taking fearful risks. You may be killed at any moment. In such a case, what will become of your property and affairs? Let me find you a confidential secretary, or some one in whose hands you can trust your great interests." His blue coat was buttoned tightly over his chest. He smiled as he pointed with his right hand to the outline of a small book in his left breast pocket, and then touching it said, "Oh, it is all here."

In the weeks and months to come the small book of which Hayes spoke would become the subject of mystery and controversy, for in it was the only accurate account (or so Ward's friends and family claimed) of just how much money Ward was owed by his Chinese backers. Thus the book had value not only to Ward but to Yang Fang and Wu Hsü: just how much value Yang and Wu would soon demonstrate.

For the moment, however, the attention of most officials and commanders in Shanghai was fixed on events at Ningpo. Since June the port had been occupied by Captain Dew's British naval units, the Chinese troops that Dew's officers were disciplining, the Ever Victorious Army troops under Major Morton (who had returned from the north, and to whom Dew's Chinese troops were attached), and Prosper Giquel and Le Brethon de Caligny's still untested Franco-Chinese unit. Although they had been assisted by instructors from Tardif de Moidrey's Franco-Chinese Corps of Kiangsu, Giquel and Le Brethon de Caligny's men had not, even as late as July, been under fire, and both commanders decided during that month that it was high time to prove the unit's worth. Modeling their strategy on that of Ward and Admiral Hope in Shanghai, the two men determined that a thirty-mile radius should be cleared around Ningpo, with their Franco-Chinese troops playing the featured role. This campaign opened at the Taiping stronghold of Yü-yao, some thirty miles northwest of Ningpo. The walled city was taken in early August by Giquel and Le Brethon de Caligny's men, supported by some fifteen hundred local pirates, as well as Major Morton and his Ever Victorious Army detachment. Captain Dew, prohibited by his superiors from playing a direct part in the attack, transported troops aboard the British gunboat *Hardy.*

But after the capture of Yü-yao, Le Brethon de Caligny was temporarily called away to other duties, and Tardif de Moidrey arrived in Chekiang to supervise the city's defense. Unfortunately, Tardif was assisted by a less than capable subordinate officer who was unable to avoid a breach with the local imperialist forces. Arrogantly insisting that the imperialists accommodate his troops when making their own movements, this Frenchman provoked an argument that turned violent: Shots were exchanged, and in the aftermath many Chinese soldiers defected to the Taipings. Recognizing that the Western-imperialist military effort in Chekiang was anything but organized, the local Taiping commanders decided in September that the time was ripe for an attack on Ningpo itself.

In this atmosphere of peril and confusion, Ward received orders to proceed to Ningpo and assume personal command of defensive efforts in the region. The call found the commander of the Ever Victorious Army ready, as a group of visiting Western officers discovered on the day before Ward's departure for Ningpo. As Charles Schmidt recalled, the officers

> expressed a desire to see the whole force under the General's command. Although it was already late in the afternoon, General Ward, ever obliging, ordered a general parade of all troops in the garrison. The whole force accordingly assembled and never have I seen the General in better spirits than that afternoon. No doubt he felt the just pride of being able to show these officers a disciplined force of several thousand Chinese entirely his own creation, and which had already shown it could withstand a rebel force ten times its strength on the open battle field. He gave them an ocular demonstration that he was something more than a mere fillibuster [*sic*], as most British officers took him to be, with the honorable exception perhaps of Admiral Sir James Hope, who seemed already to have recognized General Ward's military talent and become his warm friend. Poor General! He little thought that this parade would be his last one. Nor did the officers and men think that they would see their beloved and respected General for the last time that evening.

On September 18 Ward left for Ningpo aboard the *Confucius,* accompanied by the two hundred men of his personal bodyguard—commanded by Major James Edward Cook—as well as by Vincente Macanaya and Colonel Forester. In Ningpo he met with his friend Captain Dew and made plans for a well-coordinated effort to meet the rebel threat in the area. But on September 19 came bad news that seriously altered the theater picture: The Taipings had taken the city of Tz'u-ch'i, on the water line from Ningpo to Yü-yao. The Yü-yao garrison now faced the possibility of being cut off, and, just as important, there was a danger that the large local rice crop would fall into rebel hands. Ward moved quickly to put the situation right.

On September 20 Ward marched his bodyguard to Tz'u-ch'i. Captain Dew and Lieutenant Archibald Bogle also proceeded to Tz'u-ch'i, on board the *Hardy.* The *Confucius* went ahead to ferry Major Morton's force down from Yü-yao. According to Andrew Wilson, the grassy fields that surrounded Tz'u-ch'i had been ignited when the city was taken by the rebels and were still burning when Ward arrived: "The whole plain seemed on fire. The terror-stricken inhabitants, many of them swimming on logs, were crossing the river; and for miles the long reeds on its banks gave shelter to men, women and children up to the middle in water." Ward and his men spent the twentieth chasing Taiping looting parties back inside Tz'u-ch'i. At midnight Captain Dew received word that Ningpo was being threatened from the north, and he hurried back to the port, leaving Lieutenant Bogle and the *Hardy* with Ward.

Early on the morning of the twenty-first, Major Morton and his four hundred men arrived from Yü-yao, having left Tardif de Moidrey and his Franco-Chinese troops behind as a garrison. Immediately, Ward held a council of war and outlined an attack: Lieutenant Bogle was to shell Tz'u-ch'i's western gate and provide cover for a storming party that would be commanded by Major Cook. Cook was to feint at the city's southern wall before making his actual attempt to climb the west gate. "You must do it with a rush," Ward was heard to tell Cook, "or we shall fail, for they are very numerous."

At about seven-thirty the *Hardy* opened fire, and within an hour Cook's men were ready to scale the walls. What happened next is, in keeping with the rest of Ward's life, somewhat clouded by contradictory accounts. Forester later claimed that he and Ward supervised the preparation of the scaling ladders, oblivious to danger: "We had become so accustomed to the enemy's fire that we had grown somewhat careless. While standing side by side inspecting the position, Ward put his hand suddenly to his abdomen and exclaimed, 'I have been hit.' A brief investigation of the wound showed that it was a serious one, and I had him carried on board the 'Hardy,' where surgical attendance was promptly given."

Ward had in fact been hit by a Taiping musket ball in the abdomen. But as for Forester's being present, Lieutenant Bogle, in his account of the day's action, stated that after Ward fell command devolved on Major Morton, suggesting that Forester was still in Ningpo. And while it is true that Ward was removed to the *Hardy,* there was no medical officer on board that vessel, hence no "surgical attendance" to be "promptly given." Again, Forester's account raises more questions than it answers.

A rumor quickly spread among Ward's men that their commander had been shot not with a Taiping musket but with a Western rifle fired by a European mercenary from the walls of Tz'u-ch'i. This story may have been invented to heighten the rage of the Ever Victorious Army troops; if so, it succeeded. Since forming his first contingent in 1860, Ward had been wounded at least fifteen times—but he had never allowed anyone to take him from his men. Even at the first battle of Ch'ing-p'u, when his jaw had been shattered, Ward had refused to leave the field. But here, before Tz'u-ch'i, a sniping shot had finally broken that long battlefield bond, and in the wake of Ward's removal the men of the Ever Victorious Army climbed the walls of Tz'u-ch'i with speed and heartfelt conviction. First up, appropriately enough, was Vincente Macanaya, whose courage was duplicated by the unit's other officers: "I myself noticed," wrote Lieutenant Bogle to Captain Dew, "that all the officers led their men over the ladders." Faced with such determination, the Taipings soon abandoned Tz'u-ch'i.

But there was little rejoicing among the conquerors, for on board the *Hardy* the news was all bad. Ward was placed on a suspended cot as the ship made for Ningpo and skilled surgical care at full steam. But it was clear that Ward might not last the journey. In excruciating pain, he drifted in and out of consciousness. During one of Ward's waking moments, Lieutenant Bogle, fearing the worst, told his comrade that he was near death and asked him if he had made a will. Ward was able to whisper to Bogle that Wu Hsü owed him 110,000 taels, and Yang Fang 30,000. "I wish my wife to have 50,000 taels," Ward said, Bogle writing the words down, "and all that remains to be between my brother and my sister. I wish Admiral Sir James Hope and Mr. Burlinghame [sic] to be my executors." Bogle then witnessed the document, as did the ship's boatswain.

In Ningpo Ward was taken to the house of a missionary surgeon. The musket ball, which had become embedded in the muscles of his lower back, was removed, but the damage it had done proved too great: On the morning of September 22, after enduring almost twenty-four hours of agony, the creator and commander of the Ever Victorious Army died.

In a little more than two months, he would have been thirty-one years old.

EPILOGUE
"POOR OLD WARD"

A potential for intrigue, conflict, and chaos had always existed among the officers of the Ever Victorious Army, their Chinese superiors, and the Western soldiers, diplomats, and merchants with whom the army did regular business. By September 1862 this potential had assumed alarming proportions. Up to that point it had been kept in check only by Ward himself: The young commander's charm, determination, and ability to manage those above and below him had consistently prevented a serious crisis. With Ward's death, however, the affairs of the Ever Victorious Army, as well as conditions on the eastern front of the Chinese civil war generally, began a steady collapse into a state of dangerous confusion.

This degeneration began literally within hours of Ward's passing. In Ningpo, Edward Forester ordered his leader's remains taken aboard the *Confucius* for transfer back to Sung-chiang. As the gunboat made ready to leave, Ward's body was guarded by an officer of the Ever Victorious Army. Some years later this man gave an anonymous interview to A. A. Hayes. Knowing that both Wu Hsü and Yang Fang had proved most reluctant to recognize the legitimacy of Ward's dying claim that they owed him 140,000 taels—and further aware that neither Wu nor Yang had been above falsifying documents in order to prove their case—Hayes thought back during the interview to the small account book that Ward had always carried in the breast pocket of his frock coat. If an accurate record of Ward's dealings could have been found anywhere, Hayes suspected, it would have been in that book, and he asked the former Ever Victorious Army officer what had happened to it.

"I can tell you," the man answered. "I was guarding the general's body. The blue coat which you remember lay on a chair, and the book was in the breast pocket. Colonel ———, my superior officer, relieved me. The book was never seen again, but *I saw Colonel* ——— *buy exchange for forty thousand dollars.*" (Original emphasis.) Hayes's unwillingness to name the colonel in question was understandable: Edward Forester—the only Ever Victorious Army colonel in Ningpo at the time of Ward's death—was still alive when Hayes published his story. Hayes apparently accepted the officer's assertion that the account book had disappeared following Forester's watch over Ward's body, yet the officer had not actually witnessed its removal. There was thus no way to prove the allegation that Forester had stolen and sold the book, and had Hayes named Forester he would have opened himself to legal action. What Hayes did not know was that the account book was in fact seen again, in Shanghai after the *Confucius* returned with Ward's body.

Major James E. Cook, the commander of Ward's bodyguard, later stated in a sworn deposition that following his return from Ningpo he "had occasion to visit a house and room occupied by Col. Forrester [*sic*] and saw there a small account book which he [Cook] knew General Ward had always carried with him in his pocket. He [Cook] opened it and knew the handwriting of General Ward and saw that these were various accounts of monies with persons connected with the forces." Cook left the book in Forester's room, which happened to be in a house that belonged to Yang Fang, and he thought nothing more of the matter until some months later when Forester, claiming ill health, resigned his commission and speedily left China, just as a protracted legal battle over Ward's estate was getting under way.

If we put Cook's story together with that of Hayes's unnamed officer, we get a rough and all too disheartening picture of what happened to Ward's account book. Forty-thousand dollars amounted to about twenty-five thousand taels, or one-sixth the amount Ward claimed from Wu Hsü and Yang Fang in his will. That Yang and Wu would have gladly paid Forester such a sum to ensure the defeat of Ward's claim

is beyond doubt. But the answer to the nagging question of why Forester—a man who had always exerted himself for Ward and had enjoyed
Ward's trust in return—agreed to such an arrangement remains hidden.
Certainly, Forester had suffered during his imprisonment at the hands
of the rebels and probably knew that his health would not permit him
to serve in the Ever Victorious Army very much longer. Yet avarice
does not seem an adequate explanation of his actions: It was not simple
greed, for example, that caused Forester to warp the history of the Ever
Victorious Army as he did in his published recollections. Perhaps Forester, his seemingly faithful service notwithstanding, had been untrust-
worthy all along, yet it is doubtful that as shrewd a judge of personalities
as Ward would have failed to recognize as much during their months of
campaigning together. Or there may have been a late and specific cause
for the seeming bitterness that marked Forester's actions after Ward's
death. If so, it will in all likelihood never be discovered.

News of Ward's death had a deep and somewhat surprising effect
on the Western communities in Shanghai. Captain Roderick Dew had
already written to Admiral Hope from Ningpo, saying that it was his
"painful duty" to inform the admiral that Ward had been killed in action.
"During a short acquaintance with General Ward," Dew continued, "I
have learnt to appreciate him much, and I fear his death will cast a gloom
over the Imperial cause in China, of which he was the stay and prop."
Hope passed the news on to the Admiralty in London, saying that "[i]t
is with much regret that I have to acquaint their Lordships with the
death of Colonel Ward, who was mortally wounded at the recapture of
T'zu-ch'i, by which event the Chinese Government have lost an able and
gallant officer who had served them well, and whom it will not be easy
to replace." Hope also communicated the news to Minister Burlingame
in Peking, who, Hope was sure, would be "much grieved to hear of poor
Ward's death." General Staveley, predictably, had no comment on
Ward's passing; but his brother-in-law and chief of engineers, Captain
Charles Gordon, wrote that "I am afraid this will give the rebels much
confidence as he was a very energetic man & did good service to the
Chinese Govt."

The *North China Herald* gave the news of Ward's death a featured spot in its September 27 issue, promising to "collect information" about Ward and his death to be published later. When it finally appeared, the *Herald*'s assessment of Ward was quite typical of general Western feeling at the time:

> Without a military education, Ward displayed on many occasions the qualities of a General. The biography of this man has yet to be written; and whatever be his antecedents the chief events of his life would be interesting. All we can remark, from the little we have gleaned of his life, is that he has been an important actor in the Taiping drama; and we should be the last to register on the annals of the campaign, any circumstance detrimental to his character before he entered upon those scenes of warfare. "Tell me not of what I was, but of what I am," is a good motto for such wandering sons of fortune.

After the *Confucius*'s return to Shanghai, Ward's body was taken to Sung-chiang. According to Charles Schmidt, "It was a solemn day, and the news had a depressing effect not alone on the officers and men [of the Ever Victorious Army], but even on the inhabitants of Sung-chiang. General Ward had always been a true friend to all, and just in his dealings, irrespective of nationality. All shops were closed when the corpse arrived in this city as a token of respect for the deceased." Ward's body was taken to Sung-chiang's Confucian temple and temporarily placed in a corner of the courtyard (another rare honor for a Westerner) while plans were made for the actual funeral. Chinese astrologers and geomancers went to work selecting an appropriate burial site. Ward's Chinese soldiers braided their hair with white tape, a traditional Chinese sign of mourning. His officers wore black crepe on their sleeves. And Ward's large black-and-white mastiff wandered around the army's training grounds and headquarters for days, hopelessly seeking his master. The dog refused to eat (or perhaps, with Ward gone, could find no one to feed him) and soon died.

How Ward should be buried was as important to Chinese officials as when and where. He was, after all, a Chinese subject, and burial rites were extremely important in Confucian society. Ultimate responsibility for Ward's funeral rested with his immediate Chinese superior, Li Hung-chang. After carefully weighing the matter, Li dispatched a memorial to the throne, expressing a view of Ward and his services that would shortly become characteristic of the Chinese government generally. Relieved of any reason to be suspicious or jealous of Ward, Li recalled the American-born commander's early victories, summing them up with the statement "Thus with few he overcame the many; a meritorious deed that is very rare." Wu Hsü, said Li, had sent in a petition detailing Ward's role during the Chung Wang's January 1862 offensive; based on Wu's account, Li concluded "that the turning away of the danger and the maintenance of tranquility in those places [the Shanghai region] was chiefly due to the exertions of Ward."

But Li saved his greatest praise for a retelling of his own experiences with Ward:

> From the time of the arrival of Your Majesty's Minister, Li Hung-chang, at Shanghai, to take charge of affairs, [Ward] was in all respects obedient to the orders he received, and whether he received orders to harass the city of Chin-shan-wei or to force back the rebels at Liu-ho, he was everywhere successful. Still further, he bent all his energy on the recapture of Ch'ing-p'u, and was absorbed in a plan for sweeping away the rebels from Soochow. Such loyalty and valor, issuing from his natural disposition, is extraordinary when compared with these virtues of the best officers of China; and among foreign officers it is not easy to find one worthy of equal honour.

There was, to say the very least, some variance between this assessment of Ward and the reports from provincial officials that Peking had been getting in the weeks before the Ever Victorious Army commander's death. Li further underlined his new approach with recommendations concerning Ward's burial:

> Your Majesty's Minister, Li Hung-chang, has already ordered Wu Hsü and others to deck Ward's body with a Chinese uniform, to

provide good sepulture, and to bury him at Sung-chiang, in order to complete the recompense for his valiant defense of the Dynasty. . . . We owe him our respect, and our deep regret. It is appropriate, therefore, to entreat that your Gracious Majesty do order the Board of Rites to take into consideration suitable posthumous rewards to be bestowed on him, Ward; and that both at Ningpo and at Sung-chiang sacrificial altars be erected to appease the manes of this loyal man.

In the custom of most imperial officials, Li was recording facts not as he knew them to be but in the way that would most benefit Chinese interests. There was real purpose in his depiction of Ward as a wholly loyal and valiant defender of the Manchu dynasty: the Ever Victorious Army would need a new commander soon, and by setting Ward up as the ideal of a naturalized Chinese subject, Li Hung-chang hoped to make his successor fit a mold which Li was well aware Ward himself had never matched.

In replying to Li's memorial, Prince Kung and the Empress Dowager Tz'u-hsi echoed the Kiangsu governor's tone and intent:

We have read the memorial, and feel that Brigadier Ward, a man of heroic disposition, a soldier without dishonor, deserves Our commendation and compassion. Li Hung-chang has already ordered Wu Hsü and others to attend to the proper rites of sepulture, and We now direct the two Prefects that special temples to his memory be built at Ningpo and Sung-chiang. Let this case be submitted to the Board of Rites, who will propose to Us further honors so as to show our extraordinary consideration towards him, and also that his loyal spirit may rest in peace. This from the Emperor! Respect it!

In another decree, the imperial clique made their true motivations more apparent: "Ward was a foreigner who submitted to China. He was a little arrogant, but he has served China and died while fighting the rebels; therefore he should be rewarded and treated exceptionally well, so that foreign countries will be impressed."

An appropriate plot of ground was eventually selected in Sung-chiang, and Ward was finally laid to rest. The funeral was a solemn and elaborate affair, the heterogenous procession symbolizing all that the fallen soldier had been in life. Officers and men of the Ever Victorious Army, Chinese mandarins and military leaders, and British naval and army officers (Admiral Hope was in Japan at the time) all marched solemnly together behind a gun carriage, on which lay Ward's coffin. Ward had been dressed in his mandarin's robes, minus his blue-button cap and black Manchu boots. The gun carriage was drawn by Ward's bodyguard, preceded, according to Charles Schmidt, "by the Staff band playing the dead march in [Handel's] Saul." Schmidt reported that a British chaplain read a burial service at the grave site: hardly in keeping with traditional Chinese ceremony. An equal source of consternation for those Chinese present must have been the fact that Ward's dog was buried in a small grave next to him. Following the internment there were salvos by the rifle and artillery battalions, and the Ever Victorious Army immediately entered an official three-month period of mourning. A tumulus was built up over Ward's grave and a smaller one over that of his mastiff. And with that the principal participants in the ongoing war against the Taipings returned to the business of suppression.

There is no record of precisely what happened to Chang-mei in the months following Ward's funeral. Certainly, there was never any chance that either Wu Hsü or her father would have paid Chang-mei the money Ward wished and thus given her some hope of an independent existence. Although she had been living at Sung-chiang during the summer of 1862, there is no subsequent mention of her in connection with that city, suggesting that after her husband's death Chang-mei returned to her father's home in Shanghai. The biography of Shen Chu-jeng, the boy the Wards reportedly adopted, states only that after Ward's burial "Mrs. Ward became very ill with extreme grief and died the following year in Shanghai. Shen was in charge of her funeral, and sent her coffin back to Ningpo."

On October 2, 1862, Lieutenant Thomas Lyster of the Royal Engineers wrote to his father to say that the British regulars in Shanghai had not killed any Taipings recently, "although they have managed to kill General Ward. I saw him a short time ago, and was to have gone on an expedition with him. I liked the old fellow very much." Some weeks later Lyster, visiting Sung-chiang, further informed his father that "[p]oor old Ward is buried here in Chinese fashion—his coffin over-ground. This place was his headquarters. He came out to China as mate of a ship, outlawed from America, and has died worth a million and a half. He was often wounded, and people had the idea he could not be shot."

The discussion of who would succeed Ward as commander of the Ever Victorious Army quickly became a debate—and an acrimonious one. In his published recollections, Forester claimed that he immediately assumed overall command of the force, but in fact he was second in line behind Burgevine. Burgevine was still badly hampered by the wound he had received in the spring, but he wasted no time after Ward's death in writing to George Seward, the young American consul in Shanghai, to say that "in consequence of the death of Major-General Ward, the command of the Imperial troops stationed at Sung-chiang has devolved upon me as Senior Officer acting under the authority of this province." But certain British officers and officials—most notably General Staveley—did not immediately recognize Burgevine's claim and attempted to finally bring the Ever Victorious Army under British control by having one of Her Majesty's officers appointed to command it. The French similarly angled to gain control over the Ever Victorious Army by pointing out that, in light of the activities of Tardif de Moidrey, Prosper Giquel, and Le Brethon de Caligny, a French officer would be singularly suited to carry on Ward's work.

The issue was not settled immediately, although military developments highlighted the need for a decisive solution. Forester returned to Ningpo, where in early October he assisted Captain Dew and the Franco-Chinese troops in clearing the thirty-mile radius around that port. Forester then resigned his commission and soon cut his deal with Yang Fang and Wu Hsü for Ward's account book. In the meantime, the Chung Wang was stepping up his attack on Tseng Kuo-fan's forces outside Nanking, forcing Tseng to reconsider his position on allowing the Ever Victorious Army to support his Hunan troops. Tseng finally did authorize such a mission for the army he so deeply distrusted, but the

Ever Victorious Army could not go to Nanking until it had an unchallenged new leader.

General Staveley's attempts to block Burgevine's bid to succeed Ward were eventually stymied, not because Burgevine was clearly the best man for the job but because he had taken the fortuitous step of following Ward into Chinese citizenship: the imperial government's first requirement, at the time, for an Ever Victorious Army commander. In addition, Burgevine's cause was supported by Admiral Hope, who knew of Ward's respect for Burgevine above all his other officers and who spoke up for Burgevine largely in remembrance of his dead comrade. Against a backdrop of false Chinese praise and jealous scheming by General Staveley, Hope's genuine loyalty to Ward stood out all the more clearly during October. Not only did the admiral insist to Forester and others that the Ever Victorious Army continued to be called Ward's Chinese Corps, and that its officers maintain practices that had enjoyed Ward's special attention (such as the training of Chinese officers) but late in October he wrote to Frederick Bruce in Peking to request a series of tributes to the corps's creator:

> I shall feel obliged by your explaining to Prince Kung the practice which prevails with European Nations of placing on their colours the names of the battles in which they have been successful, and those of the Towns which they have taken, and by your acquainting him that I think it would be highly beneficial to the Esprit de Corps of Ward's Chinese if the Emperor should decree that they should carry on their colours the names of Ch'ing-p'u and Tz'u-ch'i, the former having been captured by themselves alone, and the latter having been the scene of Col. Ward's death, and stormed by them.

Hope then repeated his desire concerning the force's title: "I should further deem it a personal favor that the Corps should retain in future the name of 'Ward's Chinese,' which it now bears and which would be a graceful compliment to the officer by whom it was raised, and who fell at their head."

These and other of Hope's tributes to Ward were echoed by Anson

Burlingame in Peking, who also supported the nomination of Burgevine to take over the Ever Victorious Army. Like Hope, Burlingame knew that Burgevine would have been Ward's choice, and his advocacy was based on strong loyalty to his fallen friend. Late in October, Burlingame dispatched official word of Ward's death to Secretary of State Seward and President Lincoln in Washington. Burlingame made the most of Ward's national origins, calling his fellow New Englander

> an American who had risen by his capacity and courage to the highest rank in the Chinese service. . . . General Ward was originally from Salem, Massachusetts, where he has relatives yet living, and had seen service in Mexico, the Crimea, and, he was sorry to say, with the notorious Walker. He fought at the head of a Chinese force called into existence and trained by himself, countless battles, and always with success. Indeed he taught the Chinese their strength, and laid the foundations of the only force with which their government can hope to defeat the rebellion.

Recalling Ward's offer to contribute ten thousand taels toward the building of "the strongest[,] darkest & deepest Hotel in the country for the blackguards Jeff[erson Davis] & Cabinet," Burlingame went on to urge: "Let this wish, though unexecuted, find worthy record in the archives of his native land, to show that neither self exile, nor foreign service, nor the incidents of a stormy life could extinguish from the breast of this wandering child of the Republic the fires of a truly loyal heart."

Of Burgevine, Burlingame said that the Carolinian had "taken part in all the conflicts with Ward, and common fame spoke well of him." This opinion was shared by Frederick Bruce. And with such powerful supporters—and because he satisfied the Chinese requirement that he become a Chinese subject and submit to imperial military authority—Burgevine was finally named to command the Ever Victorious Army. But very quickly, Hope, Burlingame, and Bruce, not to mention the imperial government, were given ample reason to doubt their selection. At Sung-chiang, where Ward had used a skillful blend of guile and intimidation to nullify the power of the local mandarins, Burgevine quickly gained a reputation as a tactless bully: "The authorities," wrote England's Chaloner Alabaster some months later, "useless under Ward, were indignant under Burgevine." Doubtless this situation was adversely affected—as indeed all of Burgevine's actions were—by his ever-increasing reliance on alcohol to ease the pain of his pelvic wound. As Dr. Macgowan noted, Burgevine "had undertaken, while recovering from the wound, to fortify his constitution by the use of stimulants, which he was assured were tonic; so that, what with morning cocktails, and brandy-smashes through the day . . . it was clear that a crisis could not long be averted."

Incontestable proof of the destructive effects of Burgevine's drinking, as well as of the considerable differences between Ward and Burgevine, came during an Allied attack on Chia-ting on October 23. The only Taiping stronghold left in the Shanghai thirty-mile radius, Chia-ting was taken by a detachment of the Ever Victorious Army working with British naval forces under Admiral Hope and military units under General Staveley. Following the battle, several witnesses reported that rebel prisoners taken by the Ever Victorious Army were executed summarily, a policy Ward had carefully avoided. Furthermore, the manner of execution sparked revulsion in Chinese and Western observers alike. Apparently having heard of the same thing being done to Sepoy rebels in India, Burgevine either ordered or allowed the rebels to be strapped across the mouths of cannon and blown to pieces.

Both Hope and Staveley were understandably dismayed by such behavior, and, in the wake of the capture of Chia-ting, Admiral Hope persuaded Burgevine to agree to the appointment of Captain John Holland of the Royal Marines as chief of staff of the Ever Victorious Army, in an effort to "prevent the entire disorganisation of the Corps." But Holland soon proved a less than imaginative officer; in fact, his appointment may only have worsened the situation, for, as one of Ward's veteran officers put it, "Burgevine, instead of giving responsible appointments to competent men, was very often ruled by some of his staff officers; and men were appointed because they were favored by those around him. Burgevine was not the man that Ward was. The latter used to go by his own judgment; while Burgevine confided too much to his staff; which would have been right enough, if these men had been competent to hold their rank; but Burgevine ought to have known that they were not."

Admiral Hope—tired, still feeling the effects of his wounded leg, and ready to relinquish his command in China—tried to remain hopeful: "Colonel Burgevine," he told Frederick Bruce, "is perfectly sensible of the necessity of thoroughly organising and disciplining the Corps prior to attempting any distant operation, and will during the ensuing winter limit his operations to the protection of the Shanghai district." Following the Allied recapture of Chia-ting, however, the Chung Wang returned east to make sure that the new threats to his forces in Kiangsu did not result in the fall of Soochow. An opportunity for a decisive imperialist move against Nanking was thus created, and by late fall Hope, the only hand that could moderate Burgevine's behavior, had left for England. In November and December, Burgevine's Chinese superiors pressed him to prepare his army for an attack on Nanking in conjunction with Tseng Kuo-fan's forces. Burgevine agreed to the plan but stated that he would not move until he was completely ready and until Wu Hsü and Yang Fang supplied him with more supplies and money than they had to date.

Burgevine's position in this last regard was understandable: He did not possess Ward's magic gift for getting what he needed out of Wu and Yang, who since Burgevine's assumption of command had withheld sorely needed funds. By January 1863 the situation was so bad that the Ever Victorious Army was on the brink of mutiny. After trying to placate his men by repeating a series of empty pledges from his backers, the desperate Burgevine marched into Yang Fang's office, beat the old banker bloody, and took forty thousand silver dollars.

This was not only theft but a crime against the Confucian order: To Li Hung-chang, Burgevine was "in the sight of Chinese law, guilty in the highest degree, and even according to foreign law such a rebellious and treasonable subject cannot be tolerated in the service." Needless to say, the Ever Victorious Army's expedition to Nanking never materialized. After making repeated attempts to exonerate himself, Burgevine fled Sung-chiang with many of his officers and eventually defected to the Taipings.

Burgevine's behavior gave Li Hung-chang the excuse he had long needed to strip Wu Hsü and Yang Fang—who, as Burgevine's sponsors and superiors, were responsible for his actions—of most of their government posts. Wu subsequently left Shanghai, and Yang withdrew into the Western settlements, where he owned considerable property. As to command of the Ever Victorious Army, Li and his superiors had had enough, by this point, of foreign adventurers: They agreed to allow the British to appoint an officer to command the steadily deteriorating force.

They were encouraged to do so by the successes enjoyed during the winter of 1862–63 by the Franco-Chinese troops supporting the imperial armies in Chekiang province. In December 1862 Prosper Giquel and Lieutenant Le Brethon de Caligny had begun operations against the Taipings again. Giquel quickly received a bad wound and was forced to suspend his field participation, but in January Le Brethon de Caligny resolutely moved against the Taiping stronghold of Shao-hsing without the support of any Ever Victorious Army or Anglo-Chinese troops. Among Le Brethon's artillery force were some old British nine-pounder guns, which Le Brethon himself positioned outside the walls of the city. In the midst of this bold action, tragedy struck: "[A]t the first discharge the gun burst," wrote Andrew Wilson, "and a large portion of the breech struck Le Brethon, carrying away the whole upper part of his body and causing instantaneous death."

The wounded Giquel still could not assume field command of the Franco-Chinese troops, which now devolved on Ward's old comrade Adrien Tardif de Moidrey. Many of the Franco-Chinese soldiers were reluctant to renew the attack on Shao-hsing, whose defenders were determined. But Tardif was as unstoppable as ever. On February 19, 1863, he ordered his troops back to Shao-hsing's walls. On this occasion, however, discipline had its price: At 10:00 A.M. Tardif de Moidrey was shot in the back of the head by one of his own soldiers. Wilson recalled that "[h]is iron constitution enabled him to live for eight hours, though his brains were scattered over the hair of his head." Ironically, Tardif's troops finally took the city when the rebels evacuated it on March 18. In subsequent months, commanded by Giquel, the Franco-Chinese Corps of Chekiang became the Ever Triumphant Army and played a key role in the recapture of Hangchow.

The Ever Victorious Army, meanwhile, was enjoying no such success. In response to the Chinese agreement to allow a British officer to command the force, General Staveley—who, with Hope gone, became the dominant voice in British military policy in Shanghai—put forward his young brother-in-law, Charles George Gordon, as a candidate. The Chinese requirement that any Ever Victorious Army commander become a Chinese subject was waived, but the imperial government still insisted that Gordon at least enter the Chinese military service. To do so, however, Gordon needed permission from Staveley's superiors. As those orders were awaited, Captain John Holland was placed in temporary command of the Ever Victorious Army.

It quickly became apparent that Holland had no central understanding of what made the Ever Victorious Army work as a unit: "Everything," Dr. Macgowan wrote, "was reorganised, after the pattern of the Queen's regulations, as Holland used to term it. Even Ward's uniform, which that general had ordered to be worn when he raised the force—a kind of American style, was done away with, and instead, a new one invented *à la* Holland. It was a wonder he did not order a red coat, like the Royal Marines."

Unfortunately, Holland paid less attention to tactics than to details: When he engaged the rebels at T'ai-ts'ang on February 14, he was soundly beaten. The English-language periodical *Friend of China* commented, "It took the troops four days to reach T'ai-ts'ang;—it took them—less muskets, blankets, provisions, munitions of war, ordnance—everything,—to the tune of over a hundred thousand dollars—eight hours only to get back! Such a skedaddle was never seen."

Lieutenant Thomas Lyster of the Royal Engineers wrote to his father of the incident: "The rebels . . . beat Ward's force, killing several hundred. . . . General Holland had no idea beyond brute force. He actually told me, when I was at Sung-chiang, and had an argument with him about the last French and Austrian campaign, that he did not believe in *tactics!* . . . He, throughout all the operations, did not take the least advantage of tactics. General Ward, who was not a professional soldier, would have acted better."

The Ever Victorious Army's sad disintegration during the early months of 1863 caused many Westerners in Shanghai to wonder if the army had ever truly been the wondrous force of disciplined Chinese that they had once supposed. The *North China Herald,* for example, wrote in January that "there is reason to believe that the corps has not been of that high character it was represented to be." This attitude only deepened as time went by: Soon the *Herald* was worrying that the force would "degenerate into, what in Ward's time it too much resembled, a rabble presenting the guise only of a military organization—which in reality it never possessed." Typically, the *Herald* was encouraged by the appointment of Captain Holland, who, as a British officer, could presumably reverse the downward trend. But after T'ai-ts'ang the *Herald* was forced to admit that Holland "did not exhibit the requisite skill in generalship to command so large a force."

On March 23 command of the Ever Victorious Army was given to Charles George Gordon (now promoted major), despite the continued protests of the army's veteran officers against outside control. Charles Schmidt wrote in early April that " '[t]he ever Victorious army' [*sic*] do not want any regular Military Foreign Generals, however necessary the latter may be supposed to be. Do not intrude! We want men of Ward's and Vincente's stamp!" But the likelihood of Vincente Macanaya being given command was slim, as Schmidt himself recognized: "[H]is being a Manila man puts the damper on his chances of election to the position of Commander under the present Sung-chiang dynasty." Schmidt could see that with the arrival of Gordon the Ever Victorious Army entered on a period of transition that would leave it far from the vision Ward had originally conjured up and subsequently come so close to achieving. Schmidt further sensed that the money he and Vincente were owed by their Chinese backers would probably never be paid. Schmidt, Vincente, and other officers of the force had, like Ward, often accepted Wu Hsü's and Yang Fang's vouchers in lieu of payment. But as things stood in April 1863—with Ward dead and Yang and Wu degraded—these vouchers meant little. In bemoaning this fact, Schmidt bid farewell to Vincente Macanaya and, at the same time, to an era:

"Perhaps, Vincente, the time may come when our old Tartar masters will be tired of their new ones [the English]. They may then again ask a favor of us and let us then be wise;—have nothing to do with a necessity for vouchers;—but catching our one moon's advance first, be with that content.—Until then Adieu."

Under Charles G. Gordon the Ever Victorious Army came out of the organizational and operational tailspin it had been in since Ward's death. But it also lost much of the roguish élan that had characterized it during Ward's tenure and took on an aura that more closely matched its deeply religious and psychologically complex new commander. The contrast between Ward and Gordon was a paradoxical one, involving details of character that at once suggested similarity and extreme difference. For example, when Gordon was younger he, like Ward, had played a game that involved falling into the ocean and observing the reaction his distress created among those ashore; the difference, as Richard J. Smith has pointed out, "was that Ward could swim." Ever the pure adventurer, Ward had none of the religious intensity and fascination with death that marked Gordon, whose indulgent mother had taught him to interpret the Bible as literal truth. Gordon never belonged to any church or organized Christian sect but relied wholly on his own interpretations of the sacred book for guidance. Thus like Ward he constructed his own system of values, but unlike his American predecessor Gordon formed those values around a deep religious commitment that bordered on mysticism.

Again like Ward, Gordon had had a history of violent encounters as a boy at school. But while Ward had been a popular champion of weaker children, Gordon had been a difficult youth prone to violent outbursts that too often resembled bullying. In adulthood, both Ward and Gordon possessed undeniable charm, yet Gordon's was perhaps the less calculated. Indeed, for all his perspicacity about the world around him, Gordon could be remarkably lacking in insight about his own character and actions. For this reason his personality, while more restrained than Ward's, was also less disciplined. Never very comfortable with other people, Gordon was particularly ill at ease with women, giving rise after his death to grossly unfair questions concerning his sexuality. Harry Parkes, Britain's foremost consul in China, summed Gordon up as "a fine noble generous fellow, but at the same time very peculiar and sensi-

tive—exceedingly impetuous—full of energy, which just wants judgment to make it a very splendid type." Throughout his life it was this
occasional lack of judgment that kept Gordon from attaining the highest
level of success. It also, in the end, made him a legend throughout the
world: His final decision to stand alone at the head of a comparatively
tiny garrison at Khartoum and take on the hordes of the Sudanese
Islamic rebellion in 1885, while impractical to the point of being suicidal,
also gave him just renown as a courageous martyr.

On taking command of the Ever Victorious Army in March 1863,
Gordon made several disparaging statements that unfairly attributed the
unit's recent troubles to Ward. But he quietly took other actions that
indicated both that he knew such statements to be ungrounded and that
he had studied Ward carefully during the thirty-mile-radius campaign.
Adopting the practice of going into battle armed only with a rattan cane,
Gordon was able to form around himself the same superstitions of
invulnerability that had marked the attitude of China's peasants toward
Ward. On a more practical level, Gordon strengthened the branches of
the Ever Victorious Army that Ward, toward the end of his life, had
recognized were the most crucial: the artillery and the armed steamers.
He cleaned out officers he considered unreliable and restored a disciplined air to the army's camp. Yet this air, unlike that of Ward's day, was
all business: While the men marched, drilled, and fought effectively, they
did so with little of the enthusiasm that had so marked the Ward period.

By late July 1863 Gordon and Li Hung-chang had engaged the
Taipings extensively outside the thirty-mile radius. These engagements
had been so successful that they were closing in for an attack on Soochow, the Chung Wang's most valued prize. Now serving with the
Taipings was Burgevine, whom Gordon knew personally, and through
an extensive system of spies and contacts inside the rebel camp that he
(again like Ward) employed, Gordon was able to communicate with the
troubled ex-commander of the Ever Victorious Army. Having found the
rebel service less profitable than he had expected, Burgevine was ready
to. desert, and Gordon facilitated the move. According to Augustus
Lindley, Burgevine next proposed to Gordon that the two men abandon
both the Manchus and the rebels "and commence a system of indepen-

dent conquest." Lindley speculated that the idea might have been the result of "mental derangement, consequent upon the effects of his [Burgevine's] wound and the stimulants he used"; whatever the case, Gordon turned him down.

But the British engineer turned imperial commander soon had cause to reconsider his loyalty to the Chinese government. Surrounding the walls of Soochow and laying siege to the city, Gordon engaged in weeks of tough fighting that resulted in surrender by the seven commanding rebel wangs (the Chung Wang was not among them) on December 4, 1863. Gordon—who, unlike Ward, was not bound to China by either citizenship or inclination—had great admiration for the leaders of the Taiping cause, whom he considered "*without* exception brave and gallant men." He had arranged for the surrender of Soochow by offering the rebel leaders a pardon. But when Gordon and his army left the city, Li Hung-chang promptly had the men executed. Gordon considered the incident a violation of his own honor and flew into a rage that astounded and bewildered everyone around him. Li (most of whose family had been killed by the Taipings) was especially confused: In China, the execution of rebel leaders was common policy, and any pledges made to practitioners of the worst of the "ten abominations" could hardly be considered binding. But when Gordon threatened Li with personal violence and gave serious thought to defecting to the Taipings, Li perceived just how bad the situation was. He quickly urged his superiors to grant heavy rewards to placate Gordon, who was subsequently made a member of the emperor's own imperial bodyguard and given ten thousand dollars. As it usually did, Gordon's mood soon swung, and the Ever Victorious Army got back to business. But it had been a revealing and perilous moment.

The fall of Soochow hurt the Taiping cause badly and worsened the plight of Nanking. When the Ever Victorious Army took Ch'ang-chou on May 11, 1864, it became clear that the Taiping capital would never get the relief its defenders had long hoped for from the east. With victory against the rebels finally within reach, the imperial Chinese government felt safe in disbanding the strange force of "imitation foreign devils" that had always caused them so much anxiety. The Ever Victorious Army

passed into history shortly after the fall of Ch'ang-chou, without ceremony and largely unmourned. Gordon himself issued an epitaph that was
callous, somewhat unjust, and certainly indicative of the feelings of
Chinese and Western officials by 1864: "This force has had ever since
its formation in its ranks a class of men of no position. . . . Ignorant,
uneducated, even unaccustomed to command, they were not suited to
control the men they had under them. . . . I consider the force even
under a British officer a most dangerous collection of men, never to be
depended on and very expensive." Gordon might have thought to add
that the force had been vital to the suppression of the world's most
brutal rebellion.

The Taiping movement did not long outlive the Ever Victorious
Army. The Chung Wang, who in the spring of 1864 was desperately
fighting Tseng Kuo-fan's forces in Nanking, had known since his expul-
sion from Kiangsu that his own days and those of his comrades were
numbered. Faced with the collapse of his Heavenly Kingdom, the T'ien
Wang withdrew ever further into a world of degeneracy and insane
religious fantasy, urging the starving people of Nanking to eat grass—
which he called "heavenly dew"—to survive. Finally, in a moment of
clarity on June 3, 1864, the failed civil servant whose mad ramblings had
cost tens of millions of lives took poison, leaving his followers to shift
for themselves.

Loyal beyond all reason, the Chung Wang remained in Nanking
even as Tseng Kuo-fan's soldiers were storming it, to see to the safety
of the T'ien Wang's young son. Escorting the rebel heir out of the city,
the Chung Wang gave up all chance of his own escape by offering his
fastest horse to the boy. Captured by Tseng Kuo-fan, the Chung Wang
was imprisoned in a wooden cage and, in a rare example of leniency,
allowed time to write a short autobiography before his execution. After
vainly urging Tseng Kuo-fan to have mercy on the defenders of Nanking
(all of whom were executed), as well the T'ien Wang's followers generally, the Chung Wang ended his life with this melancholy statement:

> Now our Kingdom is finished, and this is because the former
> T'ien Wang's [appointed] span was ended. The fate of the people

was hard, such a hard fate! How could the T'ien Wang have been born to disturb the country? How could I, a man of no ability, have assisted him? Now that I have been taken and locked up, is it not because of the will of Heaven? I do not know my origins before this life. How many brave and clever men in the empire did not do these things, and I did. It is really because I did not understand. If I had understood . . .

The Chung Wang was not alone in his failure to understand the forces released by the Taiping rebellion. Burgevine, for example, had left China briefly after his defection from the rebels, then returned, apparently thinking the imperial government had forgotten or forgiven his transgressions. But the imperialists hunted Burgevine down and seized him in the summer of 1865, and while being transported on a riverboat with another group of prisoners, he mysteriously died. The official story was that the boat had capsized and all the prisoners had drowned. But in October, when a Western doctor exhumed Burgevine's body and did an autopsy, he found something peculiar: "a piece of skin, about 13 inches long and 3 inches wide, which had been removed from part of the thigh." The doctor could not conclude "whether this portion of skin was cut out," but the Chinese penchant for flaying traitors alive immediately presents itself.

To its end and through its aftermath, the Taiping rebellion was a wrenching and often fatal experience for those who became in any way involved in it; and one might have thought that in ensuing decades China's leaders would have learned from it many useful lessons and changed their governmental habits. But even Tseng Kuo-fan and Li Hung-chang, who represented China's best hope for a new political order, proved too steeped in tradition to carry any of their reform programs to the necessary lengths, and too prone to the usual Chinese habit of bureaucratic infighting to permit their alliance to gain lasting power. Following the defeat of the Taipings, Prince Kung and the Empress Dowager Tz'u-hsi ordered Tseng and Li to lead their Hunan and Anhwei armies against the Nien rebels. In the course of putting down this threat, Tseng and Li fell out, and their armies entered a factional feud that was to endure for decades and take precedence over reform and reconstruction. Tseng Kuo-fan at least died a true (if unsuccessful) defender of China, in 1871. But Li Hung-chang, in his later years, undermined his nation's strength by recklessly amassing personal power and lining his own pockets with bribes from China's enemies. As Tseng summed it up just before his death, "The dead leaves of disappointed hopes fill all the landscape."

Prince Kung and Tz'u-hsi also began to feud relatively soon after the defeat of the Taipings. The shrewd Tz'u-hsi emerged the ultimate victor in this contest, but just how unfortunate this victory was for China became apparent in 1900, when she ordered the fanatical Boxers to attack the foreign legations in Peking rather than trying to use the Western treaty system to ensure China's integrity as Kung had done. These and other private wars among the native Chinese and Manchu elites eliminated the possibility of real change in China during the late nineteenth century. Yet as that era came to an end, the Middle Kingdom's rulers clung to their ancient ways ever more tightly, making the death of the empire a certainty.

It is, therefore, hardly surprising that the important military innovations observed by Chinese commanders during their days of cooperation with the Ever Victorious Army and the forces of the Western powers should finally have amounted to so little. True, both Tseng Kuo-fan and Li Hung-chang favored China's manufacture of more modern weapons: With the help of Prosper Giquel, an extensive, modern shipyard and naval arsenal was eventually built at Foochow. But in essence the military effectiveness that China achieved during the final years of the Taiping rebellion was an anomaly. This became singularly clear when the empire was badly humiliated by the emerging Japanese nation in 1894–95.

Had the battlefield ineptitude displayed during this war been a result of the imperial government's preoccupation with goals that were higher and more peaceful than military reform one might forgive it. But it was factionalism and an addiction to social, political, and military obsolescence that actually prevented China's nineteenth-century leaders from building on the foundation of Ward's Ever Victorious Army. In the end, the fact that Ward had been born a barbarian counted for far more than the fact that he had taught the Chinese how to fight a modern war well. The history of late imperial China was full of rebellions and wars, many of which were prolonged and savage and any of which would have benefited from the presence of someone like Ward. But such flirtations with Western methods were not repeated in any meaningful way, and the Chinese went on slaughtering each other in essentially the same idiosyncratic, backward style that had marked their conflicts for centuries.

How much actual historical importance, then, did the Ever Victorious Army have? The question has been argued ever since the Taiping rebellion came to a close. In the early years of this debate, the army's importance was undeniably overestimated by Westerners. Entranced by the romantic image of "Chinese" Gordon (as the force's final commander came to be known), many foreigners, especially the British, portrayed the Ever Victorious Army as having played the most important role in breaking the back of the rebellion. We now know that that honor belongs to Tseng Kuo-fan and his Hunan troops. Yet to move in the opposite direction, as some sinologists and Communist Chinese historians have done, and portray the Ever Victorious Army's contribution as minimal is equally misleading. The force that Ward created and commanded—barred as it was from growing past five to six thousand men or undertaking significant operations in the interior—could not have helped but play a strategically supporting role to the Hunan Army. But that role was nonetheless vital. Neither Tseng Kuo-fan's nor Li Hung-chang's forces alone could have prevented the Taipings from seizing Shanghai, and it is impossible to determine how long the rebel movement would have survived had that valuable port fallen. In this sense it cannot be said with certainty when or even if the imperial government would have put the rebellion down without the Ever Victorious Army.

On another and perhaps more important level, it should be remembered that there was no governing idea behind the Hunan and Anhwei armies progressive enough to have allowed China to create an army capable of taking on an enemy such as the Japanese. A steady diet of Confucian philosophy was simply no substitute for disciplined training in the use of modern weapons and tactics. Had Ward and, more important, his work been better remembered, the disaster of 1894–95 might never have taken place, and the many humiliations that followed it—the Allied march on Peking in 1900, the steady loss of Chinese territorial integrity to the foreign powers, and finally the fall of the empire itself— might have been avoided.

Sadly, Ward was not well remembered. For a time the legal battle over his estate kept his name alive in the Western settlements in China, and he was honored as a loyal defender of the Middle Kingdom among some peasants and provincial officials for at least a few decades following his death. After that, however, as the account of his work was retooled to fit the successive waves of changing political philosophies that engulfed China, Ward's life and the history of the Ever Victorious Army became the province of specialized scholars and finally drifted into almost complete obscurity.

Pleading other pressing business, Admiral Hope and Minister Burlingame had both disqualified themselves as executors of Ward's estate late in 1862. Ward's friend Albert Freeman was eventually named administrator of the estate, and he brought the case to arbitration in March 1863. A. A. Hayes was named one of the arbitrators, whose task turned out to be a taxing one. From the first, Yang Fang and Wu Hsü disputed Ward's claim that they owed him 140,000 taels by insisting that their American employee had incurred offsetting debts to them during the operation of his army. This sum they first put at 10,000 taels, but it eventually rose, without credible explanation, to ten times that amount. The arbitrators accepted Yang's claim that the 30,000 taels he supposedly owed Ward was a private family matter, but they found the claim against Wu for 110,000 taels to be valid. Wu continued to dispute the finding, prompting a second arbitration in October 1863.

By this time, Ward's father, Frederick Gamaliel Ward, had arrived in China. The elder Ward represented himself as speaking for his family, but in fact, as the American consul in Shanghai, George Seward, told

Burlingame: "There is reported to have been a considerable rupture in Mr. Ward's family at home. This much is certain, that the only person supposed to be interested in the estate beside Henry Ward, the sister mentioned in the last words of the deceased, refused to give her father the power of attorney asked for by him." This development supports Dr. Macgowan's statement that the elder Ward was not a particularly well-loved father. Such did not stop him, however, from vigorously pursuing his son's claims: He even attempted to inflate them, to an amount that George Seward considered "essentially absurd."

At the second arbitration, Wu Hsü worked his counterclaim up to 270,000 taels by including in it monies owed by Ward to various Shanghai firms for supplies bought on credit. Since these were official expenses, Wu's argument was rightly dismissed by the arbitration board. Wu then introduced a document he claimed was Ward's actual will. Written in Chinese (a language Ward had never mastered) and signed only with a chop displaying the character *Hua,* the will was an obvious fake and was also dismissed. Wu had more success, however, in arguing that he was still owed money from Harry Ward's purchasing trip to America. None of the steamships Harry was supposed to have bought for Wu had ever reached China, nor had the money been returned. Pending an accurate accounting of Harry's purchases, said Wu, he would not pay any of the Ward claims.

Hearing of Wu's tactics, Harry Ward wrote to his father from New York:

> I am astonished at the proceedings. . . . How Mr. Seward or anyone else can sustain the "last commission!" I cannot understand—it is either a very high handed or a very low and disreputable position to take—I of course cannot advise or suggest to you but feel that you will be able to convince Mr. Burlingame of the injustice of such a course and that if carried out it would be a downright fraud and robbery of Fred's heirs. . . . Furthermore I don't see why the estate should have to pay Fogg & Co. bills—you can make them show books and prove that the articles were used for the Chinese Govt. and I fancy Fogg's people know it—All of them should blush,

if there is any blush in them for such robbery—for Fred made half
of them—If Fred were alive and in Shanghai for 24 short hours they
would all disgorge and sneak away like whipped curs.

The second arbitration board ordered Wu Hsü to pay the various
merchant houses in Shanghai the amounts he said were owed by the
Ward estate, but the board would make no judgment concerning the
original 110,000 taels claimed by the Ward family until Harry Ward's
accounts had been examined. Frederick G. Ward followed Harry's advice and went to Peking to enlist Burlingame's aid. But Burlingame and
other legal experts agreed with the arbitration board that Harry's accounts were essential if a fair decision was to be reached. With no other
course available, the elder Ward procured funds (reportedly from his
son's widow, Chang-mei) for a trip back to the United States. But before
he could reach Harry he died, of a sudden illness in San Francisco in
December 1865.

By 1867 prosecution of the Ward claims had fallen to George
Seward, who, with Anson Burlingame's departure from China, became
the new American minister to the Middle Kingdom. Burlingame left his
post when he was asked by the Chinese government to head a Chinese
mission to the Western powers and negotiate new treaties of trade and
friendship. That an American should lead such a mission was no less
significant than another American's once having led a Chinese army; and
Burlingame further echoed Ward's fate when, in the midst of vigorously
and successfully representing Chinese interests abroad, he died of ex-
haustion and pneumonia. In February 1867 George Seward visited the
United States and was able to obtain from Harry Ward, just before the
latter's death from an unnamed disease, an accurate accounting of his
boat-buying trip. Apparently Harry had commissioned the building of
river steamers as originally planned. But, when additional funds for
completion and transfer failed to arrive from China following his
brother's death, he was forced to sell the vessels to the Union government at a loss. In 1868 Seward took this information to Wu Hsü, who,
having been stripped of his government offices, was now living in comfortable disgrace in Hangchow. Wu continued to insist that Frederick T.

Ward had owed him more money than he had owed Ward, and this defiant attitude, along with the death of Yang Fang, made it obvious to all that if any satisfaction was to be had it would have to come from the Chinese government.

However, Peking claimed that it could not pay the 110,000 taels because, under Chinese law, an oral will was not binding, even if witnessed. Furthermore, Prince Kung stated that the debt was based on unpaid bonuses for the capture of cities. Kung and most other imperial officials had long disapproved of the bonus system and did not recognize its legitimacy. The will was nothing more than "the mere utterance by Ward of his hope," said Kung, "and not a recognized obligation that has been left unfulfilled." Thus did Peking—harried by foreign powers, pressed for funds, and as prone to duplicity as ever—dispense with the dying wishes of the man it had once characterized as a valiant defender of the Manchu dynasty. The legal battle was not yet over, but it was to remain in limbo for the rest of the century.

In Shanghai, Ward's legacy fared considerably better. At the time of Ward's death, Li Hung-chang and his superiors had ordered the building of shrines to Ward's memory in both Ningpo and Sung-chiang. The plan had been aborted when the American chargé, S. Wells Williams, arrogantly declared that such a shrine would not be considered an honor by an American or his family. Since one of the purposes of the planned shrines had been to gain foreign favor, the plan was quickly dropped by the Chinese, and over the next fourteen years Ward's tumulus was left untended.

But in 1876 Li Hung-chang—who throughout his life never missed an opportunity to honor Ward's memory—ordered the taotai of Shanghai to inspect Ward's grave and investigate the possibility of finally erecting some kind of a memorial. The taotai had the tumulus restored, then wrote to the American consul in Shanghai: "Now that the grave is repaired, I think of building a wall around it, and thus protect it from further depredations. I find, too, that there is near the grave a good piece of empty ground on which I am thinking of building a Hall and inscribing within it the ancestral tablet of General Ward in order that all may know that this is the grave of General Ward." The American consul responded favorably to this idea, building began, and within the year a date for the hall's dedication and consecration had been set: May 10, 1877.

On that morning a group of American and European consular officers joined the taotai of Shanghai on a cruise up the Huang-pu River. Breakfast was served aboard the river steamer that transported them, and, when the party reached the mouth of Sung-chiang Creek, they transshipped to a collection of houseboats and steam launches in order to make their way up that shallow tributary. Soon they had reached Sung-chiang, where a large number of curious citizens had gathered to greet them. The taotai's bodyguard cleared a path through this crowd, and the notables from Shanghai continued on their way.

They passed by delicately adorned yamens and pagodas, then through a ghostly stretch of open ground where the ruins of what had once been buildings lay rotting and grown over by grass and weeds: a grim reminder to the visitors of both the Taiping rebellion and of why they had come to Sung-chiang that day. Finally, a long, low wall came into sight. The group of dignitaries entered the compound and turned to face the open front of a small temple. Through its entrance could be spied a shrine. Atop the shrine's altar sat a brazier for the burning of incense. To either side stood memorial columns, both painted blue and each bearing a golden inscription in Chinese. The first declared: "A wonderful hero from beyond the seas, the fame of whose loyalty reaches round the world, has sprinkled China with his azure blood." The second inscription played on the ancient name of Sung-chiang, which translates to "among the clouds": "A happy seat among the clouds and temples standing for a thousand springs make known to all his faithful heart."

Moving on to an open courtyard behind the temple, the visiting dignitaries arrived at a high burial mound, beside which lay a similar but smaller mound. Saplings and shrubs had grown up around the graves of the famous Hua and his faithful dog in the years since their interment, but the memorial compound had been assigned a keeper, and it was hoped that future generations would more closely guard the remains and better attend to the memory of the creator of the Ever Victorious Army.

And indeed for many years an annual pilgrimage was made by officials from Shanghai to the memorial hall to offer sacrifices and pay respects to Ward's spirit, and incense was often burned at the shrine by local Chinese. These rituals gave rise to a belief in the West that Ward was worshiped as something of a god by the Chinese. In fact, by the terms of Confucian theology—in which divinities and semidivinities were arranged, quite typically, in bureaucratic order—Ward was given a rank that was closer to sainthood than godhood. But it was an important position, one that demanded (and received) real reverence. Thus if the Western interpretation was a slight exaggeration, it was an understandable one.

By the close of the nineteenth century there were comparatively few Chinese who could actually remember Ward or the Taiping rebellion, but one of these was the most powerful statesman in the empire. Li Hung-chang operated a provincial administration in Tientsin that was little short of a second imperial government, so great was his power and the respect he was accorded by foreign nations. When this great Chinese statesman embarked in 1896 on a world tour that took him to New York, he managed to squeeze half an hour out of his busy schedule to see an elderly woman who had journeyed from Maine to talk with him: Elizabeth Ward, Frederick Townsend's sister and correspondent. With Elizabeth was Harry Ward's former wife, now remarried, who was later to destroy Elizabeth's invaluable collection of letters from her adventurous brother Fred. Perhaps Elizabeth's record of her meeting with Li Hung-chang was destroyed at the same time. If so, the pity is all the greater, for Li probably revealed more of his genuine feelings about Ward during this encounter than bureaucratic politics had ever allowed him to before.

Elizabeth Ward did not live to see the settlement of the Ward claims against the Chinese government. But in 1902 her sister-in-law made the shrewd move of hiring a pair of eminent international lawyers to pursue the case. John Watson Foster had served as secretary of state under President Benjamin Harrison, and his son-in-law, Robert Lansing, would later fill the same post for Woodrow Wilson. Together these law partners carefully mounted one last effort to gain monetary satisfaction from China's imperial rulers. In doing so they provided a long overdue reminder of just who Ward had been and what he had done for China.

"When the Chinese officials declared that there were no revenues to maintain [Ward's] soldiers," Foster and Lansing wrote of Ward's days in command of the Ever Victorious Army, "he unhesitatingly used the money which he had received as a recompense for his own services, relying upon the ultimate success of the Imperialists and the good faith of the Chinese Government to be refunded the sums advanced." Foster and Lansing then carefully reviewed the claims of Wu Hsü during the estate arbitrations, characterizing the former taotai's assessments as erroneous, "to use no harsher term." Foster and Lansing's logic was irrefutable, but the two men realized that the Chinese government— which had been forced to pay huge indemnities for its sponsorship of the Boxers in 1900—might not have the money to settle accounts with Ward's heirs. Foster quickly saw that the best chance of gaining a settlement was to suggest that the money be taken from the indemnities the Chinese government was currently paying to the United States. Accordingly, he and Lansing addressed their closing arguments to Washington as well as to Peking:

> [I]t is hardly becoming the Government of the United States to allow the reputation of one of its distinguished citizens to be clouded by neglect and by failure to have his just dues recognized. . . . Mr. Burlingame stated that General Ward was a man of great wealth. Li Hung-chang during his visit to America expressed a high appreciation of his services and said that he should have died a rich man. But it is now known that all that he had accumulated had been advanced to the Chinese Government when in sore need, and that he relied upon its good faith for its return. . . . It is confidently believed that if the Government of the United States . . . shall instruct its minister at Peking to ask the attention of the Foreign Office [Tsungli Yamen] to this long delayed claim, it will now take it into its favorable consideration.

The tactic worked, and a sum of 368,237 American dollars was finally paid—out of the Boxer indemnity fund—to the Ward estate. Oddly enough, the only beneficiary was Harry's ex-wife, a woman who had not been born into the Ward family, had married out of it by the time of the settlement, and subsequently proved cataclysmically destructive to Frederick Townsend Ward's legacy and memory by destroying his letters. Irony seemed forever destined to surround Ward's name.

With the settlement of the estate claims, Ward's recession into obscurity picked up pace. In the United States, knowledge of his career seemed limited to a few interested citizens of Salem, Massachusetts. One of these citizens, traveling in Italy in 1897, had made a remarkable find, as she later recalled:

> I was coming out of the dining room at Hotel Eden in Rome at lunch time and saw Rear-Admiral Bogle, now on the retired list, but for over forty years in the English Navy, showing two bullets to a gentleman. I had got well-acquainted with the Admiral, and I said: "What are these?" He said, "There is the bullet that killed General Ward." I pricked up my ears and thought at once of General Ward of Salem, who bore a part in suppressing the Chinese Rebellion. I found it was our Ward, and that he [Admiral Bogle, formerly Lieutenant Bogle of the *Hardy*] was in the fight and knew him very well.

The bullet—actually a musket ball—was eventually sent to the Essex Institute in Salem, which, using a bequest from Elizabeth Ward, soon established a division of Oriental studies named for Frederick Townsend Ward. Ward's few personal belongings, including his mandarin's cap and boots, were collected at the institute and remain carefully stored there to this day.

As for the memorial hall at Sung-chiang, after the Chinese revolution of 1911 it fell into disrepair and was not rehabilitated until the 1920s, when the American Legion undertook the job. The Nationalist Chinese, following their assumption of power, took an interest in Ward and the Ever Victorious Army (perhaps as part of their campaign to strengthen their ties to the United States) and on at least one occasion acknowledged a debt to him: In 1934 a Nationalist general who had defended Shanghai from the Japanese visited America and stopped at Ward's empty grave in Salem's Harmony Grove Cemetery. Not without effect the general commented, "We both fought to save Shanghai—he gave his life."

But the combination of Japanese occupation during the Second World War and Communist rule after 1949 spelled the end of any appreciable acknowledgment of Ward and the Ever Victorious Army within China, or, indeed, throughout the world. That the Japanese should have ransacked Ward's memorial hall is not surprising, given their attitude toward things American during their period of expansion. But the systematic efforts of the Chinese Communist party to erase all tributes to Ward were even more disillusioning than simpleminded Japanese destructiveness. Having destroyed the memorial hall and whatever other tokens of remembrance or respect to a man they considered an imperialist servant they could find, China's Communists went on to revise the history of the Taiping era in order to paint Ward's efforts in the worst possible light. They then dug up Ward's bones—as well as those of his dog—carefully hid or destroyed them, and, having razed the memorial hall and sacked the grave, paved their grounds and built a public park. All of this seems at first simply callous. Yet the effort was so calculated, so systematic that one soon detects in it more than mere disapproval: There is fear, as well.

Such fear is understandable. Over a century after his death, with the Chinese still killing each other in the name of differing ideologies, Ward's realism, self-styled values, and basic attention to the decent treatment of "his people" continue to stand out, and are doubtless as discomforting to China's Communist dynasty as they were to the Manchus.

The most effective criticisms of Ward's career came not from Communist revisionists but from two men who personally witnessed the Taiping rebellion and Ward's campaigns: Augustus Lindley and A. A. Hayes. To Lindley, who never met Ward, the American commander "was a brave and determined man" who "left those who cherished his memory to regret that he had not fallen in a worthier cause." Hayes was one friend of Ward's who had just such regrets: He wrote Ward's imperialist employers off as "sorry allies for honorable men" and summed up his own feelings about Ward with this statement:

It is difficult to withhold praise from brave deeds, even if we be not wholly in sympathy with the cause in which they are done. While dwelling upon the striking character of Ward's achievements, and having only admiration for the many excellent traits of his character, a conscientious historian must guard himself from approval, actual or implied, of the entry of any right-minded and self-respecting foreigner into the Chinese naval or military service.

But to defend Ward against the charge of working for nefarious masters is unnecessary: He himself knew the nature of the "Rascally officials" who paid his troops and his bonuses and on at least one occasion acknowledged a temptation to "throw them all overboard." In fact, if many observers are to be believed, Ward grew so dissatisfied with Manchu corruption, brutality, and ineptitude that he gave much thought to turning his army against the dynasty once the Taipings had been defeated and then reforming not only China's military but its political system. Hayes stated that

> [h]ad the operations in which [Ward] was engaged been completed, he would have been made a Prince of the Blood Royal, and Commander-in-Chief of the armies in China. There is no doubt that he had a well-defined and consuming ambition to bring this great empire into line with Eastern nations; and an officer of his staff, with whom I was well-acquainted, told me that if he had never before believed in the Divine direction of earthly affairs, he would have done so after he had seen in Ward's death a direct interference from on high with a purpose carried on, and to be carried out, with fire and sword.

Ward's methods were, however, more complicated than fire and sword, and more unique than the kind of religious and political zealotry that drove the Taiping rebellion. Ward succeeded on the battlefield, spread fear among his enemies, antagonized his superiors, and finally achieved some measure of lasting importance not because he was a committed idealist or a simple adventurer but because he was in every sense a free-lance—perhaps the purest example of that breed the modern world has produced. In Ward's relatively untrained but keen

mind everything was up for questioning: family and religion, the authority of superiors, military doctrines, governmental policies, even
national loyalty itself. (It is well to remember that his transfer to Chinese citizenship was made without apparent philosophical difficulty,
and, while he habitually signed himself "an honest American," he also
criticized his brother for becoming "excessively patriotic" during the
American Civil War.) In every endeavor he undertook, Ward displayed
this questioning, indeed challenging, attitude, which is such an essential component of the true free-lance. To his own father, to the pomp-
ous filibuster William Walker, to the president of Mexico, to his senior
officers in the French army in the Crimea, to the Western authorities
in Shanghai, and finally to his imperial Chinese superiors he was consistently, irrepressibly forthright and troublesome. The perceptive
Prince Kung had indeed been right when he wrote of Ward: "His nature is basically unrestrained and his heart is even harder to fathom."
Ward was an aggressive realist, so determined to hold himself aloof
from any person, group, cause, or nation that did not embody or
share his own values and goals that it often seemed he would never
cease his global wandering or form personal attachments of any real
significance.

Yet in his attitude toward his wife, Chang-mei, toward China (as
distinct from the Manchus), and toward the men of the Ever Victorious
Army there is the distinct suggestion that something had finally touched
Ward. Whether or not he actually intended to carve out a warlord
domain or replace the Manchus with a native dynasty, there is about his
actions and life in Sung-chiang the unmistakable sense that he was
building toward a greater achievement than mere profit. Certainly his
naive and even foolish management of his own business affairs prevents
Ward's dismissal as a mere mercenary. Rather, his Chinese career
suggests a systematic attempt to construct an order in Sung-chiang and
around the Ever Victorious Army that would finally embody a military
and political style of which he himself would have approved. That style
was based on a simple notion: decent treatment of "his people." If his
attempts to achieve this—and, on a larger scale, to propel China toward
new methods of fighting and perhaps even governing—were piecemeal,

ingenuous, and ultimately ill-fated, they were nonetheless worthy of greater tribute than an empty grave in America, a ransacked grave in China, and the invective of ideologues, against whom Ward always fought with such brilliant determination.

CAST OF CHARACTERS

AMERICAN

Frederick Townsend Ward, American sailing officer and soldier of fortune born in Salem, Massachusetts. In the first twenty-nine years of his life, Ward traveled the world extensively on merchant vessels (making several trips to China) and participated in military campaigns in Mexico and the Crimea before contracting with the imperial Chinese government to undertake the defense of Shanghai against the Taiping rebels in 1860. Starting with foreign mercenaries, Ward later employed Western officers to train Chinese soldiers to use the most modern weapons and tactics. The force he organized along these lines was eventually named the Ever Victorious Army by the imperialist Chinese, but his troops were known as "the devil soldiers" among the rebels.

Henry Gamaliel Ward, called Harry, Frederick's brother. A shipping merchant, who often acted as agent for arms purchases for his brother's Chinese army.

Elizabeth Ward, Frederick's sister and principal correspondent, who kept his letters carefully preserved until her death. These invaluable documents were subsequently destroyed by a group of relatives headed by Harry Ward's widow.

Henry Andrea Burgevine, of North Carolina. Frederick Ward's second-in-command. An effective officer with a weakness for alcohol, Burgevine was invaluable in many battles against the rebels, but he eventually became the tragic victim of his own emotional instability.

Edward Forester, third in the line of command of the Ever Victorious Army. An accomplished linguist and efficient officer, Forester also played a vital role in the army's campaigns, although he revealed a troubling and puzzling tendency toward self-glorification and denigration of his commander's achievements following Ward's death.

Charles Schmidt, an American soldier of fortune who first met Ward in South America in the early 1850s and wrote several eyewitness accounts of his service with Ward in China.

Dr. Daniel Jerome Macgowan, an American Baptist missionary and physician who doubled as a correspondent for several English-language publications in China. Macgowan wrote the first relatively complete account of Ward's exploits, remarkable (given the conflicting sources and reports he had to contend with) for its insight and accuracy.

Anson Burlingame, American minister to China who arrived in Shanghai in 1862. Destined to become a trusted friend and servant of the imperial Chinese government, Burlingame quickly developed an attachment to Ward and his officers and often pleaded their case before officials in both Peking and Washington.

Augustus A. Hayes, a junior partner for one of Shanghai's larger Western trading firms and a fellow New Englander who knew Ward well during his years of imperial service. Hayes wrote two important magazine pieces as well as private memoranda concerning Ward.

BRITISH

Admiral James Hope, commander of British naval forces in China. Known to his men as Fighting Jimmie, Hope was bellicose and singularly confident. After the Allied march on Peking in 1860, he became a fixture in Shanghai. He headed two missions to negotiate with the Taiping leaders in Nanking for safety of trade on the Yangtze and initially did his best to stop the activities of adventurers such as Ward. Eventually, though, Hope's hostility toward the rebels, as well as strong similarities of character, made him and Ward friends and allies.

Frederick Bruce, British minister to China during the period of Ward's operations. Dedicated and capable, Bruce nonetheless embodied the contradictory commitments—to neutrality in the Chinese civil war and active protection of British trading rights—that characterized many British officials. Bruce initially opposed Ward, but impatience with Peking and disgust with the Taipings gradually changed his attitude.

General Sir John Michel, commander of British army forces in China until early 1862. A gifted commander with a real understanding of unconventional warfare, Michel appreciated the work Ward had undertaken, and saw in it the chance for China's military regeneration. Before leaving China he recommended that heavy assistance be given Ward by the British government.

General Sir Charles Staveley, Michel's successor, a capable but arrogant officer with none of Michel's appreciation for Ward. Staveley believed that the British should be responsible for training Chinese troops and that Ward was little more than a rogue and an outlaw.

Captain Roderick Dew, one of Admiral Hope's subordinates who, like Hope, initially tried to stop Ward's activities but ended up becoming the young American's friend. Responsible for the unauthorized seizure of Ningpo from the Taipings in 1862, Dew was acting in conjunction with Ward in the Ningpo area when Ward was killed.

Thomas Taylor Meadows, a noted sinologist and Taiping sympathizer who was British consul in Shanghai at the time of Ward's early operations, which he strongly opposed.

Walter Medhurst, Meadows's successor, who, while opposed to the activities of adventurers, gradually became less troublesome to Ward as the official position of his government regarding the Ever Victorious Army changed.

Chaloner Alabaster, British consular official and interpreter in Shanghai. Brave and outspoken, Alabaster served as an observer at many of the battles involving joint actions between Ward's troops and British regulars, leaving several important accounts of them.

Augustus F. Lindley, a British sailing officer who, at the time of Ward's arrival in Shanghai, traveled up the Yangtze to gain firsthand knowledge of the Taiping movement. Liking what he saw, and eventually marrying a Portuguese girl in a Taiping ceremony, Lindley ran guns to the rebels and trained their soldiers in tactics and the use of modern weapons. On returning to England, he wrote a bitter account of the end of the Taiping rebellion and of the part the British and Ward had played in suppressing it.

CAST OF CHARACTERS

Captain Charles George Gordon, General Staveley's young brother-in-law and chief of engineers. Destined to become one of Victorian England's greatest heroes, Gordon was emotionally complex but professionally brilliant, capable of absorbing important lessons from his early experiences in China (and especially from his observations of Ward in action). He put these lessons to good use during his tenure as Ward's most illustrious successor in command of the Ever Victorious Army.

FRENCH

Vice Admiral August Leopold-Protet, commander of French naval forces in China. Like Admiral Hope and General Michel, Protet was a personable and aggressive officer, with appreciable experience fighting unconventional wars. He played a key role in support of Ward's troops during the early months of 1862, and his death during an action against the Taipings caused his troops to engage in deplorable acts of vengeance.

Adrien Tardif de Moidrey, a French officer who may have originated the idea of using Western officers to train Chinese soldiers. During the winter of 1860–61 he met Ward and Burgevine, and out of these meetings came the idea not only for the Ever Victorious Army but for the Franco-Chinese Corps of Kiangsu, Tardif de Moidrey's small but potent force of Chinese artillerymen.

Prosper Giquel, a young French officer and the head of the Ningpo office of the Imperial Chinese Customs Service, which was operated for Peking by capable Westerners. Giquel was another careful observer of Ward's activities, which he emulated in Chekiang province by creating what became known as the Ever Triumphant Army.

Albert Edouard Le Brethon de Caligny, cofounder and battlefield leader of the Ever Triumphant Army, who played a vital role in countering Taiping moves in the Ningpo area in early 1862.

CHINESE

Hsien-feng, emperor of China during the early period of Ward's operations. A dissipated hedonist, Hsien-feng was controlled by reactionary advisers, most of whom favored a disastrous policy of simultaneously fighting the Taiping rebels and abusing Western representatives. His death in 1861 left imperial governmental matters in immense disarray.

Yehonala (the Empress Dowager Tz'u-hsi), Hsien-feng's favorite concubine and the mother of his son. Shrewd and manipulative, Yehonala initially favored berating and lying to Western representatives, but she eventually came to see that such a policy would have to take a secondary role—at least temporarily—to the defeat of the Taipings. After Hsien-feng's death, she emerged as controlling regent for their young son, T'ung-chih.

Prince Kung, Hsien-feng's half brother and the most capable statesman in Peking at the time. After Hsien-feng's death Kung served Yehonala and T'ung-chih well by realizing that rather than berating Westerners the Chinese should make treaties with them and then hold the Westerners to the terms of the treaties, thus limiting their aggressions. He established the suppression of the Taiping rebellion as the imperial government's first goal. Though he distrusted foreign adventurers such as Ward, Kung, like Tz'u-hsi, became willing to make use of them.

Tseng Kuo-fan, the brilliant Chinese bureaucrat and military leader who organized the progressive Hunan Army to fight the Taipings and became the architect of China's "self-strengthening movement." By reemphasizing Confucian values and dealing with the rebels in an uncompromising fashion, Tseng became the first imperial leader to check and then turn back the advancing Taiping wave. But, because he was so grounded in antiquated Chinese tradition, Tseng's determined attempts at military and political reform ultimately amounted to relatively little. Opposed to any foreign involvement in the Chinese civil war, Tseng distrusted Ward but understood that his own strategy of crushing the Taipings at Nanking with two mighty pincers—one moving from the east and one from the west—might not work without the participation of the Ever Victorious Army.

Li Hung-chang, Tseng's most accomplished student and lieutenant. Destined to become nineteenth-century China's most famous statesman, Li shared all his tutor's brilliance but little of his scrupulous honesty. Appointed governor of Kiangsu province by Tseng in 1862, Li was brought into close contact with Ward, whom he admired, if cautiously. The two cooperated in a series of crucial actions against the rebels in 1862, and it was Li who broached to Tseng the idea of Ward's playing a part in an eventual attack on Nanking.

Hsüeh Huan, governor of Kiangsu at the time of Ward's arrival in Shanghai. Hsüeh gave initial approval to the idea of Ward's force, although he did not admit to this approval until the army had demonstrated success. By then, however, his own military incompetence had been revealed, and he subsequently tried to salvage his reputation by discrediting Ward.

Wu Hsü, *taotai,* or circuit intendant, of Shanghai and Ward's initial employer. A master of all the forms of corruption that made the Chinese bureaucracy function, Wu was reluctant to reveal publicly his sponsorship of Ward until the latter had proved himself. Though deeply impressed by and fond of the young American, Wu felt no compunction about turning his back on Ward when tact demanded doing so.

Yang Fang, also known as Taki because he headed a financial firm of that name. Wu Hsü's partner in a variety of official and unofficial undertakings, Yang was the crafty veteran of decades of dealing with foreigners. He took an immediate liking to Ward and worked hard to raise the money that would supply Ward's men and pay their salaries. Yang and Ward's relationship became legendary in Shanghai and was sealed in 1862 when Ward married Yang's daughter.

Yang Chang-mei, Yang Fang's daughter, twenty-one at the time of her marriage to Ward. Healthy, attractive, and the child of a wealthy family, Chang-mei was nonetheless regarded as bad luck by most Chinese because her first fiancé had died. She survived Ward by just one year; the only known explanation for her death is "extreme grief."

Hung Hsiu-ch'üan, a peasant whose humiliation at being unable to enter the only path to social advancement open to him—the imperial civil service—led him to illness and madness. Believing himself to be the younger brother of Jesus Christ, Hung organized a band of quasi-Christian followers and set in motion the most savage civil war in world history, the Taiping rebellion (1850–1864), during which somewhere between 20 and 40 million people died.

Li Hsiu-Ch'eng (also known as the Chung Wang, or "Loyal King"), Hung Hsiu-ch'üan's most talented general. In the Taiping rebellion's later years, as Hung withdrew into a world of debauchery and mysticism and his advisers battled among themselves, Li kept the movement alive through a series of brilliant campaigns against the imperialists. His last and most crucial assignment was to seize Shanghai and its rich trade. Had he succeeded, the movement would have gained extended life. The attempt brought him into direct conflict with Ward's Ever Victorious Army.

NOTES

PROLOGUE

p.2: one American soldier: Herman N. Archer, writing in the Feature section of the Boston Sunday *Post,* August 21, 1927.

CHAPTER I

p.10: an Englishman: Augustus F. Lindley, in his *Ti-Ping Tien Kwoh: The History of the Ti-Ping Revolution* (London: Day & Son, 1866), vol. 1, pp.71–72 (hereafter Lindley). Also taken from Lindley are the descriptions of the Taiping palaces and official ceremonies.

the Chung Wang: The best translation and edition of his brief autobiography, written quickly before his execution in 1864, was done by Charles Curwen in his *Taiping Rebel: The Deposition of Li Hsiu-ch'eng* (London: Cambridge University Press, 1977), p.114 (hereafter Curwen).

p.11: the Chung Wang: Curwen, p.115.

p.13: the Chung Wang: Curwen, p.115.

p.14: one British consular official: Thomas Taylor Meadows, in his *The Chinese and Their Rebellions* (London: Smith, Elder & Company, 1856), pp.307–308 (hereafter Meadows).

one Western missionary: the Reverend Dr. Bridgeman, quoted in Lindley, vol. 1, p.215.

p.15: one Western expert: Walter H. Medhurst, in his *The Foreigner in Far Cathay* (New York: Scribner, Armstrong & Company, 1873), p.180.

p.16: the Chung Wang: Curwen, p.111.

337

p.17: the Chung Wang: Curwen, p.116.

p.18: the Chung Wang: Curwen, p.116.

p.19: the Chung Wang: Curwen, p.118.

a pair of the emperor's senior servants: Their memorial of June 26, 1860, is in the *Ch'ou-pan I-wu shih-mo* [A Complete Record of the Management of Barbarian Affairs] (Beijing, 1930). Volumes in this series are arranged by emperors; this quotation is in volume 52, covering the reign of Hsien-feng, on pages 15b–16. Future citations (including those for the Emperor T'ung-chih series, *TC*) will be abbreviated, in this case to *IWSM, HF 52*, pp.15b–16, June 26, 1860.

p.21: one early historian: Francis Lister Potts, in his *A Short History of Shanghai* (Shanghai: Kelly & Walsh, Ltd., 1928), p.19 (hereafter Potts).

p.22: one visitor: Laurence Oliphant, quoted in Potts, p.42.

p.23: drunken soldiers: *North China Herald* (hereafter *NCH*), May 26, 1860.

p.24: imperial corruption: *NCH,* January 28, 1860.

the rebel advance and executed spies: *NCH,* June 2, 1860.

p.25: Hsüeh Huan: *NCH,* July 21, 1860.

p.26: Wu Hsü: *NCH,* July 21, 1860.

Li Hung-chang on Wu: Stanley Spector, *Li Hung-chang and the Huai Army: A Study in 19th Century Regionalism* (Seattle: University of Washington Press, 1964), pp.56–57.

Wu Hsü as a mouthpiece: *NCH,* July 21, 1860.

p.28: the British proclamation: reprinted in Andrew Wilson, *The "Ever-Victorious Army"* (London: William Blackwood & Sons, 1868), p.61 (hereafter Wilson).

the "grand national principle": *NCH,* July 21, 1860.

p.29: the "Cinderella" settlement: Potts, p.63.

the American minister and the consul: John Ward to Lewis Cass, February 22, 1860, "Despatches from U.S. Ministers to China," Record Group 59, microfilm 92, roll 21, U. S. National Archives.

p.30: Augustus A. Hayes: in his "Another Unwritten Chapter of the Late War," in *International Review,* December 1881, p.521 (hereafter Hayes, "Chapter").

p.31: Charles E. Hill and the "Troy dredging machine": according to Daniel J. Macgowan, in his "Memoirs of Generals Ward, Burgevine, and the Ever-Victorious Army," *Far East,* vol. 2 (1877), p.104 (hereafter Macgowan).

one American official: George F. Seward, whose comments can be found in *Senate Executive Documents, 45th Congress, 2nd Session,* no. 48, pp.24–25 (hereafter *SED 45:2:48*).

Hill on his own dealings: part of his testimony in a later lawsuit against Wu Hsü, which can also be found in *SED 45:2:48,* p.29.

Hill on Yang Fang: *SED 45:2:48,* p.30.

p.32: Gough on Ward: as recalled by Wu Hsü, in the *Wu Hsü tang-an chung ti T'ai-p'ing t'ien-kuo shih liao hsuan-chi* (Selections of Historical Materials Concerning the Taiping Heavenly Kingdom in Wu Hsü's Archives) (Beijing, 1958), p.125 (hereafter *WHTA*).

CHAPTER II

p.36: one great-grandmother: Mary Harrod Northend, in her *Memories of Old Salem, Drawn from the Letters of a Great-grandmother* (New York: Moffat, Yard, 1917), p.50.

p.37: Robert S. Rantoul: in his "Frederick Townsend Ward," *Historical Collections of the Essex Institute,* vol. 44 (1908), p.19 (hereafter Rantoul). The Essex Institute became the repository for the few of Ward's personal effects that made it back to America and were not destroyed by his family. A library dealing with Chinese history and culture at the institute is named after Ward, following the terms of a bequest by his sister Elizabeth.

one history: Ralph D. Paine, in his *Ships and Sailors of Old Salem* (Boston: Charles G. Lauriat, 1924), p.422.

Macgowan: Macgowan, p.102.

p.38: Ward's trip to Beverly: Rantoul, p.9.

p.38: Charles Schmidt: writing as P.C., Schmidt published "Memoirs of the Late General Ward, the Hero of Sung-Kiang, and of his Aide-de-Camp Vincente Macanaya" in *Friend of China* in 1863; this quotation is on p.2 (hereafter Schmidt, P.C.).

p.39: assessments by Ward's peers: Rantoul, pp.16–17.

p.40: the Chinese tracts: John L. Nevins, trans., "A Death Blow to Corrupt Doctrines: A Plain Statement of Facts" (Shanghai, 1870), pp.11–13 (hereafter Nevins).

p.42: a British officer: J. Lamprey, in his "The Economy of the Chinese Army," *Journal of the Royal United Service Institution,* vol. 11, no. 46 (1867), p.406.

p.45: one honest mandarin: Henry McAleavy, *The Modern History of China* (New York: Praeger, 1967), p.45 (hereafter McAleavy).

p.46: one official: McAleavy, p.46.

p.46: the Chinese on war with Britain: McAleavy, pp.49–50.

p.47: one American official: S. Wells Williams, quoted in Tyler Dennett, *Americans in Eastern Asia* (New York: Macmillan, 1922), p.322.

p.48: one Chinese pamphlet: Nevins, pp.10, 18.
Meadows: Meadows, p.121.

p.50: one Garibaldi biographer: Denis Mack Smith, in his *Garibaldi* (New York: Knopf, 1953), p.51.

p.51: Schmidt: Schmidt, P.C., pp.2–3.

p.53: Hung's rantings: Eugene Powers Boardman, *Christian Influence Upon the Ideology of the Taiping Rebellion* (New York: Octagon Books, 1972), p.13 (hereafter Boardman).

p.54: Issachar Roberts: Meadows, p.192.

p.55: anti-Manchu broadsides: McAleavy, p.71.

p.56: Hung: Boardman, pp.66, 79.

p.57: one anti-Christian pamphleteer: Nevins, p.36.
one modern Taiping expert: Boardman, p.126.

p.58: Richard Harding Davis: in his *Real Soldiers of Fortune* (New York: Scribner's, 1906), p.202 (hereafter Davis).

p.59: "extravagant humor": Edward Wallace, *Destiny and Glory* (New York: Coward and McCann, 1957), p.150.
Davis: Davis, p.202.
one deserter: Arthur Woodward, *The Republic of Lower California, 1853–1854* (Los Angeles: Dawson's, 1966), p.67.

p.60: Schmidt: Schmidt, P.C., p.3.
Rantoul: Rantoul, p.23.

p.62: Humphrey Marshall: Foster Rhea Dulles, *China and America: The Story of Their Relations Since 1784* (Princeton: Princeton University Press, 1946), p.49 (hereafter Dulles).
President Franklin Pierce: Dulles, p.50.
Marshall's reverse: Dulles, p.51.

p.63: Ward on usurpation: This comment is contained in one of the two surviving letters from Ward to Anson Burlingame, American minister to China. This letter is dated August 16, 1862, and can be found among the Burlingame Papers in the Library of Congress.
one Canton official: Dulles, p.46.
the reply to McLane: Dulles, p.56.

p.65: Elizabeth Ward: Rantoul, p.24.
Hayes: in his "An American Soldier in China," *Atlantic Monthly*, 57 (1886), p.195 (hereafter Hayes, "Soldier").

p.67: William S. Wetmore: in his *Recollections of Life in the Far East* (Shanghai, 1894), p.33.

p.68: one British officer: Charles George Gordon, quoted in Richard J. Smith, *Mercenaries and Mandarins: The Ever-Victorious Army in Nineteenth Century China* (Millwood, N.Y.: KTO Press, 1978), p.85 (hereafter Smith, *Mercenaries*).

one English official: Chaloner Alabaster, in a memorandum enclosed in a dispatch from Consul W. H. Medhurst to Lord Russell, February 4, 1863. *British Parliamentary Papers* (hereafter *BPP*), vol. 63, 1864 (3295).

p.69: Ward on Lincoln and Davis, Ward on "the fate of war": Ward to Burlingame, August 16, 1862, Burlingame Papers, Library of Congress.

CHAPTER III

p.70: at least one authority: Robert Harry Detrick, in his unpublished dissertation, "Henry Andrea Burgevine in China: A Biography" (University of Indiana, 1968), p.16 (hereafter Detrick).

p.71: Burgevine: Detrick, p.13.
Burgevine: Detrick, pp.14–15.

p.72: Macgowan: Macgowan, p.104.
Ward: Ward to Burlingame, August 16, 1862, Burlingame Papers, Library of Congress.

one contemporary Shanghai author: An anonymous author with an apparently detailed knowledge of Ward and his corps wrote *The Suppression of the Taiping Rebellion in the Departments Around Shanghai* (Shanghai: Kelly & Co., 1871), p. ii (hereafter *Suppression*).

p.73: Lord Elgin: quoted in John S. Gregory, *Great Britain and the Taipings* (London: Routledge & Kegan Paul, 1969), p.80 (hereafter Gregory).

p.74: the Chinese request: as recalled by W. A. P. Martin and quoted in Marina Warner, *The Dragon Empress* (New York: Atheneum, 1972), p.48 (hereafter Warner).

p.75: John Ward: Dulles, p.60.
Ward the "tribute bearer": Warner, p.49.

p.76: Tseng Kuo-fan: McAleavy, p.75.

p.77: one Westerner: Mary C. Wright, *The Last Stand of Chinese Conservatism* (Stanford: Stanford University Press, 1957), p.74 (hereafter Wright).
Tseng: McAleavy, p.75.

p.77: the *Herald: NCH,* October 31, 1868.

p.78: Tseng: Smith, *Mercenaries,* p.47.

one American diplomat: George F. Seward, whose "Comments on Li Hung-chang" of September 21, 1894, can be found among his papers at the New-York Historical Society.

p.80: Alabaster: Medhurst to Russell, February 4, 1863, enclosed, *BPP,* vol. 63, 1864 (3295).

Schmidt: Schmidt, P.C., p.6.

p.81: one Ward biographer: Elliot Paul Carthage, Jr., in his unpublished dissertation, "The Role of Frederick Townsend Ward in the Suppression of the Taiping Rebellion" (St. John's University, 1976), p.64.

p.82: anonymous: *Suppression,* p. i.

p.83: one observer: *Suppression,* p. ii.

p.84: one British observer: William Mesny, quoted in Hallett Abend, *The God from the West* (Garden City, N.Y.: Doubleday & Co., 1947), p.120 (hereafter Abend). Abend, a *New York Times* correspondent in China, had a journalist's penchant for embellishment, and his biography of Ward must be used with care.

Schmidt: Schmidt, P.C., p.7.

one contemporary's assessment: *Suppression,* p. i.

p.85: Albert L. Freeman: quoted in Richard J. Smith's dissertation, "Barbarian Officers of Imperial China" (University of California at Davis, 1972), p.67 (hereafter Smith, Dissertation).

p.87: Hayes: Hayes, "Soldier," p.196; Hayes, "Chapter," p.520.

p.88: Wilson: Wilson, p.127.

one of Ward's successors: Charles George Gordon, quoted in Smith, *Mercenaries,* pp.129–130.

p.89: Macgowan: Macgowan, p.105.

p.90: Macgowan: Macgowan, p.104.

Ward: Ward to Burlingame, August 16, 1862, Burlingame Papers, Library of Congress.

p.91: Schmidt: Schmidt, P.C., "Vincente Macanaya," the second part of Schmidt's pieces for *Friend of China,* p.3 (hereafter Schmidt, P.C., "Vincente").

p.93: Meadows on execution: Meadows to Bruce, July 5, 1860, *Foreign Office* (hereafter *FO) 228/291.*

Meadows to Smith, Ojea: Enclosures 1 and 2, in Meadows to Bruce, July 5, 1860, *FO 228/291.*

p.94: Meadows to Bruce: Meadows to Bruce, July 5, 1860, *FO 228/291.*

p.95: Ward: Ward to Burlingame, September 10, 1862, Burlingame Papers, Library of Congress.

one expert: Prescott Clarke, in Prescott Clarke and Frank H. H. King, eds, *A Research Guide to China Coast Newspapers* (Cambridge, Mass.: East Asian Research Center, 1965), p.8.

p.96: the *Herald: NCH,* July 14, 21, 1860.

p.97: Ward: Ward to Burlingame, September 10, 1862, Burlingame Papers, Library of Congress.

p.98: Palmerston: see Kenneth Bourne, *The Foreign Policy of Victorian England* (Oxford: Clarendon Press, 1970), pp.274–275.

p.99: Lindley: Lindley, vol. 1, pp. vii–viii.

the Chung Wang: Curwen, pp.134–135.

Wilson: Wilson, pp.56–57.

p.100: Lindley: Lindley, vol. 2, pp.585–586.

p.101: one visitor: *Suppression,* p.17.

Lindley: Lindley, vol. 1, pp.345–346.

p.102: the Kan Wang: in Walter Lay, trans., *The Kan Wang's Sketch of the Rebellion* (Shanghai: North China Herald Office, 1865), p.6 (hereafter Lay).

p.103: Wilson: Wilson, p.63.

p.104: Schmidt: Schmidt, P.C., pp.8–9.

p.105: the Chung Wang: Curwen, p.119.

J. F. C. Fuller: J. F. C. Fuller, *Grant and Lee* (Bloomington: Indiana University Press, 1957), p.250.

p.106: Bogle: Rantoul, p.51.

p.108: "come on, boys": This line may well be apocryphal, but it was commonly repeated and became standard in popular treatments of Ward's life.

p.110: the *Herald: NCH,* July 21, 1860.

p.111: one expert: Curwen, p.14.

CHAPTER IV

p.113: John Hinton: Enclosure 4 in Bruce to Russell, May 23, 1861, "Deposition of John Hinton, May 2, 1861," *BPP,* vol. 63, 1862.

p.114: one observer: quoted in William Sykes, *The Taeping Rebellion in China:*

p.114: *Its Origin, Progress and Present Condition* (London: Warren Hall & Co., 1863), p.56 (hereafter Sykes).

p.115: Macgowan: Macgowan, p.120.

Wu Hsü: *WHTA,* pp.138–141.

p.116: Macgowan: Macgowan, p.120.

Schmidt: in his "A Note on Ward's Character," which can be found in *Dispatches of U.S. Consuls in Shanghai* (hereafter *DUSCS*), microfilm 112, roll 5, record group 59, National Archives.

Macgowan: Macgowan, p.120.

p.119: Schmidt: Schmidt, P.C., "Vincente," p.2.

the *Herald: NCH,* August 4, 1860.

p.120: Consul Smith: enclosure 3 in Meadows to Bruce, August 6, 1860, *FO 228/292.*

Meadows: Meadows to Bruce, August 6, 1860, *FO 228/292.*

p.121: Wilson: Wilson, p.64.

p.121: the Chung Wang: Curwen, p.118.

p.122: Schmidt: Schmidt, P.C., "Vincente," p.2.

p.125: Hayes: Hayes, "Soldier," p.194.

p.125: the Chung Wang: *NCH,* August 18, 1860.

p.126: the *Herald: NCH,* August 18, 1860.

p.127: the *Herald: NCH,* August 25, 1860.

p.127: Hayes: Hayes, "Soldier," p.195.

p.128: angry Westerner: *NCH,* August 25, 1860.

the *Herald: NCH,* August 25, 1860.

p.129: the Chung Wang: Lindley, vol. 1, p.283.

p.129: Bruce: Bruce to Russell, September 4, 1860, *BPP,* vol. 63, 1861.

p.130: letter: *NCH,* August 18, 1860.

p.131: Wu: enclosure in Meadows to Bruce, September 28, 1860, *FO 228/292.*

p.132: Meadows: Meadows to Bruce, September 28, 1860, *FO 228/292.*

p.133: the *Herald: NCH,* October 27, 1860.

p.134: Hsien-feng: Warner, p.51.

p.135: Manchu officials: Warner, p.53.

Prince Kung: McAleavy, p.100.

p.136: Gordon: Paul Charrier, *Gordon of Khartoum* (New York: Lancer, 1965), p.26.

p.139: Hsüeh Huan: Gregory, p.92.

p.140: Roberts on his trappings: *NCH,* September 7, 1861.

Lindley: Lindley, vol. 2, pp.566, 567.

NOTES

p.141: Hope: Rantoul, p.42.

p.142: Hope: Gregory, p.97.

the *Herald: NCH,* March 2, 1861.

p.143: diary: Yao Chi, "Hsiao ts'ang-sang chi," in Hsiang Ta, ed., *T'ai-ping t'ien-kuo* (Peking, 1952), vol. 6, p.245.

p.146: Hope: in "Commander Hire's Report Relative to the Recent Desertions at Shanghai," May 1, 1861, *Admiralty 125/7* (hereafter *ADM 125/7*).

diplomatic officer: Forrest to Bruce, April 20 and May 1, 1861 (enclosures 1 and 2 in Bruce to Russell, May 23, 1861), *BPP,* vol. 63, 1862.

p.147: Alabaster: "Notes by Chaloner Alabaster on a Meeting Between Hsueh Huan, Wu Hsu and Commander Hire, April 22, 1861," *ADM 125/7.*

p.148: Alabaster's quoting of the mandarin: Alabaster to Medhurst, April 23, 1861, *ADM 125/7.*

Ward's pass: "Ward Pass No. 2, April 22, 1861," *ADM 125/7.*

Ward's residence: Alabaster to Medhurst, April 23, 1861, *ADM 125/7.*

Hire: Hire's Report, *ADM 125/7.*

p.149: the consuls: Hire's Report, *ADM 125/7.*

Ward: Commander Henry W. Hire, "Memorandum of a Question Put by Commander Hire to the Person Calling Himself Ward, April 25, 1861," *ADM 125/7.*

Cleary: Nicholas Cleary to Commander Hire, April 25, 1861, *ADM 125/7.*

p.150: the second interview: Chaloner Alabaster, "Interview Between Commander Hire R.N. and H.E. the Taotai with Reference to the Capture of Colonel Ward," *ADM 125/7.*

Hire: Hire's Report, *ADM 125/7.*

the Shanghai Municipal Council: William Howard to Walter Medhurst, April 26, 1861, *ADM 125/7.*

p.151: Hire: Hire's Report, *ADM 125/7.*

the *Herald: NCH,* June 8, 1861.

Medhurst: Medhurst to Bruce, May 29, 1861, *FO 228/311.*

p.153: Forester: Edward Forester, "Personal Recollections of the Tai-ping Rebellion," *Cosmopolitan,* vol. 21 (1896), p.629 (hereafter Forester).

p.154: Forester: Forester, p.629.

the *Herald: NCH,* June 8, 1860.

p.155: Forester: Forester, p.629.

p.156: Bruce: Bruce to Russell, May 23, 1861, *BPP,* vol. 63, 1862.

Hope: Hope to Bruce, May 24, 1861, *FO 228/300.*

p.157: Alabaster: enclosure 1 in Medhurst to Bruce, May 29, 1861, *FO 228/311.*
Dew: Dew to Hope, June 18, 1861, *BPP,* vol. 63, 1862.
Hope: enclosure 3 in Dew to Hope, June 18, 1861, *BPP,* vol. 63, 1862;
Hope to the Admiralty, June 27, 1861, *BPP,* vol. 63, 1862.

p.158: Bruce: Bruce to Russell, June 23, 1861, *BPP,* vol. 63, 1862.
Compton: *NCH,* January 12, 1861
Bruce: Bruce to Russell, June 23, 1861, *BPP,* vol. 63, 1862.

p.160: Bruce: Bruce to Russell, July 3, 1861, *BPP,* vol. 63, 1862.

CHAPTER V

p.161: the T'ien Wang: Curwen, p.122.
the Kan Wang: Lay, p.7.

p.162: Schmidt: Schmidt, P.C., p.7.
Macgowan: Macgowan, p.119.

p.163: Wilson: Wilson, pp.129–132.
Wu Hsü: *WHTA,* pp.125–127; Smith, Dissertation, pp.75–76.

p.165: Harry Ward's purchases: Smith, *Mercenaries,* p.90.

p.166: two passes: The passes are contained in the Frederick Townsend Ward Collection at Sterling Library, Yale University (hereafter Ward Collection, Yale).

p.167: Macgowan: Macgowan, p.105.

p.168: Russell: Russell to Bruce, August 8, 1861, *FO 17/349.*
Macgowan: Macgowan, p.105.

p.169: Burlingame: Frederick Wells Williams, *Anson Burlingame and the First Chinese Mission to Foreign Powers* (New York: Scribner's, 1912), p.12 (hereafter Williams).
Seward: Williams, pp.22–23.

p.171: the imperial decree: Warner, p.73.

p.172: Burlingame: Burlingame to Seward, November 30, 1861, *Dispatches of U.S. Ministers to China* (hereafter *DUSMC*), R.6.59, microfilm 92, National Archives.
Lindley: Lindley, vol. 1, p.358.

p.173: Roberts's report: *BPP,* vol. 63, 1863.

p.175: the *Herald: NCH,* December 14, 1861.
the *Herald: NCH,* December 21, 1861.
one missionary: *NCH,* January 4, 1862.

p.176: British consul: Gregory, pp.109–110.

Hope: *BPP*, vol. 63, 1862.

p.177: Bruce: Gregory, p.119.

Palmerston: Gregory, pp.108–109.

p.178: British consul: Smith, Dissertation, p.127.

Bruce: Bruce to Russell, March 26, 1862, *BPP*, vol. 63, 1862.

p.180: Willes: Capt. George O. Willes to Admiral Hope, January 20, 1862, *BPP*, vol. 63, 1862.

p.181: Macgowan: Macgowan, p.105.

p.182: Wu Hsü's letters to Ward: Ward Collection, Yale.

p.183: Hsüeh: *IWSM, TC 4*, pp.25–28.

the *Herald: NCH*, January 18, 25, 1862.

Daily Shipiing and Commercial News: in *BPP*, vol. 63, 1862.

p.184: the *Herald: NCH*, February 15, 1862.

p.185: Hayes: Hayes, "Soldier," p.196.

p.187: Tseng: Smith, Dissertation, p.87.

p.189: Gordon: Smith, *Mercenaries*, p.214.

p.190: Hayes: Hayes, "Chapter," pp.522–524.

p.192: Hope: Smith, *Mercenaries*, p.49.

p.193: Hope: Hope to Paget, February 21, 1862, *ADM 125/104*.

p.194: Alabaster's account: *BPP*, vol. 63, 1862, enclosure in May 2, 1962.

Macgowan: Macgowan, p.107.

Forester: Forester, p.34.

p.195: Macgowan: Macgowan, p.107.

p.196: Hope: Hope to Paget, February 21, 1862, *ADM 125/104*.

p.197: Burlingame: Burlingame to Seward, March 22, 1862, *DUSMC*, R.6.59, microfilm 92, roll 21, National Archives.

the *Herald: NCH*, February 22, 1862.

Lindley: Lindley, vol. 2, p.450.

p.198: Sykes and the *Times:* Sykes, pp.23, 33.

Hope: Hope to Bruce, February 22, 1862, *BPP*, vol. 63, 1862.

p.199: Michel: Michel to Bruce, February 28, 1862, *BPP*, vol. 63, 1862.

p.201: Burlingame: Burlingame to Seward, March 7, 1862, *DUSMC*, R.6.59, microfilm 92, roll 21, National Archives.

Hope: Hope to the Admiralty, March 5, 1862, *ADM 1/5790*.

p.202: Hsüeh: *IWSM, TC 4*, pp.25–26.

p.203: the imperial decree: Smith, Dissertation, p.91.

p.204: the *Times:* London *Times*, June 4, 1862.

the *Herald*'s account of Hsiao-t'ang: *NCH*, March 8, 1862.

p.204: Lindley: Lindley, vol. 2, p.451.

Alabaster's account: *BPP,* vol. 63, 1862, enclosure in May 2, 1962.

p.206: Hsüeh's account: *IWSM, TC 4,* pp.49b–51b.

p.208: the *Herald*'s account of Ssu-ching: *NCH,* March 22, 1862.

Hsüeh's account: *IWSM, TC 5,* pp.5b–7b.

CHAPTER VI

p.211: Abend: Abend, pp.149–150.

p.212: edict on foreign troops: *IWSM, TC 4,* p.52a.

Hsüeh on Ward: *IWSM, TC 5,* p.6b.

p.213: edict questioning Ward: *IWSM, TC* 5, p.8a.

p.214: Smith: Smith, *Mercenaries,* p.52.

p.215: Ward: Ward to Burlingame, August 16, 1862, Burlingame Papers, Library of Congress.

Wilson: Wilson, pp.123–124.

p.216: Wu Hsü: His letters to Ward can be found in the Ward Collection at Yale.

p.218: one Western witness: William Mesny, cited in Abend, p.160.

Abend: Abend, p.151.

Macgowan: Macgowan, vol. 3, p.22.

p.219: another early Ward biographer: Cahill, p.165.

one early-twentieth-century scholar: Hosea Ballou Morse, in his fictionalized *In the Days of the Taipings* (Salem, Mass.: Essex Institute, 1927).

Yang's letter: This letter can be found in the Ward Collection at Yale.

p.220: Cahill: Holger Cahill, *A Yankee Adventurer* (New York: MacAulay and Co., 1930), p.166 (hereafter Cahill).

Wu Hsü on Ward's embarrassment: *IWSM, TC 5,* pp.51–52.

p.221: the *chop*: This object can be found among the personal effects belonging to Ward that have been stored at the Essex Institute. There is also a collection of Chang-mei's jewelry, as well as Ward's mandarin's cap (the blue button is missing).

p.222: Shen Chu-jeng's biography: A copy was graciously supplied to me by Richard J. Smith, who deserves sole credit for its discovery.

p.223: Burlingame: Burlingame to Seward, March 7, 1862, *DUSMC,* R.6.59, microfilm 92, roll 21, National Archives.

p.224: Burgevine supplying Burlingame with lemonade and soda water: as related in a letter from Burgevine to Burlingame dated May 1863, Burlingame Papers, Library of Congress.

p.225: Burlingame: Burlingame to Seward, March 22, 1862, *DUSMC,* R.6.59, microfilm 92, roll 21, National Archives.
Ward's letter: Ward to Burlingame, August 16, 1862, Burlingame Papers, Library of Congress.

p.227: Burlingame: Burlingame to Seward, October 27, 1862, *DUSMC,* microfilm 92, roll 21, National Archives.
Hope: Hope to Bruce, October 8, 1862, *FO 228/321;* Hope to Forester, October 12, 1862, *FO 228/321.*

p.228: Schmidt: his memo on Ward's character can be found in record group 59, *DUSCS,* microfilm 112, roll 5, National Archives.
Hayes: Hayes, "Soldier," pp.196–197.

p.229: Hope: Hope to Forester, October 12, 1862, *FO 228/321.*

p.230: Feng Kuei-fen: quoted in Smith, Dissertation, p.149.
Hsüeh: *IWSM, TC 5,* pp.56–76.
Wu Hsü: *WHTA,* pp.138–141.

p.231: Tseng: quoted in William J. Hail, *Tseng Kuo-fan and the Taiping Rebellion* (New Haven: Yale University Press, 1927), p.260 (hereafter Hail).

p.232: Macgowan: Macgowan, vol. 2, p.119.

p.233: Hayes: The comment is contained in a memo concerning Ward's estate dated August 30, 1864, that can be found in the *bound DUSCS* (record group 84), p.849, National Archives.
Hope: Smith, Dissertation, p.345.
Hayes: Hayes, "Soldier," p.197.
Tseng's biographer: Hail, p.259.

p.234: imperial edict on foreigners: quoted in John K. Fairbank, ed., *The Chinese World Order* (Cambridge, Mass.: Harvard University Press, 1968), p.267 (hereafter Fairbank).
Fairbank: Fairbank, pp.262, 269, 272–273.

p.237: Hsüeh's doubting memorial: *IWSM, TC 5,* pp.33–36b.

p.238: Ward to Harry: the letters can be found in record group 84, Legation Archives, Consulate Records, Shanghai, vol. 34, p.803, National Archives.

CHAPTER VII

p.240: the Chung Wang: Curwen, pp.133–134.

p.242: Bruce: Bruce to Russell, March 26, 1862, *BPP,* vol. 63, 1862, p.220.
Bruce: Bruce to Hope, March 26, 1862, *FO 17/371.*

NOTES

p.245: the *Herald* account: *NCH,* April 12, 1862.

p.246: Lindley: Lindley, vol. 2, p.505.

the *Herald: NCH,* April 12, 1862.

p.247: the *Herald: NCH,* April 12, 1862.

Borlase: Borlase to Hope, April 6, 1862, *BPP,* vol. 63, 1862, p.226.

the *Herald: NCH,* April 12, 1862.

p.248: Borlase: Borlase to Hope, April 18, 1862, *BPP,* vol. 63, 1862, p.225.

p.249: *Shanghai Daily Shipping List:* quoted in Lindley, vol. 2, p.507.

Wilson: Wilson, p.134.

p.250: Wilson: Wilson, p.131.

p.251: Li Hung-chang on Wu, Yang, and Hsüeh: in J. C. Cheng, *Chinese Sources for the Taiping Rebellion, 1850–1864* (Hong Kong: Hong Kong University Press, 1963), p.92 (hereafter Cheng).

Peking to Li: Cheng, p.94.

Li on Ward: Cheng, p.96.

p.252: Ward on Li: Ward to Burlingame, August 16, 1862, Burlingame Papers, Library of Congress.

the Allied agreement: *BPP,* vol. 73, 1863, p.410.

p.254: Gordon: Charrier, *Gordon of Khartoum,* pp.41–42.

Lindley: Lindley, vol. 2, p.510.

p.255: Macgowan: Macgowan, vol. 2, p.121.

Schmidt: quoted in Macgowan, vol. 2, p.121.

China Mail: quoted in Lindley, vol. 2, p.512.

p.256: Macgowan: Macgowan, vol. 2, p.121.

British Foreign Office: the Foreign Office to the Admiralty, May 6, 1862, *FO 17/382.*

p.257: Ward: Ward to Burlingame, August 16, 1862, Burlingame Papers, Library of Congress.

p.258: Dew: Wilson, p.102.

p.260: the *Herald: NCH,* May 17, 1862.

p.262: Smith: Smith, Dissertation, p.177.

the *Herald: NCH,* May 24, 1862.

p.263: Lindley: Lindley, vol. 2, p.517.

p.264: the *Herald: NCH,* May 24, 1862.

Lindley: Lindley, vol. 2, p.519.

Overland Trade Report: quoted in Lindley, vol. 2, pp.519–520.

Staveley: Staveley to Sir G. C. Lewis, *BPP,* vol. 73, 1863, p.396.

p.265: Forester: Forester, p.36.

p.266: Staveley: Staveley to Bruce, May 23 and May 26, 1862, *BPP*, vol. 73, 1863, p.421.

p.268: Hope: Hope to the Secretary of the Admiralty, May 31, 1862, *BPP*, vol. 63, 1862, p.253.

p.269: Montgomerie's account: Montgomerie to Hope, June 7, 1862, *BPP*, vol. 73, 1863, p.402.

the Chung Wang's surrender demand: in Franz, Michael, *The Taiping Rebellion: History and Documents* (Seattle: University of Washington Press, 1966–71), vol. 3, p.1018.

p.270: the rebel general's surrender demand, and Forester's reply: *BPP*, vol. 73, 1863, pp.404–405.

Macgowan: Macgowan, vol. 2, p.123.

Forester on mutiny: Forester, p.36.

p.271: Li Hung-chang: Cheng, pp.95–96.

p.272: Forester: Forester, p.39.

p.273: the *Herald: NCH*, June 14, 1862.

p.274: the Chung Wang: Curwen, p.136.

the T'ien Wang: Curwen, p.136.

p.275: Li Hung-chang: Cheng, pp.96, 98.

imperial edict: Smith, Dissertation, p.98.

p.276: Hope: Hope to Bruce, June 14, 1862, *FO 228/321.*

Ward: *NCH*, January 10, 1863.

Macgowan: Macgowan, vol. 3, p.23.

Kung on Ward: *IWSM, TC 6*, p.17.

p.277: Bruce to Kung, and Kung's reply: *BPP*, vol. 73, 1863, pp.448–452.

p.279: Li Hung-chang: Cheng, p.99.

p.280: Ward: Ward to Burlingame, August 16, 1862, Burlingame Papers, Library of Congress.

p.281: Tseng Kuo-fan: quoted in Smith, Dissertation, p.190.

Wu Hsü to Ward: Ward Collection, Yale.

p.282: *Peking Gazette* account: *NCH*, October 4, 1862.

Forester: Forester, p.213.

Macgowan: Macgowan, vol. 2, p.124.

p.283: Li Hung-chang: Cheng, p.100.

Ward: Ward to Burlingame, August 16, 1862, Burlingame Papers, Library of Congress.

Li Hung-chang: Cheng, p.101.

p.284: the *Herald: NCH*, July 26, 1862.

p.284: Li Hung-chang on the free city movement: Cheng, pp.100–101.
Ward: Ward to Burlingame, August 16, 1862, Burlingame Papers, Library of Congress.
Li Hung-chang on Wu and Yang: Cheng, p.101.

p.285: Ward on accounts: Ward to Burlingame, August 16, 1862, Burlingame Papers, Library of Congress.
Macgowan: Macgowan, vol. 2, p.124.

p.286: Thomas Lyster: in E. A. Lyster, ed., *With Gordon in China: Letters from Thomas Lyster, Lieutenant Royal Engineers* (London: T. Fisher Unwin, 1891), p.79 (hereafter Lyster).
Lyster: Lyster, pp.84–85, 86.

p.288: Hayes: Hayes, "Chapter," p.521.
Li Hung-chang: Cheng, p.103.
Ward's letter: Ward to Burlingame, September 10, 1862, Burlingame Papers, Library of Congress.

p.290: Hayes: Hayes, "Soldier," p.197.

p.292: Schmidt: His memo can be found in record group 59, microfilm 112, roll 5, National Archives.

p.293: Wilson: Wilson, pp.107–108.
Ward: Macgowan, vol. 3, p.24.
Forester: Forester, p.212.

p.294: Bogle: Bogle to Dew, September 21, 1862, *BPP,* vol. 73, 1863, p.482.
Ward's will: Bogle's statement can be found in record group 84, Legation Archives, Consulate Records, Shanghai, vol. 34, no. 225 (bound), p.763, National Archives.

EPILOGUE

p.297: Ever Victorious Army officer: see Hayes, "Soldier," p.199.
Cook: his deposition can be found in record group 84, Legation Archives, Consulate Records, Shanghai, vol. 34, no. 225 (bound), p.797, National Archives.

p.298: Dew: Dew to Hope, September 27, 1862, *BPP,* vol. 73, 1863, p.481.
Hope: Hope to the Admiralty, October 1, 1862, *BPP,* vol. 73, 1863, p.480.
Hope to Burlingame: Rantoul, p. 42.
Gordon: Smith, *Mercenaries,* p.79.

NOTES

p.299: the *Herald: NCH,* September 27, 1862; January 3, 1863.

Schmidt: *DUSCS,* 1847–1906, R. G. 59, microfilm 112, roll 5, National Archives.

p.300: Li Hung-chang's memorial: Rantoul, pp.47–48.

p.301: imperial decree on Ward: Rantoul, p.45.

second imperial decree: *IWSM, TC9,* p.3b.

p.302: Schmidt: *DUSCS,* 1847–1906, R.6.59, microfilm 112, roll 5, National Archives.

Shen Chu-jeng's biography: see note for p. 222.

Lyster: Lyster, pp.96, 113.

p.303: Burgevine on command: Smith, *Mercenaries,* p.108.

p.304: Hope on Ward's Chinese: Hope to Bruce, October 29, 1862, *FO 228/321.*

p.305: Burlingame: Burlingame to Seward, October 27, 1862, *DUSMC,* microfilm 92, roll 21, National Archives.

p.306: Alabaster on Burgevine: an undated memorandum to Medhurst, *BPP,* vol. 63, 1864, p.26.

Macgowan: Macgowan, vol. 3, p.47.

Hope: Hope to Bruce, October 29, 1862, *FO 228/321.*

a veteran officer: quoted in Macgowan, vol. 3, p.48.

p.307: Hope: Hope to Bruce, October 29, 1862, *FO 228/321.*

Li Hung-chang on Burgevine: Smith, *Mercenaries,* p.113.

p.308: Wilson: Wilson, p.116.

Wilson: Wilson, p.118.

p.309: Macgowan: Macgowan, vol. 3, p.49.

the *Friend of China: Friend of China,* February 18, 1863.

Lyster: Lyster, pp.128–129.

p.310: the *Herald: NCH,* January 10, March 10, 1863.

Schmidt: Schmidt, P. C., p.10.

Schmidt: Schmidt, P. C., Vincente, pp.6–8.

p.311: Smith: Smith, *Mercenaries,* p.125.

Parkes: Smith, *Mercenaries,* p.125.

p.312: Lindley: Lindley, vol. 2, p.645.

p.313: Gordon: Jonathan Spence, *To Change China* (New York: Penguin Books, 1980), p.87 (hereafter Spence).

p.314: Gordon: Spence, pp.90–91.

the Chung Wang: Curwen, p.162.

p.315: Burgevine's autopsy: Dr. Johnston to Markham, October 18, 1865, *FO 17/432.*

NOTES

p.316: Tseng Kuo-fan: Warner, p.123.

p.319: Seward: S.E.D. 45:2:48, p. 215.

Harry Ward to his father: record group 84, Legation Archives, Consulate Records, Shanghai, vol. 34, no. 225 (bound), p.819, National Archives.

p.321: Kung: Abend, p.221.

Shanghai taotai: Abend, p.238.

p.324: Foster and Lansing: in their *The Claim of General Frederick T. Ward's Estate Against the Chinese Government, Arising Out of His Military Services During the Taiping Rebellion,* a copy of which can be found in the Essex Institute, Salem, Massachusetts (hereafter Foster and Lansing).

Foster and Lansing: Foster and Lansing, p.11.

p.325: one Salem citizen: Francis H. Lee, quoted in Rantoul, p.52.

p.326: a Nationalist Chinese general: *Boston Herald,* September 23, 1934.

Lindley on Ward: Lindley, vol. 2, p.585.

Hayes on Ward's achievements: Hayes, "Soldier," p.198.

p.327: Hayes on Ward's ambitions: Hayes, "Chapter," p.522.

INDEX

INDEX

INDEX

Hsien-feng, *see* Hsien-feng,
Emperor; imperial military
hierarchy, 89; power struggle
within, 134–35, 137, 170–72,
315–18; reactive policy of,
234–37; secondary revolts against,
75; seeking foreign help in
Shanghai, 25–33; Taiping advance
to Soochow and, 14–19; treatment
of Western prisoners, 135, 136;
unreliability of troops of, 89,
108–09, 151, 158, 199, 207–08,
225, 242, 250, 265, 266; using
foreigners against Taipings,
64–67, 73, 78, 139, 187–89,
202–04, 212, 231–32; Ward's
military innovations and, 239–40,
315–18; worries about Ward,
212–15, 230–39, 242–43, 256,
275–77. *See also* China
Mandate of Heaven, 43, 66
Manilamen, 91–92, 93, 107–13, 115; as
bodyguards, 163
Marshall, Humphrey, 62
Martin White, 238
McLane, Robert M., 63
Meadows, Thomas Taylor, 48, 52, 55,
56, 124, 140, 142; attempts to end
Ward's activities, 119–21, 131–32,
149; described, 92; maintenance of
trade and, 93–94
Medhurst, Walter, 142, 266; arrest of
Ward and, 149–53
Mercenaries, 138, 139, 144; in Latin
America, 58–60, 81; Ward's army
of, *see* Foreign Arms Corps
Mexico, 57–60, 67, 68, 81, 201
Michel, General Sir John, 188, 193;
on Chinese officials, 200; des-
cribed, 177; flying columns
strategy of, 177; on Ward, 200,
241–42; on the Ward Corps,
199–200
Military armaments, 85–87; artillery,
104–05; defense of Shanghai and,

127; revolvers, 85–86; rifles, 86,
127, 162; stinkpots, 190
Ming dynasty, 11, 52
Missionaries, 41–44, 126; opium trade
and, 47–48; pro-Taiping, 66, 140
Montgomerie, Captain John, 268–69
Morton, Major J. D., 264, 268, 272,
276, 283, 291, 292–93
Muddy Flat, Battle of, 64
Muslim rebellion, 75

Nan-ch'iao, 252, 259, 278; Portet's
death at, 262–63
Nan-hsiang, 253, 287
Nanking, 61, 173, 232; British naval
expedition to, 139–42; siege of, 9,
79, 161, 267–68, 279–81, 283,
303–04, 307, 313, 314; water
gates of, 279, 280–81
Nationalist Chinese, 325–26
Neale, Colonel, 128
Neutrality of Western powers, 64,
93–95, 96, 120–21, 124, 139, 142,
156, 159, 176–77, 186–88;
British-French rivalry and, 178;
contradiction of, 124–25, 129–30;
questioning of, 139–41, 156–60;
support for Ward and, 201–02,
241–95
Nevins, John L., 40
Newspapers, China coast, 95–96
Nicaragua, 59–60
Nien rebellion, 75, 315–16
Ningpo, 157–58, 173, 178–79, 272,
276; Allied defense of, 268, 283,
285, 288–95; Allied recapture of,
257–59, 264; Taiping capture of,
174–76
Niuhuru, Empress Dowager, palace
coup of, 170–71
North China Herald, 23–26, 77, 133,
142, 143, 151, 253, 284; on death
of Ward, 298–99; defense of
Shanghai and, 28, 126–28, 204–08;
described, 95–96; on the Ever

INDEX

INDEX

68–69, 190–91, 201, 226–27, 289, 305; armies of, *see* Chinese Foreign Legion; Ever Victorious Army; Foreign Arms Corps; Ward Corps of Disciplined Chinese; arrests and escape of, 147–54; birth of, 34; bodyguards of, 163, 292; boyhood of, 36–39; Burlingame and, 201, 224–27; change in public opinion of, 184–85; as charismatic leader, 72–73, 84, 106–07, 116–17, 154, 164–65, 256, 290; as a Chinese citizen, 150–51, 201, 202–04, 209, 210–13, 234–37, 284; Chinese name of, 180–81; as "colonel," 112; commission in the imperial army, 213, 217–18, 233, 234; confrontation with Chung Wang, 267–95; "crimping" recruits, 113, 146, 150, 151; criticisms of career of, 326–29; death of, *see* Death of Ward; defense of Shanghai and, 128, 130–31, 133–34; described, 30, 33, 37, 39, 59, 68–69, 100, 106–07, 127–28, 201, 210, 228, 286, 326–29; discipline and, 40, 59, 88, 106, 113, 116, 255, 256, 260, 264; distrust of the British, 113–14, 167–68, 185, 189–92; dog of, 116, 299, 302; European support for, 193, 198, 201–02, 212, 241–95; finances of, 165, 216–17, 223–24, 238, 276, 284–85, 290, 294, 296–98; forward command position of, 108, 164–65, 206, 207, 282–83; "free city" movement in Shanghai and, 226, 284; home of, 200, 221, 238–39; intelligence-gathering missions, 166–67, 192; intolerance of superior authority, 65, 230–39; isolation of, 68, 84; last surviving letter of, 288–89; as "lionized" by Shanghai hostesses, 211; loyalty to, and control by, the Manchus, 213–15, 230–39, 242–43, 256, 275–77; as a mandarin, 203–04, 209, 212–13, 215, 217, 220, 234, 302; military bent of, 38–39, 49, 65, 103; military innovations of, 239–40, 315–18; as military tactician, 105–06, 108, 165, 194; mistakes of, 121–23, 245–47; as no longer an American citizen, 148, 149, 190; parents and, 36–39, 49, 318–20; in Paris, 133–34; Pirate Suppression Bureau and, 30–31; plans to attack the British, 190–91; pre-China exploits of, 49–51, 57–61, 65, 67–69, 282; rattan cane of, 106, 116, 206; as a seaman, 37–40; siblings of, 37; Sung-chiang and, *see* Sung-chiang; thirty-mile radius plan, 198–99, 225, 241, 250–83; understanding of Chinese methods, 80–83, 104, 289–90; uniform of, 106; wife of, *see* Chang-mei; women and, 69, 211; wounds of, 109, 118–19, 131, 181, 182, 206, 208, 293–95; Wu Hsü and, *see* Wu Hsü; Yang Fang and, *see* Yang Fang

Ward, Henry (Harry), 37, 67, 68, 211, 222, 238–39, 294; brother's estate and, 319–20; as purchasing agent for brother, 165, 216, 223–24, 320; wife of, 323–25

Ward, John E., 74, 95, 289

Ward and Company, 165

Ward Corps of Disciplined Chinese, 160–68, 179–209; arms for, 162, 165, 201; backers for, 163–64; described, 193, 199–200; early successes of, 180–85; European support for, 193–98, 201–02, 204–07, 209; flying column strategy, 178–79, 191, 198; Hope and, 167–68, 193–206; Hsaio-t'ang and, 204–27; imperial sanction for,

INDEX

The
Yangtze
Delta